In Search
of a Kingdom

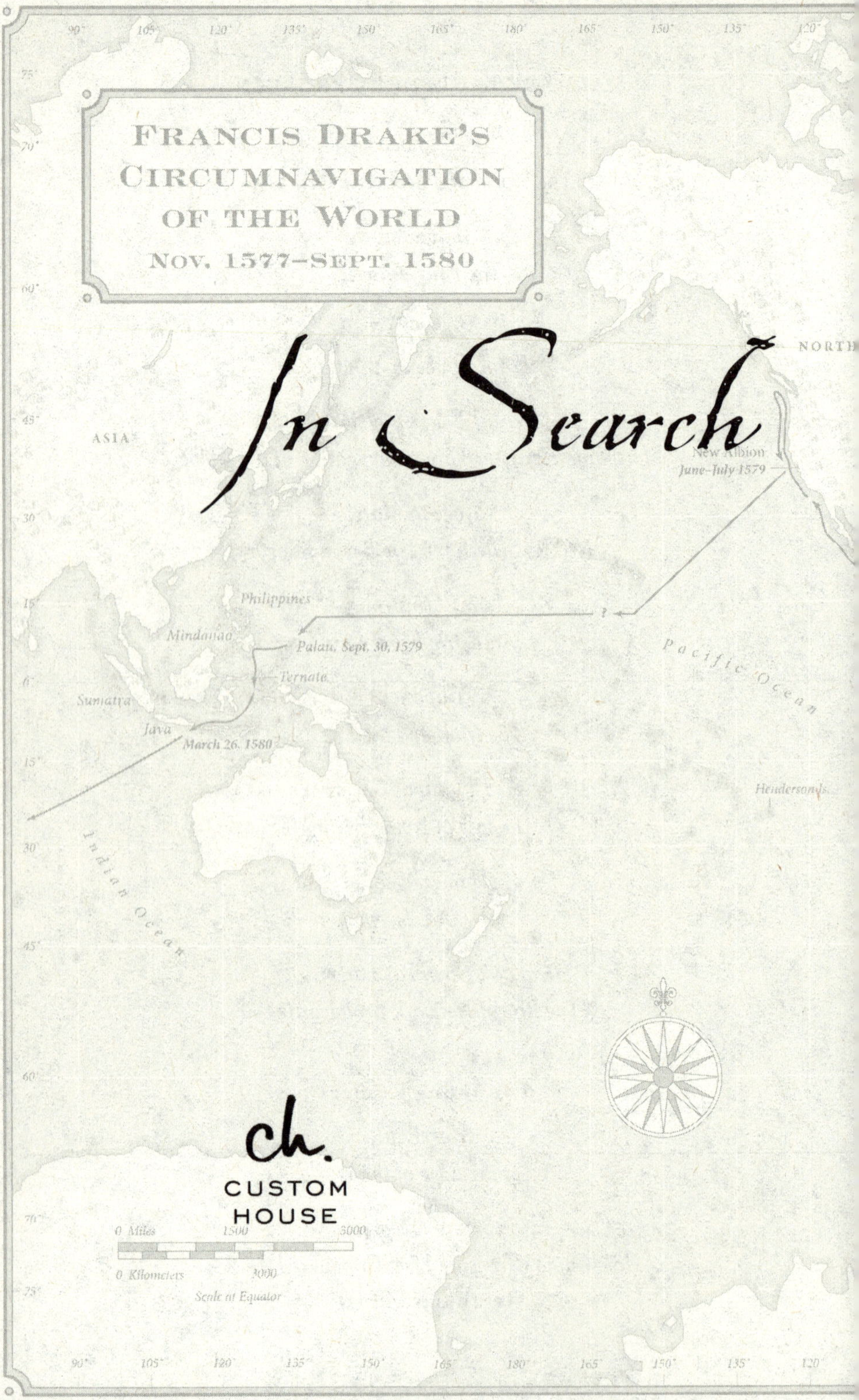

FRANCIS DRAKE'S
CIRCUMNAVIGATION
OF THE WORLD
NOV. 1577–SEPT. 1580

In Search

NORTH

ASIA

New Albion
June–July 1579

Philippines

Mindanao

Palau, Sept. 30, 1579

Ternate

Sumatra

Java

March 26, 1580

Pacific Ocean

Henderson's

Indian Ocean

ch.
CUSTOM
HOUSE

0 Miles   1500   3000

0 Kilometers   3000

Scale at Equator

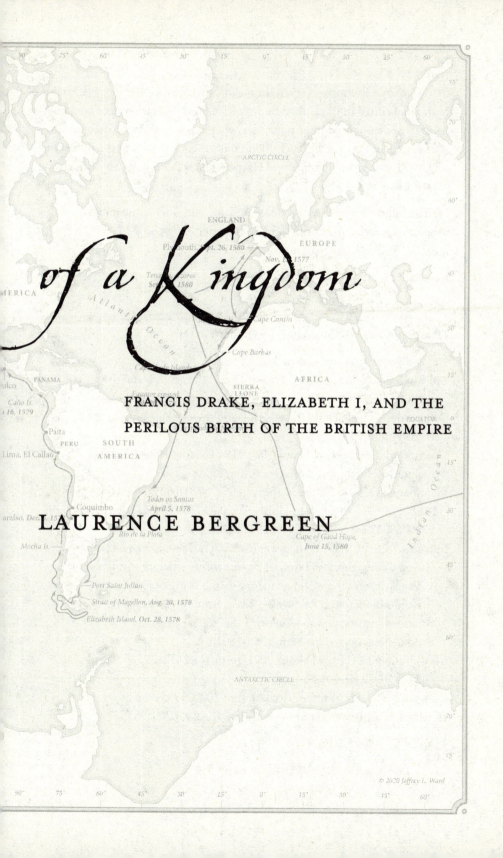

# of a Kingdom

FRANCIS DRAKE, ELIZABETH I, AND THE
PERILOUS BIRTH OF THE BRITISH EMPIRE

LAURENCE BERGREEN

HarperCollins books may be purchased for educational, business, or sales promotional use. For information, please email the Special Markets Department at SPsales@harpercollins.com.

FIRST EDITION

Maps by Jeffrey L. Ward

Library of Congress Cataloging-in-Publication Data

Names: Bergreen, Laurence, author.
Title: In search of a kingdom : Francis Drake, Elizabeth I, and the
    perilous birth of the British Empire / Laurence Bergreen.
Other titles: Francis Drake, Elizabeth I, and the perilous birth of the
    British Empire
Description: First edition. | New York, NY : Custom House, [2021] |
    Includes bibliographical references and index.
Identifiers: LCCN 2020039354 (print) | LCCN 2020039355 (ebook) | ISBN
    9780062875358 (hardcover) | ISBN 9780062875365 (trade paperback) | ISBN
    9780063062979 | ISBN 9780062875389 (ebook)
Subjects: LCSH: Drake, Francis, approximately 1540-1596. | Elizabeth I,
    Queen of England, 1533-1603. | Privateering—History—16th century. |
    Voyages around the world—History—16th century. | Explorers—Great
    Britain—Biography. | Admirals—Great Britain—Biography. | Great
    Britain—History, Naval—Tudors, 1485-1603. | Great
    Britain—History—Elizabeth, 1558-1603.
Classification: LCC E129.D7 B47 2021 (print) | LCC E129.D7 (ebook) | DDC
    942.05/50922 [B]—dc23
LC record available at https://lccn.loc.gov/2020039354
LC ebook record available at https://lccn.loc.gov/2020039355

ISBN 978-0-06-287535-8

21 22 23 24 25 LSC 10 9 8 7 6 5 4 3 2 1

To Jacqueline

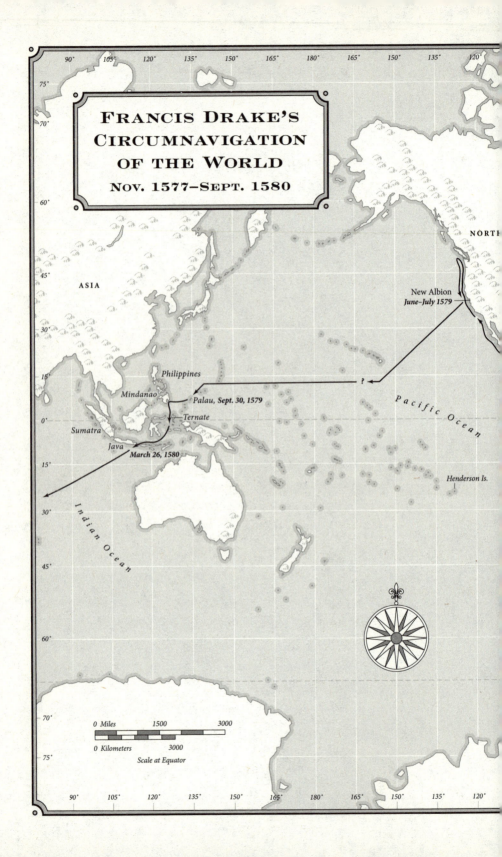

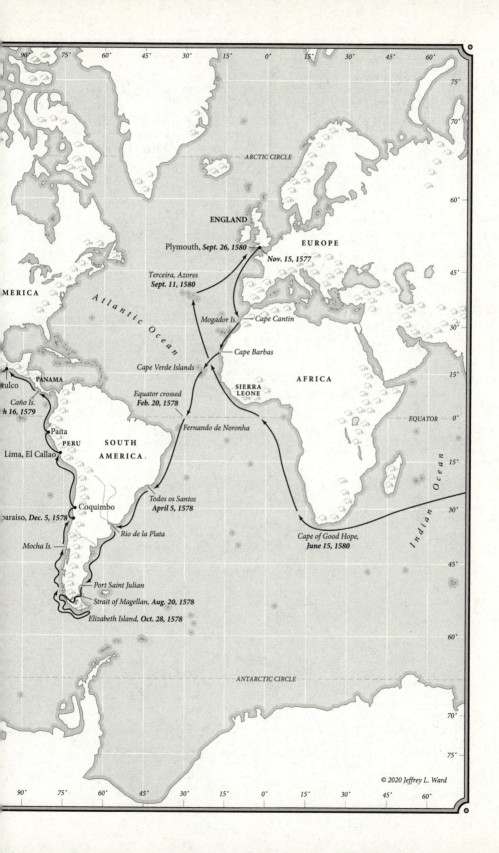

ARCTIC CIRCLE

ENGLAND

EUROPE

Plymouth, *Sept. 26, 1580*

Nov. 15, 1577

Terceira, Azores
Sept. 11, 1580

Atlantic Ocean

Mogador Is. —— Cape Cantin

MERICA

—— *Cape Barbas*

Cape Verde Islands

AFRICA

Equator crossed
Feb. 20, 1578

SIERRA
LEONE

EQUATOR

ulco

PANAMA

h 16, 1579

Caño Is.

Fernando de Noronha

Paita

PERU

SOUTH

Lima, El Callao

AMERICA

Indian Ocean

Todos os Santos
April 5, 1578

Coquimbo

araíso, *Dec. 5, 1578*

Rio de la Plata

Cape of Good Hope,
June 15, 1580

Mocha Is.

Port Saint Julian

Strait of Magellan, Aug. 20, 1578

Elizabeth Island, Oct. 28, 1578

ANTARCTIC CIRCLE

© 2020 Jeffrey L. Ward

ROUTE OF THE SPANISH ARMADA
MAY–SEPT. 1588

Shetland Islands

Aug. 21

Orkney Islands

Outer Hebrides

Aug. 24

SCOTLAND

•Edinburgh

North Sea

Aug. 12

•Newcastle

Dublin

IRELAND

WALES

ENGLAND

•London

Plymouth•

Dover•

×Dunkirk

July 19

July 23–Aug. 7

Calais

NETHERLAN

Scilly Islands

Sept. 20

•Brest

Paris•

Sept. 17

FRANCE

Atlantic Ocean

June 14

La Coruña
June 18–July 21

•Gijón

•Santander

Sept. 23

Bilbao•

•Bayonne

•Oporto

PORTUGAL

•Madrid

SPAIN

•Barcelona

Lisbon•

•Valencia

May 28

from Brazil

•Lagos Seville•

Sagres• •Córdoba

Cádiz•

Tangier• •Gibraltar
Ceuta

Mediterranean Sea

•Oran

BARBARIA

© 2020 Jeffrey L. Ward

0 Miles 300

0 Kilometers 300

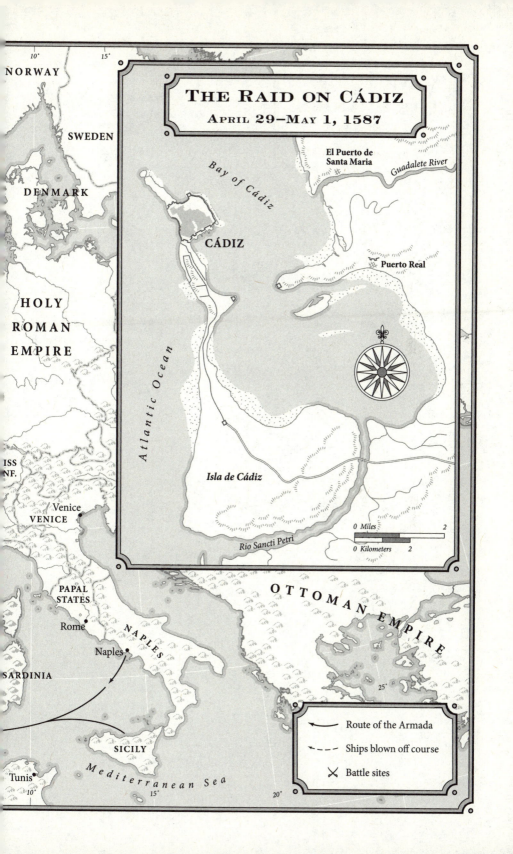

NORWAY

SWEDEN

DENMARK

HOLY
ROMAN
EMPIRE

ISS
NF.

Venice
VENICE

PAPAL
STATES

Rome

NAPLES

Naples

SARDINIA

SICILY

Mediterranean Sea

Tunis

OTTOMAN EMPIRE

THE RAID ON CÁDIZ
APRIL 29–MAY 1, 1587

El Puerto de
Santa Maria

Guadalete River

Bay of Cádiz

CÁDIZ

Puerto Real

Atlantic Ocean

Isla de Cádiz

Rio Sancti Petri

0 Miles   2
0 Kilometers   2

Route of the Armada

Ships blown off course

✕ Battle sites

Contents

Book II: El Draque

Principal Characters

England

Burroughs, William (1536–1599). Naval commander. Hanged ten masters of pirate ships in 1583. Vice admiral during Francis Drake's raid on Cádiz in 1587. Tried and acquitted on charges of mutiny.

Carder, Peter. Escaped ship's boy who claimed to walk across Brazil before catching a boat to England.

Cecil, William, Baron Burghley (1520–1598). Queen Elizabeth's chief minister. Appointed Lord High Treasurer in 1572. Died in his London home in 1598.

Dee, John (1527–1608). Mathematician, astronomer, astrologer, alchemist. Influential adviser to Queen Elizabeth. Formulated the concept of the "British Empire."

Devereux, Robert, 2nd Earl of Essex (1565–1601). Late-life intimate of Queen Elizabeth. When he ran afoul of her, she had him executed.

Doughty, Thomas. Nobleman. Mutineer. Condemned to death by Drake in Port Saint Julian, Argentina, 1578.

Drake, Sir Francis (1540–1596). Eldest of twelve sons of Edmund Drake. Second cousin of Sir John Hawkins, with whom he sold slaves in the Caribbean. Led the first successful circumnavigation, 1577–1580. Vice admiral of the English fleet during the Armada period. Died of dysentery and buried at sea near Portobello, Panama, in January 1596.

Drake, John. Francis Drake's nephew.

Dudley, Robert, Earl of Leicester (1532–1588). Fifth son of John Dudley, the executed Duke of Northumberland. Suspected of murdering his first wife, Amy Robsart.

Elizabeth I (1533–1603). Daughter of Henry VIII and Anne Boleyn, his second wife.

Fletcher, Francis. Drake's chaplain during the circumnavigation, maintained a journal of the voyage, which formed the basis of *The World Encompassed by Sir Francis Drake.*

Frobisher, Sir Martin (1539–1595). Navigator. Led three voyages to the New World. Commanded *Triumph* in Battle of the Spanish Armada. Died at Plymouth.

Hawkins, Sir John (1532–1595). Privateer, slaver, Drake's mentor. Treasurer of the navy. Commanded *Victory* in Armada battle. Knighted. Died off Puerto Rico during a campaign with Drake.

Howard, Charles, Second Baron Effingham (1536–1624). Eldest son of William Howard. Appointed Lord High Admiral of England, 1585. Led the English fleet against the Armada in 1588. Fought in the Battle of Gravelines.

Mary I (1516–1558). The sole surviving child of Henry VIII and Katherine of Aragon, his first wife. Married King Philip of Spain in 1554. Died childless in London.

Newman, Mary (m. 1569, d. 1583). Francis Drake's first wife.

Norreys, Sir John (1547–1597). Military commander involved in the notorious massacre of Scots at Rathlin Island. Knighted by Leicester. Led unsuccessful campaign with Drake to install Dom António, the Portuguese pretender to the throne, in 1589.

Oxenham, John. First non-Spanish explorer to traverse the Isthmus of Panama (1575). Fought with Drake against the Spanish in two early campaigns in Central America, captured by the Spanish in 1578, executed in Lima on September 30, 1580.

Pretty, Francis. Drake's gentleman-at-arms.

Sydenham, Elizabeth (1540–1596). Francis Drake's second wife.

Walsingham, Sir Francis (1532–1590). Queen Elizabeth's spymaster and minister. Knighted in 1577. Died in London deeply in debt.

Scotland

James VI of Scotland (1566–1625). Son of Mary, Queen of Scots. Succeeded Queen Elizabeth.

Mary, Queen of Scots (1542–1587). Only surviving legitimate child of James V of Scotland, who died six days after she was born. Heir presumptive to English crown as a descendant of Henry VIII's elder sister, Margaret. She fled Scotland in 1568, and was detained by Elizabeth I for nineteen years until she was executed.

Spain

de Antón, San Juan. Captain of *Cacafuego,* captured by Drake off Brazil.

de Figueroa, Gómez Suárez, Fifth Count de Feria (1520–1571). The Duke of Feria, as he was later known, served as Philip's representative in England from 1557 to 1559.

de Mendoza, Bernardino (1540–1604). Spanish ambassador and spy to London from 1578 to 1584.

de Zúñiga-Sotomayor, Alonso Pérez de Guzmán y, 7th Duke of Medina Sidonia (1550–1615). Commander of the Spanish Armada that was to attack the south of England in 1588.

Farnese, Alexander, Duke of Parma (1545–1592). His mother was King Philip's half sister. Failed to carry out a planned rendezvous with Medina Sidonia during the battle of the Spanish Armada.

Philip II of Spain (1527–1598). Philip the Prudent ascended to the throne after his father, Charles V, Emperor of the Holy Empire, abdicated in 1556. At various times, he was king of Spain, Portugal, Naples, Sicily, England, and Ireland. He died at the Palace of El Escorial.

Vatican

Gregory XIII (1502–1585). Pope 1572–1585. A reformer who tried to discourage the spread of Protestantism by founding new colleges for priests. He celebrated the massacre of the Protestant Huguenots in Paris in 1572 with a mass in Rome.

Pius V (1504–1572). Pope 1566–1572. Excommunicated Elizabeth I on February 25, 1570.

Sixtus V (1520–1590). Pope 1585–1590. Although fond of Elizabeth, he renewed the excommunication and promised to grant Philip II a generous subsidy after the Spanish Armada arrived in England.

A Note on Dates

For the sake of consistency, I have followed the modern, Gregorian calendar for all events in all locations.

In 1582, Pope Gregory XIII replaced the Julian calendar, in effect since 45 BC, with a new calendar to compensate for errors accumulated over time. The Gregorian calendar omitted ten days, so October 5, 1582, became October 15 in Catholic countries such as Spain. But Protestant countries continued to follow the traditional Julian calendar, some until the twentieth century. England made the switch in 1752.

The change has led to some confusion. For example, older records state that Francis Drake departed from Plymouth December 23 on his circumnavigation. In our modern calendar, the equivalent is December 13.

In Search

of a Kingdom

A wyvern, or two-legged dragon,
Francis Drake's heraldic symbol
*(The Rare Book & Manuscript Library, University
of Illinois at Urbana–Champaign)*

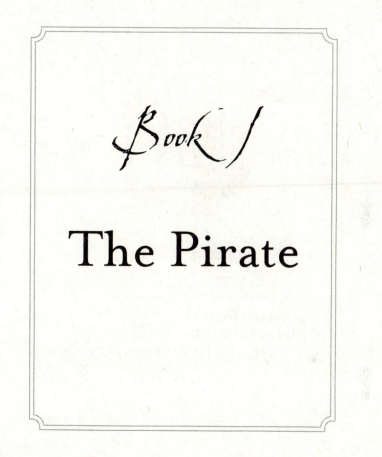

Book 1

The Pirate

CHAPTER I

The Island and the Empire

On the morning of December 13, 1577, Francis Drake, a pirate and former slaver, ordered his small fleet in Plymouth, England, to weigh anchor. The ships stood out against a bleak background. They were colorfully painted, with billowing sails, and boisterous sailors calling to one another.

Plymouth lies 190 miles southwest of London, surrounded by two ancient rivers, the Plym and the Tamar, both running into Plymouth Sound to form a boundary with the neighboring county, Cornwall. It was a tranquil town, mostly farmland gathering into a peninsula jutting into a bay. Drake, from nearby Devon, made Plymouth his base of operations. The port was recognized for its shipping, and it also served as a hub of the English slave trade. It was not an innocent place. In folklore, Devon harbored witches and the Devil himself.

The fleet's destination was unknown, but they would not be home by Christmas or even the next, not if Drake's ambitious plan was successful. Many aboard had a financial stake in the voyage, and they might return prosperous. Or, just as likely, they might never see Plymouth again. Weeks earlier, the Great Comet of 1577 had passed overhead, an event taken across Europe as a sign, portent, or warning that a great event would soon unfold. Comets, those mysterious, phosphorescent messengers from the far reaches of space, coincided with the commencement of a new age.

Two of the most consequential figures of this era, Francis Drake and Queen Elizabeth, knew the expedition's true purpose: to circumnavigate the globe. If successful, Drake would take his place in history as the first captain to command his fleet around the world—and return alive. For Elizabeth, the expedition was a challenge to the global order, which ranked Spain dominant and England a second-rate island kingdom. Both dreamed the voyage would reap riches. But for the moment, Drake and Elizabeth kept their ambitions to themselves, concealing their plans for the expedition in documents.

Drake allowed the crew to think they were going to raid the coast of Panama for gold, or perhaps set a course for Alexandria, Egypt, in search of currants. These were lucrative but not exciting pursuits. Had the crew known Drake's real intentions, they may well have deserted at the first opportunity. "The Straits were counted so terrible in those days that the very thought of attempting it were accounted dreadful," said a commentator, referring to the treacherous passage between the Atlantic and Pacific Oceans, only the most obvious of many obstacles to a circumnavigation attempt. Maintaining secrecy was essential, especially from the men expected to perform the task.

The syndicate backing his voyage had authorized Drake's fleet to cross the Atlantic, navigate the southern tip of South America, explore the west coast of that continent, and prospect for gold and silver—specifically, gold and silver stolen from the Spanish, along with anything else of value aboard Spanish ships that could be carried away. His unspoken commission was to drive out the Spanish from those mineral-rich regions. Nothing was said about a circumnavigation; it was up to Drake to take the initiative as they embarked on a journey that would transform England.

*I*f Francis Drake ever had a moment of self-doubt, he left no record of it. He respected the violence of storms, but they held no terror for him. Drake was thoroughly at ease aboard whatever ship he happened to be sailing, from a pinnace to a flagship. He was just as authoritative and quick-witted on land as he was at sea. As a loyal Englishman, he naturally respected the queen and her court, most of them wellborn and with little use for him, but he was not awed by them. Deference did not come naturally to Drake.

Ultimately, he respected only one force in this world, and that was the Supreme Being. His father, Edmund, had come to preaching late in life, and from him Drake inherited a reliance on absolutes concerning faith. When a sailor signed on to a voyage with Drake, it was understood that he would sing psalms and recite prayers as often as possible, even several times a day. Drake ordered his crew to sing psalms before battles, to give thanks for victories, and, when necessary, to give the dead a Christian burial—and that meant a Protestant burial. Roman rites infuriated Drake, even though the two were at the time far more similar than they are now. Although rough around the edges compared with the upper echelons of the nobility, he yielded to no one in his belief in queen and country, and his disdain for her enemies, especially Spain. His was a simple moral compass, but it was durable and allowed him to negotiate the perilous straits he encountered, both real and imagined.

Drake was daring and resolute. He was short of stature, at most five foot nine, probably closer to five foot seven, and stocky. He had a typically Cornish fondness for painting and drawing. He sketched throughout his travels, the better to comprehend the Lord's creation.

Where others saw the world in muted tones, Drake saw the full spectrum. Some pirates loved women, others bloodshed and swordplay. Drake lusted for gold, and when he had stolen enough for several lifetimes, he kept on stealing it, because it was deeply ingrained in his nature to plunder. He was something of a scavenger. Everything belonged to him—potentially—at least all that glittered. He thrust himself into the world, wanting to see it all in the span of years allotted to him. He understood how short life could be, as did everyone in Elizabethan England. Plague, war, and infection frequently menaced the population, to say nothing of the hazards of sailing into the unknown. Nevertheless, the populace steadily increased: two million, three million, eventually four million over the course of Elizabeth's long reign. Her subjects jostled for resources and for space, and so did Drake. The difference was that he had access to ships and, just as important, royal license to create mayhem in the name of the queen, and he happily rose to the occasion. With Drake, fame, fortune, and empire seemed possible, and his bravado made attaining these prizes look inevitable.

*T*he syndicate funding Drake's 1577 expedition included prominent Elizabethans: Robert Dudley; Christopher Hatton, the Earl of Lincoln (the Lord High Admiral); and John Hawkins. Drake contributed £1,000 from the proceeds of his previous raids on Spanish ships and outposts. Elizabeth contributed £1,000, so Drake later claimed, although no record of the transaction exists, which she would have been keen to conceal. William Winter, the surveyor of the queen's ships, added £750. His brother George, clerk of the queen's ships, another £500. (The sole copy of the document listing the other backers was partly destroyed by fire, obscuring their names.) Although she had not given the expedition her official blessing, the queen's apparent participation in Drake's syndicate signaled that it enjoyed her consent, which was almost as good. In this way, Drake's desire for revenge against the Spanish and Queen Elizabeth's budding need for an empire aligned.

The English fleet was led by Drake's 121-foot-long flagship, *Pelican*, a galleon or multidecked ship commissioned two years earlier and built to his specifications at the Plymouth shipyards. Her beam was estimated at nineteen feet, keel between forty-seven and fifty-nine feet, and length of anywhere from sixty-eight to eighty-one feet (reports vary), with a hold of about nine feet. She was sizable, but hardly overwhelming, probably the largest ship that Drake could afford to build with his loot as a pirate. She was originally called *Francis* as an indulgence, but Elizabeth preferred to name the ship *Pelican*, after one of her personal symbols. In the allegorical medieval bestiary, a pelican symbolized Christ, wounded by humanity's sins. The pelican flew with its breast open over the sea and wings outstretched, seeming to mimic Christ's death on the cross. If *Pelican* hinted at Elizabeth's involvement, the name of the "vice admiral," *Elizabeth*, revealed the expedition's pedigree. *Elizabeth*, though smaller, was a more impressive craft than *Pelican:* eighty tons, fashioned from wood taken from the queen's personal stock, with eleven cast-iron cannon.

The rest of the fleet included a barque, *Marigold;* a flyboat, *Swan;* and two pinnaces, *Benedict* and *Christopher*, the last of which Drake owned. (A pinnace signified a light boat such as a tender, and also happened to be Elizabethan slang for "harlot.") The crew came to 164, including soldiers, sailors, and apprentices, as well as a dozen "gentlemen."

Although Drake was the captain, he did not belong to that exalted social rank. But he was unquestionably Protestant and loyal to the queen, and his years of experience in the company of Hawkins, as well as his own daring exploits, testified to his courage, resource-fulness, and skill as a mariner. And the ships arrayed before him would make his ambitions attainable.

Their provisioning was, by the standards of the time, ample: biscuit, powdered and pickled beef, pickled pork, dried codfish, vin-egar, oil, honey dried peas, butter, cheese, oatmeal, salt, spices, mus-tard, and raisins. (Nearly all these items were provided by Drake's longtime Irish supplier, James Sydae.) Scurvy—the loss of colla-gen, one of the body's building blocks—devastated sailors, and not until 1912 would it become widely understood that ascorbic acid, or vitamin C, available in citrus, vegetables, and beer, prevented it, yet even at this early date, English captains including Drake relied on oranges and lemons as a remedy without understanding why they worked.

English sailors were known for drinking quantities of ale and wine, but the record is silent concerning the expedition's supply of alcohol. More is known about the objects Drake brought along for trading, including knives and daggers, pins, needles, saddles, bri-dles, bits, paper, colored ribbons, looking glasses, cards and dice, and linens. Carpenters packed staples such as rosin, pitch and tar, twine, needles, hooks, and plates, together with pikes, crossbows, muskets, powder, and shot. Drake himself was fond of luxury items, including perfume (a necessity in an age of negligible hygiene) and dishes made of silver with gilded borders, embossed with his coat of arms.

For navigation, Drake relied on a Portuguese map of the globe as well as a detailed chart of the Strait of Magellan. He carried a copy of the famous account kept by Ferdinand Magellan's chief chron-icler, Antonio Pigafetta, *The First Voyage Around the World*, and consulted it as a guide for both navigation and the management of mutinous sailors. The young Venetian had traveled with Magellan, been at the right hand of the captain general at that fateful hour in Mactan harbor, and was fortunate to be among the handful of survivors of the voyage. His account made it clear that everything—even survival—came with difficulty for Magellan, who perished in the Philippines. It stood as a reminder that attempting to cross the Atlantic, let alone sail all the way around the world—ever changing, poorly understood, and immense—was more than dangerous, it was fated to end in disaster and oblivion. Those drawn to it were likely to be reckless, fearless, and rapacious. They had little to lose and perhaps fame to gain.

Books about the New World were a new and expanding genre at the moment, and Drake brought several state-of-the-art volumes with him, including *L'Art de naviguer*, published at intervals between 1554 and 1573. This work was a French translation of Pedro de Medina's authoritative *Arte de navegar*, originally published in eight volumes in Valladolid, Spain, in 1545, and dedicated to the future king of Spain, Philip II. Then there was Martín Cortés de Albacar's *Breve compendia*, published in Seville and translated into English in 1561. Profusely illustrated, this was the basic text for many captains and covered technical matters such as magnetic declination (the angle between magnetic north and true north) and the celestial poles, hypothetical points in the sky where the Earth's axis of rotation intersects the celestial sphere, a projection of the sky onto a hemisphere. These measurements were useful for a ship to fix her position when out of sight of land. Cortés also discussed the nocturnal, an instrument that allowed a navigator to determine the relative positions of stars in the night sky and to calculate tides, critical for ships in determining when to enter ports. Drake's nautical library included two other standard references: *A Regiment for the Sea* by William Bourne (1574), which was a translation of Cortés's popular work, and *Cosmographical Glasse* by William Cunningham, a physician and astrologer (1559).

*D*rake did not expect to command the expedition. The original leader was Sir Richard Grenville, a wellborn mariner from Devon who had served as a member of Parliament in addition to trying his luck as a privateer. In 1574, he had proposed to rob Spanish ships, establish English colonies in South America, sail through the Strait of Magellan, and proceed across the Pacific to the Spice Islands. At the time, Drake was attempting to put down a bloody rebellion by Irish and Scots in the Rathlin Island massacre off the coast of Ireland. Hundreds died, and Drake, who had not been paid for his efforts, moved on. Grenville received his license from the English crown, but it was later withdrawn because England was reluctant to provoke the powerful, reclusive Spanish monarch, Philip II. Diplomacy, not conflict, was the watchword of the day. Drake inherited the role that had once seemed destined for Sir Richard, who resented the redheaded upstart for the rest of his life.

The Spanish had gotten a decisive jump on England in global commerce and exploration. In July 1525, just three years after Magellan's battered *Victoria* returned to Seville, King Charles dispatched García Jofre de Loaísa to explore the Spice Islands with a fleet of seven ships and 450 men, including Juan Sebastián Elcano, the Basque mariner who had sailed with Magellan and was among the few survivors. Loaísa was assigned to rescue lost ships from Magellan's ill-fated Armada de Moluccas, but this ambitious goal proved impossible to achieve.

After weathering storms and a mutiny, Loaísa's much reduced fleet entered the Strait in May 1526. The next leg, across the Pacific, proved devastating, as one ship after another ran aground. *Santa María del Parral* made it all the way to the coast of Sulawesi in Indonesia. There members of the crew were either killed or enslaved, with the exception of four survivors. Just one ship of the original seven made it to the Spice Islands. By that time, both Loaísa and Elcano had succumbed to scurvy. Their corpses were wrapped in linen and deposited in the sea. Only twenty-four men remained by the end of the voyage, and they all returned to Spain. Among them was Hans von Aachen, Magellan's gunner, who therefore became the first person to circumnavigate the globe *twice*.

Later, in 1533, Francisco de Ulloa was sent from Valdivia, on the coast of southern Chile, to investigate the Strait. Ulloa thus became the first European to enter the *western* mouth of the Strait. He made it partway through before determining he would run out of provisions and headed back to Chile. In November 1557, Juan Ladrillero became the first explorer to traverse the Strait in *both* directions. And he was followed by other Spanish explorers.

Their efforts raised the stakes of Drake's voyage. It was vital that Elizabeth establish an English—and Protestant—presence in the New World before it was too late. But Drake was not one to feel desperate or agitated. The sheer scale of the Central and South American landmass was too great for any power, even Spain, to control completely. Although it was not yet apparent, the Spanish navy was overextended, undisciplined, and indolent.

Yet Drake's diverse crew seemed barely equal to the ambitious tasks he set for them. Only one, William Coke, had reached the Pacific, not as an explorer but as a Spanish detainee. Drake did include men skilled in crafts they would need: a blacksmith, coopers to maintain and fashion barrels, and carpenters. Drake adored music, and he included several musicians along with a selection of instruments to perform at the change of watch and to accompany the singing of psalms.

There were about a dozen gentlemen on board, notably Thomas Doughty, a nobleman and investor in the voyage, along with his younger half brother, John, also present. Thomas Doughty probably knew of Drake's real intentions, and his status led him to think of himself as cocaptain, a dangerous delusion. The resulting insecurity unnerved Drake and affected the entire crew to the point where it would threaten the voyage.

Other crew members included a naturalist named Lawrence Eliot; a botanist; several merchants, among them John Saracold, a member of the Worshipful Company of Drapers, a powerful trade association whose origins went back to 1180.

Then there was Francis Fletcher, a priest in the Church of England, tasked with religious observance. Records indicate that he studied at Pembroke College, Cambridge, but did not graduate, and for a brief time he served as rector of St. Mary Magdalen parish in London. Few crew members were literate, so it fell to Fletcher to function as a chronicler. He maintained a detailed narrative of the voyage that would later be gathered and published under the title *The World Encompassed*. He was an engaging eyewitness, sensitive to the moods of the crew, capable of eloquent descriptions, and appeared to be wholly loyal. Drake followed the example of other captains by taking his personal retainer, Diego, an African who had escaped Spanish enslavement, with him. He was probably the only black member of the crew. They had met in 1572, when Drake attacked the Spanish port of Nombre de Dios in Panama. Because he spoke both Spanish and English, he was particularly useful to Drake and became not merely his servant but also his employee, receiving wages like the other hired hands. And there were relatives, including Drake's younger brother Thomas; his cousin John, only fifteen years old; and a nephew of Drake's cousin and mentor, John Hawkins, who had introduced Drake to the sordid, treacherous, and lucrative slave trade.

With the exception of Thomas Doughty, who signed a will on September 11, 1577, shortly before they departed, and Drake himself, none of the personnel sensed that they were about to commence

the most ambitious voyage in English naval history. And even Drake
was not sure where he would end up. He would be guided by his
hunger for gold and status.

All the while, Spanish spies watched and worried. Their concerns regarding England and especially Drake intensified week by
week. On September 20, 1577, Antonio de Guarás, a Spanish ambassador to Queen Elizabeth's court, warned, "As they carry on their
evil plans with great calculation, there is a suspicion that Drake the
pirate is to go to Scotland with some little vessels and enter into a
convenient port, for the purpose of getting possession of the prince
of Scotland for a large sum of money; whereupon he will bring him
hither convoyed by the Queen's ships that are there."

Drake's calm demeanor gave nothing away. Perhaps he was em-
barking on another escapade and would go wherever the winds of
fate took him—across the entire length of the Mediterranean to the
commercial port of Alexandria, Egypt, or along the coast of Africa,
or across the Atlantic. As Francis Pretty, Drake's gentleman-at-
arms, or military guard, noted: "The 15th day of November, in the
year of our Lord 1577, Master Francis Drake, with a fleet of five
ships and barques, and to the number of 164 men, gentlemen and
sailors, departed from Plymouth, giving out his pretended voyage
for Alexandria." Just then the first of many unexpected occurrences
altered their plans. "The wind falling contrary, he was forced the
next morning to put into Falmouth Haven, in Cornwall, where such
and so terrible a tempest took us, as few men have seen the like, and
was indeed so vehement that all our ships were like to have gone to
wrack. But it pleased God to preserve us from that extremity and
to afflict us only for that present with these two particulars: the
mast of our Admiral, which was the *Pelican*, was cut overboard for

the safeguard of the ship, and the *Marigold* was driven ashore, and somewhat bruised. For the repairing of which damages we returned again to Plymouth."

Drake spent weeks restoring the damaged vessel, until "we set forth the second time from Plymouth and set sail the 13th day of December following." The days were short, the air cold and damp, in contrast to the expected warmth of the Alexandrian sun, if Egypt was their destination. Unlike his inspiration, Magellan, who called his fleet the Armada de Moluccas to proclaim his objective, Drake never named his fleet, and kept his options open. They might be headed toward Alexandria; then again, they might not. Another possibility, which promised to be both quick and lucrative, concerned Brazil. If he could reach the coast, avoid vicious Spanish soldiers, and return with quantities of silver and gold, the queen would likely consider his voyage a success. Drake had no intention of dying on a distant beach, as Magellan had, with his body dismembered and his memory disgraced.

*M*uch of Drake's knowledge of South America derived from the controversial records compiled by the Florentine navigator Amerigo Vespucci, who had died in 1512. Vespucci claimed he had made as many as four voyages to the land he called "The New World," and put his name to several influential letters about his adventures (the authorship of the first and fourth letters is contested)—accounts that popularized his discoveries across western Europe. A skillful propagandist, Vespucci composed a vivid portrait of the enormous land known as Brazil, after the pau brasil, the flowering tree growing there in abundance at the time. He told of naked locals rushing to the water's edge to greet (fully clothed) European arrivals. He described how communication was tentative at first, largely in sign language, helped along by the exchange of gifts as proof of peaceful intentions. The Brazilians were "very great swimmers, with as much confidence as if they had for a long time been acquainted with us." The ability made an impression because many Europeans, even sailors, simply could not swim. The women were even more capable in the water than the men: "we have many times found and seen them swimming two leagues out at sea without anything to rest upon." They had ample weapons, "such as fire-hardened spears, and also clubs with knobs, beautifully carved," and they did battle "against people not of their own language, very cruelly, without granting life to any one, except (to reserve him) for greater suffering. When they go to war, they take their women with them, not that these may fight, but because they carry behind them their worldly goods, for a woman carries on her back for thirty or forty leagues a load which no man could bear."

Vespucci cautioned his readers not to underestimate the native peoples of the New World simply because "in their conversation they appear simple." In reality, "they are very cunning and acute in that which concerns them: they speak little and in a low tone: they use the same articulations as we, since they form their utterances either with the palate, or with the teeth, or on the lips." They were highly verbal, the idioms constantly shifting. "For every 100 leagues we found a change of language, so that they are not intelligible each to the other."

At least one of their innovations captivated him: "They sleep in certain very large nettings made of cotton, suspended in the air: and although this fashion of sleeping may seem uncomfortable, I say that it is sweet to sleep in those (nettings): and we slept better in them than in the counterpanes." The hammock, a rope mesh suspended by cords at the ends, was ubiquitous, and caught on with the Europeans, who adapted them to their ships. One sturdy hut, covered with palm leaves, sheltered as many as "600 souls." A village with only thirteen huts contained several thousand souls.

Their concepts of value and property also varied greatly. "The wealth that we enjoy in this our Europe and elsewhere, such as gold, jewels, pearls, and other riches, they hold as nothing; and although they have them in their own lands, they do not labour to obtain them, nor do they value them." Instead, they prized "bird's plumes of many colours," and "rosaries" made of fish bones. They embedded "white or green stones" in their cheeks, lips, and ears. And they were generous, "for it is rarely they deny you anything: and on the other hand, liberal in asking, when they show themselves your friends."

One of their customs was beyond the pale. "They eat all their enemies whom they kill or capture, females as well as males with so much savagery, that (merely) to relate it appears a horrible thing: how much more so to see it, as, infinite times and in many places."

Vespucci was, at the same time, a slaver. He boasted that his ships returned on October 15, 1498, carrying 222 slaves to Cádiz, Spain, "where we were well-received and sold our slaves."

Vespucci's reputation would have faded were it not for a quirk of fate. The New World might have been called "Columbia," after the most celebrated and notorious explorer of the continent, even though he thought he was approaching India. But, in 1507, a year after Christopher Columbus died, a German cartographer, Martin Waldseemüller, produced an enormous world map naming the newly discovered continent "America" after the feminine Latin version of Vespucci's first name, Amerigo. Protests were raised on Columbus's behalf, but Waldseemüller insisted, "I do not see why anyone should justifiably forbid it to be called . . . America, from its discoverer Americus [Vespucci], a man of perceptive character; since both Europa and Asia have received their names from women." The name stuck.

*D*rake's early efforts to wage undeclared war against King Philip II of Spain eventually came to the attention of Elizabeth. Reluctant to antagonize the formidable Spanish empire, which might weaken her position abroad and at home among English Catholics, she came to rely on pirates such as Drake, who were out for themselves as much as they acted on behalf of the Crown.

"Drake!" Her Majesty exclaimed, "I would gladly be revenged on the King of Spain for divers injuries that I have received." This was much easier said than done. Spain was unquestionably the most powerful nation in Europe, its influence augmented by the Catholic Church. England, on the other hand, was a Protestant—actually a semi-Protestant—upstart, isolated and second-rate compared to Spain's preeminence. It was Spain, not England, who ruled the waves. Challenging Spanish dominance required a carefully considered strategy combined with a devil-may-care attitude and fearlessness. It required a captain who thrived on confrontation rather than shrank from it. Drake met and exceeded those requirements. For him, faith and loyalty were matters of life and death. His instincts included a zeal for revenge against Spain and an inordinate fondness for gold.

Emboldened, Drake developed a plan to attack Spanish interests on the Pacific coast of Panama, "by way of the Straits of Magellan." Elizabeth put a thousand crowns behind it. Secrecy was essential. "Her Majesty did swear by her crown that if any within her realm did give the king of Spain to understand," Drake recalled, "they should lose their heads."

Spain had the advantage of size and wealth, but England had Francis Drake. Of all English navigators, only Drake possessed the raw courage and skill to deliver the global influence Elizabeth and her advisers sought. He was never satisfied, always striving for more, as expressed in the opening stanza of a prayer he once wrote: "Disturb us, Lord, when we are too well pleased with ourselves, when our dreams have come true because we have dreamed too little, when we arrive safely because we sailed too close to the shore." No one would ever accuse Drake of hugging the shore; he preferred to be far out at sea, on a broad reach, riding the wind where it would take him, or fighting it when circumstances demanded.

Elizabeth's realm was poor and isolated by comparison with the great Spanish empire, more *Beowulf* than Camelot. It seemed likely that Spain, led by the methodical Philip II, would soon invade England and replace the Protestant queen, who had already been excommunicated by the pope, with a suitable Catholic monarch, bringing the country into the Vatican fold. The country was half-Catholic, and many of the populace would welcome the development. But Elizabeth's improvised strategy and Drake's daring defied this likely outcome and set England, Europe, and eventually much of the world on a different course. It marked the moment when England, overshadowed by Spain and Portugal, shook off Catholic authority. Drake became the catalyst in England's great transition from an island nation to the British Empire.

All that Drake accomplished on his voyages, especially acts of piracy and violence, he did on Elizabeth's behalf and, as a result of her largesse, for himself. Piracy offered his surest route to wealth and status, and, as the eldest son of a clergyman, he was unlikely to attain these prizes any other way. Elizabeth's reputation in England was never higher than in the years surrounding Drake's voyages. And he might have fancied becoming her beloved, joining the lengthy list of men whose affections she had ensnared. The farther he sailed around the world, the deeper he would sail into her heart, or so he hoped. It would be a long and unlikely journey.

Francis Drake, born in Devonshire in 1541, was the son of Edmund Drake (1518–1585), a farmer turned minister to the faithful at the Royal Dockyard in nearby Chatham, and his wife, Mary Mylwaye. The Drake name resonated across Devon, and his father beseeched a member of the nobility, Francis Russell, to sponsor the infant's baptism, to little avail. Francis Drake spent his youth in obscurity, perhaps because his father became embroiled in religious controversy. William Camden, a British historian and contemporary of Drake, explained, "Whilest he was yet a child, his father embracing the Protestant Doctrine was called into question by the Law of the Six articles, made by King Henry the Eighth against the Protestants, fled his country, and withdrew himself into Kent. After the death of King Henry he got a place among the sea-men of the King's Navy, to read prayers to them: and soon after he was ordained Deacon and made Vicar"—that is, a parish priest—"of the Church of Upnore."

Drake's father was too poor to keep his son at home, a circumstance that made all the difference in Francis's life. "By reason of his poverty, he put his son to the Master of a Bark"—a ship with at least three masts—"his neighbour, who held him hard to his business in the Bark, with he used to coast along the shore, and sometimes to carry merchandise into Zeland [Denmark] and France. The youth . . . so pleased the old man by his industry, that being a bachelor, at his death he bequeathed the bark unto him by will and testament."

*I*n need of money, young Francis began his career as a slaver under the command of his cousin John Hawkins, who was prominent in the booming English slave-trading enterprise. In 1562 they sailed from Plymouth with three ships and kidnapped four hundred Africans in Guinea, selling their captives in the West Indies. Many prisoners died en route. But in the horrific calculus of slavery, their voyage was a commercial success. During the next five years, Drake and Hawkins completed three more voyages to Guinea, where they captured and enslaved another 1,200 Africans.

By summer of 1568, Drake, only twenty-seven years old, was still part of Hawkins's fleet, but now he was leading eight ships carrying fifty-seven slaves, stolen silver, and jewelry to England, where they hoped to receive a modest profit. On August 12, a storm blew up and walloped the ships for eleven days, scattering the fleet. After weeks of wandering at sea, Hawkins and Drake happened on a Spanish vessel, whose crew told them of a harbor at San Juan de Ulúa. Located near Veracruz, Mexico, this fort was supervised by Spanish bureaucrats who regularly tortured suspects in the dungeons of churches. His worst fears about Catholicism confirmed, Drake recoiled. As Hawkins and the other English captains brought their battered vessels close to the harbor, a large Mexican fleet ensnared them. Only Drake's ship *Judith* escaped—all the more remarkable because she was unarmed.

Drake spent four grueling months guiding *Judith* across the Atlantic, arriving at Plymouth on January 20, 1569. Two weeks later, Hawkins limped home to Plymouth, cursing his luck, the Spanish, and Drake, whom he denounced as a deserter. The claim reached the highest levels, and Queen Elizabeth jailed Drake for several weeks to placate Hawkins and to maintain the fiction that she neither condoned nor sponsored piracy.

Drake emerged from captivity seething with resentment—not against the queen, whose tacit approval he needed, or even Hawkins—but against the Spanish, and with good reason. Drake learned that his cousin Robert Barret had been arrested by the Inquisition in Mexico after the governor there, Don Martin Enriques, had given his word that the English adventurers would be safe. The governor then decided there was no need to keep his word when it came to heretics. He took several men prisoner and confined them to a dungeon. Some of the men were forced to renounce their religion while being tortured.

An even worse fate awaited Barret. He was burned at the stake. Drake never forgot and never forgave the outrage. From that time forward he despised Spanish tyranny and saw himself engaged in a crusade against this spreading evil. He had glimpsed their version of a world empire, one based on torture and the exploitation of local tribes, and he was repelled. He renounced slaving and vowed to seek revenge (and his fortune) against those who trafficked in human lives. He became a cunning, enthusiastic pirate, living by his wits, raiding Spanish forts, and taking but not killing Spanish prisoners. He told them he was simply getting back "a bit of his own" for the indignities he had witnessed at San Juan de Ulúa.

*T*he previous circumnavigation came to a tragic conclusion fifty-five years earlier. In 1518, the Portuguese navigator Ferdinand Magellan, after repeatedly trying and failing to win support from his own king, Manuel I, persuaded Charles V of rival Spain to back the project. Magellan led a fleet of five little ships and 258 sailors from a variety of nations, many of them risking their lives at sea to avoid prison at home. In a time when it was widely believed that ships could sail over the edge of the world, the armada planned to sail beyond the horizon to the distant Moluccas. There nutmeg, cinnamon, and cloves, among the most valuable crops in the world—more valuable, even, than gold—grew in abundance. European traders wishing to reach the Spice Islands previously had traveled east rather than west, a journey by land and sea, until they reached their goal. A round-trip to the far side of the world lasted seven years or longer, if the traders survived the rigors of long-distance travel. And the herbs they brought back with them to Europe lost considerable potency along the way. Magellan hoped that by going west, in the opposite direction, over water, he would complete the trip in a year or less and return with fresher, more potent spices. All of that was speculation; no one had ever succeeded.

Throughout the voyage, Magellan, equipped with a set of hopelessly inaccurate maps, relied on his navigational instincts to sail from Seville across the Atlantic to the coast of Brazil, all the while fleeing Portuguese ships in pursuit, battling storms, and quelling violent mutinies.

After several disappointments, Magellan located a rumored passage near the southern tip of South America. By this time, he had lost two ships. The three remaining vessels ventured into the passage without benefit of maps. Thirty-eight days later, Magellan spied the Pacific Ocean and wept with joy. His relief did not last long. He faced the largest body of water on the planet, about which almost nothing was known in Europe. On this leg of the journey, his diminished fleet was assailed by storms and menaced by ocean-going warriors in their highly maneuverable proas. Magellan's crew, confined aboard their ships, relied on worm-eaten biscuits and flying fish that landed on the decks. They slowly succumbed to scurvy, which Magellan and other officers escaped by accident. Because of their rank, they were entitled to an allocation of jam made from quince, a tart little fruit rich in vitamin C. Without realizing how or why, those who had access to quince were protected.

By March 6, 1521, the fleet reached the island of Guam, covering a little more than two hundred square miles barely rising above the surface of the ocean: their first sight of land in ninety-nine days. Ten days later Magellan's fleet reached what is now called the Philippines, just four hundred miles from their goal, the Moluccas. They had sailed three-quarters of the way around the world. In the Philippines, Magellan blundered into a confrontation with a combative local chieftain, Lapu Lapu. Feeling secure with their Western firearms and shields and swords, Magellan and eighteen stalwart loyalists squared off against hundreds of warriors charging into harbor, brandishing fired-hardened swords under the command of Lapu Lapu. The men focused their wrath on Magellan, easily identifiable in his gleaming helmet, and cut him down.

After Magellan's violent death, *Victoria*, laden with precious spices, continued on a westerly course. She was commanded by Juan Sebastián Elcano, a Basque navigator, who guided her across the Indian Ocean, around the Cape of Good Hope, and finally to Seville on September 6, 1522, three years after her departure. The battered ship's arrival astonished the authorities, who had assumed that the entire fleet had come to grief in a remote part of the world. They were not far from wrong. Of the 258 sailors and five ships that had set out, only one ship with eighteen emaciated sailors completed the circumnavigation.

For the next fifty years, Magellan's ill-fated mission was considered a cautionary tale rather than a great step forward in exploration. It demonstrated that circumnavigation was folly, an endeavor for overreaching kings and reckless captains in search of elusive wealth. The Portuguese navigator had established that the world was larger than anyone in Europe imagined—and far more hazardous.

That was how matters stood for more than half a century, when England challenged the Catholic—and Spanish—world order.

At the time of *Victoria's* return to Seville, Henry VIII had ruled England for thirteen years. His was an exceedingly violent reign. He sent twenty-seven thousand people to their deaths, or nearly one percent of the population of England and Wales. In Germany, Martin Luther, having published his ninety-five Theses, had become the focus of controversy and launched a revolution. In 1520, Pope Leo X, thoroughly corrupt and highly intelligent, issued a bull—an official document—condemning Luther's propositions as heretical. The pope gave the monk 120 days to renounce his Theses, but Luther refused, and on January 3, 1521, the pope excommunicated him. Several months later, on April 17, Luther appeared before the Diet of Worms, in Germany, still defiant, and declared, "Here I stand. I can do no other. God help me." In response, Magellan's onetime sponsor, Charles V of Spain, ordered Luther's writings to be burned.

Henry had condemned Martin Luther, the German monk who launched the Protestant revolution, as "a venomous serpent, a pernicious plague, infernal wolf, an infectious soul, a detestable trumpeter of pride, calumnies and schism"—a description endorsed by Pope Leo X. Several years later, Luther further challenged Roman orthodoxy by marrying a nun, Katherine of Bora, with whom he had five children, and retreating from the revolution he had launched.

But for now, in 1521, Leo X, nearing the end of his life, looked to Henry VIII to champion the church. The king in response wrote

"Defence of the Seven Sacraments," which attacked Luther's theology and earned Henry the title "King of England and France, Defender of the Faith and Lord of Ireland." But matters did not rest there. Tension between England and the Vatican grew until, in 1538, Pope Paul III excommunicated Henry and deprived him of the title "Defender of the Faith."

Seeking a male heir to the throne, the king had tried in 1527 to persuade the pope to annul his twenty-three-year marriage to Catherine of Aragon, with whom he had a daughter. When the pope refused, Henry formed the Church of England, which would permit him to marry his longtime mistress, Anne Boleyn. Henry had previously bedded and spurned Anne Boleyn's sister, Mary. Anne, not wanting to repeat this pattern, insisted that they marry before they embarked on sexual intimacy. But would the pope agree?

Henry dispatched his influential chancellor, Cardinal Wolsey, to request an annulment of his marriage to Catherine. Wolsey was unsuccessful and found himself in jeopardy with the king. He offered a magnificent new palace at Hampton Court to Henry in a bid to save his status but died before Henry subjected the cardinal to the humiliation of a mock trial for disloyalty.

Lusting for Anne and tantalized by the prospect of a male heir at last, Henry married her in secret under the auspices of the newly constituted Church of England. When she became pregnant, his court astrologers agreed with their king's prediction that the child of his second marriage would be a boy. Instead, Anne Boleyn gave birth to a girl: Elizabeth.

He was so disheartened by the newborn's gender that he did not attend the baby's christening, and he blamed her mother for the treachery of giving birth to a girl. Condemned as a witch, Anne Boleyn became known as "the great Whore." Henry was not one to forgive. Two years later, he determined to behead his second wife.

"I have only a little neck," Anne pleaded while placing her hands over her exposed throat. An experienced executioner imported from Calais dispatched her with a stroke of his massive sword as she stared at him with open eyes.

Later, the story spread that Anne Boleyn had a sixth finger—a sign of the devil. In England at the time, the devil was considered real and powerful. (Some paintings of Anne Boleyn indicate a small bump, possibly an extra nail, protruding from the little finger of her left hand.) Her daughter, only a toddler, was declared illegitimate, and it was said that Henry could not bear to set eyes on little Elizabeth. Her nanny had to beg for essentials for the girl, "for she hath neither gown, nor kirtle, nor petti coat, nor no manner of linen, nor foresmocks, nor kerchiefs, nor sleeves, nor rails, nor body-stitchets, nor mufflers, nor biggins" (a sleeping cap). With the birth of Prince Edward to Henry's next wife, Jane Seymour, Elizabeth remained outside the line of succession until 1544, two years after Henry beheaded Catherine Howard, his *fifth* wife, on suspicion of adultery.

Despite her straitened circumstances, young Elizabeth learned Latin and Greek from Roger Ascham, a scholar and scribe. Later, she was trained in public speaking—a rare skill for a woman of that era.

Henry lived on a while longer, injuring his leg at a jousting tournament at Greenwich Palace on January 24, 1536, when he was thrown from his horse, which proceeded to fall on him. He lay unconscious for two hours. His leg became ulcerated. Unable to exercise, he became morbidly obese, expanding to well over three hundred pounds. His eyesight failing, subject to spells of paranoia, he lived for eleven more years, marrying six times in all. He died on January 28, 1547, at the age of fifty-six, leaving the religious and political landscape dramatically transformed.

*T*hese were the darkest years for young Elizabeth. During this time, Catherine Parr, Henry's last wife, married Edward VI's uncle, Thomas Seymour of Sudeley. The couple took Elizabeth into their household at Chelsea. There Seymour, nearly forty years old, was said to have sexually harassed Elizabeth, who was only fourteen. Entering her bedroom dressed only in a nightgown, he tickled the girl and smacked her buttocks. Strangely, Catherine Parr participated. She, too, tickled Elizabeth and restrained the girl as her husband slashed her gown "into a thousand pieces." But when Catherine discovered her husband embracing Elizabeth, she put a stop to the outlandish behavior. In May 1548, she moved Elizabeth out of the household.

It has been theorized that these episodes had a formative effect on Elizabeth's character. The victims of sexual abuse can manifest an unusual interest in or avoidance of sexual activity. They can suffer from sleeplessness, or nightmares, or other symptoms of what is now called post-traumatic stress disorder. Elizabeth experienced all of these symptoms throughout her life.

On Henry's death, his young son, Edward, ascended to the throne. England's first Protestant monarch was plagued by a series of debilitating illnesses, and he died in 1553, just fifteen years old. Edward's untimely death precipitated another succession crisis. Edward's Protestant cousin, Jane Grey, highly educated, and herself only sixteen years old, briefly succeeded him. While Lady Jane was awaiting coronation, Edward's oldest sister, Mary, a Catholic, and Henry VIII's daughter with his first wife, orchestrated the trial and execution of both Jane Grey and her husband for treason.

Mary ascended to the throne in 1553 and plotted to return England and Ireland to the Roman Catholic Church. During her five-year-long reign of terror, Mary ordered 280 dissenters burned at the stake. Protestants denounced her as "Bloody Mary." She relished her role as an avenging angel but worried that her much younger half sister, Elizabeth, would spark a Protestant insurrection. To prevent that circumstance, Mary confined Elizabeth to the Tower of London, a medieval fortress and prison rising above the north bank of the Thames.

Determined to prevent Elizabeth from succeeding her, Mary married Prince Philip II of Spain and hoped for an heir. In September 1554, she began to gain weight, stopped menstruating, and developed nausea. It seemed an heir was on the way. Only Philip had doubts. Elizabeth, languishing under house arrest, was summoned to observe the birth of Mary's successor, but Mary had suffered a false pregnancy. She considered the outcome divine retribution for having "tolerated heretics" in her realm. After another false pregnancy, she died on November 17, 1558, possibly of ovarian cancer.

Despite Mary's machinations, Henry VIII's second child, Elizabeth Tudor, age twenty-five, became queen, a Protestant monarch. Her hold on power was tenuous, and few had any inkling that she was destined for greatness on the throne as she did her best to juggle the competing claims of Protestants and Catholics.

During the same period in Spain, the old order was yielding to the new. The most powerful man in Europe, Charles V, the Emperor of the Holy Roman Empire, became ill and depressed and withdrew to the Monastery of Yuste in Extremadura, where amid the bucolic surroundings he contemplated his mortality. Suffering from debilitating gout, he abdicated his throne in 1556 in favor of Philip. In March 1558, Charles was said to have staged his own funeral. During the ceremony, he concealed himself in his coffin as mourners wept with as much feeling as they would at a real funeral. When the mock service concluded, Charles rose from the casket and sequestered himself in his apartment, where he died on September 21.

Philip II, or Felipe el Prudente, came to power at the peak of the Siglo de Oro Español: the Spanish Golden Age. Before anyone referred to Great Britain as the "empire on which the sun never sets," the concept applied to Spain—*el imperio donde nunca se pone el sol*. At its peak, the empire included much of Central and South America including Argentina, Bolivia, Colombia, Mexico, Paraguay, Uruguay, and Venezuela, and wide swaths of Africa. And it was the source of great wealth for Spain, particularly gold from Central and South America.

During this period, the artists Diego Velázquez and El Greco flourished. Tomás Luis de Victoria, Cristóbal de Morales, Francisco Guerrero, Luis de Milán, and Alonso Lobo advanced Renaissance music. Nor was the flowering confined to the visual arts and music. Spanish literature also thrived. Miguel de Cervantes, born north of Madrid, created *Don Quixote*. And Spain's celebrated playwright Lope de Vega wrote a thousand plays abounding with stylistic innovations. He was so prolific that Cervantes called him *Monstruo de la Naturaleza*, the Monster of Nature.

In his mid-forties, Philip decided to subdue Protestant England. He ordered the Duke of Alba to invade the island nation, deploying an army of only six thousand. Spain's best general, the duke insisted this task was pure folly, but Philip proclaimed it was God's will that Spain would prevail. Elizabeth ruled England by means of "tyranny," Philip believed, and Mary, Queen of Scots, a Catholic, was the "true and legitimate successor" to Elizabeth. But Mary was both unlucky and unwise. She was the only child of King James V of Scotland and succeeded him upon his death when she was only six days old. She married three times, the first time to Francis, King of France, at the age of fifteen. With Lord Darnley, she had one child, in 1566, who

later became James VI and I of Scotland and England. Mary's imprudent marriages allowed Elizabeth, free of similar entanglements, to
keep her rival at bay. As their rivalry played out, Philip postponed
the inevitable confrontation between the two nations. Spain and England meanwhile fought one another with proxies on the Continent
and in South America. In the years to come, the Spanish empire,
though wealthy, slowly stagnated, and Philip increasingly functioned
as a cautious caretaker known for his pale complexion and melancholy demeanor. He passed his days sequestered in a small office
within the massive walls of the Monasterio de El Escorial, arriving at
decisions—or more often, deferring them—according to his ministers' written recommendations.

All the while, the Holy Inquisition, designed to combat heresy,
deprived Spain of some of its most accomplished and wealthiest inhabitants, as it had since the twelfth century, when the influential
Pope Innocent III declared, "Anyone who attempts to construe a
personal view of God which conflicts with Church dogma must be
burned without pity." The Inquisition's rituals, especially the auto-
da-fé, travestied legal proceedings and inflicted cruelty for which
Spain became notorious across Europe and later South America. The
auto-da-fé was intended to instill fear, and it accomplished its goal
with ruthless efficiency.

The rite usually commenced with a procession of monks followed by officials and finally those condemned to perform public
penance or, even worse, be burned at the stake. These were prolonged
exercises, beginning at daybreak and lasting throughout the day, by
which time the stink of burning flesh and shrieks of those being
tortured filled the air.

The prisoners destined to be burned at the stake held green candles as they went and wore miters painted with flames as well as a
halter or noose around their necks. Many wore the dreaded san-

benito, a tunic made of linen and adorned with images of flames or demons delivering a heretic into hell.

Not everyone was condemned to death. Some penitents, wearing a yellow gown with two red bands in the shape of a St. Andrew's Cross, kneeled, recited a catechism, and stated "Yes, I believe" in response to each statement of dogma. They were then subjected to various forms of penance, including serving as a soldier in a distant outpost or aboard a galley, which was nearly tantamount to a death sentence. Survivors convicted of heresy could not hold office, nor could they work as a physician, apothecary, surgeon, merchant, advocate, or even grocer. They were subject to severe sumptuary laws, forbidden to wear silver, gold, pearls, other gems, silk, and other luxury fabrics. They were barred from riding horses and bearing arms. These prohibitions extended to the second and even the third generation, so their grandchildren, perhaps unborn, endured the same stigma as their forebears, on an equally irrational basis.

In Mexico, where the Inquisition was active, these grotesque practices extended to English sailors—the "Lutherans" and Protestant heretics, whom the Spanish despised. In 1569, Drake's cousin John Hawkins narrowly escaped capture by the forces of the Inquisition in Veracruz. Had he been captured, the English role in the Age of Discovery would have been diminished.

Others were not so fortunate as Hawkins. A band of English sailors left behind in the region lived for six years in relative peace until the Inquisition, established in Mexico in 1571, caught up with them, placed them under arrest, and transported them to Mexico, where they were subjected to an auto-da-fé. One of the survivors, Miles Philips, made it back to England, where he recounted the suffering he and his compatriots endured. Everyone was tortured on the rack and forced to recant Protestant beliefs. The ordeal did not end there. The Inquisition erected a scaffold "in the middle of the market place in Mexico right over against the head church." On the day of execution, the heretics were placed in yellow sanbenitos with red crosses to await their fate. Fires were lit, filling the air with smoke mingled with a primal instinct for slaughter. Then came the verdicts. Some English prisoners were condemned to serve in Spanish monasteries for years while wearing the humiliating sanbenito while others were "burned to ashes" on the spot.

Sixty-eight survivors, including Philips, "were carried back that night to prison again." On Good Friday 1575, the captives were whipped, forced to mount horses "naked from the middle upward" as a "spectacle for all the people to behold throughout the chief and principal streets of the city" and to display stripes "most cruelly laid-upon their naked bodies with long whips by sundry men appointed to be the executioners." As they proceeded, three hundred criers announced, "*Behold these English dogs, Lutherans, enemies of God!*"

Some English captives—John Gray, John Brown, John Rider, John Moon, James Collier, and Thomas Brown—suffered two hundred lashes, and were sentenced to serve aboard Spanish galleys for eight years. "And then was I, Miles Philips called, and was adjudged to serve in a monastery for five years, without any stripes, and to wear a fool's coat; or sanbenito, during all that time." Philips was relatively lucky. He was among the survivors, although he would bear the psychic scars of the ordeal.

This fate constantly threatened Drake and every other "Lutheran" who ventured into Central America or other territory controlled by Spain. Only the boldest, the most reckless, or the most foolhardy risked falling into the Inquisition's snares.

In contrast to the powerful and pious global empire that was Spain, England was an island mired in debt and drifting into poverty. In

January 1558, France invaded England's sole territorial possession, the port city of Calais, formerly the "brightest jewel in the English crown," and reclaimed it. Without this little colony, the ancient kingdom was more isolated than ever. Her penurious subjects were divided on the crucial matter of religion and demoralized by a frail economy that depended on exporting woolen cloth, the proceeds of which could not offset dire conditions at home. Burial mounds were often ransacked by desperate "hill-diggers" in search of buried wealth. Famine drove people to survive on acorns, grass moistened with milk, sawdust, and the blood of animals. To one visitor, the starving populace resembled "walking skeletons."

It seemed unlikely that England would soon reverse its downward spiral, yet there were those at Elizabeth's court and scattered throughout the land who envisioned a more glorious and prosperous future for the nation, especially across the seas.

CHAPTER II

The Monarch and the Mystic

In 1570, Robert Dudley and Christopher Hatton, two of Elizabeth's confidants at court, commissioned the Cambridge-educated John Dee, equal parts mathematician and mystic, to report on the state of the nation's political, economic, and social affairs. A man whom Elizabeth called "my philosopher," Dee inspired the character of Prospero in Shakespeare's play *The Tempest*. And he helped to create the British intelligence service. To enhance his mystique, he signed his letters to Queen Elizabeth with a pair of O's to indicate watchful eyes, followed by the number 7, believed to be lucky, drawn across the O's: **007**, from which Ian Fleming, a former British intelligence officer turned spy novelist, is said to have taken James Bond's code number. The spirit of James Bond, combining absolute loyalty to the Crown with a cavalier attitude toward danger, extends back to Drake. (Elizabeth, with her penchant for secret codes, assigned nicknames to her closest associates; Drake became known as "Water" and Dee, "Eyes."

In search of more sophisticated education, the young Dee had traveled to Louvain, Belgium, where he encountered leading-edge scientists and the eminent cartographer Gerardus Mercator, who integrated Columbus's discoveries into his maps. No longer did depictions of the world show the Garden of Eden and Tower of Babel as actual, if unlocated, places. Mercator showed geographical features on a rectangular map with precision. Dee and the thirty-year-old Mercator became close. "It was the custom of our mutual friendship and intimacy that, during three whole years, neither of us willingly lacked the other's presence for as much as three whole days."

By now Dee was turning away offers of royal patronage. He returned to an England recovering from the excesses of the reign of Henry VIII and became a prominent figure at the court of the young Edward VI. He received a generous pension at a young age, tutored the sons of nobility, and earned renown as an "expert astronomer." But his fortunes turned when, on May 28, 1555, during Queen Mary's reign, an order went out to apprehend Dee and seize his books as evidence. It would be three years until Elizabeth became queen. Dee, who had once had an audience with Elizabeth, was considered a member of a clandestine group supporting her claim to the throne, but his real crime, according to the authorities, concerned his practicing mathematics, "calculating" being considered a form of witchcraft. After interrogation, he escaped with his life but was deprived of the means to make a living and suspected of heresy. The death of Mary and the ascension of Elizabeth to the throne changed everything for Dee. He still had her ear and, as a fervent believer in astrology, drew up charts concerning her reign, selecting January 15, 1559, as the most auspicious date for her coronation.

Dee went abroad soon after the great event. He immersed himself in Kabbalah, a focus of interest because Hebrew was thought to contain in coded form the secrets of the cosmos. Dee's studies took him into the realms of numerology and another preoccupation of mystics: angels. Dee believed that the study of such symbols would melt away religious obstacles and bring him closer to a universal tongue. He also took care to keep Elizabeth current with his work. After his return to England, he had an audience with the queen on two solemn occasions, immediately after the death of his second wife and again after the death of his mother. Following these meetings, she regularly summoned him to court to consult about personal matters, including her plans for marriage.

When not at court, Dee lived with his third wife in his mother's modest house in Mortlake, a pleasant village on the south bank of the Thames River, about eight miles from London. There he acquired other buildings, which came to house one of the biggest libraries in Europe, and which included works on magic, mathematics, zoology, marriage, tides, weather, and many other subjects, the more esoteric the better. Works by Copernicus, Ptolemy, and Boethius adorned his shelves. There were 2,670 texts in all, compared with 451 manuscripts at Cambridge and 379 at Oxford.

Beyond his library, Dee introduced crucial mathematical symbols such as $+$, $-$, and $\div$ to England. At the same time he became ever more absorbed in mysticism. By 1581, he believed he could communicate with angels with an obsidian "scrying mirror" intended to conjure spirits. This object, similar in size and shape to a woman's pocket mirror, but shiny and black, was intended to connect with the spirit world. Unable to see spirits himself, a source of frustration for such a dedicated mystic, he relied on a professional scryer, or medium, to carry out the work for him by gazing into the device in the hope of seeing visions or messages from the great beyond.

On a more rational level, Dee devised the *Brytannicæ Republicæ Synopsis*—"Summary of the Commonwealth of Britain" (1570)— in which he argued that only through maritime preeminence could England colonize newly discovered lands and resources and assemble them into an empire. He singled out economic problems afflicting England such as unemployment. And he was the first person to use the term "British Empire" to describe his vision. Dee's bold plan challenged the Spanish and Portuguese hegemony over the New World, but Elizabeth knew that giving the scheme her official blessing would surely provoke King Philip—something she could not afford to do at this time.

Dee proposed a solution for England's chronic economic insufficiencies in the form of buried treasure. Many in England concealed their riches in the earth in those days; there was no better way to secure gems and coins. The practice came to the attention of Dee, whom some people implored to use his gifts to lead them to buried treasure, but to do so was illegal, and it would have opened him to a charge of using magic to recover stolen goods. The first conviction for such a crime meant a year's imprisonment, and the second, death. He refused, although the idea of seizing others' treasure remained alive at court, which looked beyond England for riches.

Dee had long been an effective promoter as well as necromancer. Now he entwined the queen herself in his web of prophecy. When he visited Elizabeth in late November 1577 at Windsor Castle, Drake had just departed from Plymouth on his mysterious voyage. Dee met with Queen Elizabeth on November 25, a fraught moment.

At about this time, the Great Comet of 1577 appeared in the skies over Europe, prompting predictions of cataclysm and doom from philosophers and soothsayers. Elizabeth formed a different interpretation, according to Henry Howard, Earl of Northampton, who was present: "Behold a woman and a Queen, which seem to be the kinds and callings, upon which the Comets (if Astrologers speak truth) are wont to prey: and yet not only she relenteth not to common fear, but insulteth rather upon common folly," he noted. She placed her faith in God, not in superstitions about comets.

Under Elizabeth's influence, Dee advocated the revolutionary

idea of challenging the Spanish empire, which had been sanctioned by
Pope Alexander VI and the Treaty of Tordesillas. The treaty divided
the entire world, known and unknown, between Spain and Portugal.
On June 7, 1494, the two countries agreed that the line of demar-
cation should follow an imaginary north-south vertical line, which
was positioned west of Cape Verde and extended around the world,
even before Europeans had an idea of what lay beyond the American continent. Under the terms of the treaty, signed in the town of
Tordesillas, in northwestern Spain, the lands to the east of this line
would belong to Portugal and the lands to the west to Castile. Later, in
1529, the Treaty of Zaragoza divided the other side of the world. Both
treaties assumed that the Catholic Church had the final say over the
matter, and various popes gave their blessing to the arrangements.
But Protestant countries such as England ignored it for official purposes. Even so, ships venturing into regions associated with Spain and
Portugal remained wary. For a time, a surprising number of nations
complied with this arbitrary arrangement.

In time, the treaty had the opposite of its intended effect. Rather
than keeping Spain and Portugal at bay, it touched off a contest between them for global control. All the while Dee wondered why
this circumstance should prevail. Why should a Protestant nation
like England be excluded? He studied the matter with his colleague
and friend Gerardus Mercator, who referred him to an invasion by
the legendary King Arthur in 537. According to Mercator, who took
Arthur to be a real person, thousands of members of this invasion
survived, as did their descendants. On this tenuous basis, Dee contemplated extending the English sphere of influence across the globe.

He expounded on the idea in what he believed would be his
magnum opus, *General and Rare Memorials Pertaining to the Perfect
Art of Navigation*, a mystical four-volume description of a potent
new concept, the "Brytish Impire." The title page depicted Elizabeth

at the helm of a ship tending toward Lady Occasion (that is, opportunity). In this deeply idiosyncratic work dating from 1577, Dee discussed the formation of a navy designed to secure English shores, which had long been vulnerable to invasion by foreigners. At the time, England's tiny navy, hardly more than twenty vessels, most of them the worse for wear, paled in comparison to Spain's fleet of two hundred vessels. Dee warned "neither France, Denmark, Scotland, Spain, nor any other country can have such liberty for invasion, or their mutual conspiracies or aids, any way transporting, to annoy the blessed state of our tranquillity." That sense of security derived largely from the English Channel. Three hundred and fifty miles long, it is among the most heavily trafficked shipping channels in the world. But in Elizabeth's time, the Channel was nameless, unclaimed by any nation, and little understood.

To maintain this natural obstacle to invasion, Dee proposed a "Petty Navy Royal" of sixty "tall ships," as he called them, and twenty smaller vessels designed "greatly to displease and pinch the petty foreign offender at sea." They would be "very strong and warlike" and require crew in excess of six thousand, including pirates. He reminded his readers that these English buccaneers were "already hardened to the seas." They were courageous and fierce. The need for such a fleet, and the inevitability of it, struck Dee as "almost a mathematical demonstration . . . for a feasible policy to bring and preserve this victorious British Monarchy in a marvellous security." He recommended that the queen not attempt to finance this fleet from her own resources but from taxing the people; after all, the people would benefit from the activities of a robust navy.

The second volume, now lost, contained navigational charts. A third volume and its secret contents disappeared, and much of a fourth volume was also destroyed. In addition to this lost magnum opus, Dee composed a shorter surviving work designed for an audience of one—the queen—called *Brytanici Imperii Limites* (*The Limits of the British Empire*). Of course Britain could claim lands far beyond the tight cluster of British isles, Dee explained, basing his argument on the exploits of fabulous figures such as King Arthur and Madoc, a Welsh prince who sailed across the Atlantic in 1170, centuries before Columbus. In Dee's feverish interpretation, Madoc's exploration of America's eastern coast signified these lands belonged to Britain. Although fanciful, his theories evoked the Arthurian past and looked ahead to the creation of the British Empire as the modern-day version of that myth. For the next few years, Dee communicated with the queen to promote his imperial scheme. It would be England's answer to the Treaty of Tordesillas.

Just as Dee was aligning himself with the queen, he became distracted by the pursuit of alchemy. Elizabeth resolved to keep her savant on course. On September 17, 1580, she arrived at his home in Mortlake. "She beckoned her hand for me," he recorded. "I came to her coach side: she very speedily pulled off her glove and gave me her hand to kiss: and to be short, willed me to resort to her court." What choice did he have?

Within a matter of days, an invigorated Dee completed a new version of *Brytanici Imperii Limites*, placing the text in Elizabeth's hands as she walked through the gardens at Richmond Palace, built by her grandfather King Henry VII. The residence was a favorite of Elizabeth, who would die there in 1603. Dee spent several days discussing his dreams of a "Brytish Impire" with the queen and two of her closest advisers, Robert Dudley and William Cecil, Lord Burghley. Although Dudley embraced it, the cautious Cecil wanted no part of a scheme that was certain to draw the ire of Spain. It seemed that

Dee's moment had passed, and according to his own calculations, the very stars plotted against him.

Dee took refuge in his home in Mortlake, on the Thames, amid his books and manuscripts. Soon after, on October 10, 1580, his mother died. The queen herself called to pay her respects and to affirm that she would continue to study his proposals, although she stopped short of endorsing them. Nevertheless, without explicitly linking developments to Dee's treatise, Elizabeth gradually brought about his prescriptions.

*T*he queen was accustomed to charting her own course. Years before, on February 25, 1570, Pope Pius V had excommunicated Elizabeth, paradoxically liberating and condemning her. The declaration ended any pretense that she was simply leading an English offshoot of the Church of Rome. The pope declared her "a heretic and in favour of heretics." This papal bull was the equivalent of a declaration of war between two adversaries, Elizabeth I and Philip II, for the prize of global control. It appeared to be an unequal match between the island and the empire. Spain, along with the rest of Europe, regarded England as a backward nation populated with farmers and laborers. It was a natural breeding ground for pirates, whose immoral and heretical queen, Elizabeth, encouraged them and helped herself to the fruit of their larceny. Her court seemed rude and slipshod in comparison to Spain's customary formality. There was more: Philip had an heir at the ready, whereas Elizabeth was childless, unmarried, and determined to remain that way. England was torn by religious dissension and teetered on the brink of a religious war between Protestant and Catholic factions; Spain stood unified on matters of religion. Dee's bold plan for a British Empire to replace the Spanish hegemony over the New World, appealing though it was, was likely to provoke King Philip to invade England. Such an outcome would be a disaster for England, and Elizabeth hesitated to bless the scheme. An uneasy balance of fear between the opposing factions of Christianity took hold. Elizabeth conveniently made Drake her proxy in an undeclared war against King Philip as she struggled to outwit the Spanish and lay the groundwork for an English empire.

After Queen Mary's death, Elizabeth appeared powerless to stem the Catholic tide. She was educated and a Tudor, but at twenty-five she was inexperienced and unknown to the public—not a warrior or a zealot but a young Protestant woman doomed to vanish into a Catholic marriage. A Venetian envoy characterized Elizabeth as a "lady of great elegance both of body and mind, although her face may be called pleasing rather than beautiful." For all intents and purposes, "she concealed her religion"—Protestant—"and comported herself like a good Catholic." She had more than religion to contend with. There was the issue of her gender. After the havoc wrought by Bloody Mary, countless people in England were aghast that another queen would succeed her. In 1558, John Knox, the Scottish founder of Presbyterianism, warned: "It is more than a monster in nature that a woman should reign and bear empire over man." He could not bring himself to address the idea of two such "monsters."

Elizabeth was determined to confound her skeptics. She would have them all believe in their queen, that is, in *her*. Her tortuous path to the throne had marked her. She had learned the uses of adversity. She had little of her father's tyrannical temperament, although she could at times be brutal in performing her duties. She approached matters of state hesitantly and strategically, always re-

serving a chance to change course. She played to people's percep-
tions and expectations. She could be both pious and blasphemous,
virginal and sensual, compassionate and cruel. She walked the path
of monarchy as if on slippery stones, always managing to maintain
her balance, rarely faltering. She appeared to be lucky, but good fortune derived from constant wariness and anticipation. She had the
rare ability to learn from the mistakes of others, so she would never
define herself, or let herself be defined, by a single issue, as Mary
had. Nor would she marry and become subservient to her husband.
Although she often seemed reluctant to exert control, she always
maintained her preeminence, even if it meant changing her mind
once, twice, or three times. She derived strength from flexibility and
restraint, and understood perfectly what Niccolò Machiavelli meant
when he urged rulers to "abstain from threats or any contemptu-
ous expressions, for neither of these weaken the enemy, but threats
make him more cautious, and the other excites his hatred and a desire for revenge."

Her coronation on January 15, 1559, demonstrated that she knew
how to galvanize a crowd. The ceremony took place under the auspices of the Roman Catholic Church and was the last of its kind in
Latin. It included five spectacular pageants—Elizabethans would become extremely fond of masques and plays of all kinds—and let the
realm know what to expect of her reign. She made the point that she
was fully English, and not half-Spanish like her half sister, Mary, by
banishing foreign merchants from participating in processions. And
she restored her disgraced mother, Anne Boleyn, to respectability.
The result was more than pomp and circumstance; it was magic and
mysticism that would resonate with the English people. In this way
she revived a dying monarchy and made it her own. Observing the
ceremonies, an Italian nobleman living in England noted Elizabeth's
ability to connect personally with her subjects: "She returned very

cheerfully with a most smiling countenance for every one, giving them all a thousand greetings, so that in my opinion she exceeded the bounds of gravity and decorum."

Elizabeth's exuberant display derived from her belief that she depended on the support of the people as well as the Church to guarantee the monarchy. She would act in partnership with her subjects. Witnessing this upsurge of English patriotism, the Spanish ambassador to England, Gómez Suárez de Figueroa, Count de Feria, warned King Philip: "She is a very vain and clever woman. She must have been thoroughly schooled in the manner in which her father conducted his affairs, and I am very much afraid that she will not be well-disposed in matters of religion, for I see her inclined to govern through men who are believed to be heretics and I am told that all the women around her definitely are." Feria found another reason for Philip to be wary of Elizabeth: "She is highly indignant about what has been done to her during the queen's lifetime. She puts great store by the people and is very confident that they are all on her side." Not only that, "She declares that it was the people who put her in her present position, and she will not acknowledge that your majesty or the nobility of this realm had any part in it, although as she herself says they have all sent her assurances of their loyalty. In fact there is not a heretic or a traitor in all the kingdom who has not joyfully raised himself from the grave to come to her side." As a result, "She is determined to be governed by no one," especially not the Church and King Philip. From Spain's point of view, a renegade queen was a catastrophe in the making.

This was especially true because she was the first unmarried queen of England. To her many detractors in England and across Europe, she was primarily a heretic. And she was a usurper, not to mention illegitimate. Finally, she was, of course, a woman. All of these characteristics undercut her claim to the English throne. If she married, and if she produced a son to succeed her, a measure of legitimacy might return to the throne, but at the same time, she would lose her hard-won independence, and perhaps England's independence, to her husband. For as long as she remained single, ran the conventional wisdom, England would be feeble and liable to succumb to a bitter religious war. The situation was not sustainable. But Elizabeth had other ideas.

Her resolve became apparent to all when she presided over the Church Settlement that formally returned England to Protestantism. Prayers and worship took place in English, not Latin. The Book of Common Prayer became a staple of religious observance. Celebrating the Roman Catholic mass was outlawed, but that was not the same as outlawing Catholicism itself. She cleverly allowed Catholic symbols such as the cross and clerical robes to be displayed despite strenuous objections from Puritans—those English Protestants committed to "purifying" the Church of England from Catholic practices.

And as queen, Elizabeth faced one other immense task: getting England's financial house in order.

In 1558, when she became queen, Elizabeth inherited a debt of £227,000. There was no Bank of England to extend credit; the bank would not be established until 1694, during a subsequent debt crisis. Banknotes would not come into general use for another century. At the time, money consisted of gems, coins, and precious metals. England owed more than £100,000 to the Antwerp Exchange, the oldest stock exchange in Europe, and central to the world's economy. To make matters worse, Antwerp charged an interest rate of 14 percent.

At the start of her reign she was advised by Thomas Gresham, an extraordinarily wealthy and successful merchant and financier

best known for "Gresham's law," which held that "bad money drives
out good," that is, cheaper currency will flood the marketplace. (It
is possible that Gresham himself never articulated this principle,
but it is now irrevocably associated with his name.) From the start
of Elizabeth's reign, Gresham made it clear that Elizabeth's father,
Henry VIII, had suffered from a bad credit rating among European
moneylenders because of his practice of debasing coins. (Bad money
was driving out good.) Gresham cautioned Elizabeth that England's
entire financial system was being hampered by obsolete regulation.
In 1560, he urged Lord Burghley, William Cecil, to enact reforms to
permit the market to grow. If the queen needed to borrow money—
and she did—she could do so from within the nation instead of looking abroad for loans. Gresham knew it would appear unseemly for
the Queen of England to approach moneylenders throughout Europe, but if she dealt with the issue internally, that need not be the
case. It took a decade for Gresham's advice to be put into practice,
and by 1571 England had begun to reform usury laws, a step that
Gresham considered necessary for internal financial modernization.
Remarkably, by 1574 Elizabeth announced that she was no longer in
debt. When she needed money, she raised as many loans as she could
at home. As queen, that was easy for her to arrange. Failure to offer
a loan needed for "national interests" would have been deemed un-
patriotic. And the arrangement meant that those who loaned money
could be easily controlled. Not only that, news of such loans could
be restricted.

While Elizabeth may have been cautious with money, long-term
improvement in England's financial situation was threatened by the
lack of financial sophistication. She was against raising taxes, fearful
that this would alienate those whose support she wanted. Parliament
also granted money to the queen. Local gentry collected this, and
few believed that the amount collected was the actual sum sent to

London. Her life was complicated by the fact that the rich were also allowed to assess their own contribution, and it was an accepted fact that the money they gave was not proportionate to their wealth. However, Elizabeth needed these men on her side, so nothing was done to correct this anomaly. One way of coping with this situation would have been for the queen to have an efficient bureaucracy— but this she did not have.

England and Wales also suffered from natural disasters. A series of poor harvests in the 1590s devastated the nation's economy, and Elizabeth was forced to borrow from financiers. In 1600, the Crown estimated its expenditures in both domestic and foreign affairs to be £459,840, most of which went to Ireland. England's contribution to the Low Countries came to only £25,000. However, the queen's income for 1600 was estimated at £374,000—a shortfall of £86,000.

There were a few groups, such as members of the Merchant Adventurers, who prospered during Elizabeth's reign. But these same individuals stifled fiscal reform, since they did well under the existing system. Those who suffered the most were the poor. The price of food increased over time by about 75 percent—yet the pay of agricultural laborers fell sharply during the same period. Those with work could barely afford food, and those out of work starved.

*T*hree years after the Elizabethan era began, it nearly ended. On October 10, 1562, the twenty-nine-year-old queen fell ill at Hampton Court Palace, an immense retreat near London built by Cardinal Wolsey. What seemed to be a mere cold became a high fever accompanied by a blistering rash. Her Majesty had contracted smallpox (*variola*), a scourge with a 30 percent likelihood of mortality. (The term "smallpox" was new and distinguished the malady from its more sinister cousin, the "great pox," or syphilis.) There would be

no vaccine for smallpox until 1796, and in the absence of an effective cure, Elizabeth received the so-called red treatment, described
by Gilbertus Anglicus in his thirteenth-century encyclopedia, *The
Compendium of Medicine.* She was wrapped in a red blanket on the
theory that red light would weaken or eliminate the smallpox. No
other treatment beyond prayer and isolation was considered. Those
who survived twelve days of this ordeal usually lived, although tiny
scars disfigured them, as happened to Elizabeth. For the rest of her
life she applied white lead paint to her face to conceal the legacy of
smallpox. The disfigurement became a source of shame—she ejected
anyone who intruded on her privacy—and a warning to others, including any potential husband, to remain at a safe distance.

Her illness triggered plots to overthrow her reign. Three conspirators under the influence of a Catholic necromancer predicting
Elizabeth's impending death were swiftly caught, tried, found guilty
of treason, and condemned to execution. Elizabeth placated her
Catholic adversaries by commuting the sentence to life imprisonment in the Tower of London, perhaps a fate worse than death.

These shocks—illness and treason—transformed Elizabeth
from a vulnerable child, often the victim of circumstances, into a
canny adult constantly seeking advantage. The populace rejoiced
at Elizabeth's recovery from the smallpox, and coins were struck
to commemorate her reemergence. From then on, she showed the
world—lovers and rivals, Protestants and Catholics—the face she
wanted others to see during the forty-five years of her reign. They
observed a simulacrum—a term coming into use in England at the
time—rather than the disfigured reality. For Elizabeth, artifice and
dissembling became her modus operandi.

Her daily routine assumed the form she would maintain for the
rest of her life. Dressing consumed hours as her ladies-in-waiting
painstakingly laced and pinned Her Majesty into her clothes. Her

sense of fashion was acute. She wore shifts of the finest linen available, as well as wrist ruffs to shield her gowns from perspiration. Elizabeth bathed herself no more than once a month. In between, her maids scrubbed and washed Her Majesty. The absence of regular hygiene meant a surfeit of unpleasant odors. Elizabeth and others disguised them with sachets of oil and dried flowers pinned into their clothes. There were no toothbrushes, and she did not brush her teeth; in later years, she suffered from myriad dental problems and stuffed her mouth with rags to avoid the appearance of sunken cheeks. Nor did she wear knickers. Attempting to dehumanize Elizabeth, Catholic mouthpieces claimed she had no need because she never menstruated. Her household accounts told a different story, documenting that she employed a length of linen as a sanitary towel.

Elizabeth wore velvet slippers when young, and later, shoes made of Spanish leather, and in her sixties, an Elizabethan version of high heels. Comfort also mattered. She spent most of her waking hours in the Privy Chamber, transacting business and consuming many of her meals there. This imposing room featured a crystal fountain and a mural composed by Hans Holbein the Younger. Security was managed by the Captain of the Guard, the Lord Chamberlain, and two chief gentlemen of the Privy Chamber. These were traditional arrangements. What was novel was that as queen, she commanded the services of six or seven women in the Privy Chamber and three or four women in the Bedchamber. Even more women of lower rank stood by, as did six maids of honor in the Bedchamber. Elizabeth selected every individual, and they all followed detailed "ordinances" outlining their duties.

In the Privy Chamber, Elizabeth could dine without being scrutinized and without a great deal of formality, speeches, and distractions. Her ever-present ladies-in-waiting brought her food on plates, each item having been tested for poison. Elizabeth would help herself to whatever she wished and distribute the rest to the ladies. If time permitted, she hunted with her courtiers, attended bearbaiting and dog-baiting events, went hawking, and played tennis.

Rules governed the behavior of everyone at court. Elizabeth's head was supposed to be higher than anyone else's, which meant a lot of kneeling, and no one dared to turn their back to her, which meant a lot of walking backward. Supper was served at an early hour, between five and six P.M., while there was still daylight. After supper, she entertained with gusto. She was a talented harpsichordist, she adored gambling, and she imbibed copious amounts of white wine. On occasion she invited Italian dancers and musicians to perform, generally without incident, except for a troupe of female acrobats who drew complaints about their "unchaste, shameless and unnatural tumbling." Like many monarchs, she had a fool entertain her, but in her case, the fool was female, a dwarf known as Tomasin de Paris. On occasion, Elizabeth kept an African page boy in attendance, attired in white taffeta with gold and silver stripes, and stockings and shoes all in white.

At night, she insisted on beeswax candles to shed light, and she slept on silk sheets adorned with Tudor roses. She retired at nine in the evening to the accompaniment of maids softly singing, but sleep did not come easily. The windows to her bedchamber were shut tight to keep out the foul night air, and heavy curtains obscured the moonlight, believed to endanger unwary sleepers. Despite these precautions, she suffered from insomnia and dreaded a surprise attack in her bedchamber—and with good reason. During her reign, she survived fourteen assassination plots.

She slept late, explaining, "You know I am no morning woman," and even then, it took her ladies and maids two hours to get her prepared for the day. It was said that it was easier to rig a ship for the royal navy than to outfit the queen.

She remained available yet unattainable, the only queen of England who never married. Elizabeth turned this limitation, the lack of a king, into a source of strength and popularity. Her accession day, November 17, became the most important holiday in the English calendar and was celebrated with bonfires, bells, and knights jousting. The cult of her virginity took on quasi-religious significance. Despite her Protestant allegiance, items associated with the Virgin Mary—the phoenix, ermine, crescent moon, rose, and pearl—became associated with Elizabeth, the Chaste Queen—even though her chastity was more an article of faith than a reality. She dressed provocatively; when the weather was hot, she exposed her breasts to seek relief. Her ghostly white makeup imparted an ethereal glow to her flushed skin.

*E*lizabeth carried on for years with her chief consort, Robert Dudley, the 1st Earl of Leicester. The couple took outlandish physical liberties with each other in public, and they had adjoining apartments. But romancing the queen made Dudley a target for murderous rivals. He took to wearing a coat of mail under his shirt to protect against attempts on his life. Dudley hoped to wed Elizabeth, even though he was already married to a beauty by the name of Amy Robsart, who was rarely seen at court. In September 1560, while at home in Oxford, Lady Dudley, alone "in a certain chamber" (perhaps the water closet), fell down the stairs and broke her neck. Dudley was suspected of arranging his wife's demise so he could marry the queen. The scandal drove him apart from Elizabeth, who could not be seen cavorting with a suspected murderer.

Instead, she set out to seduce Sir Christopher Hatton, an obscure member of Parliament, who became so infatuated with her that observers feared for his sanity. When not in her presence, he became physically ill. Elizabeth dispatched him to a spa to recover from his lovesickness, and from there he wrote to her, "I love you. I cannot lack you . . . Passion overcometh me. I can write no more. Love me for I love you." Although Hatton and Dudley answered her need for a fleeting measure of intimacy, neither could join her on the throne.

*E*lizabeth's other preoccupation concerned the risks and temptations of empire. She sustained her balancing act between Protestant and Catholic. An act of Parliament made her head of the Church of England, but in private, her chapel services retained Catholic ritual. Her excommunication proved a turning point. Designed to extinguish her authority, it had the opposite effect. It emboldened both her and her enemies. English Catholics, placed in an impossible position, schemed to replace her with a Catholic monarch. She retaliated by taking measures against priests and other religious enemies. The challenges posed by excommunication proved liberating, and she retained her popularity with her preferred constituency, the people. She conveyed the impression of evenhandedness, which only added to her stature. "I see and I say nothing" became her watchword. Later, she won admiration from a most unlikely source, Pope Sixtus V, who offered compliments tinged with regret: "She certainly is a great queen. Were she only a Catholic, she would be our dearly beloved. Just look how well she governs," he exclaimed. "She is only a woman—only mistress of half an island—and yet she makes herself feared by Spain, by France, by the Empire, by all." This cantankerous and unattractive pontiff was smitten by the heretical queen. "A pity we cannot marry, she and I, for our children would have ruled the world," he lamented. Nor was he alone. English poets called her "Gloriana" in tribute.

These tributes were chimerical. Insecurity gnawed at the foundations of her reign. To the north, she faced threats from Scotland, home of her cousin Mary and a stronghold of Catholics. On the Continent, the massed forces of Spain, Portugal, and France ruled the seas and commerce. Philip II of Spain loathed her and sent spies to England to undermine her reign like so many termites, but it would be years before the mutual antipathy broke out in open warfare. Her version of Protestantism gradually took root, and she favored adventurers who belonged to that faith.

All the while, intimations of empire inspired receptive minds in England. In 1555, a graduate of Cambridge University named Richard Eden published *Decades of the Newe Worlde*, a compendium of accounts of exploration, including Antonio Pigafetta's *First Voyage Around the World*. Inspired by Magellan, English explorers took up the challenge. Elizabeth dabbled in a bit of piracy of her own as early as December 1568. Spanish ships bearing gold to pay troops in the Netherlands encountered a storm and unwisely sought shelter in various English harbors. Although England and Spain were not officially at war, Elizabeth's agents took the opportunity to relieve the ships of their cargo of gold for safekeeping, and never returned it.

A few years later, attention turned to the legendary "Northwest Passage," a shortcut to the riches of Asia. It was believed to run from the Arctic Ocean along the northern coast of North America to the Pacific. Although proponents in Spain and in England claimed it was possible to navigate the passage from west to east, and a Spanish friar named Antonio Urdaneta claimed to have done as much, the Northwest Passage remained elusive. Undeterred, Humphrey Gilbert, in Devon, offered to claim it for England. The offspring of wealthy gentry and a graduate of Eton and Oxford, he had studied French and Spanish, war and navigation. He served in the English military intervention in Ireland, where he was wounded in battle.

He adopted ruthless measures to bring the Irish to heel, refusing to spare women and children, and notoriously advocating the display of the victims' heads on stakes to scare the populace into subservience. He urged the English to keep the bit firmly in the teeth of the Irish.

Gilbert devoted the rest of his career to promoting exploration, especially of Asia. He wrote to Elizabeth to volunteer for the Northwest Passage initiative, personally funding the venture. All that he asked in return was a monopoly on all trade through the passage during his lifetime. To further his argument, he composed *A Discourse of a Discoverie for a New Passage to Cataia*, interspersing his argument with quotations from antiquity designed to persuade Elizabeth and the English public of his scheme. He included a map to show how easy it would be to outdo Catholic explorers. His proposed route ran along largely imaginary geographical features to the eastern boundary of the Pacific Ocean. From there it was but a short run across the Pacific to China and the Moluccas and their spices, precious metals, silks, and "cloths of gold." English merchants in that part of the world could sell these precious items locally to realize a quick profit. As for the strait, it could become a home for "such needy people of our Country, which now trouble the common wealth, and through want here at home, are daily enforced to commit outrageous offences, whereby there are daily consumed by the Gallows"—in other words, a colony comprised of misfits and criminals.

In 1578, Gilbert received "letters of patent" or official authorization for a voyage of exploration. This was a major undertaking for a neophyte, seven ships in all, one of them commanded by Gilbert's well-connected Protestant half brother Walter Raleigh, who later rivaled Drake as the most celebrated—and tragic—Elizabethan explorer. Gilbert set sail from the port of Plymouth, in Devon. Winter storms in the Atlantic pummeled the fleet. Gilbert was not the master mariner he believed himself to be. Defeated by rough weather, the ships limped back to Plymouth six months later. In 1583, Gilbert went to the bottom aboard his own ship.

*J*ohn Oxenham initially proved more successful than Gilbert. He made two incursions into Central America, the first time with Francis Drake as his captain. This voyage left Plymouth in May 1572, and included two of Drake's brothers, John and Joseph, neither of whom survived, along with seventy other men aboard two ships. When they reached the Isthmus of Panama, they assailed the Spanish with raids on nearby mines. They ambushed a mule train transporting silver across the isthmus, put the guards to flight, and returned to England in August 1573 carrying a substantial treasure stolen from the Spanish to benefit themselves and Queen Elizabeth. The successful voyage later encouraged Drake to dream of an even more daring voyage of plunder.

Oxenham tried his luck again. Departing from Plymouth on April 9, 1576, on an armed frigate (a maneuverable warship) accompanied by two pinnaces, he proceeded to Panama, where he surprised the Spanish who had established themselves there, and were not expecting any intruders, least of all from England. The audacious pirate and his crew seized two Spanish barques (small sailing vessels with at least three masts) laden with Spanish silver and gold coins, along with other valuable booty. Oxenham planned to capture the entire Isthmus of Panama, almost five hundred miles of twisting waterway. Control of this strip of land would give him a chokehold on global trade.

As he and his men made off with their loot, the Spanish, led by Gabriel de Loarte, tracked them down by following the trail of trash they had scattered along the banks of the Tuira River. Following the practice of pirates, Oxenham buried the stolen fortune, and then he engaged in a pitched battle with the Spanish who had spied on him, barely managing to escape. Months later, in the middle of 1578, Spanish forces trapped him. He would never see Plymouth again. On September 30, 1580, the Spanish executed him in Lima, Peru.

Rumors reached England that Drake had been executed along with Oxenham. On hearing this false information, Elizabeth drafted an official document in which she announced that she was extremely "glad" about this development, which, had Drake heard of her reaction, would have been most disconcerting. She later toned down her comment and said she "took no exception to the news," which was hardly more reassuring. In either case, Elizabeth's statements were nothing more than posturing. She had surreptitiously backed his voyage and wanted him to succeed, but at the same time she needed to maintain the appearance of strict neutrality to keep the peace with vastly more powerful Spain.

The Monarquía Hispánica, the largest, wealthiest, and cruelest empire in the world, was built on slavery and the confiscation of wealth, especially gold and silver. The far-flung realm rapidly gained strength during the fifty-five-year reign of Philip II and evolved into a highly organized system of convoys and plunder of the New World. By the 1560s, after French privateers sacked Havana, the Spanish government, under the direction of Pedro Menéndez de Avilés, began systematically protecting the Caribbean, Cuba, and the Canary Islands from pirates while transporting silver to Spain in ships known as the treasure fleet.

There were actually two treasure fleets, each with its own route, or sea-lane, managed by the Casa de Contratación, or House of

Trade, founded in Seville in 1503. The first, the Flota de Indias, ran between Seville and the Caribbean Spanish West Indies. Ships arrived in ports as far-flung as Veracruz and Cartagena before stopping in Havana and returning to Spain. A second route, the Galéon de Manila, ran from the Philippines across the Pacific to Acapulco, where precious commodities from the other side of the world were transferred by mule train to Veracruz and loaded onto treasure ships bound for Spain. The Casa levied a 20 percent tax, known as the *quinto real,* or royal fifth, on precious metals coming into the country, mostly silver.

Record keeping was meticulous, even as corruption flourished. On land, the crown trained legions of clerks to staff the immense new bureaucracy. There was a growing demand for *letrados,* or men of letters who had graduated from universities such as Valladolid, Salamanca, and Alcalá, to work in the Casa and other government bureaucracies as the empire expanded year by year. In 1513, Vasco Núñez de Balboa traversed the Isthmus of Panama and became the first European, or at least the first European expedition leader, to reach the west coast of the New World and to lay eyes on the Pacific Ocean, which he claimed for Spain. More territory to exploit, administer, and tax. At sea, each ship had her own clerk who oversaw goods and transactions.

The Casa did more than levy taxes. It ran a school dedicated to training pilots for ocean navigation. No other European country except Portugal had anything like it. The Casa also maintained a massive, evolving cartographic database originally known as the Padrón Real, or Royal Register. Begun in 1508, it was a compilation of routes for the treasure fleet, and every ship in the fleet carried a copy. (By Drake's era, it was called the Padrón General.) A number of prominent navigators—Amerigo Vespucci, Juan Lopez de Velasco, and Sebastian Cabot (who was Venetian)—consulted versions of this map for their voyages, but Drake preferred to rely on an improvised collection of maps dating back to Magellan's circumnavigation.

With its Casa, Padrón, and centralized administration, the Spanish system proved efficient. Each year two fleets guarded by military ships departed from Spain carrying goods for Spanish America. Their route followed the coast of Africa to the Canary Islands, where they took on provisions prior to heading west across the Atlantic to the Caribbean. The fleets went their separate ways, one bound for Mexico, to load up on porcelain and silk from China, and the other for Cartagena, to receive silver, especially Peruvian silver from the seaport of Callao, near Lima, and from Potosí, in the southern highlands of Bolivia. Some silver was transported by mule train, especially near the Isthmus of Panama, one of the few places where it was vulnerable to marauders. After loading, the treasure fleet's ships made for Havana, where they formed a convoy to return to Spain.

One ship in the treasure fleet carried as much as two million pesos, or pieces of eight, equivalent to the U.S. silver dollar. Of four billion pesos mined during this era, about two and a half billion found their way to Western Europe, and the rest went to Asia, or remained in Spanish America. This economic phenomenon led to the Spanish Price Revolution, which lasted more than a hundred years, during which prices rose steadily, as people and governments with more gold and silver than ever chased a finite number of goods. As a result of these imbalances, the Spanish economy remained in flux, despite Philip's micromanagement. State bankruptcies were declared over and over—in 1557, and again in 1560, in 1569, and, as if nothing had been learned from these crises, in 1575 and 1596.

This chaotic economy coexisted with appalling suffering. During the early years of the Spanish empire, an estimated seventy million people perished, more than 80 percent of the entire indigenous population of Central and South America. The toll was so high that it is considered the worst genocide in history. Many died simply because they lacked the immunological capability to combat the germs brought by the Spanish invaders. As a result, indigenous people, languages, and cultures vanished. The survivors lived stunted lives under the yoke of Spain, reduced to a subsistence level of existence. Legally, they were considered minors. The sudden and surprising labor shortage led to another evil. Those engaged in colonizing for Spain instigated the Atlantic slave trade, importing cheap labor from Africa. In time, the Spanish crown made concerted efforts to convert indigenous peoples, as well as African slaves, to Christianity. At the same time, the crown tried to limit Jews (expelled from Spain in 1492) and Protestants from emigrating to South America.

The systematic administration of the treasure fleet, with its meticulous record keeping, carefully maintained sea-lanes, organized transfer of precious items, and substantial royal taxes, made Spain the wealthiest country in Europe. Drake might have believed he was striking at the heart of the Spanish empire by depleting its resources and mocking its security, but by the time of his circumnavigation, Spanish influence was so entrenched and far-flung that he could do little more than embarrass the Spanish and carry off some of the excess wealth for himself and England.

The Spanish treasure fleet expanded quickly in Drake's day, with seventeen ships in 1550 and more than fifty by the end of the century. As a result, the sum of the West's wealth increased dramatically. The peso became the first global currency. But there was a catch: the treasure fleet was high-maintenance, and not much of the treasure remained in Spain. The ruling Hapsburg dynasty devoted most of Spain's imported wealth not to the benefit of the Spanish people, but to finance foreign wars and to protect its outsize empire against enemies, whether they were other European nations or the

Ottoman Empire. A lot of wealth went in trade to France, Italy, the Dutch Republic, and Portugal. According to popular lore, the ships of the treasure fleet, laden with silver and gold, were sitting ducks for privateers, but that was far from the truth. In reality, the ships plied their assigned sea-lanes undisturbed. Drake the disruptive pirate was the exception, not the rule.

At the height of the Spanish empire, Philip, the only legitimate son of Charles V, became King of Castile and Aragon in 1556. Soon after, he became King of Portugal, King of Naples, King of Sicily, the Duke of Milan, and lord of the Seventeen Provinces of the Netherlands. For four anxious years, from 1554 to 1558, he was the *jure uxoris* king of England, that is, the husband of Queen Mary, the grim, intensely Catholic "Bloody Mary." She was eleven years older than Philip, who was twenty-seven at the time they wed, and her youth had fled. Her sour disposition remained. It was said that she revered her husband, whose elegant visage and fine slim figure struck everyone as admirable. His calm demeanor belied a pronounced morbid streak. He collected body parts of well-known religious figures. In his peculiar morgue could be found a dozen corpses, no less than 144 heads, and 306 arms and legs. Even this collection was not enough to put off ardent Mary.

Philip made the most of their wedding, bringing ten thousand soldiers with him to England in 180 ships. There was pressure for him to put Elizabeth on trial to prevent her from inciting a Protestant rebellion, but he resisted the idea. The royal couple expected to have a child to rule the Catholic empire one day, and return England to the Catholic fold. That was how he understood God's plan. But English Protestants rebelled. "Bloody Mary" ordered the execution of the conspirators, and confined Elizabeth to the Tower of London for two months. (Elizabeth denied involvement in the conspiracy, and the idea of Mary's executing her possible successor was highly problematic.) Upon release, Elizabeth lived under house arrest near Oxford. The ordeal made the shy, intellectual girl into a tough and astute young adult. In William Scrots's well-known portrait of her at this time, she appears to be a serious and observant young woman. When Mary unexpectedly died in 1558 without issue, her half sister, Elizabeth Tudor, became queen. For Mary, this was the worst possible outcome, but for England, it meant deliverance from civil strife. Although she was Protestant, Elizabeth observed Catholic forms of worship, and tried to keep religious matters to herself, without success. This was a twist of fate few would have predicted, and it set England on a course different from that of Spain.

During this period of centralization, Philip, the most important monarch in Europe, married four times, and he pursued liaisons with mistresses in and around his marriages. Inevitably, his empire building led him to woo Elizabeth, six years his junior. It was an impossible quest. Their backgrounds contrasted sharply. Elizabeth had survived years of neglect and incarceration, yet there was an air of ebullience about her. She knew how to act the part of a queen. Melancholy, dogmatic Philip had been groomed by his father to maintain an empire, but instead of radiating confidence, he was trapped by distrust of his advisers and of the world at large. His unassailable position as the son of Charles V made him virtually friendless as a child. He was bred to be aloof, cold, isolated, and joyless. Etiquette in his presence was very strict. Laughing was out of bounds. He was surrounded by clerics, who offered moral instruction in the guise of companionship. He despised Protestants. He would never share his kingdoms with one, and Elizabeth resisted with every fiber of her being the thought of converting and becoming subservient to a Catholic husband—or, for that matter, any husband.

Philip visited England twice, for more than a year beginning in 1554, and for three months in 1557, before Elizabeth became queen. His visits filled him with dislike for the island nation. The language posed an obstacle, and the English shunned foreigners, especially those from the Continent. It was impossible to conceive of these two disparate empires profitably linked through a strategic marriage. The difference was partly a matter of religion and partly one of temperament, of Spanish severity versus English boisterousness. Spain was the land of the somber and gruesome auto-da-fé; in England, the executioner joked as he went about his business.

Philip had married his cousin Maria Manuela, Princess of Portugal, in 1543. Their son and presumed heir, Carlos, Prince of Asturias, was born sickly and deformed. Carlos led a circumscribed life and suffered the physical and emotional consequences of endogamy—generations of royal inbreeding. On January 18, 1568, Philip, accompanied by a cadre of courtiers, arrested and imprisoned Carlos.

According to one account, Philip decided he owed it to his country to rid it of the menace posed by Carlos. One night, when Carlos was sleeping, Philip, along with a retinue of gentlemen and guards, undid the bolts securing the door and approached the sleeping prince, who reached for a firearm or sword, but without luck. All the instruments of self-defense had been removed. He tried to strangle himself but was prevented from doing so. Realizing his plight, from which there was no escape, Carlos cried out, "I am not mad, only desperate!"

Philip avoided referring to Carlos after that. Protestants whispered that the young man had been punished, perhaps murdered, for heresy. Philip directed suspicion concerning Carlos's condition toward a bitter enemy, Antonio Pérez.

In reality, Carlos lived on in secrecy and misery. At times he swallowed any object he could force into his mouth. At other times, he refused to eat for days. He died in seclusion on July 24, 1568, at the age of twenty-three, an enigma to the end. Later, endless discussions, essays, plays, and a five-act grand opera by Giuseppe Verdi, *Don Carlo*, grappled with the prince's ill-fated life and death, the cause of which was not some sinister plot but the defects inherent in his limited gene pool.

Philip spent much of his time in his enormous castle, the Monasterio de El Escorial, northwest of Madrid. It served as palace, hospital, school, pantheon, and library. A vision of Catholicism (as it appeared to Philip) in stone, the monastery was dedicated to Saint Lawrence, a deacon of Rome martyred by the emperor Valerian in the third century. The design, a grid, was meant to evoke the grid on which Saint Lawrence had been burned. For the reclusive Philip, it was like living in his own tomb. Each morning he rose before dawn for Holy Mass. He often remained at his desk until nine o'clock at night, as two clocks counted off hours and minutes, marking the time until his rendezvous with immortality.

During that period, according to the French ambassador, Philip reviewed several thousands of pages of official documents a day, correcting grammatical errors and demanding rewrites whenever he spotted a flaw, as if he were a clerk or a schoolteacher. He avoided those who sought him out by taking long, unexplained retreats. Ministers on urgent business often had to wait for months to obtain an audience with the king. "His exits are predictable, his returns are unpredictable," it was said of him. Despite these pressures, he rarely lost his temper. He spent hours a day in religious contemplation and considered his interests identical with those of God. He ascribed success and failure alike to divine will.

On occasion, Philip got out and about. He hunted birds in Brussels, participated in jousts, and well into his fifties he could often be found on horseback. He was enthusiastic about bullfights, the ancient, pagan sport that offers a glimpse into the depths of the Spanish soul, where death and pageantry mingle, and he enjoyed witnessing a spirited auto-da-fé. In the Spanish empire, intolerance was a virtue.

From his secluded office in El Escorial, he oversaw all correspondence, hampered by arthritis in his right wrist and hand, the one he used for signing. His eyesight steadily deteriorated. "I am writing with my eyes half shut," he complained. When he received a pair of spectacles, he was embarrassed to wear them in public but grudgingly adopted them for work—not that the spectacles helped his powers of observation and analysis. His lack of comprehension of royal finance hampered his imperial designs. During his reign, the debt he inherited from his father, Charles V, grew rather than shrank, despite the infusion of wealth transported from the New World. With resources constantly flowing out to a succession of foreign wars, Spain remained impoverished.

Although Drake's plunder barely registered with the clerks at the Casa de Contratación, it was massive by English standards. From this time on, he was driven by the search for wealth to present to Queen Elizabeth (and, according to custom, to keep for himself)—more wealth than anyone expected from a buccaneer, more than his island nation had ever seen.

CHAPTER III

"Contrary Winds and Foul Weather"

On Christmas Day, 1577, Drake's diminutive fleet sighted Cape Cantin, on the Barbary Coast, Morocco. They had sailed a thousand miles only to gaze at forbidding mountains rising above a stony ocher beach. Concerning the question that everyone was asking—what *was* their destination?—Drake provided only "occasion to conjecture in part whither he intended." If he could make it to the Strait, he would cross it and reach the Pacific. If he could make it to the Spice Islands, he would gather spices and trade with the rulers there. If he could locate the Northwest Passage connecting Europe and Asia, he would take that route. For Drake, everything was conditional—except treasure. Once he stole enough gold and silver from the Spanish, he could return to Plymouth and claim success. His voyage would likely not end in that manner because he possessed signed orders from Elizabeth herself, or so he said, to circumnavigate the globe. No one else had seen these directives, and he invoked them only when convenient. For the moment, he made for Mogador, about 110 miles west of Marrakech. They dropped anchor at the flat, featureless island, a mile offshore.

Fletcher noted that Mogador was "uninhabited, about a league in circuit"—that is, roughly three miles—"not very highland, all overgrown with shrub, breast-high." The shrubs sheltered goshawks, doves, and "divers sorts of seafowl." On the other side of the island, the reverend noted "a great store of very wholesome but very ugly fish."

Drake took the opportunity of landing on a desolate island to bring the fleet up to full strength. He set up a pinnace, or tender, to enable the sailors to maneuver in shallow water and guard against attack. Sure enough, according to John Cooke, one of the voyage's chroniclers, "there came to the waters side some of the inhabitants of the country, showing forth their flags of truce." Drake dispatched the pinnace to inquire about their intentions. "They being willing to come aboard, our men left there one man of our company for a pledge, and brought two of theirs aboard our ship, which by signs showed our General that the next day they would bring some provision, as sheep, capons, and hens." Drake reciprocated with bolts of linen and shoes, which the locals were happy to have. Cooke neglected to mention that these inhabitants were Muslims. But Fletcher wrote that Drake was fully aware of the situation and noted that despite the Muslims' prohibition against alcohol they returned "by stealth . . . to have it abundantly."

The next morning, the Muslim traders brought their camels "laden with wares to be exchanged for our commodities." All went well until one of the fleet's men, John Fry, recklessly waded ashore, wanting only to give the locals a friendly hug. Instead of the expected embrace, said Cooke, "they set violent hands on him, offering a dagger to his throat if he had made any resistance, and so laying him on a horse, carried him away." The obvious conclusion was that "a man cannot be too circumspect and wary of himself among such miscreants." Fletcher added that the "cause of this violence" was the intense curiosity of the King of Fez about the mysterious visitors. What did they intend? Were the Portuguese close behind?

They replied they were Englishmen "bound for the Straits" under the command of "General Drake." Tension between the two sides declined, and the crew members lingered for a week, beginning with Christmas Day, during which time they happened on an old fort built by the Portuguese and later pillaged "by the King of Fez." Drake weighed anchor on the last day of 1577 without John Fry, who was released shortly afterward, only to find "to his great grief the fleet was gone." Eventually he found passage home aboard another English ship.

*T*he first day of 1578 brought "contrary winds and foul weather," Fletcher noted. The fleet proceeded south to rocky, windswept Cape Barbas, where Arabs prepared to either trade or raid were lurking just out of sight. Here Drake spied a small Spanish ship riding at anchor, having been abandoned by her crew, with the exception of two who had stayed behind. He had made his name preying on the Spanish and their cargo, so naturally the crew secured the ship, which could come in handy, as did the unspecified contents of three more caravels in the region, all plundered by the English.

Drake decided the location was just right "to make his abode, both for the place afforded plenty of fresh victuals," said Fletcher, for the moment and for the future. He marveled at the rich store and variety of fish to be found in the harbor, "the like of which is hardly to be found again in any part of the world." More than just an endless supply of fish tempted the Englishmen. The inhabitants included "a woman, a Moor with her little babe hanging on her dry dug, having scarce life in herself, much less milk to nourish her child, to be sold as a horse, or a cow and calf." Drake refused to deal in that kind of "merchandise." The former slaver had come to abhor the trappings of slavery.

Instead, the visitors were fascinated by gray, misshapen clumps of ambergris, a substance that forms in the intestines of sperm whales. The clumps were stuffed into balls known as pomanders—from the French *pomme d'ambre*, "apple of amber"—containing the scents of processed ambergris, civet (a small mammal), and musk (a pungent secretion). Elizabethans of all classes wore fragrant, perforated pomanders dangling from chains around their necks, belt, or girdle to ward off infections and foul smells, especially body odors. In an era when people generally bathed just once a year, or at most once a month, aromatic pomanders disguised objectionable aromas, and ambergris served as a key ingredient.

The Arabs of Cape Barbas, in contrast, craved drinking water and brought leather bags to carry it away. "They cared not at what price they bought it, so they might have [it]. A very heavy judgment of God upon that coast!" Drake's heart went out to these strangers, and he "freely gave it"—water—to them. He also fed them. That gesture turned out to be a mixed blessing, because in Fletcher's estimation, the mere sight of the inhabitants eating and drinking was not only "uncivil and unsightly to us, but even inhuman and loathsome in itself." Another outrage: the residents performed all bodily functions in full view of the English visitors. "There were not to be found in all those parts of the world more beastlike people than these inhabitants about this cape, as well in manners as in religion," Fletcher wrote. "Their religion altogether consisteth in worshipping of the sun . . . in this manner. They never come out of their dens till the sun be above the horizon, at which time they . . . bow their bodies and set their knees upon some hillock or stone." As distressing as their habits were to Fletcher, "I prefer them (in my opinion) before the Papists in their religion, for the ones following instinct of nature make a choice of that which in reason seemeth to be likeliest to do them good and to give them help." It was unfortunately true that they were "ignorant of the Living God," and so "worship the same as other nations of Infidels do." Matters could be worse, as far as Fletcher was concerned; at least they were ignorant of "the Pope and his malignant synagogues of Satan, who profess themselves to be the only spouse of Christ, and to have the keys of all knowledge and power of life and death," but who, Fletcher insisted, belonged to the "base work and vile things of the earth."

After six days of cleaning the ships and adjusting the sails, the fleet departed in mid-January for Cape Verde, a group of ten volcanic islands located four hundred miles due east of Dakar. They remained uninhabited isles of mystery until the fifteenth century, when the Portuguese, driven by a perpetual need for labor, became the first Europeans to occupy the archipelago. Beginning in 1526, the islands served as a hub for the Atlantic slave trade until well into the nineteenth century, attracting both freelance pirates and government-commissioned privateers carrying letters of marque authorizing them to attack and capture vessels, later dividing the spoils among the sponsor, owners, captain, and crew. It was here, at Cape Verde, that Drake, a privateer, planned to take on provisions, especially fresh water, in preparation for running a "long course (even to the coast of Brazil) without touch of land."

Benefiting from a steady offshore breeze bearing the fleet toward the cape, Drake arrived at a "great number of desolate and ruinous houses, with a poor naked chapel." To the skeptical Protestant Fletcher, the chapel "seemeth only to make a show" on behalf of the Catholic Portuguese who had preceded them. "The reason of this ruin being, we considered to be not the want of idolatrous affections in the Portuguese which possessed the island," he wrote in his early draft, "but the generation of . . . pirates, who, bearing a special grudge and hatred against the Portuguese, in the hope of purchase, take the opportunity of this place to lie in wait for such ships and goods."

Dangers aside, the soil was "very fruitful," with "plenty of fig trees, with fruit upon most of them." They surveyed valleys dotted with cottages, and vineyards, and tall trees "without any branch to the top, which bare the coconuts." There were plantains "in clusters together like puddings, a most dainty and wholesome fruit." In fact, "all the trees in this island, as well these as others, now being the dead of winter in England, were flourishing, with blossoms and green fruit and ripe fruit upon them," thanks to the strong equatorial sun. And they savored "most sweet water, bearing the taste of milk, which I conceived to be qualified"—that is, improved—"from the roots of the Muscatine vine, from whence it sprang, which bore the fairest and most pleasant grapes that I had seen in all my former travail in any kingdom." Cape Verde also abounded in goats and wild hens, as well as "huge heaps of salt like drifts of snow, and most fine and perfect in nature." In England, salt was considered a delicacy, generally imported from France, and preserved in a large saltcellar, or container, placed next to the host at a dinner table. That this immeasurable quantity of "perfect" salt in Cape Verde "was produced without art, skill, industry, or labor of man" made it seem "one of the wonders of the world." Fletcher lamented this land should "either be possessed by so ungrateful, ungracious a people, as are the Portuguese, or be so subject to such caterpillars of every kingdom and nation as are pirates and hyenas of the sea" without pausing to ask himself if Drake was just another "caterpillar."

The primary task of fetching water posed another difficulty. Two of the nobles on board, Thomas Doughty and John Winter, led an expedition deep inland on the tiny Isle of Maio but returned without water. It was at this time that Doughty began a campaign of criticism of Drake, to delegitimatize his authority and to persuade the crew to consider mutiny. He loudly complained of being mistreated by Drake, but the reverse appears to have been the case. Mindful of Doughty's status, Drake had treated the young man with such consideration that the others were resentful. Several officers loyal to Drake accused Doughty of stealing items "of great value" expressly to "enrich himself and make himself greater to the overthrow of all others"—in other words, to mutiny against Drake. "The General," as Drake was known among the men, "speedily went on board to examine the matter." There he found gloves, coins, and a ring, probably stolen, but "not worth the speaking of." Nevertheless, he replaced Doughty with Drake's half brother Thomas Drake. Doughty protested that the General had been "too peremptory and exceeded his authority." This affront—from a person of lower social rank such as Drake—proved too much for the aristocratic Doughty, who insisted that these items were not stolen; he had received them as gifts. Drake suspected that Doughty was trying to undermine his authority. By way of retribution, he assigned Doughty to *Pelican*, and had further demotions in store for his enemy, but Doughty's friend, a lawyer named Leonard Vicary, prevailed on Drake to make a show of forgiving the accused for the good of the expedition. The gesture temporarily restored an uneasy peace. Before they left for good, the English "espied two ships under sail, to the one of which we gave chase, and in the end boarded her with a ship-boat without resistance; which we found to be a good prize, and she yielded unto us good store of wine. Which prize our General committed to the custody of Master Doughty; and retaining the pilot, sent the rest away with his pinnace, giving them a butt of wine and some victuals, and their wearing clothes, and so they departed." The haul, including another pilot, was so rich that Fletcher considered it "the life of our voyage, the neck whereof otherwise had been broken for the shortness of our provisions."

On January 30, the Portuguese pilot Nuño da Silva, "well-travelled both in Brasilia and . . . India," declared himself "most willing to go with us." (Fletcher nervously considered this operation "the expedition's first act of war.") Drake immediately realized that da Silva could be a valuable asset, welcomed the pilot aboard, and treated him as an honored guest.

The next day, the fleet set sail, her crew refreshed and ready for whatever the sea brought their way. Of all the pilots Drake cajoled or kidnapped on the voyage, da Silva remained with Drake the longest. Although he proved an accurate guide, and Drake relied on him, his skills were limited. Like other pilots of the era before longitude, da Silva employed only "latitude" sailing. This crude but effective technique meant that a ship got onto the desired latitude and stayed with it until the destination.

*T*he fleet called at Santiago, the largest of the Cape Verde islands, explored more than a hundred years earlier by the Genoese explorer António de Noli and later by the Portuguese. The English visitors in turn scorned the Portuguese. Fletcher reported that their slaves, having been subjected to years of "extreme and unreasonable cruelty," hid in the nearby mountains. It seemed to him they suffered as much from "bondage in mind" as they did physically. The Protestant sailors were also distressed to encounter Roman Catholic images wherever they went, "for upon every cape and small head they set up a cross, on most whereof is engraved an evil-faced picture of Christ." Oblivious to his own religious hypocrisy, Fletcher urged members of his seagoing congregation to destroy the crosses with their bare hands.

When the sailors returned to the ships and departed, they were greeted with the sound of cannon, or shot, as a warning not to return, "but they all fell short of us, and did us no harm," recalled Francis Pretty with satisfaction.

*D*rake placed Thomas Doughty in charge of the stolen *Santa Maria*. Doughty was a personal aide to Sir Christopher Hatton, who was rumored to be Elizabeth's lover. Three years earlier, when Drake had seen military action in Ireland, he had become acquainted with Doughty, but the two were hardly close. At this point in the voyage Drake was still sharing authority with both Doughty and the much younger John Winter, barely twenty, the scion of a distinguished naval family. The two aristocrats were so prominent that, despite their lack of seafaring experience, many thought of the expedition as the Drake-Doughty-Winter voyage. Unhappy with his place in the hierarchy, Doughty addressed the crew to explain his differences with Drake and to encourage a smoother relationship in the future. "Whereas there have been great travails, fallings out, and quarrels among you and that every one of you have been uncertain whom to obey, because there were many who took upon them to be master . . . therefore, the General [Drake] by his wisdom and discretion set down to order that all things might be better done with peace and quietness." The General could not be in two places at once, Doughty explained, so he sent Doughty "to take charge in his place" and, more crucially, "all matters by-past are forgiven and forgotten" on condition that there would be no more "evil dealing." And he wanted the crew to keep in mind that the queen had given Drake other powers that she had given almost no one else, that is, "to punish at his discretion with death or other ways offenders," and Drake, Doughty claimed, had given the same authority to him. Anyone who offended them would "feel the smart." Still Doughty insisted that he would "rather be your friend than your enemy." It was unlikely that Doughty possessed the same authority to discipline as Drake did. In fact, it was troubling that he would even make the claim, but its import can be summarized in a word: *beware*.

*T*he fleet made for the volcanic island of Fogo, or Fuego, the Portuguese word for "burning furnace," which Fletcher judged "one of the rare wonders of the world." It rose out of the water, "like a steeple's spire, being hollow," visible for miles around, and "within the bowels whereof is a consuming fire, maintained by sulphury matters, seeming to be of a marvellous depth, and also very wide." Four times every hour it exploded into flames, "with such violence and force, and in such main abundance, that besides it giveth the light like the moon a great way off, it seemeth that it would not stay still till it touch the heavens themselves," said Fletcher. The explosions sent "infinite numbers of pumice-stones scattered abroad in the air." They fell to the water's surface as if they were "sponges swimming upon the face of the seas." Finally, there appeared an "abundance of heavy, black, hard substances congealed as smith's cinders, which no sooner touch the air but they fall down the side of the spire with a great noise to the lower part, where resting, they increase continually the outside of the hill."

In contrast to this continual uproar, "Upon the south side thereof lieth a most pleasant and sweet island, the trees whereof are always green and fair to look upon; in respect whereof they call Isla Brava, that is, the Brave Island. From the banks thereof into the sea do run in many places reasonable streams of fresh water easy to come by, but there was no convenient path for our ships; for such was the depth that no ground could be had for anchoring. And it is reported that ground was never found in that place; so that the tops of Fogo burn not so high in the air, but the roots of Brava are quenched as low in the sea." Of the inhabitants of Brava Island the crew glimpsed none except for a hermit who fled the moment he caught sight of the English visitors, "leaving behind him the relics of his false worship; to wit, a cross with a crucifix . . . and certain other idols of wood of rude workmanship."

The fleet headed south toward Brazil, with the goal of arriving at the Strait of Magellan becoming more certain every day. It was not an easy crossing. The weather inflicted misery even as nature dazzled the intruders. "We drew towards the line," Pretty recalled, meaning the equator, "where we were becalmed for the space of three weeks, but yet subject to divers great storms, terrible lightnings and much thunder. But with this misery we had the commodity of great store of fish, as dolphins, bonitos, and flying-fishes, whereof some fell into our ships, where they could not rise again for want of moisture, for when their wings are dry they cannot fly." In the unfamiliar surroundings, the expedition's three leaders found themselves at odds with one another. There could be only one leader to give orders, but it was not yet settled as to who it would be.

On February 20, the fleet crossed the equator. The weather turned monotonous and soporific, with stifling heat interrupted by stabbing flashes of lightning, booming thunder, and sheets of rain, useful at least for drinking water. Lice that had bedeviled the men since leaving Plymouth withered and died in the heat. Pelicans appeared out of nowhere and alighted on deck, where the sailors fell on them with cudgels.

Nuño da Silva, the Portuguese pilot, had by this time ingratiated himself with the crew. He informed Fletcher, mesmerized by the ungainly pelicans, that "they cannot abide to touch the water with their feet, and therefore being never so hunger but they would not take out of the sea any slain bodies of the fishes they killed themselves. Again, when they slept they mounted up into the air, and casting their wings abroad, descended without waking, fast on sleep, till they came near to the water, which nature abhorring, they presently awake, and flying up again to fetch out the rest of their sleep as before."

*D*rake renamed the leaky and decaying *Santa Maria*. She was now *Mary*. The name was inspired by his first wife, Mary Newman, or by perhaps his mother, Mary Mylwaye. And da Silva remained at his side for the next fourteen months. Not everyone fell in behind him. William Markham, the voyage's master, complained that Drake had hired him for a voyage to Alexandria, with its promise of warmth and luxury, and if he had known Drake's true purpose, he would have preferred to be "hanged in England rather than have come on this voyage." John Winter, the youngest member of the triumvirate, became livid at the sight of the upstart Francis Drake carrying away *Mary*'s store of wine "for what he now declared to be a two-years' journey."

The ships faced a journey of at least five thousand miles. Unease gripped the crew as they confronted distances and latitude. How would they get there? And how would they return home?

*A*t the time, navigators relied on three devices: the astrolabe, the quadrant, and the compass. The astrolabe determined latitude by measuring the angle between the horizon and the North Star, or Polaris, less than one degree from the north celestial pole, that is, the geographic pole directly overhead. The astrolabe of the Elizabethan era consisted of a brass ring fitted with a sighting device known as an alidade. The user turned the alidade to sight the star along its length, and read the altitude from a scale etched on the ring. These were tricky tasks to perform from the lurching deck of a ship. Mistakes were common and dangerous. A latitude reading only one degree off could produce an error of sixty nautical miles, more than enough to lead a ship to disaster. To minimize this problem, two sailors would take the same sight with different astrolabes.

The quadrant was shaped like a quarter-circle, made of wood or brass, and it measured the altitude of Polaris by sighting through an aperture and taking a reading with a plumb line intersecting the scale etched on the outer edge of the arc. Because all-important Polaris was often hidden from view, or below the horizon in the Southern Hemisphere, navigators improvised workarounds with several instruments, none of them perfect. Finally, captains and pilots kept declination tables and astronomical charts of calculated heights of the sun above the equator at noon for every day of the year. These precious records were kept under lock and key.

Sailors also relied on the magnetic compass, an instrument developed by the Chinese as early as the eleventh century. The original Chinese compass consisted of a wooden fish floating in a bowl of water, holding a magnetized needle. As European sailors later learned, the compass always points north. A typical sixteenth-century compass consisted of a magnetized needle attached to the underside of a circular card on which many directions were drawn. The compass rose, as this design came to be called, contained thirty-two points, each one 11.25 degrees apart, or north, north by east, north by northeast, and so forth. Sailors knew how to "box the compass," that is, recite all the points in clockwise order. The compass card was suspended by gimbals that permitted the card to stay level regardless of the ship's motion. The needle pivoted on a brass pin, allowing it to swing freely. The entire mechanism resided in a box attached to a cupboard called a binnacle, attached to the deck in front of the helm. A lodestone, or piece of naturally magnetic iron ore, was kept on hand to remagnetize the compass needle when necessary.

Unlike a modern compass, the magnetic compass does not always seek true north. The magnetic pole is not at the top of the world, but a variable distance away in the Canadian Arctic. Sailors in Drake's time recognized the issue, relied on the North Star to approximate true north, and worked out these compass variations with other instruments. But cards with needles mounted at different angles only served to increase navigational confusion, and unreliable maps made the issue of navigation still more uncertain. For all these reasons, experienced local pilots, familiar with the seas and tides, were valuable to a visitor like Drake.

Navigators also relied on a sandglass or hourglass for timekeeping. At sea, days were divided into six four-hour shifts, called watches. During a watch, a ship's boy supervised the half-hourglass, turning it when the sand ran through it, and calling out or striking a bell to mark the passage of time. Because the sand's texture and consistency affected the rate of flow, several glasses were generally employed for greater precision. The ship's glass often worked in combination with the log, nothing more or less than a piece of wood attached to a line knotted at identical intervals. A sailor threw the log from the stern and let the line play out as the ship pulled away. When the sailor felt the first knot pass over his fingers, he barked a signal to another sailor, who rotated a one-minute glass. The first sailor counted aloud the number of knots that passed until the sand ran out. Using simple arithmetic, the sailors worked out the ship's speed, or knots, in nautical miles per hour. The lead line consisted of a sounding lead attached to a line with evenly spaced knots or pieces of colored cloth worked into it. The lead was tossed overboard and allowed to sink to the sea floor.

Since the distance between marks was constant, water depth was measured by the mark, or by the deep. By using such simple, tactile means of measurement Drake proposed to sail not just from Plymouth to Cádiz, or to Cape Verde, or across the Atlantic, but around the entire world.

*T*he misery of life at sea was universally acknowledged. "No man will be a sailor who has contrivance enough to get himself into a jail," Samuel Johnson pronounced, "for being in a ship is being in a jail, with the chance of being drowned." Operated by convicts, ships were crowded, noisy, filthy, and dehumanizing. Personal space did not exist, except in the cramped, semiprivate quarters of the captain's cabin. Danger was ubiquitous. Climbing the rigging, sailors were liable to fall or to be tossed by the ship's movement into the sea, and few sailors knew how to swim. Below deck, amid foul odors, sailors were hurled about like satchels. Sailing in a storm was particularly wretched, beginning with the first intimations of waves reaching twenty, thirty, or even forty feet, accompanied by stinging needles of rain blown by strong wind. Even experienced hands would suddenly heave and spew as waves crashed into the boat and howled through the rigging. In foul weather, surging seas peaked overhead before crashing on the deck, and all the while the ship kept heaving, hour after hour, day after day. To avoid being swamped, the captain would keep his vessel at right angles to oncoming waves, but the whitecaps could be as tall as the ship, and when the boat pitched forward into the trough between these rotating cylinders of water, the hull slammed into the bottom with shattering force. It was not enough for a sailor to tie himself to a mast to be secure, he had to remember to clench his teeth so that he did not bite off his tongue. If the mast collapsed, he had to scuttle out of its way. And he had to keep an eye out for towering rogue waves. A moment's inattention and a sailor could be swept overboard, and no one would hear his cries above the cacophony of the wind.

The crew became accustomed to wearing soaking wet clothes, to pulling their matted hair and beards out of their eyes and mouths. Sleep was almost impossible. Sailors improvised catnaps by propping themselves between sturdy trunks. They wrapped themselves in coarse ropes affixed to a nail, but even that arrangement offered no guarantee of safety when cascades of green seawater flooded below decks and threatened to carry away the sailors. They dozed during lulls in the storm, but their dreams were grim and threatening, and when they awoke, they were disoriented, not knowing whether it was dawn or dusk. After a few days of this type of adversity, sailors were reduced to a simple desire to survive.

When the weather finally broke, and patches of blue sky appeared between ribbons of clouds, the sailors gradually revived, hungry, shivering, and finally able to think about food. They were able to walk about again, to dry out in the sun, to be heard above the roar of the sea. Albatrosses, petrels, shearwaters, phalaropes, jaegers, and other pelagic birds soared overhead, diving for mussels or fish, rotating a quizzical eye in the direction of the sailors drifting past. They took a moment to appreciate the damage wrought by the storm, the broken ribs, smashed fingers, torn scalps, the occasional fractured spar and torn sail, not to mention the rope, clothing, and innumerable personal items swept overboard during the storm, as well as the detritus that found its way onto the ship: clumps of seaweed, dead or dying fish, and stagnating pools of seawater.

Fletcher marveled at the immensity of the vistas unfolding before them, "nothing but sea beneath us and air above us," as he contemplated the "wonderful works of God in his creatures . . . both great and small." It seemed to him they existed "not alone for the relief of our necessities, but also to give us delight." Even the relentlessly optimistic Fletcher admitted, "the truth is, we often met with adverse winds, unwelcome storms, and . . . less welcome calms," that is, interminable doldrums, whose stillness gave rise to irascibility in sailors, especially those inclined to mutiny.

Fletcher monitored the fluctuations in the crew's agitation in what he called "the burning zone," where they "felt the effects of sultry heat, not without the affrights of flashing lightnings, and terrifying . . . claps of thunder, yet still with the admixture of many comforts." The lack of water remained a constant concern, but "not one day went over us but we received some rain, whereby our want of water was much supplied." At such times, it seemed as if a divine presence oversaw their transatlantic passage, making their way through the watery wilderness safe.

They filled the hours marveling at the "many strange creatures" of the deep. If the universe provided for them, Fletcher wondered, would it not provide for the crew, as well? They remained at a safe distance from the coast, where they observed "great and huge fires" made by the inhabitants "in sundry places" to offer a "sacrifice to devils," or so Fletcher assumed. Any ship that strayed too close to these rites might wind up wrecked and the crew drowned. He reminded himself that Portuguese explorers "by the loss of divers of their ships have often had that experience."

The Europeans who circumnavigated kept records, accounts, and recorded impressions. There are no written records from those whom they encountered. Those reading the European accounts could only guess at the motivations and experiences of indigenous peoples from Cape Verde to Cape Horn, from Brazil to the Moluccas. No matter where the Europeans ventured, they remained steadfastly Eurocentric.

As English ships explored, and chroniclers recorded their travels, storms that assailed Drake and others inspired writers and poets, especially William Shakespeare, whose late play *The Tempest* pulled out all the stops available to an Elizabethan dramatist to immerse the audience in the terror of life at sea. Shakespeare was not a seaman, but he might have been inspired to write his play soon after reading an account by William Strachey in 1610 about a fleet of English vessels encountering a "cruel tempest" off the coast of Bermuda. Some of the crew were lost at sea, and others were stranded on a small island. A few sailors made it back to England, and Shakespeare might have met some of the survivors of the disaster and listened to their stories, and captured their panic and desperation, beginning with a "tempestuous noise of thunder and lightning," followed by anxious sailors—"mariners," Shakespeare calls them—shouting orders at one another:

Heigh, my hearts! cheerly, cheerly, my hearts!
yare, yare! Take in the topsail. Tend to the
master's whistle. Blow, till thou burst thy wind,
if room enough!

The boatswain, or officer on deck, warns the alarmed passengers to remain in their cabins; otherwise, "You mar our labour: keep your cabins: you do assist the storm." Even the presence of a king and duke on board gives the boatswain no comfort. They are all equally powerless before the tempest. "If you can command these elements

to silence, and work the peace of the present," the boatswain challenges, "we will not hand a rope more; use your authority: if you
cannot, give thanks you have lived so long, and make yourself ready
in your cabin for the mischance of the hour, if it so hap. Cheerly,
good hearts! Out of our way, I say."

When it seems the situation cannot get any worse, the ship
breaks up in the storm: "'Mercy on us!'—'We split, we split!'—
'Farewell, my wife and children!'—'Farewell, brother!'—'We split,
we split, we split!'" And another passenger, Gonzalo, beyond hope
or prayer, plaintively implores the bedlam surrounding them:

Now would I give a thousand furlongs of sea for an
acre of barren ground, long heath, brown furze, any
thing. The wills above be done! but I would fain
die a dry death.

Going to sea, Shakespeare implies, amounts to surrender—to the
elements, to the madness of others, and to the chaos of the universe.

Brazil entered the European consciousness in January 1500
when a Spanish explorer, Vicente Yáñez Pinzón, who had led _Niña_
during Christopher Columbus's first expedition to the New World
in 1492, touched the coast of northeastern Brazil in what is now
the state of Pernambuco. This is a region of broad, pristine, inviting beaches. Entranced, Pinzón explored the Brazilian shoreline all
the way to the equator and the mouth of the Amazon River. A few
months later, on April 22, 1500, a Portuguese explorer, Pedro Álvares
Cabral, leading a fleet of thirteen ships, sighted a mountain on the
northeast coast of Brazil after forty-four days at sea. It was Easter,
so they called the landmark Mount Pascoal. He thought they had

discovered an enormous, fertile island, and he immediately claimed it for Dom Manuel I. All at once the Kingdom of Portugal became vastly richer and greater.

Fletcher recalled reports from the Armada de Moluccas, as Magellan's fleet was known, concerning heathens who "pray to no manner of thing but live only according to the instincts of nature." He speculated these people had once lived contentedly in a state of nature until the Portuguese intruders put them "in the most miserable bondage and slavery, both in body, goods, wife, and children, and life itself." They belonged to their masters, "whose most cruel dealings against them forceth them to fly into the most unfruitful parts of their own land."

Drake sailed on, undeterred by such concerns in his search for the Strait.

*I*n late February, his fleet arrived at the archipelago of Fernando de Noronha, slightly more than a hundred miles east of the Brazilian mainland. Under brilliant sun, broad sheets of crystalline white sand disappeared beneath glistening turquoise seawater. Despite the seductive surroundings, Drake did not avail himself of a scenic idyll. He made straight for Todos os Santos, or the Bay of All Saints, in search of drinking water. He had been preceded by Amerigo Vespucci, who had arrived on All Saints Day, November 1, 1501. Vespucci named the bay, the largest in Brazil, after his parish church in Florence, Holy Savior of All Saints. The bay, or *bahia*, became known as the Bay of All Saints, and the Brazilian state in which it was located was called Bahia. When Drake arrived, Portuguese galleys stood guard on either side of the bay. To avoid a confrontation, Drake remained out of sight of land, heading south.

On April 5, Drake approached the shore, where he planned to clean his fetid ships, but at that moment an impenetrable fog arrived to cloak them all. Blinded, they were in danger of running aground, or being attacked, or colliding with one another. One of the ships scraped bottom but fortunately avoided disaster. Da Silva, the Portuguese pilot whom Drake had enticed to join their crew, maneuvered her to safety. According to da Silva, the dense fog stemmed from an ancient conflict between the Portuguese and the inhabitants, who had formed an alliance with local devils. Whenever strange ships approached, da Silva explained, the devils tossed beach sand into the air to create an impenetrable miasma, and when the sand fell to the sea, it created an additional hazard in the form of shoals.

April 7 brought more hardship as the ships made their way south through a fierce three-hour storm. *Christopher* disappeared in the swell, followed by *Marigold,* now captained by Drake's brother Thomas. After eleven anxious days of searching and waiting, said Francis Pretty, "we found [*Marigold*] again; and the place where we met our General called the Cape of Joy, where every ship took in some water."

Throughout these trials, Drake adhered to a few critical goals: keep the fleet together, make fresh water available, and give the exhausted sailors an opportunity to rest. All the while, Fletcher compiled his log, tracking both the voyage and the meanderings of his mind: "We continued 34 days without sight of land, and being now entered into *torrida zona*, that is, the burning zones, we found the vain guesses and imagined conjectures to be untrue and false concerning the same, and the surmised opinion of the ancient and great philosophers to be contrary to appearance and experience, and indeed to reason: whereas Aristotle, Pythagoras, Thales, and many others, both Greeks and Latin, have taught that *torrida zona* was not habitable for the exceeding heat and intolerable burning reflection of the sun, which suffereth, say they, no radical moistures to abide in nature of creatures to live, we proved the same to be altogether false, and the same zone to be the earthly Paradise in the world."

All was calm, except "sometimes we had thunders, some few storms, and momentary tempests, which suddenly coming were quickly gone without harm or dangers." Providence assisted the fleet, sending fish right up to the decks of their ships, as if on cue, and not just any fish, but "rare fishes, which are not common . . . [such] as the dolphin, bonito, flying fishes, with many such others." They were five hundred leagues from land, Fletcher estimated; it would have taken time and energy each day to kill and eat and store sufficient food. Instead, the fish "fell upon all parts of our ships to rest themselves, taking them as it seemed for mooring rocks, with out any fear or doubt of harm or danger, in so much they suffered themselves to be stricken dead with cudgels one by one, to be snared with lines put about their necks with poles, and to be taken with hands without motion . . . as if they had been commanded of God to yield themselves to be meat for us." The only hazard was "salted and dried" fish that could lead to "pestilent fevers." Do not consume, Fletcher warned.

Of all the creatures in their midst, he most admired the flying fish, "of the length and bigness of a reasonable pilchard"—about five or six inches—"having two fins reaching from the pitch of the shoulder to the tip of the tail, in length and in breadth and form like to the wing of a swallow, and being full of small bars instead of quills, are knit together with most thin, fine, and clear film, wherewith she flyeth as any feathered fowl in the air." No other fish possessed "this kind in freedom from corruption and slimy nature, and so in wholesomeness and purity of substance. The cause whereof I gather to be, their continual exercise in water and air; for in the seas they are for the most part pursued by the schools of the dolphins. As a result, the flying fish, having such mighty and devouring enemies, by means whereof they are forced to practice their flying in the air to free themselves from so present danger." They flew as well as a pigeon, both in speed and height, and a range of "at least a quarter of a mile," limited only by their wings drying "and so will easily split asunder or burst for want of moisture, which, if they do, they end their flight, and fall down a prey to their enemies into the sea." And to their enemies above, the "multitude of strange birds did ever attend upon the schools of the dolphin." Fletcher compared the sight to a covey of partridges as hawks fall upon them "with all violence to make havoc," killing a thousand victims "before they held one fast for their own use, wherewith they pleasured their friends, the dolphins and bonitos in the sea, which received them with greediness, looking for more."

*T*heir next destination presented itself: the Rio de la Plata, the Silver River, a broad funnel-shaped estuary between Uruguay and Argentina, formed by the confluence of the Uruguay and the Paraná Rivers. Explorers had been surveying this silt-filled basin for years. Decades earlier, Magellan had been tempted to penetrate it, thinking it might be the strait he sought, until he realized it was a nautical dead end and beat a retreat, but to a less perceptive navigator in search of safe passage, the surroundings were enticing. "The country hereabouts is of a temperate and most sweet air," said Fletcher, "very fair and pleasant to behold." The one curious feature the men observed appeared to be outsize footprints, although there were no people to be seen in any direction. Still, they suspected they were

being followed by mysterious "men of great stature." These might
have been a group of so-called Patagonian giants whom Magellan
had encountered.

They surveyed the Bay of Montevideo, originally known as
Bahía de la Candelaria, where the ships found refuge among miniature islands. Sailors tiptoed up on seals sunning themselves on these
rocky outcroppings, banged the creatures on the nose, and killed
them. The younger seals were good to eat; they produced a soothing
oil; and their thick skins offered warmth and protection.

The seals learned to protect themselves from the onslaught.
When threatened, they launched rocks with their fins at their antag-
onists and scurried toward the safety of the ocean, with their young
clinging to their undulating backs.

When the men ventured out on land, they "chanced with a plant
very rare and strange, having but one leaf." Their appearance was
peculiar, "one side green and full of white specks, as the belly of
a toad, and the other perfect green and frayed over with a kind of
whitish small down or cotton, full of pricks of a poisoned nature."
These were prickly pears, *Opuntia*, distinguished by a head of a cactus bursting with brilliant red or yellow flowers, reaching a height
of about eighteen inches. The fruit was sweet, and as the men gathered them, the cactus's thorns buried themselves in their clothes, and
were impossible to remove. "If they come in touch with the body,
they convey their poison into the pores of the skin and work there a
most vile effect, raising red and fiery pimples, with extreme itching
and burning." Many of the crew "were mightily afflicted; for the
fruit being pleasant they gathered abundance of it to bring on ship-
board, and putting them in their bosoms within their shirts, or in
their pockets, and some in their hats, they had sour sauce with their
sweet meat, the fruit being wholesome." But "the juice of the leaf
is poison," potent enough for the locals to employ on their arrows.

*A*ll the while, the fleet had been running more or less south, remaining well offshore, away from the inhabitants. On May 12, the ships dropped anchor off a cape. On the following day, Drake decided to reconnoiter for himself, boarded a skiff, and rowed himself into a bay, to the dismay of Fletcher, who believed such risky exercises were best left to others. As Drake's little craft approached land, a man appeared onshore, "seeming very pleasant, singing and dancing, after the noise of a rattle which he shook in his hand," as he invited Drake to land.

And so he would have, had it not been for a sudden change in the weather. Fog descended, and an "extreme storm and tempest" blew up. Three leagues out—a "league" equals three miles—Drake returned to the flagship, guided by his nemesis Thomas Doughty, still loyal to the captain general, who believed him a witch and had banished him to a pinnace. Although Drake was safe, "our other ships," Fletcher wrote, "were so oppressed with the extremity of the storm, that they were forced to run off to sea for their own safeguard."

The following day, under tranquil skies, Drake made a second attempt to go ashore. He set fires to signal to the other ships to assemble, and so they did, except *Swan*, "lost long time before," Fletcher noted, and *Mary*, which still had not been found.

Once they landed successfully, Drake's men came across a novelty: a "great store of ostriches, at least to the number of 50." More precisely, the English explorers had probably encountered a large, flightless creature similar to the ostrich: the rhea. Like an ostrich, rheas are tall, the males more than six feet high. They weigh as much as ninety pounds, display grayish brown plumage, feature elongated necks, and have only three toes, a rarity among birds. On the run, they spread their wings for balance and momentum, like retractable sails.

Fletcher observed these large, ungainly creatures with wonder. "They cannot fly at all; but they run so swiftly, and take so long strides, that it is not possible for a man running by any means to take with them." It was difficult even to approach closely enough to have a shot at them. The rheas fled, but the locals who took their place "rejoiced greatly in our coming, and in our friendship, and in that we had done them no harm." The local inhabitants proved docile, "showing themselves not only harmless but also most ready to do us any good and pleasure: yea they showed us more kindness than many Christians would have done, nay more than I have for my own part found among many of my brethren of the ministry in the Church of God." Seeing the beleaguered, downcast sailors, they "pitied our case, being so weather beaten, and had been in so great danger, wherefore they were most diligent to do any good to us, and with all expedition brought to us some such victuals as their country yielded in most kind and familiar sort, thinking themselves most happy as they could first do us any pleasure." The Patagonians plied their guests with the flesh of ostriches, "whereof their land is full." The men feasted on the legs, "which are bigger than the greatest legs of mutton in the province of Peru, and the meat thereof is equal to any red deer." Nothing else on the ostrich body was fit to eat, it was all "skin and bones," too "scarce for a sparrow."

Yet the surroundings lacked the necessary wood or water, and on May 15, the fleet departed, heading south and west under light sail in search of these essentials.

By May 18, they went ashore again, in a different bay, where they waited fifteen days for the missing ships. During the interval, the men, sent in search of supplies for the next leg of the voyage, came across "a store-house of victuals for a king's army; for such was the infinite store of eggs and birds." The birds were so thick on the ground that there was nowhere to step. The sight and sound of an approaching man would not dislodge them. Instead, "they were enforced with cudgels and swords to kill them to make our way to go, and, the night approaching, the fowls increased more and more, so that there was no place for them to rest in; nay, every third bird could not find any room, in so much that they sought to settle themselves upon our heads and shoulders, arms, and all parts of our body they could, in most strange manner, without any fear." The men were being smothered by feathers and scratched by claws. "We were driven with our hands to pull them away one from another, till with pulling and killing we fainted, and could not prevail." The creatures' daring amazed the men. What a strange land this was, where the giants were peaceful and the birds terrifying.

To the fleet's great relief, *Swan*, missing since their departure from the Rio de la Plata, reappeared. But Drake had no intention of keeping her. Doughty had once been assigned to the ship and his resulting influence over the crew meant that *Swan* could become a staging ground for a mutiny, witchcraft, or other distractions. So he ordered her broken up for firewood, ironwork, and other supplies for the rest of the fleet. Which left the question of what to do with the subversive Doughty. Drake had no choice but to transfer him again, this time to the flagship, the better to keep an eye on him.

The would-be mutineer tried to poison his shipmates' minds against Drake, telling them that the General owed his position to him, and that he had special influence over Drake and even knew secrets about his life. When he finished spewing these falsehoods, he attempted to persuade a fellow mariner, John Chester, to take up the sword and, cutting whatever throats were necessary, seize the ship. Another sailor, John Saracold, later testified that he spoke up to encourage Drake to deal with potential mutineers as Magellan had, "which was to hang them up to be a sample to the rest." Doughty insisted, by way of contrast, that Drake's authority "is none such as Magellan's was. I know his authority as well as he does himself. And as for hanging, it is for dogs and not for men." Drake might not have had the power of life and death as Magellan did, but he possessed broad license to punish given to him by Elizabeth, who had told him, "We do account that he which striketh at thee, Drake, striketh at us." It was a watchword that would echo in Drake's mind.

Discussion of Magellan's experience continued aboard ship, as did Doughty's provocations. He urged Drake to give up on the idea of entering the Pacific Ocean, saying it was too dangerous and would lead to the destruction of them all. Drake was risking their lives for no reason. Better to confine his pillage and plunder to the Atlantic. But for Drake, that restriction meant no Spice Islands, and no glory. Finally, Drake had had enough. John Cooke, another participant who chronicled the voyage, observed, "The General did not only strike him but commanded him to be bound to the mast."

Freed from this humiliating ordeal, Doughty was shifted to *Christopher*—a thought that terrified him, for he believed that Saracold and others might come after him. Heedless, Drake commanded a tackle to fling him onto the waiting ship. The matter did not end there. After a furious argument with Drake, the master of *Pelican*, Cuttill, waded ashore, shouting as he went that he preferred to cast his lot with cannibals rather than be swept up in a plot to accuse Doughty. When Drake's ship prepared to sail away, Cuttill fired his gun, which Drake took to be a call for help, or surrender. Drake dispatched a pinnace to retrieve him, and as soon as he was on board, Drake weighed anchor.

No sooner had that problem been solved than foul weather separated *Christopher*, the ship carrying Doughty, from the fleet. Drake spent the next three days trying to find her. He eventually did, but from then on, Cooke observed, Drake blamed Doughty for any foul weather. By now the General was convinced that he was practicing sorcery. Drake boarded *Elizabeth*, assembled the company, and vented his frustration with Doughty, whom he denounced as a "conjuror, a seditious fellow, and a very bad and lewd fellow." Doughty's younger brother was no better, a "witch, and poisoner . . . I cannot tell you from whence he came, but from the devil, I think." He warned those aboard ship not to speak to either of the Doughty brothers, John or Thomas. If they did, he would consider them enemies, as well. If they obeyed, Drake promised to fill their ships with all the gold they could carry, and to elevate the humblest ship's boy into a gentleman. And if they disobeyed, they would all go to a very dark place. Immediately thereafter, he sent the Doughty brothers to *Elizabeth*, warning them on pain of death to avoid spells. Although he had succeeded in isolating the brothers, their mortal threat remained.

*D*rake faced a more urgent problem: the disappearance of *Christopher*. He leaped to the conclusion that Thomas Doughty, whom he now believed to be a "conjuror and witch," was responsible. The assumption that a witch was meddling with the expedition is not as strange as it sounds. Elizabethans believed the occult created disorder, even havoc in daily life. Few questioned the existence of the Devil, and a witch was, at bottom, someone who had made a pact with the Devil, thereby relinquishing hope of salvation in exchange for supernatural powers.

Over time, the reputation of witches became more sinister. In days gone by, there were good witches and bad witches. They devised homemade medicines to cure sickness, chanted incantations, made the odd prediction, and occasionally acted as a force for good. In the fourteenth century the idea took hold that witches brought about the horrors of the plague, which killed nearly half of Europe's population. Dedicated to eliminating this evil, Christians launched witch hunts in Scotland and England, as well as in countries on the Continent. In Elizabethan England, witches were believed to rely on a "familiar," perhaps a black cat, or toad, even a bird, to facilitate mayhem. When people or animals died from terrible diseases, when a crop failed, when houses burned to the ground, when soup or milk turned sour and curdled, witches were held responsible. Superstitions regarding witches abounded. Spilled salt brought misfortune. (Salt was expensive.) Walking under a ladder was considered bad luck. (A ladder resembled the gallows.) If someone sneezed, others immediately recited "Bless you" to prevent the Devil from entering the body through the mouth. Gruesome tests sprang up to detect witches. The accused might be lashed to a stool, or simply bound, and cast into the water. If she sank, she was innocent. But if she floated— most, but not all witches were female—she was guilty and would be executed. Anyone who had fallen into severe disfavor was liable to be branded a witch, including Anne Boleyn, Elizabeth's ill-starred mother.

In 1563, Queen Elizabeth passed a law intended to suppress the madness. Any witch convicted of murder would be hanged. (France and Spain, meanwhile, burned their witches at the stake.) Even minor witchcraft could land the offender in a pillory, subject to abuse from passersby. In 1578, while Drake was in search of the Strait, the court of Elizabeth I was gripped by fear. The suspicion spread that someone was working magic against Her Majesty. As the queen made a progress, or official tour, in East Anglia, three wax images about a foot high were found in a dung heap in Lincoln's Inn Fields, London's largest public square. One bore the name ELIZABETH on its forehead. The other two images, or poppets, were taken to be her advisers. It was assumed that whoever made the poppets intended them to melt in the warmth of the dung heap, bringing pain and death to the real-life counterparts.

Elizabeth had been ailing at the time, and gossip linked her illness to the evil effect of the wax images. In fact, she was suffering from severe dental problems, to which she was prone, and from which she recovered. Nevertheless, to be on the safe side, her closest adviser, John Dee, mystic, mathematician, and astrologer, set about performing counter magic. She had trusted Dee to select the date of her coronation twenty years earlier, and she trusted him now to save her.

Doughty himself lent strength to Drake's accusation by bragging that he possessed supernatural powers. According to one witness, both he and his brother "could conjure as well as any." Not only that, they could "raise the devil . . . in the likeness of a bear, or lion, or a man in harness." By accusing his former friend and ally of witchcraft, Drake had unleashed a potent force. It was only a matter of time until there would be a reckoning between the highborn Doughty and the lowborn Drake, or as Drake conceived the struggle, between the Devil and Christianity.

Still there was no news of *Mary*. In the meantime, wrote Francis Pretty, "there came down of the country certain of the people naked, saving only about their waist the skin of some beast, with the fur or hair on, and something also wreathed on their heads. Their faces were painted with divers colours, and some of them had on their heads the similitude of horns, every man his bow, which was an ell [about forty-five inches] in length, and a couple of arrows."

A cluster of people emerged from the leafy shadows, "leaping, dancing, and holding up their hands, and making outcries after their manner." Pools of water, the result of high tide, separated them from their English visitors, and Drake in a gesture of goodwill sent them a boat filled with "things he thought would delight them, as knives, bells, bugles, etc." After retrieving the gifts, the group dispatched a delegation of two men "running one after the other with a great grace . . . by degrees descending towards the waterside very swiftly." They came full stop, afraid to go a step farther.

Drake's crew offered more gifts tied by strings to a rod. The inhabitants exchanged them for feathers worn on the head "with a bone made in the manner of a toothpick, carved about the top, and in length about six inches, being very smoothly burnished." In another mystifying ritual, the men broke ranks, one by one, and ran back and forth, pointing out the moon and the sun, which Drake's men took to signal "that they meant nothing toward us but peace." Still, when the Englishmen approached, "they [would] have none of our company, till such time they were warranted by oracle from their god Setebos, that is, the Devil, whom they name their great god." The name Setebos had been handed down from Magellan's chronicler, Pigafetta, whose account, translated into English by Richard Eden in 1555, eventually came to the attention of William Shakespeare, who put it into the mouth of the magnificent monster Caliban in *The Tempest* (1611): "O Setebos, these be brave spirits indeed!"

*F*letcher had seen enough of the inhabitants by this point to arrive at a threat assessment. Even if they put on a display of hospitality when the ships arrived, would they murder the visitors while they slept? Steal their vital supplies? They might be innocents, or they might be in league with the Devil, to judge from appearances. "They go naked, except a skin of fur, which they cast about their shoulders when they sit or lie in the cold . . . Some of them . . . stick on either side of their heads (for a sign of honour in their persons) a large and plain feather, showing like horns afar off: so that such a head upon a naked body (if devils do appear with horns) might very nigh resemble devils."

Their appearance was impressive: "Their whole bravery and setting out themselves standeth in painting their bodies with divers colours, and such works as they can devise. Some wash their faces with sulphur, or some such substance: some paint their whole bodies black, leaving only their necks behind and before white, much like our damsels that wear their squares, their necks and breasts naked. Some paint one shoulder black, another white; and their sides and legs interchangeably, with the same colours, one still contrary to the other. The black part hath set upon it white moons, and the white part black suns, being the marks and characters of their gods." Fletcher supposed the body paint was functional as well as decorative, a "defence . . . against the piercing and nipping cold. For the colours being close laid on upon their skin, or rather in their flesh, as by continual renewing of these juices which are laid on, soaked into the inner part thereof, doth fill up the pores so close that no air or cold can enter." Devils or not, he admitted "they have clean, comely, and strong bodies; they are swift of foot, and seem very active."

As Drake's men marched about, noisily shooting "birds and fowl," the local dwellers silently hunted with bows and arrows made of reeds, "headed with a flint stone, very cunningly cut and fashioned." They ate their food raw. On occasion the visitors found the "remnants of seals all bloody, which they had gnawn with their teeth like dogs."

To the Reverend Fletcher, their unexamined lives lacked the essential element of redemption from original sin. "Neither is anything more lamentable (in my judgment) than that so goodly a people, and so lively creatures of God, should be ignorant of the true and living God." If only something could be done. He judged these people "tractable" and "easy to be brought to the sheepfold of Christ" along with their fertile and breathtaking land that would be enough to "recompense any Christian prince in the world . . . with a wonderful enlarging of a kingdom."

Despite this unresolved issue, Drake's men won the affection and respect of the people of the New World without firing a shot or making a convert to Christianity. They treated the captain general, said Fletcher, as they would a father, and the other sailors "as with brethren and their nearest friends."

The little things mattered most. One morning a Patagonian, "standing by the General, and seeing upon his head a scarlet sea-cap, seeming to be delighted in the colour, he boldly took it from his head and put it upon his own." But he feared Drake would disapprove, and so he "presently took an arrow, and setting out his leg, did deeply wound the calf of the same with and receiving the blood in his hands offered to the General." This unanticipated gesture seemed "to signify to him that he loved him so dearly that he would give his blood for him, and that therefore he should not be angry for so small as a cap." Magellan or Columbus might have treated the incident as a casus belli, but there is no evidence that Drake took it as anything other than a poignant apology.

When a Patagonian tried to emulate the English, his gesture veered from the comic to the pathetic. Standing alongside the sailors, who were drinking their morning draft, the Patagonian decided to take a "glass in his hand." The "strong Canary wine came not to his lips." Instead, it "took him by the nose, and so suddenly entered into his head, that he was so drunk, or at the least so overcome with the spirit of the wine, that he fell flat upon his buttock, not able to stand any longer." His countrymen drew back in dismay, as if the Englishmen "had slain the man but yet he, holding the glass fast in his hand, without shedding of the wine, thought to try again," this time sitting, not standing. The thirsty giant "smelled so long and tasted so often, that at the last he drew to the bottom, from which time he took such liking to wine, that . . . every morning would come down the mountains with a mighty cry of 'wine, wine, wine,' till he came to our tent, and . . . devoured more wine . . . than twenty men could have done."

The more Fletcher and his crewmates studied the Patagonians, the more intriguing they appeared. "No sooner are their children brought into the world, but the mother bringeth them between two or more fires made of purpose," where, on a pad of rushes, "she layeth the child, and basteth the body with the oil of ostriches," mixed with sulfur or other material, until it "entereth in the pores of the skin and stoppeth them," sealing the skin against the elements.

Adult men "have holes bored through the middle gristle of the nose and through the nether lip, with a peg of wood or bone, finely burnished, of three or four inches long, put in either of them, standing like a cross to make them seem terrible to the enemy. The men have also their hair growing at length as nature will yield, and is never cut all the days of their lives, which being loosed out at large covereth all their bodies to the buttocks, and lower much sometimes, but for the most part they bind it up with a hair lace of ostrich feathers, and make it a store house for all things (their bows excepted) they carry about them, so that it is a quiver for their arrows, a sheath for their knives, a case for their tooth picks, and a box for their fire sticks."

As impressive as the Patagonian men were, the women "in height and greatness are so extraordinary that they hold no comparison with any of the sons of men this day in the world." For instance, "as the men never cut their hair, so the women are ever shorn, or rather shaven, with a razor of a flint stone, whereof they make all their edged tools and cut one of them with another."

It was easier for Fletcher to understand the Patagonians' amusements—up to a point. "Their men being delighted much with dancing, make instruments of music, which being made of barks of trees, and sewed together with threads of guts of ostriches, like lute strings, and little stones put in them and painted over, are like our children's rattles in England, these they hang by strings at their girdles . . . which no sooner begin to make a noise but they begin to dance, and the more they stir their stumps the greater noise or sound they give and the more their spirits are ravished with melody." In the end, "they dance like madmen." When they are finished, "they stand as not knowing what has become of themselves for a long time."

When they heard Fletcher rummaging through his store of vials and bottles that had been shattered in the fierce storms, "one of the giants supposing it to be an instrument of music, must of necessity have it." When Fletcher gave the broken objects to him, "he and his companions were so overcome with the sweetness of the music, that he shaking the glass and dancing, they all followed and danced after his pipe, over mountains and valleys, hills and dales, day and night, till all the strings were consumed; for the glass being continually labored did become small powder, and wasted by little and little, quite away, and, the music ended." Without the makeshift rattle, the giants "made great moans to have another." In general, "they did admire at our still music," but there were important exceptions. "The sound of the trumpet, noise of the drum, and especially the blow of a gun was terrible to them."

*T*he jovial Englishman with the ginger beard had demonstrated his affection for local people over the course of several voyages to the New World. In this respect, he was a notable exception among explorers. He often appeared to be more at home among non-Christians, and they responded by spontaneously considering him a friend and leader rather than an antagonist.

CHAPTER IV

Traitor

Six years earlier, Drake had formed an alliance with escaped African slaves in Panama known as the Cimarron people. Their congenial name might have come from the Spanish word *cimarrón*, or "wild," referring to runaways. Or it might have come from *si'maran*, signifying in the Taíno language "the flight of an arrow." (The Taíno were, at the time, the most prevalent indigenous peoples in Central America.) Cimarrons living near the coasts traded profitably with all manner of pirates, and carefully sized up their opportunities. They were more sophisticated and varied than Europeans realized. Those of Indian and African descent practiced metallurgy, logging, and canoe building, according to a Spanish priest. They cultivated a wide variety of essentials—cotton, rice, sugarcane, cassava, tobacco, corn, and plantain—as well as chickens and pigs. Women were responsible for the agriculture, and men for hunting and fishing.

Drake became a particular favorite of the Cimarrons. In 1572, they helped him seize a fortune in Spanish silver. After that raid, he became their de facto ruler, probably because of his sheer effectiveness at smash-and-grab and his effort to establish rapport with them. Although a former slaver, he had grown disgusted not only with slavery but also with the Spanish soldiers and merchants who practiced it. He described the Cimarrons as "a black people which about eighty years past fled from the Spaniards their masters, by reason of their cruelty, and are since grown to a nation, under two kings of their own." Runaway slaves were common. At various times called *palenques* or *cumbes* or *quilombos*, they built their own settlements far from the mines where they had been forced to work and blended African, indigenous, and European elements with the local populations. To discourage this, the Spanish issued strict laws of punishment, *Ordenazas para los negros*. If a slave ran away from his Spanish master and joined the Cimarron outlaws, he would be hanged.

Among the runaways was Diego, the African who became Drake's longtime personal servant, and who helped to build an alliance between the English and the Cimarrons. Drake's Cimarrons were African slaves who had escaped or been abandoned by their Spanish masters. They intermarried with the local population, and several thousand settled in the proximity of Nombre de Dios ("Name of God"), occasionally hiding in inaccessible mountains from which they organized attacks on the Spanish and stole their treasure. Spain in turn threatened to burn down Nombre de Dios, fearing that it might become a staging area for larger confrontations, a permanent settlement, or even a nation. As a warning against such measures, Spanish forces constructed gallows on the main highway, vowing to hang and decapitate their adversaries.

*T*hat was the situation when Drake led two ships from Plymouth in May 1572 to conduct raids on the Spanish in the region of Nombre de Dios. It was his first independent expedition, too dangerous and provocative to be endorsed by England, and he did not have an easy time of it. He planned to attack the Isthmus of Panama, which the English had taken to calling the Spanish Main, and seize gold and silver

treasure stored at Nombre de Dios. He captured the town, and he captured the treasure, but he was wounded in battle by the Spanish and
abandoned the fortune to tend to his injuries. While recuperating, he
spent the better part of a year in the area, raiding Spanish shipping
and transports and strengthening his alliance with the Cimarrons.

During this period, the Cimarrons led Drake and his men to a
mountain peak where they could view both the Atlantic and the
Pacific. This mystical location revealed that these two great oceans
were connected. By this time, Drake knew his Atlantic reasonably
well, but the Pacific remained a vast unexplored realm of wonders
and dangers.

When they arrived at the location of their ambush in Nombre
de Dios, they dispatched a Cimarron spy to find out when the mule
train bearing the treasure would begin to move. Two Cimarrons kidnapped a sleeping Spanish guard, shook him awake, and interrogated
him about the Spanish treasure. The guard confirmed what the English already knew and begged not to be killed.

Drake intended to raid the Spanish mule train carrying gold
and silver across the Isthmus of Panama. In addition to Cimarrons,
his company included French privateers, among them the eccentric
Guillaume Le Testu, who had previously explored Brazil and fancied
himself a cartographer. In France, Le Testu presented King Henry II
a suite of fifty-six of his maps, one of which included a nonexistent
continent. Le Testu later joined the rebellious French Huguenots in
the struggle against the Catholics and their Spanish allies, and he
spent four years in prison for his trouble. After his release, he abandoned France and resurfaced in Panama, galvanized by the same goal
as Drake: to raid the Spanish for their treasure. Drake was cautious
about forming an alliance with Le Testu, which could lead to misunderstandings, but the French knight errant had far more resources at
his disposal.

Drake's daring, luck, and persistence paid off, and his raid on the mule train proved extraordinarily successful. He seized twenty tons of silver and gold. That was enough to see him and his men through several lifetimes, to prop up the faltering English economy for years to come, and to blacken his name in Spain forever. As a reward, he presented one of the Cimarron leaders with a gold-encrusted scimitar. (The Cimarrons would have appreciated iron, which they used to fashion their arrowheads, more than gold.) In any case, his tribute illustrated his progress from slaver to partner of former slaves. But he was still a thief, only now he dealt in gold and silver instead of people.

The plunder was too large and heavy to transport from this remote location to the waiting ships. Drake and his men buried most of it—some accounts consider this haul to be the original "buried treasure" associated with pirates—and fled. On April 1, 1573, Le Testu, who had been endlessly resourceful, was wounded in a skirmish with Spanish scouts who had been tracking him and forced him to remain where he was. The Spanish soldiers caught up with Le Testu, decapitated him, and set his head on a stake in the marketplace in Nombre de Dios. If they found Drake, he would receive similar treatment.

Drake and his small crew moved as much gold and silver as they could manage across eighteen miles of mountains to their ships' mooring, only to find when they arrived at the end of April 1573 that the boats had vanished, along with their hope of survival. The Englishmen were spent, trapped, and awaiting the arrival of the unforgiving Spanish. It appeared that their heroics had been for naught.

Drake rallied his band of pirates. They buried the treasure along the beach and constructed a flimsy raft that carried Drake and two other men miles along the turbulent coast to the flagship. When he materialized on deck, Drake's disheveled appearance shocked those on board. They carefully inquired about the raid, assuming it had failed, and Drake confirmed their fears by affecting a downcast expression. All at once, the unkempt pirate reached under his collar and produced a necklace of Spanish gold.

"Our voyage is made, lads!"

He retrieved the other sailors and the concealed treasure, which was loaded safely onto the flagship, and returned to Plymouth by August 9, 1573, in the sixteenth year of Elizabeth's reign. The last leg of the trip took only twenty-three days, a testament to Drake's growing skill as a sailor.

*D*rake's treasure offered a vital boost to the struggling English economy, but if he expected official recognition for his feat, he was disappointed. As a defensive measure, England had signed a truce with King Philip II of Spain, and Drake's blatant acts of piracy violated the pact. Nevertheless, the raid made Drake an unofficial hero in England and a villain in Spain.

The Spanish feared this unholy alliance of marauders in the New World would lead to more raids, and worse, the establishment of permanent English-Cimarron colonies. It was time to put a stop to this development.

At first, the Spanish invaded Cimarron settlements and set fire to their crops and villages. Later, the Spanish forged a truce with the Cimarrons, promising them land and self-rule. This arrangement thwarted the English for a time, but the truce collapsed, and the conflict resumed. The English considered themselves apart from European nations engaged in the slave trade, even as they contemplated a colony in southern Brazil including the Rio de la Plata, the Strait of Magellan, and Patagonia. In this visionary scheme, Drake would lead a remote colony of freed slaves allied with England. But it was not to be. Elizabeth's court considered Drake a pirate and explorer, not a colonial governor.

The antagonism persisted until 1579, when the Cimarrons, after enduring years of Spanish cruelty, agreed to live in a large settlement where they hoped to enjoy limited independence under Spanish rule. With this alliance between the Spanish and the Cimarrons in place, Drake's ambition to govern a Cimarron settlement unfettered by the English, the Spanish, or anyone else melted away. He had no choice but to return to his primary expertise, which was maritime exploration, which meant stealing gold and silver and gems from Spanish ships. At least it had the virtue of excitement, which Drake craved even more than stability or prestige.

*B*y June 3, 1578, Drake's fleet was under sail once more in the Atlantic, heading south in search of the Strait. Or had they passed it while in a storm or mist or fog? If so, they would take the perilous passage around the southernmost headland of Tierra del Fuego, later named Cape Horn. For the next two weeks, they sailed on, praying to locate vanished *Marigold* and friends whom we lost in the great storm." By the time the fleet finally entered the Strait, it would be too late for a reunion with the missing ship and its crew.

On June 19, their supplications and efforts were rewarded. "Within a few leagues of Port Saint Julian, we had our ship in sight, for which we gave God thanks with most joyful minds." Needless to say, "the ship was far out of order, and very leaky, by reason of extremity of weather which she had endured," and on that basis Drake decided to make for Port Saint Julian "because it was so convenient a place." There, he intended to "refresh his weary men, and cherish which had in their absence tasted such bitterness of discomfort." And he led them in prayer. Whenever possible, Drake, the oldest son of a clergyman, prayed twice a day, kneeling on a cushion in front of a stand as he softly chanted and his crew murmured their responses.

The marvelous reappearance of *Marigold* at that moment con-firmed the efficacy of their entreaties to a Higher Power and rein-vigorated the crew's morale. For weeks they had been anxiously cruising along the shore in search of the Strait, fearing but avoiding outright confrontations with the indigenous peoples, who called this land their own, and mourning the loss of those who had now re-turned to them. They rejoiced, but not for long.

They were still in search of the Strait, and the sight of Port Saint Julian fed their anxiety, for in the middle of a clearing stood the scaffold used by Magellan, still "sound and whole," in the words of one of the men. The crew's cooper, who repaired and maintained casks, repurposed it for "tankards or cans for such of the company as would drink in them." This deed repulsed Fletcher, for one. "I had no great liking, seeing there was no such necessity." And now, fifty-eight years later, Drake arrived to face his own mutiny. The world was larger than even Drake realized, but it could also be a very small place. Would he never escape Magellan's tragic example?

*O*n June 20, the fleet arrived at Port Saint Julian, a natural harbor located in Patagonia. In Plymouth, summer was approaching, but here in the southern latitudes it was winter, with days in the forties, and nights in the thirties, or even colder. The fleet sailed through a narrow inlet into Saint Julian bay. Once inside the bottleneck, sailors could be excused for feeling they had entered a trap. According to Fletcher, the southern perimeter was bounded by "rocks like towers, and within the harbour many islands."

The gallows that Magellan had erected still cast a shadow over a hill, and the sailors picked out bones scattered here and there. Per-haps they belonged to Gaspar de Quesada, a mutineer whom Magellan had executed on this spot. At that moment, the English explorers were interrupted by another apparition: two Patagonian giants. Magellan had glimpsed them, and Pigafetta had written about them. Part of their odd name—Pata—might have come from the Portuguese word for "duck," and it referred to their large boots, which resembled duck's feet, which added to the impression of height. At the sight of Drake and his company, "they seemed greatly to rejoice at his arrival, so did they show themselves very familiar, receiving at our general hands whatsoever he gave them and taking great pleasure in seeing the master gunner of the admiral to shoot an English arrow."

Fletcher noted "the hideousness of their voice" and that they were not nearly so "monstrous or giant-like as they were reported." He expected to see men seven and a half feet tall, but no one approached that height. There were even some Englishmen as tall as the so-called giants. Perhaps the Spanish never imagined the English would make it all the way to Port Saint Julian to disprove their exaggerations, "but this much is certain," he decided, "the Spanish cruelties there have made them more monstrous in mind and manners than they are in body."

The arrival of a second wave of Patagonian giants led to conflict. According to da Silva, the captured Portuguese pilot, "One of the Indians cried to them, and said 'Magallanes, this is my country.'" It seemed that Magellan's influence still held sway after all these years. "The Indians fled upward into the land," da Silva continued, "and being somewhat far off, they turned back again, and with their arrows slew two of the English sailors."

John Winter let loose an arrow, but his bowstring snapped. The sight of an unarmed Englishman gave the inhabitants "great encouragement and boldness, and, as they thought, great advantage in their treacherous intent and purpose," said Fletcher. The Patagonians failed to realize that their opponents had swords and firearms at their disposal.

As Drake and a few others returned to their ship, the Patagonians fired a volley of arrows at Winter before he could restring his bow. One shaft struck his shoulder, and as he turned and ran, another hit him from behind, "which pierced his lungs, yet he fell not." Just as he was about to retaliate by discharging a caliver, a cumbersome firearm with a long barrel, a sailor, known only as Oliver, "was presently slain outright." At that moment, the captain general "valiantly thrust himself into the dance against these monsters."

Drake ordered his men to keep moving from place to place, and to break any arrows they came across. Once the Patagonians had expended their supply of projectiles, the English would "have these enemies at their devotion and pleasure, to kill or save." One of Drake's company "dispatched the same man which slew our master gunner," Fletcher noted, "for the piece being charged with a bullet and hail shot, and well aimed, tore out his belly and guts." At that moment, Drake "made a shot at him that first began the quarrel, and striking him in the paunch with hale shot, and sent his guts abroad."

The victim let out "so hideous and horrible a roar, as if ten bulls had joined together in roaring, with great torment, as it seemed by his cry." Other Patagonians had emerged from the surrounding forest by this time, but they were all "flying away to save themselves." The English sailors, infuriated and frightened, obeyed Drake's order to depart rather than "take further revenge of them." Drake loved the fallen Oliver dearly, Fletcher insisted, "and would rather have saved him than slain a hundred enemies."

A second English sailor had also died in the skirmish. Curiously, Oliver's body was temporarily abandoned while the men transported the other casualty to the ship. Not until the next day did Drake and a few others return to Oliver's corpse, "which they found lying where it was left, but stripped of the uppermost garment, and having an English arrow stuck in his right eye." Removing him from the site, his countrymen laid Oliver and his fellow victim side by side in a grave "with such reverence as was fit for the earthen tabernacles of immortal souls, and with such commendable ceremonies as belong unto soldiers of worth in time of war."

After that, Drake and his crew returned to Port Saint Julian, where they faced a new adversary: hunger. "Our diet began to wax short, and small mussels were good meat, yea the sea-weeds were dainty dishes; by reason whereof we were driven to search corners very narrowly for some refreshing, but the best we could find was shells instead of meat; we found the nests but the birds were gone, that is, the shells of cockles upon the banks of the shore where the giants had banqueted." The discarded shells were, said Fletcher, "so extraordinary that it will be incredible to the most part, for a pair of shells did weigh four pounds," and the meat within he estimated "weighed one pound at least, so that it was a reasonable bit for a giant."

Their bellies were full, but they now confronted a more urgent danger, this time from within their number.

Fletcher claimed that Drake first heard about Thomas Doughty's plan to mutiny even before leaving England, as he sat in the garden of his home in Plymouth, "yet he either would not credit as true or likely of a person whom he loved so dearly." Drake believed that if he showed Doughty "all countenance, credit, and courtesies," everything would go well. Aboard ship, he gave Doughty a free hand, and when others tried to warn him about Doughty's premeditated treachery, Drake took offense.

As time went on, "perceiving that his lenity and favours did little good," Drake called Doughty's constant slights into question "before it was too late." He convened his captains and "gentlemen of his company" to consider letters of admonition about Doughty that Drake had received, "not only at sea but even at Plymouth." They all warned about the "overthrow" of Drake and "making away of his person." In other words, mutiny, even murder. One anonymous accuser became so overwrought in reporting these threats that he was afraid he would have no choice but to "take his own hands against his bowels," that is, disembowel himself, "or otherwise become his own executioner."

There was a lingering mystery about Doughty's purpose in joining the voyage in the first place. He might have been a secret agent planted by William Cecil, 1st Baron Lord Burghley, Elizabeth's trusted adviser, Secretary of State, and Lord High Treasurer, to prevent Drake from plundering Spanish ships and ports in America, and thus avoid outright war with Spain. If he thought he could prevent Drake from flamboyant piracy, Doughty was mistaken. Drake would never let the likes of Doughty interfere. But if Doughty actually was Cecil's plant, he could not be dismissed, for Cecil was reputed to be so close to Elizabeth that he spoke for her, and she spoke for him.

Furthermore, in matters of religion, Cecil was stern, unyielding, pragmatic. To his way of thinking, open-mindedness could never be an option. The state, he said, "could never be in safety where there was a toleration of two religions. For there is no enmity so great as that for religion; and therefore they that differ in the service of their God can never agree in the service of their country."

If Drake took action against Doughty, would the deed defy the wishes of both Cecil and his queen?

Drake discussed the matter with his confidants, who concluded that Thomas Doughty "deserved death," or as they put it, "that it

stood, by no means with their safety, to let him live." The date was
June 30. Afterward, the islet on which they had arrived at this decision was known as the "island of true justice and judgment." Drake
denounced Doughty in these terms: "You have here sought by divers means . . . to discredit me to the great hindrance and overthrow
of this voyage." Doughty stubbornly challenged Drake to produce
proof, at which point the volatile captain lost all patience and ordered
the accused to be bound.

"My masters," he declared, "this fellow is full of prating. Bind
me his arms, for I will be safe of my life."

*O*n July 2, 1578, Drake summoned Thomas Doughty and read
aloud to him the "guilty verdicts" that he and the others had composed. According to Fletcher, Doughty acknowledged their accuracy
"for the most part (for none had given heavier sentence against him
than he had given against himself)" and offered little in self-defense.
An unsigned deposition accusing Drake of bribing the queen and
council to disregard his acts of piracy did nothing to advance Doughty's case. And a further admission that he had offered a share of
the proceeds to the Lord Treasurer, Lord Burghley, sent Drake into a
full-blown rage. "What this fellow hath done! God will have all his
treacheries known." The queen had told Drake that the Lord Treasurer must not know of this secret voyage, and Doughty had be-
trayed that confidence.

Drake relished having this damning piece of evidence brought
into the open. He proceeded to summarize the case against Doughty.
"You must judge for yourselves whether or not this fellow has tried
to undermine my authority," he told the jury, "for no other reason
than to abort this voyage, first by taking away my good name and
altogether discrediting me, and then by taking my life, which being

taken, what would become of you?" He warned they would be "re-duced to drinking one another's blood." As far as returning to En-gland, without Drake to guide them, "you will never be able to find the way." Once those chilling thoughts sank in, he urged the jury to consider what a "great voyage" lay ahead. "The least in this fleet will become a gentleman," he reminded them. But if they found in favor of Doughty and allowed him to live, "the simplest here must appreciate what a reproach it will be." In other words, Doughty had implicated them all, and the only way they could dispel their collec-tive guilt was to execute him for his treachery. And so, "let they who think this man deserves to die hold up their hands, and let they who think he does not deserve to die hold down their hands."

Before they could carry out the sentence, Doughty's friend Vi-cary, the lawyer, complained that the trial was illegal, drawing a re-buke from Drake, who said he would have nothing to do "with you crafty lawyers. Neither care I for the law, but I know what I will do." Vicary raised objections. How could they justify taking this prisoner's life? "You shall not have to do with his life," Drake re-torted. "Let me alone for that. You are but to see whether he be guilty in these articles." When the quarrel ended, the jury, consisting of twelve men, including Vicary, returned with a unanimous verdict: guilty on all counts. Drake had the outcome he wanted.

Drake offered the condemned man three choices, each more ter-rible than the other: "Whether he would take to be executed in this island? Or to be set aland on the main? Or return to England, there to answer for his deed before the Lords of Her Majesty's Council?"

As these were read aloud, Doughty maintained his composure and "thanked the general"—Drake—"for his clemency, extended towards him in such ample sort," and promised to reply the follow-ing day.

Doughty admitted to being "justly condemned" but expressed one overriding concern: "to die a Christian man, that whatsoever did become of his clay body, he might remain assured of an eternal inheritance in a far better life." To be "set aland," or marooned, seemed the worst option of all. How would he avoid the "contagion of lewd custom"? Only slightly better was the option of returning to England to stand trial. He would require a ship, "and men to conduct it, with sufficient victuals." It was easy enough to come by the first two items, but "he thought no man would accompany him, in so sad a message to so vile an issue, from so honourable a service." After deliberating, the only option he could endorse was execution on this insignificant little island. His lone consideration was that he "might receive Holy Communion once again before his death, and that he not die other than a gentleman's death." The others tried to persuade Doughty to choose a more lenient course of action, but he remained "resolute." His capitulation, coming after his strenuous denials, implied that Drake's most damning accusation, that Doughty had conspired with Lord Burghley, the Lord Treasurer, to shield Spain from English provocation, contained more than a grain of truth.

Francis Fletcher, "preacher and pastor of the fleet," celebrated Communion. Drake himself participated in the rite alongside Doughty, "who showed great tokens of a contrite and repentant heart." Then Drake and Thomas Doughty dined together, "as cheerfully in sobriety as ever in their lives . . . each cheering up the other, and taking their leave, by drinking each to other, as if some journey only had been in hand." A journey there would be, taking one to the ends of the earth, and the other to the end of time.

According to another eyewitness, John Cooke, often accused of a pronounced anti-Drake bias, Doughty asked to speak privately with the man who had condemned him, after which "he was brought to the place of execution where he showed himself no less valiant than all the time afore, for kneeling on his knees, he first prayed for the queen's majesty of England his sovereign lady and mistress, he then prayed to God for the happy success of this voyage, and prayed to God to turn to the profit of his country." Then he asked John Winter to "commend him to that good knight, all which he did with so cheerful countenance as he had gone to some great prepared banquet." But this was not a banquet, this was an execution. "So at the last, turning to the General, he said, as did Sir Thomas More, that he that cuts of my head shall have little honesty, [for] my neck [is] so short." Doughty's gaze swept the entire company, and maintaining his composure, he asked them to forgive him, "and especially some that he did perceive to have displeasure borne them for his sake." It appeared that Doughty was determined to extend his time on earth with apologies for slights real and imaginary, until, "bidding the whole company farewell, he laid his head to the block."

Doughty kneeled in an appointed place, "preparing at once his neck for the axe, and his spirit for heaven." He encouraged everyone present to pray for him, and "willed the executioner to do his office, not to fear nor spare." His manner of death was so dignified and "worthy" that it seems to have "fully blotted out whatever stain his fault might seem to bring upon him."

The executioner prepared to dispatch Doughty into eternity. He brought the blade down swiftly through Doughty's soft neck, but a stubborn tendon interfered. The executioner slashed away until the job was complete.

Drake plucked the severed head by the hair, dribbling blood and almost alive, displayed it to the company, and intoned the customary formula:

"Behold the head of a traitor."

The death of Thomas Doughty did not sunder these two antago-
nists; it drew them together in a spiritual bond extending from this
world to the hereafter. By ordering the execution, Drake was not
merely punishing the offender; he was assuming responsibility for
his immortal soul, an obligation without end.

CHAPTER V

Golden Hind

After Doughty's execution, the crew's morale collapsed, and a full-scale mutiny threatened to erupt. Drake needed to act immediately. He assured the company that the queen would "pay every man his wages" because, as he saw matters, it was not Drake whom they served, but Elizabeth, "and this voyage is only her setting forth." He went as her representative and with her authority. Drake might well have exaggerated his status. He was, after all, a pirate—a very well-connected pirate, but a pirate nonetheless.

He preached a sermon instead of Fletcher in which he established a code of conduct at sea. With the exception of officers, all on board, gentlemen and seamen alike, would work as equals, with everyone subject to his command; there would be no other captain. Unified in this way the voyage could proceed, and it later came to be seen as establishing a tradition in English maritime command. Having established this principle, Drake made every effort to rally his crew. "We are very far from our country and friends, we are compassed in on every side with our enemies, for which reason we are not to value any man lightly, because we cannot find another even if we would give ten thousand pounds for him." They must neutralize dissent and mutinies, "for by the life of God even to think about it has disordered my wits." Conflict among his men "drives me mad even to hear it." Cooperation was the key to their survival: "I must have the gentleman to haul and draw with the mariner, and the mariner with the gentleman . . . Let us show ourselves all to be of a company and let us not give occasion to the enemy to rejoice at our decay and overthrow." He expressed exasperation with the unruly temperament of the typical seaman. "I know sailors to be the most envious people of the world, and so unruly without government," he said, "yet may not I be without them." If anyone still wanted to sail back to England without completing their great enterprise, he offered *Marigold*, "a ship that I can very well spare," for that purpose. They had until the next day to think it over, "but for now I must speak to you plainly: I have undertaken something that I do not know how in the world that I can carry out; it is a greater burden than I can bear alone." Just thinking about it "has driven me to distraction." In other words, he required their loyalty to succeed. Drake's confessional tone combined with his humility in the face of the task ahead calmed the sailors. No one accepted Drake's offer.

He urged the men to consider how the voyage stood in the global scheme of things. "Let us consider what we have done. We have now set by the ears three mighty princes, as first Her Majesty and then the Kings of Spain and Portugal; and if this voyage should not have good success, we should not only be a scorning or a reproachful scoffing stock unto our enemies, but also a great blot to our country forever. And what a triumph it would be to Spain and Portugal!" But they would not allow themselves to become objects of scorn. Drake intuited that they had reached a turning point not only in the voyage but also in relations among England, Spain, and Portugal. Their efforts, here and now, on these ships, would make the crucial difference. By highlighting the importance of their mission, Drake expected to enlist the absolute loyalty and best efforts of them all. He depended on them. The queen relied on them. England needed them. At the time, as a subtext, Drake sought to justify the execution of Thomas Doughty by invoking the patriotic principles that were at stake, and Doughty's unseemly efforts to subvert them.

*T*he ghostly presence of Magellan and his tragic overreaching seemed stronger than ever. Drake, for his part, appeared satisfied with the bloodletting, considering the expedition purged of evil. But Fletcher, the chaplain, harbored private misgivings about the execution of Doughty. "He feared God, he loved his word, and was always desirous to edify others and confirm himself in the faith of Christ," the preacher confided to his journal. "For his qualities, in man of his time they were rare, and his gift very excellent for his age, sweet orator, pregnant philosopher, good gift for the Greek tongue, and reasonable taste of Hebrew." Although the affair made Fletcher miserable, there was nothing that he could do about it here, at the end of the earth.

*A*fter the beheading, the men digging Doughty's grave unearthed a "great grinding stone, broken in two parts." They set one part of the stone at the head of the mound, the other at the foot. Doughty's name was carved on one of the stones and a "memorial of our General's name, in Latin, that it might better be understood of all that should come after us."

Then Drake disposed of *Mary* "because she was leaky and troublesome," said Fletcher. Purging themselves of this ship connected with the stain of Doughty's execution, the men stripped her and dismantled her. They deposited her ribs and keel like discarded bones on the island where they had pitched their tents.

Next, Drake relieved the officers who had been chosen by the ship owners, and reappointed them himself, invoking the authority of the queen. They now owed their loyalty to him, and he depended on them for a successful completion of the voyage, indeed, for survival itself. He was now the sole leader, as well as a target for criticism and resentment.

By the time the ships left Port Saint Julian, Fletcher, who had written approvingly of Drake's conduct before and during the beheading of Doughty, began to doubt his captain's motives, and even his sanity. What manner of man ordered the beheading of his close friend on the basis of mere suspicion?

*I*t seemed as if the execution of Thomas Doughty had occurred in a vacuum, far removed from Elizabeth and the reach of the Spanish empire, but that was not the case. King Philip, sequestered in his office, depending on his minister's reports for news of the world, received an intriguing communiqué from Bernardino de Mendoza, a son of the 3rd Count of Coruña, from one of Spain's most prestigious families.

Mendoza had already distinguished himself as a soldier in the Netherlands and had written a book on military strategy. He was a man of formidable gifts and ambition, exactly as Philip needed. In 1578, Philip named Mendoza Spanish ambassador to London. He kept up a steady stream of encrypted letters to the king about the news at court. Under cover of his official title, Mendoza pursued his real job, that of spy. It would be years before the various codes he employed were cracked and Mendoza's reports were translated into English, and when they were, they afforded a secret history of Spanish attempts to subvert England, Elizabeth, and especially Francis Drake, whom Mendoza recognized as the chief threat to Spain's imperial ambitions. Mendoza cultivated a far-reaching network of anonymous informants, whose reports he shaped to fit his agenda. No military strategy was too grand or bit of gossip too small to escape his notice.

On this occasion, he had much to say about Drake's recent activities in Port Saint Julian, written with such conviction that it was almost as if Mendoza had been there. "Various news has been current here with regard to them," he wrote to Philip, hidden away in his monastic refuge, with "some saying that they were lost and others that they had landed at Camaroons" in equatorial Africa. That was not the case. Mendoza had learned from an unnamed "shipmaster" that, after taking on supplies in Barbary, they had arrived at the Strait of Magellan, "but at the entrance thereto they experienced so great a tempest that most of the sailors mutinied and refused to proceed on the voyage. Drake, understanding that the principal ringleader was an English gentleman on board of his ship, arrested him and put him on his trial, the judges being the sailors themselves, who condemned him to death, but, as none of them would execute the sentence, Drake himself did so and with his own hand cut off the man's head and proceeded on his voyage through the Straits." This account was, in its major outlines, true enough. Drake was so ruthless that he had executed one of his own men, with his own hands. In Mendoza's telling, the captain general appeared ready to gouge out his victim's eyes and devour his brains if that was what it took to maintain order.

From this time on, Drake became a preoccupation for the Spanish, who condemned him as a "Lutheran heretic."

Drake was not the only English privateer seeking to expand England's influence. Two other English explorers were also in search of wealth and empire. They operated under the same semiofficial arrangement with Elizabeth as Drake and for the same reason, to keep Spain from attacking. The first, an expert seaman considered one of England's leading navigators, was Martin Frobisher, who was about Drake's age. With wealth inherited from his wife's deceased husband, Frobisher ranked much higher than Drake on the social scale. Antonio de Guarás, who preceded Bernardino de Mendoza as King Philip II's ambassador to London, ranked Frobisher "the best seaman and the bravest in the country." Frobisher's dreams went beyond mere wealth. Before departing on what would be his second of three voyages of exploration, he petitioned the queen to be confirmed as High Admiral of the northwestern seas and governor of all lands discovered, and to receive 5 percent of profits from trade.

As Drake approached the Strait in the Southern Hemisphere, Frobisher, journeying farther north, arrived in Newfoundland. At the moment Drake began to traverse the Strait of Magellan, Frobisher was rejoicing over his discovery of a rich seam of ore. He loaded two hundred tons of rocks onto his ships and brought them back to England amid high expectations. The queen herself received him at Windsor Castle, then as now the royal residence. He might as well have been carrying ballast across the Atlantic. When the ore was melted down, it turned out to be fool's gold, and was later used for road metal.

Another rival was Walter Raleigh, a gentleman, soldier, poet, spy, and writer who had attended Oxford, although he left without a degree. He was also a particular favorite of Elizabeth, who would knight him in 1585. In November 1578, he took command of a fleet with Humphrey Gilbert, his half brother, to establish an outpost in North America. Heading into the Atlantic late in the year proved to be a mistake, as storms battered the ships. Six months later, Raleigh and Gilbert were forced to return home without reaching their goal.

With potential competitors having been eliminated by bad luck or sheer incompetence, Drake became all the more important to Elizabeth and the fortunes of England. He was not a wealthy gentleman explorer but the genuine article, rough-hewn and resilient. No one intimidated Francis Drake—with the exception of Queen Elizabeth.

*D*rake's reduced fleet, now consisting of three ships and two pinnaces, followed the course pioneered by Magellan in search of the Strait with a newfound sense of discipline, as if the blood shed by Doughty's sacrifice had consecrated their cause to a higher purpose. Drake had a single goal in mind—treasure, specifically, Spanish treasure. To his way of thinking, it was pointless to try to avoid offending Spain. Now that he was the indisputable leader of the fleet, his behavior was more confident. There was no longer any doubt about his entering the Strait of Magellan and following it all the way to the Pacific. "And so, having wooded, watered, trimmed our ships, despatched all our other businesses, and brought our fleet into the smallest number, even 3 only, besides our pinnaces, that we might easier keep ourselves together, be the better furnished with necessaries, and be the stronger manned against whatever need should be, [on] August 17, we departed of this port, being now in great hope of a happy issue to our enterprise," wrote Fletcher.

At Drake's order, "we set our course for the Straits, south-west."

*O*n August 20, 1578, Drake's ships arrived at Cape Virgin Mary, four leagues from the entrance of the Strait. It was night when the little fleet arrived, the "high and steep grey cliffs, full of black stars, against which the sea beating, showeth as it were the spoutings of whales." Drake ordered his crew to strike their topsails "to his dutiful obedience to Her Highness," who he affirmed had "full interest and right" in their voyage of discovery.

At that moment, Drake startled his company with an announcement: he was changing the name of the flagship from *Pelican* to *Golden Hind*, and as *Golden Hind*, she would eventually become the most celebrated vessel of the Age of Discovery. It would take time for the new name to become current. For the moment, many aboard ship and, later, in England, would continue to refer to her by her traditional name, *Pelican*. It was only later that she would be known as *Golden Hind*. This gesture was a striking departure from maritime custom. No matter; he would make his own rules. He selected the name because the crest of one of his closest associates, Sir Christopher Hatton, contained a golden hind—that is, the rear legs of a female red deer—moving nimbly across the landscape. This image suggested that Drake's flagship was endowed with wealth and speed. And because Hatton enjoyed Elizabeth's favor, the name hinted at an association, however vague, with the queen.

Until Drake's circumnavigation, the most popular ships for war and transport were known as carracks. With three or four masts, square-rigged on the foremast and mainmast, they featured a lateen or Arab-style sail on the mizzenmast for maneuverability. It was hard to miss a lumbering carrack. They rode high in the water and offered an ample target for cannon. By way of contrast, English warships, or galleons, were "race built," meaning "razed," or flattened. This design was sleeker and faster, with simplified rigging that could be handled by a skeleton crew even in heavy weather.

Da Silva, the Portuguese pilot whom Drake had enticed aboard ship in remote Cape Verde, gave the galleon *Golden Hind* qualified praise. She was "in a great measure stout and strong. She has two

sheathings, one as perfectly finished as the other. She is fit for warfare and is a ship of the French pattern, well fitted out and finished
with very good masts, tackle and double sails. She sails well and the
rudder governs her well." Still, da Silva detected flaws. "She is not
new, nor is she coppered nor ballasted. She has seven armed port-
holes on each side, and inside she carries eighteen pieces of artillery,
thirteen being of bronze and the rest of cast iron, also an abundance
of all sorts of ammunition of war." Although "watertight when navigated with a moderate stern wind, but in a high sea she labours and
leaks not a little, whether sailing before the wind or with the bow-
lines hauled out." And for a vessel meant to sail the seas, she was on
the small side, hardly more than a hundred feet long.

Yet *Golden Hind* had distinct advantages. She was capable of negotiating shallow water. Even laden with Spanish silver, she drew
only thirteen feet. And she was made of the best timber available to
English shipwrights, flexible elm and sturdy oak. She could carry a
lot—enough to endure six months at sea, if need be. An inventory of
her supplies included the following: "wood, coal, candles, wax, lan-
terns, platters, tankards, jackes of leather, dishes, bowls, buckets, taper
candles, scoop shovels, mattocks, hatchets, crows of iron. Compasses,
running glasses, lamps, water cask. Hoops of iron & wood. Cordage,
canvas, pitch, tar, rosin, flat lead, rough lead, nails, spikes, sounding
lead" and much more, down to the hooks and needles to repair fishing
nets and caps to keep sailors warm.

Storing these supplies followed a scheme designed to stabilize
the ship in rough seas. The heaviest items—cannon shot, anchors,
and disassembled pinnaces and, later on, gold and silver stolen from
Spain—were kept in the hold, the lowest level, where they functioned as ballast. The level directly above the hold, known as the
orlop (the name derived from the Dutch word *overloopen*, or extension), held fresh and dried victuals: salted beef, pork, cod, and wal-

nuts, not to mention poultry and livestock. Above the orlop was the gun deck, on which rested the barrels of the cannon, or culverins. Nuño da Silva, the Portuguese pilot, observed, "On the bronze cannon that he carried in the pinnace, there was sculptured the globe of the world with a north star on it, passing overhead. He said these were his arms and that the Queen had conferred them upon him, commanding him to encompass the world." Drake was anticipating events; the Queen did not formally grant arms to him until after he returned home, but for him, expectation led predictably to reality.

The tiller, connected to the rudder, was located on the gun deck. An extension was often attached to a vertical bar or lever known as a whipstaff, which aided steering. And another binnacle was affixed nearby. The gun deck also housed the crew, although "house" might be an overstatement. The seamen slept in hammocks suspended between the cannon or on piles of straw arranged on planks. The galley, sometimes called the cook room, was nearby, as were water casks. They required constant replenishing, in rough weather or smooth, during a battle or not.

Meals aboard ship were surprisingly formal occasions. Drake and his officers dined off gilt-edged plates. And they were accompanied by music played on viols, which Drake adored. One of the Spanish pilots accompanying Drake recalled spine-tingling peals of "trumpets and clarions" during meals. The musical instruments made an even greater impression on the Indians who found themselves in the presence of Drake at mealtime. The music did more than set the mood; it lent an air of drama to the proceedings, as if the repasts were entr'actes between scenes of a marathon performance known as the circumnavigation. Drake, like many Elizabethans, often behaved in a theatrical manner, especially during worship services, when he emphasized ceremony and spectacle, such as the trial and beheading of Doughty, when Drake appeared to follow a script

compiled for just that occasion. He saw himself performing a leading role; his stage happened to be the ship's deck, and the audience
a crowd of indigenous peoples, Indians, and onlookers fortunate
enough to observe him making English history. For a self-conscious
actor like Drake, the world was a stage, and cannon, guns, swords,
pinnaces, and whatever else came to hand served as props in an all-
embracing drama.

The forecastle was located in the forward part of the ship, and
held a pair of bow chasers, or forward-facing cannon. The waist, or
center of the ship, was open to let light and air enter and circulate
around the gun deck and relieve the noisome effluvia of confined
livestock. The afterdeck, at the stern, contained the grand cabin, that
is, Drake's personal living quarters. And on the poop, there was a
small cabin known as the roundhouse where Drake and his officers
could assemble or relax.

The distance between decks was only five and and a half feet,
which meant that the crew crouched or stooped when they went
below. The captain's cabin was hardly more than six feet high, but
Drake, who stood perhaps five and a half feet tall, felt at home within
its confines, which he furnished with his bunk, desk, chair, and a
leather-covered sea chest. It would not be an exaggeration to say that
he felt more at home in his cabin aboard ship than in his lodgings
on land. For Drake, this was home. The sea chest, when its lid was
lifted, displayed an image of *Golden Hind*. The coffer contained the
important documents for the voyage, including official instructions,
which had the queen's approval if not her actual seal. In Drake's case,
the captain's cabin contained a large red cylinder, which came to be
known as Drake's Drum. When he wanted to muster the crew, he
struck it, and its authoritative boom would reverberate around the
crowded ship.

When circumstances demanded, Drake would dash to his cabin, fling open the sea chest, and flourish his official instructions to remind everyone that he enjoyed Elizabeth's support. He might be a pirate to the enemy, but he was the queen's representative. He was happy to have it both ways, and so was Her Majesty. In reality, she did not want to be seen sponsoring such flagrantly illegitimate behavior, and out of caution had not signed the papers, despite what Drake told his company, but that was a mere technicality. The existence of the document was enough to persuade sailors not to go against the queen's will, or Drake's. Otherwise, they risked treason, punishable by death.

Golden Hind, as Drake knew, was a fast ship. With topgallants hoisted above her topsails, she could easily outrun the Spanish vessels hunting for her. Her foremast and mainmast were square-rigged for stability, and a lateen sail on her mizzen, attached to a short, sturdy spar known as an outlicker, added speed. She deployed about 4,150 square feet of sail, and carried three anchors and a single kedge, or small anchor, attached to a hawser, or cable. Da Silva, an experienced pilot, was mildly impressed by the nautical gear. "All in all, she is a ship which is in a fit condition to make a couple of voyages from Portugal to Brazil."

Yet Drake's semiofficial instructions outlined a bolder trajectory, ordering him to proceed through the Strait of Magellan into the "South Sea," or Pacific. He was also directed to "have traffic for the vending of commodities of her Majesty's realms. Whereas at present they are not under the obedience of any Christian prince so there is great hope of gold, silver, spices, drugs, cochineal [scarlet dye] and divers other special commodities, such as may enrich her Highness' dominions and also put shipping a-work greatly." Drake would spend thirteen months voyaging and another thirteen months "tarrying up the coasts to get knowledge of the princes and countries there." With these instructions, Elizabeth hinted that Drake might be exploring the limits of an empire in the guise of trading.

Superstitious sailors generally recoiled from renaming a ship in midvoyage. The deed was considered an ill omen, but Drake enjoyed more good luck with *Golden Hind* than anyone had any right to expect. Even though it was winter, and the fleet was battling strong headwinds, he negotiated the labyrinthine waterways of the Strait. As they went, Drake laid claim to several islands and landmarks in the name of Queen Elizabeth and England, the same lands Magellan had once reserved for King Charles V and Spain.

On August 20, the fleet turned away from the open sea and entered the Strait. Drake remained vigilant about Spanish ships and soldiers who might patrol its waters and shoreline. The channel was, as anticipated, narrow, "carrying with it much wind, often turnings, and many dangers," Fletcher observed. Passing through safely "requireth an expert judgment in him that shall pass the same," and it was a skill that Drake displayed. Before the fleet put the mouth of the Strait astern, it appeared that the fleet disgorged from a broad river, "into a large and main sea." They proceeded, and the next night passed an island that appeared as if it "burneth . . . aloft in the air, in a wonderful sort, without intermission."

The sailors expected the sea to flow through the Strait from east to west, "but our experience found the contrary," although with an orderly ebb and flow. So far, so good, as they sailed deeper into the Strait's embrace.

A strait or inland waterway is a type of fjord, or inlet, that comes about when a glacier, having carved through rocks, retreats. The overall effect of these contrasting landscapes was uplifting, majestic. Drake's gentleman-at-arms, Francis Pretty, wrote of the scene: "The land on both sides is very huge and mountainous; the lower mountains whereof, although they be monstrous and wonderful to look upon for their height, yet there are others which in height exceed them in a strange manner, reaching themselves above their fellows so high, that between them did appear three regions of clouds."

According to da Silva, the captured pilot, "they passed along without any let or hindrance either of wind or weather: and because the high land on both sides lay covered with snow, and that all the strait is fair and clear." As they made their way through these mysterious water pathways, they realized they were not alone. In the distance they made out "Indian fishermen in their canoes or skiffs" peacefully going about their business. For the moment, the world seemed big enough to accommodate all its varied inhabitants.

$\mathcal{D}$rake was at that moment engaged in reconnoitering three triangle-like islands, one of which he found especially "fair and large and of fruitful soil," in Fletcher's description. Drake called it Elizabeth Island.

The two neighboring islands swarmed with "strange birds" smaller than geese, with plump, compact bodies. Instead of feathers, a thick mat covered them. "This fowl cannot fly, having but stub wings, without feathers, covered over with a certain down, as it were young goslings of two months old," Fletcher observed. They were penguins. "In their heads, eyes, and feet, they be like a duck. . . . They breed and lodge at land, and in the day time go down to the sea to feed, being so fat that they cannot but go, and their skins cannot be taken from their bodies without tearing off the flesh because of their exceeding fatness." Not only were they sturdy, they were strong. When his men tried to pry them loose from their nesting areas with cudgels, they fastened their bills around the instrument and held tight. And the creatures stank, although the men, who also reeked, might not have noticed.

The penguins seemed awkward in all respects except for one. They could swim, "both to prey upon others and to escape from any others that seek to seize upon them." And they were amazingly numerous; Fletcher writes of the men slaughtering three thousand penguins in a single day—and because they made for a "very good and wholesome victual" their abundance was seen as a blessing.

So much for blessings. Why was the corpse of a strange man stretched out across one of the islands? When they tried to move him, "his bones would not hold together." The Strait would not yield its secrets all at once. Before leaving this group of islands, Drake ordered a tree to be felled, and he carried off the trunk with him to prove to Elizabeth at some future date that he had arrived at the Strait.

*F*amilies of sea elephants lolled along stony beaches. The marvelous creatures reached about ten feet in length, their flippers placed close to their torpedo-like heads, and a broad stabilizing tail lazily patting the sand, scattering damp grains. Penguins crowded other beaches as massive black-and-white condors wheeled overhead. Miniature white orchids bloomed in the mud. The Strait's thick vegetation released an intoxicating fragrance. The breezes were scented with a damp mossy odor mingling with the scent of wildflowers, freshened by the cool glaciers, and faintly tangy with salt from the sea. Monumental glaciers, tinged blue, gray, and brown, towered above Drake's small ships. And when they calved, or crumbled, a deep roar reverberated through the chasms and across the turbid water.

Further inland, an impenetrable canopy of leaves created perpetual darkness. "So thick was the wood, that it was necessary to have constant recourse to the compass," wrote the young Charles Darwin when he visited the Strait aboard HMS *Beagle* in 1834. "In the deep ravines, the death-like scene of desolation exceeded all description; outside it was blowing a gale, but in these hollows, not even a breath of wind stirred the leaves of the tallest trees. So gloomy, cold and wet was every part, that not even the fungi, mosses, or ferns, could flourish." When he at last worked his way out of the enchanted forest to the summit, Darwin beheld a view glimpsed centuries before by Drake's crew: "irregular chains of hills, mottled with patches of snow, deep yellowish-green valleys, and arms of the sea intersecting the land in many directions."

When Drake reached the halfway point of the Strait, the crew consulted the logs maintained by pilots on Magellan's circumnavigation and made careful comparisons between their experience and that of their predecessors. "It is true which Magellan reporteth of this passage," Fletcher remarked of the crooked channel in which they found themselves, "namely, that there be any fair harbours and store of fresh water," yet the ships had to battle "contrary winds" that brought "no small danger."

Fletcher likely referred to williwaws—violent, frigid winds blowing from the tops of mountains. Still more violent weather occurred when "two or three of these winds would come together, and meet as it were in one body, whose forces being become one, did so violently fall into the sea, whirling, or as the Spaniard saith, with a tornado, that they would pierce into the very bowels of the sea, and make it swell upwards on every side" until "the banks ran down again a mighty rain."

This brief mention hardly begins to express the suffering of those who succumbed to hypothermia in the Strait's unpredictable and violent storms. Life-threatening symptoms set in when the surrounding environment is cold enough to bring the body's core temperature to 95 degrees. The brain triggers involuntary shivering in an effort to maintain the body's warmth. Other symptoms include chattering teeth, exhaustion, clumsiness, a weak pulse, sleepiness, tachycardia, and rapid breathing. If the body's temperature falls below 89 degrees, additional indications of hypothermia involve slurred speech, a slower heart rate, impaired mental function, and stiffness. The nervous system goes haywire. Paradoxical undressing, in which the sufferer strips off all clothing, often occurs, caused by a malfunction of the hypothalamus, which regulates body temperature. The muscles contracting peripheral blood vessels relax, creating a surge of blood to the arms and legs, which causes the sufferer to feel overheated.

As hypothermia progresses, the skin turns bluish and the pupils dilate. Loss of consciousness ensues. Finally, severe hypothermia, in which the body's temperature falls below 82 degrees, brings with it low blood pressure, fluid in the lungs, and eventually, a loss of reflexes. The heart stops beating. The body enters a state of profound unconsciousness: a coma. If the cold continues unabated, this descent into death can take from fifteen minutes to more than an hour. There were many ways to perish on the voyage—disease, drowning, attack from indigenous people, scurvy, starvation—but hypothermia was surely among the worst.

In search of shelter, the fleet paused at a compact, thickly vegetated island (now called Carlos III) rising from the water as if on spindly, leaf-covered stilts. The ships were now at the narrowest point in the passage, protected from the oceans and completely isolated, "the land on both sides high and mountainous, having on the north and west side the continent of America, and on the south and east part nothing but islands, among which like innumerable frets or passages in the South Sea," or the Pacific. The channels were too shallow to accommodate the ships. Without charts, and using only a simple weighted rope as a sounding device, they proceeded from point to point, keeping their voices low, partly out of a sense of awe at the towering mountains on either side of the channel, and partly to remain alert to the crunch of the keel plunging into sand, grinding to a halt on a concealed sandbar, or getting trapped by concealed rocks that could shred the keel or rudder. In that predicament, either the stranded ship would wait for high tide to lift it free, or those aboard would lighten the ship by discarding heavy items such as cannon until it could float. To minimize the possibility of these calamities, Drake held to the center of the Strait itself, where the water was deepest.

Fletcher blamed their navigational predicament on their reliance on "the common maps of the Spaniards," which left them "utterly deceived." Those relying on false Spanish maps would "likely perish at sea."

Fletcher saw this deceit as part of a master plan of Spanish misdirection. "The reason why the Spaniards have abused the world with such an untruth and falsehood is that thereby they would prevent all other nations to . . . attempt to travel that way."

*N*atural splendor overawed them as they advanced. "The mountains arise with such tops and spires into the air, and of so rare a height, as they may well be accounted amongst the wonders of the world," Fletcher observed as they slid past majestic glaciers. The sight of "the cold and frozen mountains rearing their heads" transfixed him, "yea, the greatest part of their bodies, into the cold and frozen region, where the power of the reflection of the sun never reacheth to dissolve the ice and snow."

All of the Lord's works were on display in this remote location. The air smelled so sweet "that no art or labour of man can make closer and sweeter arbors than they be." Strange herbs blanketed the ground. The English voyagers had no name for many of them. "I neither had seen them in other countries in my travels nor found them mentioned in any approved herbals," Fletcher said. They seemed "always to be green and to flourish as it were in our summer." Among those plants "naturally growing, without industry of man," he could identify thyme, marjoram, "Alexander's scurvy grass (as seamen call it), and divers others well known to us," and they were all "more excellent in their natures than we find them in these parts in our gardens." Another aromatic, succulent plant caught his attention, "so gummy and full of fatness that touching them the fat and the gum would stick to our hands, being so pleasant that it yielded a most comfortable smell to our senses, whereby we received great help, both in our diet and physick, to the great relief of the limbs of our men."

Fletcher marveled at the Arcadian realm, the trees evergreen and the air temperate. There was an aura of timelessness about the landscape; it seemed as if the ordinary laws of nature were suspended at this latitude. It was enough to make a visitor wonder if those who inhabited these forests and glaciers lived in an endless present combining the past and the future, neither Christian nor pagan, yet filled with spiritual potential. The place lacked for nothing—except people to inhabit it for the sake of the "Creator's glory and the increasing of the Church."

Now the question confronted Drake: Which of the many channels zigzagging across the landscape should he follow to reach the Pacific? Those leading north seemed to go nowhere, and those heading south, with "large and open frets," or a sequence of conduits, were equally puzzling. Further investigation was needed. Drake brought the fleet around to ride at anchor in the lee of an island, and then took a rowboat with a small crew of his loyalists. Their careful inspection revealed a passage to the north, but at that moment, a canoe carrying four people floated into view.

The strangers rode in a dugout fashioned from bark, with a raised prow and stern, all of it in "most comely fashion and excellent workmanship." The sides were stitched together with strips of sealskin "or other such beast, and yet so close that it received very little or no water at all." Drake and his men could scarcely believe that the finely wrought craft belonged not to a "noble personage" or "some prince," but to "so rude and barbarous a people" as those living there. They wore skins and were beardless, unlike the shaggy English intruders, and they displayed their faces painted with red circles around their eyes and red stripes running along their foreheads. The party included women adorned with chains of white shells draped around their necks or over their arms, "whereof they seem to be very proud."

After careful observation, Drake and his men felt safe enough to disembark, and they studied their fellow humans with mingled wonder and bewilderment. They were "people of a mean stature, but well set and compact in all their parts and limbs." Their houses were simple: skins of beasts stretched across poles, sheltering "fire, water, and such meat as commonly they can come by, seals, mussels, and the like."

The ingenious tools and utensils of these uncomplicated people impressed the Europeans. Even their cups, made of bark like their canoes, showed "a very formal shape and good fashion." Their tools for cutting and scraping were "knives made of the most huge and monstrous mussel shells (the likes whereof have not been seen or heard of lightly by any travellers, the meat thereof being very savoury and good in eating), which, after they had broken off the thick and brittle substance of the edge, they rub and grind them upon stones . . . till they have tempered and set such an edge upon them, that no wood is so hard but they will cut it at pleasure." The English sailors took the mighty mussel shells in hand to try for themselves and found they would cut even "bones of a marvellous hardness." Their investigations ended there. Drake and his crew departed as abruptly as they had come.

By September 6, Fletcher recorded, "we had left astern of us all these troublesome islands and were entered into the South Sea." They had made it through 350 miles of the Strait, an extraordinary accomplishment, the first Europeans to do so since Magellan. Even more impressive, they had done it in only sixteen days, compared with the thirty-eight days the Portuguese explorer required. Drake had the benefit of maps and descriptions compiled by Magellan's fleet, and as a result he expended less time on guesswork and dead ends, but the successful passage was a spectacular feat nonetheless and a testament to Drake's unsurpassed skill as a navigator, not to mention his good luck. Yet the achievement carried a steep price. Silva noted that "many of Drake's men died of cold in passing the strait."

Now that Drake had entered the Pacific, he planned to drop anchor and order every man ashore, deliver a speech to reconsecrate the voyage in the name of the queen, and leave "a monument of Her Majesty, engraven in metal, for a perpetual remembrance." He would wear his finest clothes and remind the crew of how far they had come and how far they had to go.

At the moment, however, his ships had nowhere to tie up, and he had no opportunity to deliver a bracing sermon. Instead, a blast of "nipping cold, under so cruel and frowning a winter" urged him on. Already the chill had "impaired the health" of some of the men. He realized now he should be making haste to sail north to the line, or equator, "and not sail any farther toward the Antarctic, lest . . . we might . . . be overtaken with some great danger of sickness." Preserving his men's well-being and keeping his ultimate goal in mind required every bit of Drake's presence of mind, stamina, patience, sailing skills, and luck. A wrong turn might have spelled disaster, as could an outbreak of disease or starvation, or a group of confrontational local inhabitants armed with bows and arrows. It was true that he had Magellan's example to point the way, but it was an imperfect guide at best. Drake had to devise his own solutions.

*M*any men were too sick to eat, and some suffered from the agonies of scurvy as their bodies began to discolor and dismember. As if the prospect of starvation was not enough to give Drake pause, the fleet encountered another devastating storm. The body of water they approached might be "called by some Mare Pacificum," Francis Fletcher noted, "but proving to us rather to be Mare Furiosum." He complained, "God, by a contrary wind and intolerable tempest, seemed to set Himself against us." Fletcher feared the Almighty had "pronounced a sentence, not stay His hand, nor to withdraw His judgment, till he had buried our bodies, and ships also, in the bottomless depths of the raging sea." The ordeal persisted, hour after hour, day after day. By September 15, the "incredible storm" was undiminished, the days endless. Awful days they were, "without the sight of the sun, moon, or stars."

On or about September 28, "the storm being so outrageous and furious," *Marigold* was lost along with twenty-eight souls, all of them "swallowed up with horrible and unmerciful waves, or rather, mountains of the sea." At that moment, Fletcher and John Brewer, the trumpeter, who were on the second watch of the night—from 10:00 PM until 2:00 AM—"Did hear their fearful cries when the hand of God came upon them."

All the while, the seas drove them back toward the Antarctic pole. Fletcher recalled the unending nightmare of the storm as they continued "without hope . . . in the violent force of the winds, intolerable working of the wrathful seas, and the grisly beholding (sometimes) of the cragged rocks and fearful height and monstrous mountains, being to us a lee shore, where unto we were continually driven by the winds, and carried by the mountain-like billows of the seas, to look every moment to have the like end as our other ship had, in which state we continuing, if at any time we had a little opportunity to seek some harbor for refuge to come to anchor, and rest till God in mercy might give us more safe sailing at the seas." It was not to be. Instead, they experienced a series of sickening ascents and descents. "Such was the malice of the mountains that they seemed to . . . join their forces together to work our overthrow and to consume us, so that every mountain sent down upon us their several intolerable winds, with that horror that they made the bottom of the seas to be dry land, where we anchored, sending us headlong upon the tops of the mountains and swelling waves of the seas, over the rocks, the sight whereof at our going in was as fearful as death itself." Finally, the terrifying ride ended as they were "driven as through the eye of a needle into a great and large bay, by a most narrow passage of rocks."

Even in the bay, hazard awaited the diminished fleet. "Our cables broke, our anchors came home, our ships were separated, and our spirits fainted as with the last gasp unto death."

All the while, *Golden Hind* threaded her away among islands, and the crew awaited the challenge of negotiating another channel, where the "frets" they negotiated proved as daunting as anything they had experienced in the Strait of Magellan.

At last they were able to rest for two days amid an archipelago, "finding divers good and wholesome herbs, together with fresh water," and just in time. The men, formerly "weak and much impaired in their health," received comfort from imbibing an herb that reminded them of pennywort, a medicinal plant with small round or kidney-shaped leaves, "which, purging with great facility, afforded great help and refreshing to our wearied and sickly bodies," by which Fletcher meant that it soothed their upset stomachs.

The shifting wind "and the seas raging after their former manner" ended the brief idyll. The skies darkened, the wind picked up, and soon everything "was setting itself against our peace and desired rest." Death was all but certain "if God Almighty should not make the way for us." The storm was of such force that it was "as if the bowels of the earth had set all at liberty, or as if the clouds under heaven had been called together to lay their force upon that one place." The seething waves "rolled up from the depths, even from the roots of the rocks, as if they had been a scroll of parchment," and carried the ship aloft "in most strange manner and abundance, as feathers or drifts of snow by the violence of the winds to water [level] exceeding the tops of high and lofty mountains." It was a scene of primal intensity. Amid the turbulence, the ship's anchors proved themselves nothing but "false friends in such a danger" as they "did shrink down to hide themselves in this miserable storm, committing the distressed ship and helpless men to the uncertain and rolling seas, which tossed them like a ball in a racquet." Dropping more anchors in an effort to gain stability would be useless. They had been driven so far out to sea "that 500 fathom"—three thousand feet—"would fetch no ground."

The tempest persisted "without intermission," depriving the

ship of the ability to come to anchor or to spread sail. Instead of that slender hope of deliverance, they faced "the most mad seas," and "the lee shore" toward which the "contrary and most intolerable winds" inexorably carried them under bare poles, and finally the rocks where they would meet disaster. They gained a fearsome glimpse of their own end. Amid the "perils on every side" lay "so small a likelihood to escape" that only God could have found a way for the ship to endure "that woeful state." It was more likely, in the preacher's estimation, that the mountain "should have been rent asunder from the top to the bottom and cast headlong into the sea by these unnatural winds" than any crew member survive. But, if God could "deliver Jonah out of the whale's belly," was it too much to expect that a similar miracle could happen to them?

At that moment, Providence intervened, or so it appeared to Fletcher. "He changed the stern looks of the grisly mountains to yield a favorable countenance, the heavens to laugh, the seas to obey, and the winds to cease; yea, every place we looked upon to yield us kind entertainment to refresh our weatherbeaten bodies and lives." The peril had not yet ended. Incidents took on an aspect of allegory, of stark lessons gleaned from an ancient text. "John Brewer, our trumpeter," for example, "standing upon the poop sounding his trumpet, being now as great a calm as it had been a storm, without any wind to move or shake a silken thread, most strangely a rope was so tossed and violently hurled against his body that it cast his body over into the sea." It had happened in the blink of an eye, illogical and appalling. The sailors tossed many ropes in his direction, "but he could not catch hold of any one at all to help himself, till he called one by name to cast one to him, which no sooner was done, but he received and was saved at the last pinch." John Brewer had lived. Other crew members were not so fortunate.

As Drake coped with one hardship after another, eight crew members were lost at sea. Exactly what happened to them all remains something of a mystery. Most of what is known about the disaster comes from a fantastic account narrated by a ship's boy, Peter Carder, the sole survivor, who turned up in England almost ten years later.

CHAPTER VI

"The Most Mad Seas"

After the disappearance of *Elizabeth*, Drake sent Peter Carder and seven other crew members in their pinnace to find the missing ship. At first, they survived on a diet of oysters, crabs, and penguin. Without a chart or even a compass to guide them, they rowed north along the coast, pausing at an island to slaughter and eat seal. But there was no sign of *Elizabeth*. The ship was lost.

When Carder and the others went ashore in search of food and water, seventy or so indigenous people—whom Carder called *Tapines*—took aim at the intruders with their arrows and captured four sailors. Two captives died in agony from wounds they received in the skirmish. Later, "our pinnace was dasht against the rocky shore and broken." Of the original eight, only Carder and a crewmate, William Pitcher, survived.

Over the course of two months, if Carder can be trusted, they survived on fruit and "white crabs creeping in the sand." Without fresh water, they resorted to drinking their own urine. They used jars salvaged from the wreck of the pinnace, filled them with urine at night, let them cool, and drank it in the morning. Relying on this method turned their own urine red—much to their dismay.

They constructed a raft that took them to the mainland, where they finally found the fresh water they craved along with eel and crab for sustenance. Wild with thirst, Pitcher "over drank himself" so much that the level of salt in his blood dropped—a life-threatening condition known as hyponatremia, or water intoxication. The castaway proceeded to drink himself to death, "to my unspeakable grief and discomfort." With his bare hands, Carder said, he buried the man he called "his only comfort and companion" in a shallow, sandy grave.

Now Carder was alone, but he would not be for long. He came across "some thirty of the savages of the country . . . armed with bows and arrows, and having two or three great rattles with stones in them, and a kind of tabrets [a small drum] . . . they went dancing before me about a musket shot off, and then they stayed and hanged up a piece of a white net of cotton-wool upon a stick's end of four foot high." After they had strung up their hammock, they turned their attention to Carder, "beckoning and waving with their hands, cried unto me, 'Iyorie, Iyorie,'" which he took to mean "Come hither." So he went along with a friendly group of men as well as women, who "led me along some half mile" until they came to another river, "where they hanged up their beds," or hammocks, "tying them fast to a couple of trees, being a kind of white cotton netting, which hanged two foot from the ground, and kindled fire of two sticks, which they made on both sides of their beds, for warmth and for driving away of wild beasts." After sharing a late meal, "we took our rest for that night."

His sojourn among these people was just beginning. In the morning, they took down and tied up their beds, all the while crying "tiasso, tiasso," meaning "away, away," and marched twenty miles, or so Carder estimated, in the direction of Brazil until they arrived at a settlement comprised of dwellings fashioned from "small trees like an arbor, being thatched over down to the ground with palm tree leaves." These windowless shelters featured thirty or forty doors on every side. Families entered and exited each of these openings. Within, their "chief Lord," Caiou, who appeared to be about forty years old, lived with his nine wives. The other men had just one, with the exception those considered "more valiant than the rest," who were permitted two wives, one to look to their children and the other to go to war with them.

The people in the settlement treated Carder well. Their leader dispatched many of his followers to bring food to their young guest, "to see which of them I liked best." He chose among "many types of fresh water fish, a variety of fowl, a wide selection of roots," and a certain "land-beast" that he called an armadillo, which he found to be "very good meat." All this plenty was far more than he could consume himself, so he distributed the excess among the grateful children, "which procured me no small good will among them."

At ease, and well-fed, he lived among his hosts for months, learning their language and observing them in combat. "They went out to the wars armed at my first coming, only with Bows and Arrows, some three or four hundred at a time." After bludgeoning their enemies into submission, they would truss up one of them "with Cotten cords fast arm to arm" and frog-march him to their village, where they would bind their victim to a post and "with a massive club of red wood, one of the strongest of the company (after they have drunk a certain strong drink with dancing round about him) at one blow splits his head asunder."

Carder's tale grew more wonderful and mysterious in the telling. He decided to walk alone across the South American continent. An escape from this folly materialized when thirty-eight indigenous people, men and women, whom he designated as Tupinambás, arrived to escort him to a city of four thousand people—again, Carder's estimate—living in four spacious shelters neatly laid out in a square.

In his new surroundings, Carder was treated as both an honored guest and a captive. He spent six months with his hosts, learning a few words of their language, such as *aipam*, or *cassava*. He became so close to the tribe that he participated in one of their raids against their enemy, whom he called by their correct name, *tapuias*.

Carder's colorful account, written after his return to England, raised more questions than it answered, chiefly, how would the Portuguese slavers have known of Peter Carder, the English ship's boy? How would they have heard of Drake's exploits? The details concerning his ambitious voyage were still unknown in Europe. No matter. The indigenous people killed, cooked, and devoured the Portuguese intruders. Carder might not have wanted to dwell on it, but he was held captive by cannibals.

*P*ublished accounts of cannibalism reached Europe, accompanied by macabre woodcuts depicting dismembered body parts. Carder's tribe, the Tupinambá people of Brazil, were notorious for the outlandish practice, and for that reason attracted the attention of Michel de Montaigne, the French philosopher. Among his most famous essays was his study of the Tupinambá people and his vision (at a safe distance) of their custom, which he believed worthy of consideration because it was part of the natural world. Writing in 1580, Montaigne drew on two recent accounts, André Thevet's *Cosmographie universelle* (1572) and Jean de Léry's *Histoire d'un voyage faict en la terre du Brésil* (1578). Although Montaigne never visited Brazil himself, he did meet three Brazilians who had made their way to Rouen, France, at the invitation of King Charles the Ninth, who was only thirteen years old at the time. The three visitors were astonished that "so many tall, bearded men, all strong and well armed" obeyed a child's commands. And they were also stunned by the extreme inequality of the French, some of them "gorged to the full with things of every sort" while others were "beggars at their doors, emaciated with hunger and poverty." That gross inequality could never happen in Brazil, where people were viewed "as halves of one another" and so "found it strange that these poverty-stricken halves should suffer such injustice."

Influenced by this alternate worldview, Montaigne commenced his own work with a benign description of the Tupinambá lifestyle, "in a country with a very pleasant and temperate climate," where people rarely suffered illness, in contrast to Europe, where plague and other diseases repeatedly devastated the population. He imagined their lives as nearly Edenic, with a "great abundance of fish and flesh which bear no resemblance to ours, and they eat them with no other artifice than cooking." In this state of nature, they had their limitations, such as killing the first man they ever saw on horseback with their arrows simply because they had never seen anything similar. But Montaigne still found much to admire about them.

His description of the Tupinambá town matched other accounts: "Their buildings are very long, with a capacity of two or three hundred souls; they are covered with the bark of great trees, the strips reaching to the ground at one end and supporting and leaning on one another at the top, in the manner of some of our barns." And he mentioned their distinctive hammocks, "of a cotton weave, hung from the roof like those in our ships, each man having his own, for the wives sleep apart from their husbands." (Montaigne was so fond of hammocks that he kept one in his own house.) They ate just one meal a day, and drank frequently a concoction made of a root that was "the color of our claret wines." He observed that their "whole day is spent in dancing." Or so it seemed. As the younger men hunted, the women busied themselves brewing the claret-colored beverage. Their "priests and prophets," as he called the elders, stress only "these two articles: resoluteness in war and affection for their wives." But if he fails, he pays the ultimate price: "He is cut into a thousand pieces if they catch him, and condemned as a false prophet."

The Tupinambá people at war reminded Montaigne of ancient combatants: "They have their wars with the nations beyond the mountains, further inland, to which they go quite naked, with no other arms than bows or wooden swords ending in a sharp point. . . . It is astonishing what firmness they show in their contests, which only end in slaughter and bloodshed." At the conclusion of battle, "each man brings back as his trophy the head of the enemy he has killed, and sets it up at the entrance to his dwelling." Of more immediate interest to Carder, had he known of the custom, was the Tupinambá's grotesque manner of dealing with a prisoner. They lavish hospitality on him until they bind his arms with ropes, and "kill him with their swords. This being done, they roast him and eat him and send some pieces to their absent friends." This practice was not, Montaigne advised, for "nourishment." Rather, it symbolized "extreme revenge." When the Portuguese arrived, they "improved" on this custom by burying their prisoners to the waist, shooting them with arrows, and finally hanging them. As a result, the Tupinambá regarded the Portuguese as "much greater masters than themselves in every sort of wickedness," and learned to emulate "the Portuguese style of execution."

Montaigne refrained from passing judgment on the Tupinambá people of Brazil. He preferred to understand their way of life, which, he suggested, was more civilized than the customs found in Europe or in antiquity. "I am not sorry that we notice the barbarous horror of such acts, but I am heartily sorry that, judging their faults rightly, we should be so blind to our own." He went on, "I think there is more barbarity in eating a man alive than in eating him dead, and in tearing by tortures and the rack a body still of feeling"—as was the practice in much of Europe—"in roasting a man bit by bit, in having him bitten and mangled by dogs and swine . . . and what is worse, on the pretext of piety and religion." One could call these people "barbarians," he argued, but only "in respect to the rules of reason, but not in respect to ourselves, who surpass them in every kind of barbarity." Compared to Europeans, "their warfare is wholly noble and generous."

Montaigne's "noble savage," seemingly more primitive than Europeans, actually ranked higher in his estimation, as if civilization, especially in Europe, was deteriorating over time rather than advancing.

*C*arder's odyssey took another improbable turn when, after he had lived with the Tupinambá people for about six months, "the king [Caiou] requested me to go to the war with him against his enemies the Tapwees." Carder agreed, and before they set out, he showed his hosts how to fashion shields made of the bark of a tree, "for defence against arrows, whereof we made some hundred and withall wished them to make some two hundred of clubs. Which being done we marched forward some seven hundred in number."

The next day, his contribution to his hosts proved crucial. "We set upon the town about four of the clock in the morning, the enemy standing upon defense of their arrows, were much deceived by reason of our targets"—shields—"which being seconded by our clubs, we immediately knocked down to the number of two hundred, [and] the rest, except some twenty prisoners escaped into the woods." After a day, the leader "caused many of their carcasses to be broiled upon coals and eaten." Carder moved in for a closer look: "This is to be noted, that how many men these savages do kill, so many holes they will have in their visage, beginning first in their nether lip, then in their cheeks, thirdly in both their eye-brows, and lastly in their ears." Those ritual mutilations were their way of tallying their victims, and they proceeded to add "those twenty prisoners which we brought home, [which] were afterward killed, roasted and eaten."

Nor was this Carder's only exposure to cannibalism. During his sojourn a group of Portuguese, their African slaves, and "Brazilians" approached their settlement "to see whether they could surprise any of our savages"—note that Carder considered the indigenous people to belong to him in some fashion by this point—"and to harken what was become of me." The rescue mission did not go as planned. Carder's hosts captured several of the Portuguese and Africans, "and after their confession of the intent of their coming hither, they were brained with clubs, broiled, and eaten."

Carder had finally seen enough of life in the wild. He implored Caiou to allow him to depart, "to see if I could spy out any English or French ship to pass me into my country." The king not only agreed, he provided four men to accompany Carder on the trek to the east coast of Brazil, roughly 2,300 miles through uncharted wilderness teeming with poisonous insects, snakes, and enemy tribes. In one of the more suspicious passages in his account, Carder writes of appearing eventually without warning in Bahia, all the way across the continent. It was unlikely that he had walked this great distance. Perhaps he had sailed around the cape to Bahia, surely as great an adventure as traveling across land, but Carder left no clue as to how he accomplished this exploit.

When Carder was next heard from, he had been found by a Portuguese navigator searching for Drake. Instead, he came across

Carder and six others, all wounded by arrows. They had sought refuge on a beach somewhere along the coast of Brazil. The Portuguese listened in fascination to this young man who had sailed with the English pirate Drake, and who told them about his fleet running aground, and about the wreck of an enormous galleon carrying four hundred soldiers and one hundred passengers, not to mention a fleet consisting of ten ships. Carder created the impression that hundreds of shipwrecked Englishmen were lurking in the forest, ready to attack at any time. (In reality, no such fleet existed.)

The Portuguese held Carder in confinement for a time and released him in the custody of a certain Antonio de Paiva, who "could speak good English, and was a lover of our nation, and brought me directly unto his house. This Antonio de Paiva, pitying my case, and advising me not to be known . . . brought me to the governor, whose name was Diego Vas," who promptly committed Carder to prison, with orders for him to sail for Portugal to spend the rest of his life in jail. Carder explained that he had "sought them out and came and yielded my self into their hands, laying down my weapons at one of his nation's feet." His argument worked, and a fortnight later, he was freed into the custody of de Paiva, as the officials wrote to Portugal "to know the King's pleasure concerning me."

More than two years passed before an answer arrived.

During this interval, he became the "overseer of my friends' Negroes and savages in their planting and dressing of their sugar canes, and in planting of gingers, which grow there exceeding well." He also occupied himself "cutting down of Brazilwood, and in bringing it down by rivers upon rafts unto the port where the ships do lade and in seeing them gather their cotton wool, and picking the seeds out of and packing the same, and in gathering of the long pepper both white and red."

Later, he put his navigational skills to use piloting boats belonging to Antonio de Paiva along the Atlantic coast from Salvador to Ilhéus, Porto Seguro, and Rio de Janeiro. He awaited the day when a ship would carry him away to prison in Portugal. De Paiva expressed regret that he could no longer help Carder himself, "but kindly offered me his help to convey me away."

Carder devised a careful response to this offer. "I took his boat and four of his Negroes, pretending to go on fishing," he said, "to the sea." When he came ashore, his four sailing companions were questioned about what they were doing, but, "being utterly ignorant of mine intent, answered that they were drawn thither by fierce weather." They "returned home with the next wind, myself secretly behind them." Months later, he talked his way onto a ship with eight Englishmen and fourteen Portuguese, most likely departing from Recife, a port founded forty years earlier. When the ship, bound for Portugal, encountered two English warships in the vicinity of the Azores, Carder surrendered "as their lawful prizes." He was in custody once again, but this time it was English custody.

He arrived in Chichester on England's southern coast in late November 1586, "nine years and fourteen days after my departure out of England with Sir Francis Drake in his voyage about the world." By the time Carder returned, England and Spain were on the brink of open warfare. Amid these global intrigues, the hapless Carder seemed destined for obscurity, but then, "My strange adventures and long living among cruel savages being known to the right honorable Lord Charles Howard, Lord High Admiral of England, he certified the Queen's Majesty thereof with speed and brought me to her presence at Whitehall."

There they stood, the renegade and the monarch. "It pleased her to talk with me a long hour's space of my travails and wonderful escape, and among other things of the manner of M. Doughty's execution; and afterward bestowed 22 angels [equivalent to eleven pounds] on me, willing my Lord to have consideration of me." This audience gave Carder a much-needed sense of affirmation. "With many gracious words I was dismissed; humbly thanking the Almighty for my miraculous preservation, and safe return into my native country."

Carder's flamboyant description of his adventures in Brazil reflected the European public's fascination with the New World, and it was included in an immense collection of travel accounts called *Purchas his pilgrimage; or, Relations of the World and the Religions observed in all ages and places* (1626) compiled by an English cleric and armchair traveler named Samuel Purchas. Despite its inconsistencies, Carder's tale of survival made him celebrated as an Everyman counterpoint to Drake's Superman. Unlike Drake, motivated by an unrelenting desire to explore, to plunder, and to win fame, Carder simply wanted to survive. He came so close to extinction on so many occasions that his ability to endure became a kind of heroism. Like Odysseus, who wandered for ten years before reaching home, Carder was wily and cunning; he lied not because he loved dissembling, but because he was trying to outlast his circumstances, and in this pursuit, the truth was often his enemy and deceit his ally.

*M*eanwhile, Drake struggled to resume his voyage. After leaving the western mouth of the Strait and heading north, his diminished fleet veered precariously off course, and the storm intensified. They were unable to make landfall until October 7. An attempt to get within hailing distance of the shore brought the storm-tossed ships to the brink of disaster.

When the ships cautiously came to anchor, "we were hoping to enjoy some freedom and ease till the storm was ended," but they were soon struck by "so deadly a stroke" that Drake "not only left the anchor behind her, through the violence and fury of the flaw, but in departing thence, also lost the company and sight of our vice-admiral, the *Elizabeth*." Fletcher attributed the unusual separation of the two ships "partly through the negligence of those that had the charge of her, partly through a kind of desire that some in her had to be out of these troubles and to be home again." Fletcher implied that the crew of *Elizabeth*, under the command of John Winter, had embarked on a second mutiny.

Drake gave no sign of being upset about the loss of either *Elizabeth* or, especially, Winter. Doughty and Winter had been his chief rivals, and the three of them had ruled the fleet as an awkward triumvirate: two gentlemen and one red-haired Devonshire pirate. Without the aristocracy breathing down his neck, Drake was in command of the reduced armada. All the risk would be his, as would all the reward. At the same time, the fleet lacked what a modern mission would call redundancy in case of catastrophic failure, that is, the loss of the flag-ship. If he failed, he would be disgraced, forgotten; if he succeeded, he would enlarge on Magellan's legacy, and just as important, become immensely wealthy. Magellan sailed for a rival of his native Portugal, and could never, in the most favorable circumstances, go home, but Drake could, so long as the queen was there to welcome him.

According to Edward Cliffe, a mariner who transcribed Winter's account, *Elizabeth* "lost company" of Drake on or about October 7. The day after, "hardly escaping the danger of the rocks, we put into the strait again, where we anchored in an open bay for the space of 2 days, and made great fires on the shore" to help Drake find them.

Matters turned out differently. Under the command of John Winter, part of the original Drake-Doughty-Winter triumvirate, *Elizabeth* anchored within the Strait for three weeks so that the crew could recover from the ordeal. The dislocated mariners called it the Port of Health, where, "for the most part of our men being very sick with long watching, cold, and evil diet, did here (God be thanked) wonderfully recover their health in a short space" as they feasted on twenty-inch-long mussels, "full of seed-pearls" as a bonus.

Elizabeth was under sail again on November 1, 1578, and called at Saint George's Island—named by Drake months earlier when the fleet first entered the Strait—on November 11. Winter guided the ship to the eastern mouth of the Strait, and by the end of November, they had reached an island near the mouth of the Rio de la Plata, the false strait that Drake (and Magellan before him) had reconnoitered. By this time, Winter had decided to take his ship back to England rather than follow Drake, and persisted "full sore against the mariners' minds." He had determined that the two of them could not exist as cocaptains, not after what had happened to Doughty.

Before making the leap, Winter paused at a landmass he called Seal Island—"There is such an infinite number of seals as may seem incredible to any man that hath not been there, some of them being 16 foot long, not fearing the presence of our men"—to take on provisions, especially water, and outfit a small pinnace to accompany them on the next leg of the voyage, all the way to England. The layover on Seal Island lasted fifteen days, "during which time the seals would come and sleep by them . . . unless mortal blows forced them to yield."

They set out again on January 1, 1579. Cliffe noticed that as he approached the Tropic of Capricorn, "by reason of foul weather we lost our pinnace, and 8 men in her, and never saw them since." The same storm nearly destroyed *Elizabeth* and forced her to anchor off-shore, where the cable parted and the anchor was lost. "The captain ran about so violently with the rising of the ship in the sea that it threw men from the bars, and broke out the brains of one man; one other had his leg broken and divers others were sore hurt."

The storm-battered ship found refuge on an island off the Brazilian coast. When sickness afflicted the men, Winter dispatched a contingent of sailors to hunt for medicinal herbs. They returned with *Drimys* bark, stripped from the tall, slender trees that flourished in coastal evergreen forests. Thick, pulpy, and grayish, *Drimys* bark was believed to prevent and cure scurvy, which proved to be the case. It was later known as *Drimys winteri*, after the captain fleeing Drake.

Without warning, three Portuguese soldiers appeared, demanding to know the origin of the damaged vessel. It was believed that no English ship had visited these waters until this time. The Portuguese went to speak to the governor about the arrival, but not before Winter kept one of them "for a pledge."

Soon after, another canoe arrived, this one bearing a Portuguese and "all the rest naked men of the country," who gave the visitors "two small oxen, one young hog, with certain hens, also pomeranites, lemons, oranges, and other fruits of the country." In return, Winter offered linen cloth, combs, knives, and "other trifles." Just when it appeared a trade had been successfully consummated, the governor "sent word that we should have nothing, unless we would bring our ship into the haven." And that Winter was not prepared to do, "for all their practice was to have gotten us within their danger." The sudden shift confirmed Winter's suspicion that the haughty Portuguese were not to be trusted. Instead, the English mariners approached the shore, feigning to disembark and possibly attack, "but we never meant it." They recovered their hostage and returned their Portuguese "pledge." But the English were not done with the Portuguese yet. One of their slaves indicated with gestures that the Portuguese were approaching in their canoes, and they were coming in force.

In the morning, Winter and his men spied more than a dozen oversize canoes approaching, some carrying as many as forty passengers. Most of the English fled to safety, but the Portuguese managed to capture at least two sailors, who were never heard from again.

By March 17, Winter was intent on putting as much distance as possible between him and the treacherous Portuguese. Heading north, *Elizabeth* retraced her route past the island of Fernando de Noronha, rising from the sea like a fragment of Eden, crossed the equator on April 13, and six days later the crew spotted Polaris, the North Star. The earth's axis points at Polaris, so it does not appear to rise or set in the night sky, remaining in more or less the same place while the other stars revolve around it.

In early May, *Elizabeth* arrived at one of the most remarkable places on earth, the Sargasso Sea, the *only* sea defined not by land barriers but by ocean currents: the Gulf Stream to the west, the North Atlantic Current to the north, the Canary Current to the east, and the North Atlantic Equatorial Current to the south. Together they produce an ocean gyre, which is formed by global wind patterns, the Earth's rotation, and landmasses. When wind drags on the ocean surface, it pushes in the direction the wind is blowing. At the same time, Earth's rotation deflects, or changes the direction of, the wind-driven currents. This deflection sets up the phenomenon called the Coriolis effect (named after the French scientist Gaspard-Gustave de

Coriolis). In the Northern Hemisphere, the Coriolis effect shifts surface currents by an angle of about 45 degrees in a clockwise motion. In the Southern Hemisphere, the opposite occurs: ocean currents are pushed in a counterclockwise motion. A set of different currents, called an Ekman Spiral, percolates beneath the surface, where the deflection of deeper layers decreases. The spiral descends more than three hundred feet below the surface, turning the water into a shade of dark blue inviting meditation or thoughts of self-abnegation.

Sailors feared the weeds—Sargasso weeds—in this sea, because they could foul ships and even conceal monsters. In reality, it is home to the free-floating brown *Sargassum* seaweed, which nurtures and harbors a surprising variety of sea life ranging from turtles to shrimp, whales, and sharks. In 1492, Christopher Columbus partly demystified the region. His sailors had ample time to study the olive and gold fronds that stretched from horizon to horizon, and to observe the berrylike, gas-filled bladders that keep the seaweed suspended near the water's surface. The crew called them *Sargazo* because they were reminiscent of small grapes growing in the vicinity of the Mediterranean.

Elizabeth crossed the Sargasso Sea without incident, and on May 5 sailed northeast into the North Atlantic. On May 30, they raised the ancient fishing village of St. Ives on the Cornwall coast, and on June 2, 1579, they arrived safely in Ilford Coombe, Devonshire. Edward Cliffe wrote, "And thus, after our manifold troubles and great dangers in having passed the straits of Magellan into the South Sea with our General Francis Drake, and having been driven with him down to the Southerly latitude of 57 degrees, and afterward passing back by the same straits again, it pleased God to bring us safe into our own native country, to enjoy the presence of our dear friends and kinfolks, to whom be praise, honour, and glory, for ever and ever. Amen."

Days later, on June 10, Winter returned to London. The unexpected arrival caused a sensation at the highest levels. Mendoza, relying on his anonymous sources at court, described Winter's reception with a combination of alarm and amazement. "The captain has since arrived here and has been received with extraordinary favour by the Queen, who was closeted with him alone to hear an account of his voyage," he gossiped to Philip. "He has been treated in the same way by the council at large and by each member in particular, so that it has been impossible to get at him yet. The Queen has ordered that both he and the crew should be very well treated, considering their having returned without finishing the voyage or bringing anything back with them, and the execution of the gentleman"—the unfortunate Doughty—"by Drake is not to be spoken about until his return." Mendoza had more intelligence regarding Winter to share, all of it remarkably accurate: "The captain affirms that he entered the Straits with his ship and arrived at fifty-five degrees south latitude in the southern sea, where he found an island with traces of habitation, and a gallows erected, whereon, it is said, Magellan had executed a man. The description he gives of the Straits is similar to that given of Magellan's discovery, and he says that, at its widest part, it is about seven leagues across, narrowing in some parts to less than two. He came across two islands in the Strait itself, one of which was crowded with birds like geese [actually, penguins] and the other had on it a large quantity of fish [seals], which came on shore. He said that these stood him in great good stead for his maintenance. He left Drake ten months ago and came to the coast of Brazil to victual for his voyage hither."

The circumstances surrounding Winter's return struck Mendoza as peculiar. Why would the queen greet Winter, a mutineer, with open arms? The answer arrived a few weeks later by caravel from the Indies "with news that Drake, about whom I wrote, had passed through the Straits of Magellan, and had stolen in the southern sea gold and silver worth 200,000 ducats belonging to his Majesty, and 400,000 the property of merchants. The adventurers who provided money and ships for the voyage are beside themselves for joy." The English triumph resonated all the way to London. "The people here are talking of nothing else but going out to plunder in a similar way."

It was time for King Philip to act. The authority of the Spanish crown was being mocked. "Although the courier was sent specially with this news alone, I do not believe it, as in a matter of this importance, if it were true, some steps would have been taken by his Majesty ere this. I am making every possible effort respecting the prizes taken by English pirates from his Majesty's subjects, although I only get to know of the cases through Englishmen, as the owners themselves do not tell me." What they did tell him confirmed his worst misgivings about the English, not just Drake. "One of these ministers of theirs has been convicted of the dreadful and nefarious crime of consorting with his own daughter, and, although the affair is public, all they have done is to put him for a little while in the pillory. You can judge by this how they would punish other smaller peccadilloes." Mendoza maintained his facade of moral outrage concerning the English even as the Spanish Inquisition raged.

Drake's capture of a Portuguese vessel at the Cape Verde islands came to the attention of the Portuguese ambassador, who demanded that action be taken against both Francis Drake and Winter. Drake was thousands of miles away, and no one knew if he was dead or alive, but Winter, in London, was thrown into prison for deserting the captain general. Drake's younger brother John believed that

Winter would have been hanged, except that Francis, on his eventual
return to England, pleaded successfully for his release from jail.

The scandal surrounding this unauthorized voyage obscured
several important details, beginning with Winter's successful nego-
tiation of the Strait from west to east, a nautical challenge of the first
order. Not only that, but Winter had navigated the Strait not just
once, as Magellan and Drake had, but twice. Unlike his predecessors,
Winter had not lost any men during the passage. His voyage went a
long way toward demonstrating that it was possible to traverse the
Strait from end to end without devastating consequences. Winter
made himself useful to the Crown during the course of the next two
years, as Elizabeth's ministers tried to understand exactly how Drake
had accomplished his navigational feat. As overheard by Spanish
ministers—spies—Drake was not forthcoming, but Winter freely
speculated on his former captain's maneuvers, as did Bernardino de
Mendoza in London.

"That the straits are really formed by islands is proved by what
happened to Winter," Mendoza noted, "because, after having proceeded for 80 leagues, the storm carried him back to Port St. Julian
without his again passing out of the opening by which he had arrived, which made cosmographers here think that Winter had not
entered the straits at all. Although he affirmed that the straits
were formed by islands, he was not believed until Drake himself
returned." In fact, they were formed by a collision of pieces of the
Earth's crust known as tectonic plates. At some point in the distant
past, a massive plate from the east smashed into a massive plate from
the west. The eastern plate slid on top, the western underneath to
form a unique landscape. It rains every day of the year on the western mountaintops, sustaining a lush cover of vegetation. Strikingly
dimorphic, the kelp goose—snow-white males, black-and-brown
females—inhabited a landscape covered with thirty kinds of ferns—

plants without seeds or flowers, which reproduce by means of tiny spores. Penguins and dolphins caroused offshore, while white swans with black necks, too heavy to fly, remained earthbound. The dense forest began only a few yards from the shoreline. Tiny white orchids poked out of a thick covering of leaves, and the whole landscape was enveloped in mist and gloom.

Drake's men beheld a primordial landscape of windblown trees. In the meandering channels leading to and from the Strait, diminutive aqua-tinged icebergs floated along the speckled surface of cloudy green water.

*D*rake's circumnavigation-in-progress set in motion events across Europe and the world, long before his eventual return. The effects were felt unevenly—England of all places appeared slow to recognize the global revolution in the making—but Spain, already in possession of an empire, was a different story. Merchants plying their routes close to home saw themselves as pawns in a global struggle between Spain and England. Said Mendoza, "These merchants are in great alarm lest his Majesty"—King Philip—"should order the seizure of English property in retaliation of the robberies committed by Drake."

Mendoza decided to investigate Drake's whereabouts himself. "I sent a man to Plymouth, a Spaniard residing near there, to inform me of his arrival." Mendoza learned the conspiracy to undercut Spain was much wider than he had imagined. His source revealed that "very secretly, from the wife of one of the justices there, these councilors, who have a share in the venture, have sent orders to all the justices and governors to help him [Drake] to land and place his plunder in safety, and I therefore fear that it will be difficult to recover it, if anything of value reaches the country." Not only that, but the intelligence also suggested that Mendoza was part of a conspiracy to deceive the English, with whom he was supposed to maintain civil relations. The next move in this game of global chess belonged to Drake. "Those who are well informed on the subject do not expect Drake to arrive before January, as he has to return through the same Straits, and he cannot do this until November, which is summer in those parts, as the council of the Indies will know, if true." Drake appeared poised for a major success, and Mendoza found himself in the awkward position of having to inform his sovereign of the news.

Disoriented, Drake proceeded southward toward what we now call Cape Horn and sought refuge in an archipelago where they were reassured to "find the people of the country travelling for their living from one island to another, in their canoes, both men, women, and young infants wrapped in skins, and hanging at their mothers' backs." They traded with these placid locals for necklaces made of shells and other "trifles" while resting for three days.

Even then, "the troubled seas and blustering winds did every hour threaten unto us." It seemed they had overstayed their welcome, for they were "more rigorously assaulted" by a violent squall that drove them out to sea and caused the cable connecting the ship to her anchor to part as the ship was "chased along by the winds and buffeted incessantly." Drake opined that God had sent the ordeal on purpose as a test or warning, his way of perceiving purpose in the chaos. At last they found themselves coming up on "the headland of all these islands." A limitless expanse spread before the men. "There is no main nor island to be seen southwards, but as the Atlantic Ocean and the South Sea [as the Pacific Ocean was called] meet in a most large and free scope." They had reached the end of the continent. The cape seemed to rise from the sea like the petrified spine of an extinct creature. From their vantage point, they could dispel centuries of accumulated myths and misunderstanding, or so Fletcher assumed. "It hath been a dream through many ages that these islands have been a main [open sea], and that it hath been terra incognita, wherein many strange monsters lived." But the only monsters existed in the imagination. No "traveller that he had ever heard of" discovered them. Terra incognita failed to appear. It did not exist; the way was clear, weather permitting. Nor did a powerful current, as he had once believed, run past this point. And so, he deduced, it could be possible to travel back and forth from one great ocean to the other. "There is one large and main sea," he concluded, and if anyone did not believe him, "he should be advised to suspend judgment till he have tried it himself by his own travel." Contemporary explorers and scientists refer to this concept as "ground truth," that is, information gathered by direct observation. Fletcher had just experienced his own ground truth at Cape Horn.

*I*n the Pacific, storms pummeled Drake's ships as they attempted to make their way along what they took to be the western coast of South America. On October 24, 1578, he found anchorage off Cape Horn beside a landmass that Drake considered the end of the world, "the utmost island of terra incognita, to the Southward of America." He stayed in the area—which might have been Cape Horn Island—for a little more than a week. (Accounts are unclear if not contradictory concerning his exact whereabouts at this point.)

During this time, or shortly after, Drake decided he had arrived at one of the most isolated parts of the globe, uninhabited since prehistoric times. Years later, in 1593, his cousin Richard Hawkins recalled Drake describing for him that moment: "He was not able to double [sail around] the southernmost island, and so anchored under the lee of it; and going ashore carried a compass with, and seeking out the southernmost part of the island, cast himself down upon the point groveling and so reached out his body over it." (By "grovel," Hawkins meant lying prone.) When he returned to his sailors, he explained that he had been to the southernmost part of the world, farther south "than any of them, yea, or any man yet known." It was a heroic thought, but in all likelihood, it was not the case.

Soon after, Drake had another revelation. Although Magellan had pioneered the route through the Strait to the Pacific Ocean decades before, cartographers and explorers still failed to grasp the relationship of oceans and landmasses in the extreme Southern Hemisphere. For this reason Drake and his company were astonished and grateful to realize that "The West Occidental [the Pacific] and the South Sea are but one!" The connection between the seas meant their circumnavigation could continue.

By this time, October 28, "Our troubles did make an end, the storm ceased, and all our calamities (only the absence of our friends excepted) were removed," wrote Fletcher. It seemed to him that God had led them to the place to make this discovery, and now wanted them to linger a while to enjoy it. Even more remarkable, in this extreme southern latitude, the nights lasted only two hours. There were twenty-two hours of daylight to explore and recover from their torments at sea.

Two days later, Drake and his men traveled north along the continent's western coast toward Chile, pausing at a pair of islands that on closer inspection proved to be "storehouses of most liberal provision of victuals for us." Refreshed and fed, they sailed on. It was possible to imagine that they had put the worst of their troubles behind them, having crossed the Atlantic and traversed the Strait of

Magellan. Drake had put down a mutiny, and collectively they had overcome the threat of starvation.

In this confident frame of mind, the fleet came to a "fruitful place, and well stored with sundry sorts of good things: as sheep and other cattle, maize (which is a kind of grain whereof they make bread), potatoes, with such other roots; besides that, it is thought to be wonderful rich in gold"—*gold!*—"and to want no good thing for the use of a man's life." It was November 25, and the little band of Englishmen had journeyed a thousand miles north of the Strait. They had no way of knowing they were about to encounter their most serious crisis yet.

*W*e fell in sight of an island named Mocha," Fletcher wrote. "We thought best to leave the mainland and not to discover for ourselves" whatever dangers lurked there. Mocha is tiny, less than twenty square miles, a speck in an immense and menacing sea. (Many years later, the waters surrounding the island would become home to a seventy-foot-long albino sperm whale named "Mocha Dick," the inspiration for Herman Melville's epic novel, *Moby-Dick*.)

When Drake and his men rowed themselves ashore, they realized they were not alone. The inhabitants, on whom chroniclers have bestowed many names, probably belonged to the Mapuche people, specifically, the Lafkenches, or "people of the sea" dwelling along the coast. Initially, the Lafkenches made a "great show of friendship, and roundly entered into traffic with our men," much to the visitors' pleasure, "for their commodities were such as we wanted, as fat muttons, hens, maize." The English sailors made signs that they also needed water, and immediately "they gave us assurance by signs . . . that we should have it at pleasure." The food supplied by the Lafkenches turned out to be luscious, mouthwatering, in fact.

"That night, our mutton and hens was to us so sweet that we longed for the day that we might have more such bargains at their hands, yea every man desired to be a South Sea merchant."

All the while, Drake was studying his hosts, and he concluded that unlike the unpredictable Patagonian giants, who had killed two of his men, the generous inhabitants of Mocha "had neither bow nor other shot, as they were in Port Julian when they met with the giants, when they slew two of our men." He considered the Lafkenches peaceful beings, even harmless, and for a time they were. They invited Drake to guide his ships into a "narrow creek . . . on both sides whereof did grow [an] abundance of Indian reeds, high and thick." Lulled into a false sense of security, Drake followed their prompting. It was a rare lapse of judgment.

Unknown to Drake, "a multitude of bloody soldiers on both sides" were hiding behind this thick curtain of reeds, waiting to attack. The exposed English ships ventured farther as the Lafkenches remained motionless, silent, and closely packed "till they had their opportunity they looked for." When Drake's men, still oblivious of the danger they faced, approached, "some were appointed to stand at the landing place to receive our men," and show them where to collect water. Two men, most likely Thomas Flood and Tom Brewer, went ashore with containers. One "took the boat's rope with him to draw the boat nearer to land" and placed it on the ground. Everything had been calm until that moment, but in an instant, the routine chore turned into a life-and-death confrontation. "No sooner was [the rope] out of his hand but an Indian took it up, holding the boat fast to the shore . . . [as] others laid violent hands upon our men which were landed and carried them away."

Just then, the Lafkenche warriors emerged from their hiding places in the reeds, "well armed with bows, arrows, and darts made of cane." The English sailors taken hostage were unable to "defend themselves or annoy their enemies" and so "were forced to be butts to every arrow at the pleasure of the shooter, behind and before and on every side." In this way, the Lafkenches methodically slaughtered them and attacked other sailors. There was no escape, no way to appeal for help or mercy, and no way to surrender. The "arrows came so thick and every way upon them, cribbed up into so narrow a place as the boat, not one able to stir by another to help themselves, so that not any one person escaped without some grievous wound."

Nearly all the soldiers bore multiple gashes. One suffered ten injuries inflicted by the arrows, another twenty-one, "some in [the] head and face." The sight of their bloody, broken bodies horrified the other sailors. The gunner, Great Niel, a Dane, sustained serious blows and succumbed two days later. Drake's longtime servant, Diego, received twenty wounds, although John Drake, the captain's young nephew, noted that "the arrows did not enter the flesh deeply." He probably survived for another year before dying of unknown causes.

During the mêlée, one arrow in particular found its mark. Drake himself was shot in the face. Based on Fletcher's description, the arrow entered near Drake's eye but did not pierce the globe itself. In such cases, the cornea—the transparent surface of the eyeball—and the sclera—the white outer layer—provide sufficient resistance for the eye to deform and move aside. If the arrow had passed into the orbit, or eye socket, it might have traveled all the way through the superior orbital fissure to the carotid artery, causing extensive bleeding. It might have lodged in the temporal lobe at the base of the brain. Removing the arrow would have aggravated the trauma, and the victim would have suffered tremendous hemorrhaging. Loss of consciousness and death would likely follow. But in Drake's case, the arrow was far enough from his eye to allow him to keep the eye and his vision, along with a prominent scar.

At this moment of extreme peril, "one of the simplest of the company" had the presence of mind to grasp his sword and "cut the boat's rope, and by that means set them at liberty to help themselves by shifting away" from their attackers and saving their lives in the process. As they frantically paddled, "arrows were sent to them so thick as gnats in the sun, and the sides of the boat within and without stuck full of them as almost one could stand by another, so that a man might by sight of the boat a far off judge what was the state of their bodies which were in it."

When they reached safety, and their comrades came aboard to rescue them, "the horror of their bloody state wounded the hearts of all men to behold them. Notwithstanding, prayers being made for their comfort, it was endeavoured to ease their extremity, to save them whom the Lord had appointed to live, so that it pleased God not any but one died of that accident." Both luck and resourcefulness were on their side.

Once the injured soldiers had been rescued, a fresh contingent of sailors attempted to liberate those who had been seized by the Indians, "but all in vain and impossible, for when our men came in view of them, the multitude was great." Indeed, two thousand Indians, "well appointed, with bows, darts, spears, shields, pikes, and other weapons, most of them headed with pure silver, which in the light of the moon made a wonderful show," stood ready to attack a ragtag group of sailors who had wandered far from home.

The rescue party came upon a gruesome scene. Trapped in the Lafkenches' midst "were our two men in their execution and torments." They were bound and lay on the ground, "and the people cast themselves into a ring round about them, hand in hand with a dance, still turning or going about with a song; in the meantime, tormentors, working with knives upon their bodies, cut the flesh away by gubbets"—lumps—"and cast it up into the air, the which falling down, the people catched in their dancing, and like dogs devoured it in [a] most monstrous and unnatural manner, even most horrible to nature, and thus continued till they had picked their bones." That was shocking enough, but even more sickening, there was "life yet remaining in them." They were being eaten alive.

Observing this grisly display, Drake's company fired their weapons at the Indians, only to watch the ammunition sputter and fall to the ground. "We might have taken a revenge upon them at pleasure with great shot out of our ship, but the General would not for special causes consent to it." So the cannon remained cold and silent, but Drake's order to hold their fire probably saved them from a massacre.

Fletcher devised an explanation for this appalling behavior. "We understood that this people were natural Indians," he mused, "and did inhabit at mainland; but by the bloody cruelty of the Spaniards (as were the Brazilians by the Portuguese) were driven to fly from their natural country to this island to purchase to themselves peace and safety." Here they maintained a little island kingdom by "continual shedding of the blood and eating of the flesh of the Spaniards, when or howsoever they can come by them, as the people of Brazil deal with the Portuguese when they overcome them." Because they knew no other outsiders except the Spanish, they persuaded themselves "that we were the same, and because one of our men rashly spake in the Spanish tongue, they determined to bestow upon us a Spaniard's reward, which they effected indeed to our great grief and hazarding of our state." The "Spaniard's reward," of course, meant revenge. So it was all a misunderstanding between Drake and the Lafkenches, a case of mistaken identity—but a deadly one.

Drake's eagerness to move beyond the fatal ambush was telling. Others in his place would have been more cautious or vindictive, but Drake above all wanted to survive—martyrdom had no place in his worldview—and he was inclined to trust the Indians and to ascribe their hostile behavior to their dealings with the Spanish. His willingness to rely on the goodwill of indigenous peoples and to make common cause with them had served him well in years gone by with the Cimarrons. There was no reason why this approach could not work again, so long as the Indians were free of the deceitful Spanish. The ultimate goal of his voyage was neither conquest, nor conversion to Christianity, nor the slave trade. It was gold—Spanish gold.

As the fleet slipped away from the disaster, night came on. Some of those on board panicked, frightened that their ships would be attacked in the darkness by Indians or by Spaniards posted along the shore. A growing need for fresh food and water intensified the "extreme and crazy state of our hurt men advising us to use expedition to find some convenient place of repose." There was none for several days until, on November 30, Drake arrived at Phillips Bay, as Fletcher called it, where they "came to anchor, and forthwith manned and set our boat"—that is, the pinnace—"to discover what likelihood the place would offer to afford us such things as we stood in need of . . . yet after long travel could find no appearance of hope for relief, either of fresh victuals or of fresh water."

In the distance, they made out "huge herds of white buffalo," but no sign of people until the pinnace spied "within the bay an Indian with his canoe, as he was fishing." Drake invited him aboard *Golden Hind,* "canoe and all, as he was in it." His hosts found him a "comely personage, and of a goodly stature; his apparel was a white garment, reaching scarcely to his knees; his arms and legs were naked; his hair upon his head very long; without a beard, as all the Indians for the most part are." Even better, "He seemed very gentle, of mild and humble nature, being very tractable to learn the use of every thing, and most grateful for such things as our General bestowed upon him. In him we might see . . . how grievous a thing it is that they should by any means be so abused as all those are, whom the Spaniards have any command or power over."

At last they had located the unspoiled Indian for whom they had been searching. With that, "we sent him away with our boat and his own canoe (which was made of reed straw) to land him where he would."

He was greeted by two or three friends, to whom he displayed the trinkets the English visitors had given him. A few hours later, he returned with other members of his clan with gifts of their own: hens, eggs, and a "fat hog" aboard an unmanned canoe. Meanwhile, their leader sent his horse away so that the visitors could see that he was alone and unarmed. He offered to lead them to a safe harbor where they could refresh themselves.

*T*he crew had come to realize that they had signed on for a voyage of outright piracy under a captain who obeyed no limits. They faced life-threatening conditions: sudden storms, mutiny, attacks by indigenous peoples, poisoning, dehydration, scurvy, dysentery, and the limits of their endurance and sanity. There was no guarantee that any of them would live to see Plymouth again, or even another day.

There was grumbling below deck as they realized Drake would not hesitate to sacrifice their lives to achieve his goals. One officer in particular, John Doughty, the brother of Thomas, whom Drake had executed, became a lightning rod for these malcontents. He had close connections to a clique at court opposed to Drake; they had encouraged him to join the voyage expressly to keep an eye on the upstart captain and, if possible, curb his tendency to excess. Doughty was soon stirring up anti-Drake sentiment among the crew. And to further demean the captain, Doughty claimed he had bedded Drake's wife just before the ship departed from England. Whether this was the unlikely truth—there was no independent confirmation of the situation—or merely an idle boast designed to enhance Doughty's stature in the eyes of the other men, the assertion could only infuriate Drake. That vendetta would have to wait while Drake attempted to complete the circumnavigation.

CHAPTER VII

"Cruel Courtesy"

With renewed clarity of purpose, Drake ordered his fleet to sail north along the coast of Chile. Accounts of this leg of the circumnavigation often diverge, depending on the teller and the length of time between the event itself and the effort to recall it. What is certain is that Drake and his men were menaced by both the Spanish and indigenous people, and barely escaped with their lives as they haltingly proceeded north.

The Spanish lurked everywhere. Wherever Drake found Spanish encampments, he sent out raiding parties to taunt the guards. The sense of mischief became contagious. Even the fleet's chaplain, Francis Fletcher, wrote with glee about startling a Spaniard who had fallen asleep while guarding thirteen barrels of silver, sheep, and a store of dried beef. The English raiders spared the guard's life but made off with his possessions, leaving him shouting in frustration. El Draque, the dragon, as the Spanish had taken to calling Drake, had struck again.

On December 5, 1578, "by the willing conduct of our new Indian pilot, we came to anchor in the desired harbor," Fletcher wrote. The Spaniards had first visited as early as 1536 and called the place Valparaíso, but with only nine modest households, it came as a letdown to Drake. Imagining a more populous settlement, he had envisioned a rendezvous there with missing ships in his small fleet, but they were nowhere to be seen. On the other hand, the harbor served as a storehouse for wine from Chile and, more promisingly, a Spanish ship that went by the name *Capitana*. Her crew assumed the new arrivals were Spanish and broke out liquor to welcome them to this remote haven. Instead of the greeting and toasting they had expected, the crew was overwhelmed by Drake's men, who ransacked the ship, which carried 1,770 bottles of wine, lumber, and leatherbound cases bearing "fine gold of Baldania," in other words, gold that was considered 99.9 percent pure. At last Drake had found a prize worth the time, effort, and sacrifice he had expended: quantities of fine Spanish gold.

"We spent some time refreshing ourselves," Fletcher nonchalantly noted, "and easing this ship of so heavy a burden"—in other words, stealing the precious gold objects along with provisions such as wine, bread, and bacon in preparation for a long journey. All the while, no one challenged them; not a shot was fired. In case his crew had wondered what the purpose of this voyage was, it was now apparent that it was not a single destination so much as a global campaign to do what Drake did best: steal quantities of gold from the Spanish. Over the next few days, the English occupied *Capitana* and won the indigenous tribes to their side with quantities of gifts. And he invited the inhabitants to join him in the cause of driving away the Spanish. He would provide them with weapons and explained, "With a few people you can attack many and will always be the conqueror with many of us on your side." He was following a strategy similar to the one he had employed years before with the Cimarrons, but he had no intention of remaining here, not with all the gold he had seized.

olden Hind raised anchor and set sail, "carrying again our Indian pilot with us, whom our general beautifully rewarded and enriched with many good things, which pleased him exceedingly," and then, mission accomplished, they landed him "in the place where he desired" and departed with their illicit haul. Their next chore was to locate the missing ships in the fleet, "so long severed from us; neither would anything have satisfied our general or us so well, as the happy meeting, or good news of them," Fletcher plaintively noted. A determined search took them to every harbor or inlet where the other ships might be concealed. At the same time, Drake feared "the malice or treachery of the Spaniards . . . who are used to show no mercy where they overmaster." Even though they were not visible, it was always possible they would appear suddenly and overcome the English brigands.

So as "not to hazard ourselves to their cruel courtesy"—in the form of torture, dismemberment, and death on a distant shore—Drake would search for a cove in which to hide his ship "in peace and safety." Then his men would outfit a light, agile pinnace, "in which we might have better security than in our boat" to explore "each creek, leave no place untried, if happily we might so find our friends and countrymen."

Matters did not proceed as planned. No sooner had their pinnace entered a bay near Cyppo, or Coquimbo, a town controlled by Spaniards, and landed several men, than they faced a hostile party of "300 men at least, whereof 100 were Spaniards, everyone well mounted upon his horse: the rest were Indians, running as dogs at their heels, all naked, and in the most miserable bondage." Here was the reality of life under Spanish rule.

The moment they became aware of their adversaries, they

scurried from the shore to a rock, and from the rock to the pinnace, which swiftly conveyed them to safety, out of reach of the Spaniards' weapons. One exception, a sailor named Richard Minivy, "being bold and over and careless of his own safety," had ignored the pleas of his friends to return to the ship. He was in charge of twelve men, who confronted hundreds of the enemy bearing down on them. When a mounted Spanish soldier approached, Minivy had ordered his tiny band to retreat to the pinnace while he faced the Spanish. He brandished his weapon and fired. A Spanish bullet pierced his skull, killing him instantly. After ordering their Indian slaves to drag his lifeless body to the shore, the Spaniards beheaded Minivy, severed his right hand, and "plucked out" his heart. A booklet containing excerpts from Holy Scripture was removed from his clothing, declared heretical, and burned. The Indians made off with the body parts, shot arrows into his disfigured carcass, and would have "left it to be devoured of the beasts and fowls" had not a few English sailors buried it to spare the remains from "a most extreme and barbarous cruelty."

Later, a Spanish force appeared on the shore where Minivy had been slaughtered, waving a flag of truce, but Drake, having none of it, set sail for safety.

*F*letcher reflected on the Spanish reign of terror over the "innocent and harmless Indians," keeping them in "shameful slavery" or cutting their throats and making sure to "murder strangers." He noted that the Indians' arrows were fashioned from green wood, which he took to mean that the Spanish allowed them weapons, newly fashioned for this purpose, only when they were in service to their masters. With blistering irony, he added, "They suppose they show the wretches great favour when they do not for their pleasures whip them with cords, and day by day drop their naked bodies with burning bacon," to name two of the tortures the Spanish inflicted.

The next day, December 20, saw Drake easing into a "more convenient harbor" to the north of Coquimbo. Once the expedition had dropped anchor, and the men were mourning for the lost Richard Minivy (who had been their *friend,* Fletcher stressed), Drake alarmed them by announcing he would head south again with a small party to see if he could find the missing *Elizabeth* and perhaps *Marigold* as well. Fortunately, a contrary wind forced him to turn back, and the next day he found refuge for the next several weeks in Salada Bay, whose placid waters, in alternating shades of cobalt, emerald, and gray, offered shelter and plentiful fish "as no place had ever afforded us." Dropping four or five hooks and lines at a time, the men caught four hundred fish or more within a span of two or three hours.

During the first part of the layover, Drake kept his men occupied. They built a new launch, bent the sails, fastened them to the yard, "greased and rigged" *Golden Hind,* and lugged artillery that had been stored below onto the deck. Not everything went smoothly. As he prepared to careen the ship, that is, turn her on her side for caulking (a necessary maintenance procedure), she tumbled off the trestles on which she had been positioned for repairs, but she was saved from disaster by the rapid and skillful deployment of a pulley or winch.

They also found time to rest. Drake gave his men, who had been away from home for about a year by this point, a week off from work, and on New Year's Day, 1579, they enjoyed a feast. They had much to look back on during their eventful year away from home—heroism, trauma, and sheer endurance—but the journey was less than halfway complete.

Once the ship was righted, they were underway again on January 19, 1579. Three days later they arrived at an island populated with four lonesome Indians, who directed them to fresh water. Drake rewarded them—"as was his manner towards all strangers"—with copious amounts of wine, and they proceeded to get drunk.

More reconnaissance along the reefs and beaches of Spanish-controlled territory . . . more searching for fresh water without realizing they were skirting the Atacama Desert, a six-hundred-mile-long strip of sand that ranks as one of the driest places in the world. They saw nothing of note until, at Tarapacá, off the coast of northern Chile, they came across a slumbering Spanish sentry who never suspected that a company of Englishmen would come calling. Thirteen bars of silver were neatly stacked beside him. Fletcher recalled that the sentry slept so deeply that they could not have awakened him from his nap even if they had tried. Instead, they quietly "freed him of his charge" as he slumbered. Drake's larcenous energy, fueled by his animosity toward Spain, began to show results. Magellan had passed up the opportunity to seize precious metals to save space aboard ship for spices, and Drake also recognized the value of spices, but silver was silver.

Soon after this robbery, more luck came Drake's way: a Spaniard accompanying an Indian boy driving eight "Peruvian sheep," or llamas, a wonderful novelty to the English. Their necks appeared similar to those of camels, but their heads resembled those of sheep.

Each animal carried two leather bags, "and in each bag was 50 pounds of refined silver," for a total of 800 pounds. It would make for a magnificent heist. "We could not endure to see a gentleman

Spaniard turned carrier," Fletcher mocked, and so they offered to help transport the heavy load, "only his directions were not so perfect that we could keep the way which he intended." Before anyone realized what was happening, the helpful English visitors had transferred the stolen silver from sheep to ship. The notion that they were engaged in theft never troubled the Reverend Fletcher's conscience, nor anyone else's. To their way of thinking, the Spanish had brought it on themselves.

*T*he fleet departed with the men in high spirits, heading north past Indian hamlets, where the locals sailed out to them in lightweight craft fashioned from sealskins, partly wind driven, partly rowed. They bore gifts of fish and prepared to trade for knives, gleaming margarites resembling pearls, spyglasses, or "any trifles we would give them." It seemed to Fletcher that men in their sixties or even seventies treated these inexpensive items "as if they had received some exceeding rich commodity, being a most simple and plaindealing people."

After this success, Drake was emboldened to deal with the Spanish directly. At a large town that Fletcher called Mormorena, the English captain came ashore on January 26 to deal with the two Spanish officials who held sway over the obedient Indians, "or at least to try their courtesy." The Spanish, in turn, had likely heard about Drake's exploits and responded to him "more for fear than love."

They came to another town situated in the mouth of a "most pleasant and fertile valley, abounding in all good things," even if Spaniards lived there. Drake's men appropriated two Spanish boats containing about forty bars of silver, each weighing twenty pounds. With a wink, Fletcher boasted there was nothing else to do except relieve the Spaniards of their burden. Hauling the bars one by one, they made a quick departure, arrived at another settlement for more of the same larceny, and sailed for Lima, the most important city in Peru.

*F*orty-seven years earlier, the conquistador Francisco Pizarro and his forces overpowered the Inca ruler Atahualpa. A Franciscan monk, Brother Marcos de Niza, was sickened by the brutal Spanish treatment of the ruler, who had welcomed them peacefully and given them a massive amount of gold in an effort to buy amity. When that was not enough, he gave the Spanish his land without a struggle. In return, and without provocation from the Indians, Pizarro's forces captured Atahualpa, his second-in-command Chalcuchima, among other Inca leaders, and burned them alive. They burned the feet of others to force them to divulge the location of still more gold. Brother Marcos testified that they gathered as many people as they could find and locked them into large buildings "to which they set light, burning to death those inside even though they had done absolutely nothing whatever to merit such treatment." When one of the locals rescued a boy from the conflagration, a Spaniard "thrust him back into the inferno where he was burned to a cinder along with all the rest." Brother Marcos witnessed Spaniards cut off the hands and ears of Indians "simply for the fun of it." They tore babies from their mothers' breasts and "made a game of seeing who could throw the infants farthest." Sickened and outraged, Marcos condemned the atrocities as "an offence to God and a disservice to the Crown." The possibility that the Spanish and Incas could have coexisted peacefully, to each other's benefit, made the brutality all the more sickening.

The Spanish crown saw matters differently from Brother Marcos and appointed Pizarro governor of the lands he had conquered. He selected Ciudad de los Reyes (City of the Kings) as the capital. Insurgent Incas besieged the metropolis, but Spanish forces and their Indian allies defeated them. Under the new regime, Lima, as the city was later known, flourished as the nexus of a wide-ranging trade network linking the Spanish province known as Virreinato del Perú (Viceroyalty of Peru) with the Americas, Europe, and Asia. It was immense, consisting of two thousand Spanish households; only Mexico City boasted a larger European population in the New World. The Spanish empire had come to stay, seemingly forever.

Few considered Drake, an obscure Lutheran pirate, a serious threat to Spain, if they considered him at all.

CHAPTER VIII

Treasure Fleet

*T*he farther north Drake went, the more arid and depopulated the coast became; still he sailed in a northerly direction, never straying far from the shore. His course took him past the Andes Mountains, the longest above-water mountain range in the world. For the first time, his route differed dramatically from Magellan's.

He would search for the elusive Northwest Passage.

*D*rake was oblivious to the disastrous changes that had taken place onshore. Malaria, typhus, measles, influenza, smallpox, and the common cold had devastated the sun-worshipping Inca empire, the largest in pre-Columbian America. Epidemics of measles and smallpox led to internecine warfare beginning in 1530. Over forty years the population declined from an estimated ten to fifteen million before the arrival of the Spanish to only three to five million. The Spanish conquistador and chronicler Pedro de Cieza de León, who traveled across Peru during this era, noted the demographic collapse.

An area near Lima had been home to twenty-five thousand people, but only five thousand survived. By the time Drake arrived, the population had plummeted below three million, and it decreased until the eighteenth century. Every ten years, on average, a new pandemic decimated the populace, which was too weak to recover and regenerate.

To add to the extreme hardship of this era, the Spanish demonstrated a penchant for cruelty and torture in the New World. In 1552, Bartolomé de Las Casas published *A Short Account of the Destruction of the Indies*, dedicated to Philip II, which described the havoc the Spanish wreaked on the Indians. Born in Seville, Las Casas had himself participated in Spanish massacres before becoming a Dominican priest. In his account, torture was the norm for the Spanish, emblematic of power and an assertion of superiority.

Now he bore witness against this attitude. "There is no way the written word can convey the full horror of the atrocities committed throughout this region," he wrote of the Spanish presence. They had turned Peru into a "hellish round of atrocities, robberies, and enslavements." He wrote about Spaniards tracking down local men and women with wild dogs. "One woman, who was indisposed at the time and so not able to make good her escape, determined that the dogs should not tear her to pieces as they had her neighbors and taking a rope and tying her one-year-old child to her leg, hanged herself from a beam. Yet she was not in time to prevent the dogs from ripping the infant to pieces."

When a Spaniard demanded that a boy, the son of a local chief, accompany him, and the boy refused, saying he did not want to leave home, the Spaniard "took out his dagger and lopped off first one of his ears and then the other. When the boy insisted that he did not want to go with him, he hacked off his nose, laughing out loud as though he were no more than playfully pulling his hair."

Las Casas reported that the same Spaniard boasted that he "always labored to make the local women pregnant so that they would fetch a high price as slaves." When a Spaniard, out hunting, realized his dogs were hungry, he took a knife and cut the arms and legs of a little boy into chunks to feed the dogs. After the dogs consumed them, he fed them the rest of the child. And there was worse, Las Casas lamented, of the "unforgivable behavior and consummate wickedness of the Spaniards."

He told of indigenous people rounded up and transported to an island to be sold as slaves. "They are naked, and so weakened by hunger that many—old and young alike, men and women, simply drop where they stand. They are separated from their families and sold off." What about biblical injunctions? How could the Spanish behave this way and consider themselves Christians? Why would an Indian observing this behavior ever wish to become a Christian?

The Spanish treatment of pearl fishers struck Las Casas as even more troubling, their lives "worse than any other on the face of the earth; it is even worse than that of the native gold-miner, ghastly though that undoubtedly is." They toiled in the ocean from dawn till dusk, often at a depth of twenty or thirty feet, rarely permitted to surface for air as they gathered pearl-bearing oysters in their nets. When they did surface to hand over the oysters and gasp for air, their Spanish overlord "will punch them and grab them or grab them by the hair and push them back under, making them dive once more."

On occasion, they dove and did not surface, having been swallowed by sharks, or choked to death in the frigid subsurface water, their lungs hemorrhaging. When not forcing the pearl fishers to risk their lives at work, the Spanish starved them, providing only a small amount of cassava bread and fish. At night, the pearl fishers were shackled to the ground to prevent escape. Their hair, naturally black, took on the "singed appearance more typical of sea wolves," and sores disfigured their backs "so they looked more like deformed sea monsters than men." Those who managed to survive these ordeals often suffered a wretched death from dysentery.

In other areas of New Spain, the Spanish brutalized the indigenous people by throwing them into prison or locking them in stockades. "In this fashion, a whole province, once populous and rich in gold, was devastated, ravaged, and depopulated." The Spanish burned down homes and manacled their slaves together when they moved about the countryside. "Whenever one of these poor wretches fainted from hunger or became too exhausted to carry on, they cut his head from his body at the point where the iron collar bound him to his companions so as not to have to waste time unshackling him." Then "his head would fall to one side and his decapitated body to the other."

These examples were but a small part of the misery the Spanish inflicted, Las Casas said. If he were to document the entire spectrum of atrocities, no one would believe him. To make matters even worse, the Spanish embezzled much of the wealth they seized. He estimated that these "foul enemies of God" had, over the course of fourteen years, stolen more than the "official returns from the entire kingdom." That was merely the financial cost. The human cost could never be recouped "unless God at some future date be pleased to resurrect many millions of souls." On the basis of this history, Drake had every reason to fear and detest the Spanish.

After the loss of *Elizabeth* and *Marigold*, Drake's expedition hovered on the verge of extinction. But he still had *Golden Hind* in his possession, a rugged ship that had seen him through many confrontations, and now he guided her on a northerly course along the coast. Wherever he found Spanish encampments, he sent out raiding parties more in the spirit of fun than in earnest, to taunt the Spanish rather than kill them.

And so it went as the fleet made its way along the South American coast—surprise attacks, humiliation of the Spanish, and Drake exhibiting unexpected mercy toward his many victims, and sparing the lives of nearly all. In fact, he startled his own men by getting to know their Catholic captives and speaking to them in Spanish. He apparently enjoyed their company, and they in turn were taken by his charm and vitality—so much so that several of Drake's captives, on regaining their freedom, pleaded with the Spanish authorities to be lenient with him if they ever captured him, for he had treated them well, and even bestowed decorative presents on them while they were in captivity: souvenirs of their time with El Draque, as if that were a distinction to be envied.

Among his admirers happened to be the Portuguese pilot whom he had detained. Nuño da Silva later left a vivid description of the pirate in his prime, scars and all: "Francis Drake is a man aged 38. . . . He is short in stature, thickset and very robust. He has a fine countenance, ruddy of complexion, and a fair beard. He has the mark of an arrow-wound in his right cheek which is not apparent if one does not look with special care. In one leg he has a ball of an arquebus [a musket] which was shot at him in the Indies." Da Silva found Drake to be a man of many talents. "He carries a book in which he enters his log, and paints birds, trees and sea lions. He is adept in painting and carries along a boy [John Drake], a relative of his, who is a great painter. When they both shut themselves up in his cabin they were always painting."

By February 1579, his company had plundered more than a dozen Spanish settlements. Drake distracted himself by sketching the local flora and fauna as they went. His men meanwhile occupied themselves desecrating Spanish churches, destroying Spanish art, and stealing Spanish silver. On most occasions, they found it easy to separate the indolent, overconfident Spanish from their treasure. Occasionally, Spanish troops roused themselves to defend their holdings, but even when they charged on horseback, El Draque's men always escaped to the safety of his ship. Hearing that the notorious Drake was in the region, the Spanish viceroy sent two vessels in pursuit, but *Golden Hind* evaded them both. One Spanish observer wrote home in frustration, "In this South Sea there is no vessel that can harm him, for they are small in size and their crews inexperienced."

When it became too dangerous for his men to raid Spanish settlements, they ransacked twelve unsuspecting Spanish ships in the port. They were helpless, without sails, which had been stored for them onshore, "for the masters and merchants were here most secure, having never been assaulted by enemies," wrote Francis Pretty. "Our General rifled these ships, and found in one of them a chest full of reals of plate, and good store of silks and linen cloth; and took the chest into his own ship."

While looting the ships in the harbor, Drake had learned of a Spanish vessel, casually called *Cacafuego*, that had sailed twelve days earlier. This particular ship was laden with treasure. "Whereupon we stayed no longer here, but, cutting all the cables of the ships in the haven, we let them drive wither they would, either to sea or to the shore; and with all speed we followed the *Cacafuego* toward Paita"—a seaport in northwestern Peru—"thinking there to have found her."

CHAPTER IX

Cacafuego

On March 1, 1579, Drake caught sight of the Spanish treasure ship and commenced the most famous pirate operation of his career. Success was hardly assured, for by the time they gave chase, their target, *Cacafuego*, was on the move. But Drake was not about to let the prize slip from his grasp.

Once again fortune favored him. As the pursuit of *Cacafuego* got underway, he happened upon a barque "laden with ropes and tackle." He boarded the vessel and ordered a search. For his trouble he found eighty pounds of gold and a crucifix, also made of gold "with goodly great emeralds set in it," along with some cordage, which would be useful for rigging his own ship." (He later had the pleasure of presenting those "goodly great emeralds" to Queen Elizabeth.)

This was merely a pleasant distraction. His instincts suggested that greater fortune awaited him aboard *Cacafuego*—wherever she might be. Drake promised his chain of gold to whoever was the first to spot her. The ship's real name, incidentally, was *Nuestra Señora de la Concepción*, which was more dignified than the jaunty-sounding nickname by which everyone knew her: "Shitfire."

In the afternoon, his young nephew John Drake, climbing to

the top of one of the masts, "descried her about three of the clock."
Young Drake duly collected his prize as the first to sight her, amid
some grumbling about favoritism on the part of the captain, but that
was a minor matter. *Cacafuego* was rumored to be carrying a fabulous sum of gold, silver, and jewelry. While continuing his search for
the elusive ship, Drake plundered additional smaller Spanish vessels,
but their booty only whetted his appetite for the treasure he hoped
to find aboard *Cacafuego*. And now here she was, riding low in the
water—the phantom, at last.

To avoid detection, Drake kept *Golden Hind* well back and ordered his slender pinnace to hide behind her. He lowered the English
royal standard that normally flew from the main mast and draped
wine-filled jugs over the railings to slow his speed. The simple disguise was designed to convey the impression that *Golden Hind*
was just another harmless merchant ship plying her trade on the
high seas.

Those aboard *Cacafuego* had not heard of the much larger *Golden
Hind* when she drew up beside her. As luck had it, her captain, San
Juan de Antón, was a Basque based in Southampton, England. At
first, he heard Spanish coming from *Golden Hind;* Drake had forced
one of his Spanish prisoners to hail *Cacafuego* in respectful terms.
Golden Hind looked so honorable that Captain Antón allowed her to
grapple alongside his ship. Then matters took an unexpected turn.
"We're English. Strike sail!" shouted one of Drake's men. "If not,
look out, for you will be sent to the bottom!"

"What England is this?" Captain San Juan de Antón shot back.
"Come on board and strike the sails yourselves!" Drake ordered the
bosun's whistle to trill, and his gunner let loose a deafening volley. The shot sent *Cacafuego*'s mizzenmast crashing to the deck.
As if that calamity were not enough to intimidate the Spanish into

submission, he ordered his pinnace to sail around to the exposed side of the defiant ship, whereupon English archers armed with crossbows—the most lethal weapon of the day—leaped on deck and seized the ship. "About six of the clock we came to her and boarded her, and shot at her three pieces of ordnance, and strake down her mizen," according to Fletcher, whose role as chaplain did not prevent him from thrilling to the operation. Captain Antón, unprepared and overwhelmed, was hustled to the skipper's cabin aboard *Golden Hind*. Casually removing his armor, Drake gestured for Antón to sit and indicated that his guest had nothing to fear. "Have patience," Drake told the bewildered Basque. Drake's men quickly secured *Cacafuego* and sailed both ships far out to sea for the night, beyond the range of other Spanish vessels.

*W*hat a trove *Cacafuego* carried. "We found in her great riches, as jewels and precious stones, thirteen chests full of silver reals, fourscore pound weight of gold, and six-and-twenty ton of silver," noted Francis Pretty. Drake ordered the treasure ship stripped of her valuables, and his men carried away the twenty-six tons of silver from her hold. One of the Spanish officers frantically bargained with Drake to leave behind the valuable silk, linen, and taffeta aboard *Cacafuego*. In exchange for these rich fabrics, he gave Drake a golden falcon set with an emerald in the breast. There was more. "Amongst other [silver] plate that our General found in this ship he found two very fair giltbowls of silver, which were the pilot's," wrote Pretty. "To whom our General said, '*Señor Pilot*, you have here two silver cups, but I must needs have one of them'; which the pilot, because he could not otherwise choose, yielded unto, and gave the other to the steward of our General's ship."

When Drake released the Spanish crew, he gave each man clothing, simple knives, powder, and a letter promising safe passage in case he came across other English ships. He presented Captain Antón with a silver bowl inscribed with the legend FRANCISQUS DRAQUES, a souvenir of the most successful pirate raid ever carried out in the name of England. He allowed one of the captives to keep the royal Spanish ensign. "Leave the arms of King Philip where they are," he declared with a wink, "for he is the best king in the world." This king was making Drake wealthy, rescuing England from bankruptcy, and securing Elizabeth's throne—without realizing it. And the gallant way in which Drake conducted his raids made it seem an honor of sorts to be looted by such a charming pirate.

Throughout, the English remained disciplined and frugal. "We gave the master a little linen and the like for these commodities, and at the end of six days we bade farewell and parted." *Cacafuego*, humiliated and somewhat lighter than before, hastened to Panama, while Drake and his men busied themselves "plying off to sea, that we might with more leisure consider what course henceforward were fittest to be taken." Along the way, they counted and recounted their newfound riches.

*D*rake's run of luck continued. On March 16, 1579, he reached tiny, uninhabited Caño Island, off the southern coast of Costa Rica. Nuño da Silva, the Portuguese pilot, noted "they found a small bay, wherein they anchored at five fathom deep close by the land, and there they stayed till the twentieth day." Drake brought *Golden Hind* and a pinnace ashore for caulking. So far, these maneuvers were routine. But then the sharp-eyed men aboard the pinnace caught sight of a barque approaching from the north, "which with their pinnace they followed, and taking her, brought her to the English ship, which frigate was laden with sarsaparilla, and Botijas or pots with butter and honey, and with other things." (Sarsaparilla was a tropical root believed by Europeans to have medicinal properties and was used for treating diseases such as syphilis. As such, it had particular importance for randy sailors.) This frigate was bound for Panama, with a crew of thirteen, a fraction of the number of men accompanying Drake.

Drake's pinnace boldly approached the Spanish as his men blew their trumpets and fired harquebuses. The gunners struck two men, who hastened to surrender along with the other Spaniards on the ship. This incident marks one of the very few times that Drake actually wounded the Spanish, despite their many encounters on land and sea.

Drake took his prisoners to a nearby bay, where he dealt with them in his customary courteous style. His gallantry yielded not one but two pilots, Martín de Aguirre and Alonso Sánchez Colchero. Even better, they carried "sea-cards" or charts with them showing the route from Acapulco to the Philippines. Drake immediately confiscated these precious items. All proceeded within the bounds of pirate propriety until his men smashed a crucifix to bits and tossed it into the sea as the Spanish prisoners looked on in revulsion. This act of desecration was far worse than mere theft. With such callous deeds Drake's notorious reputation grew in Spain.

Drake for his part retained his visceral dislike for the Spanish and especially for their religious objects. At the same time, the Spanish charts he captured were a major find. They were more accurate and up-to-date than the crude representations on which he had been relying. At that time, maps erroneously extended Asia too far to the east and America too far to the west. The result made oceans seem smaller and landmasses larger than they were. And the layout of these maps was most frustrating for the aspiring circumnavigator, for they put Europe squarely in the center, and the Pacific Ocean merely a jagged strip, at the periphery. (Only a globe could show these features in correct relationship to one another.) Drake considered Colchero's information so valuable that he proceeded to confiscate his letters and rutters—the Anglicized name for a routier, or handwritten sailing chart.

Rutters were prized because they contained much information beyond basic sailing directions. They traced shorelines, islands, and harbors, and included comments about tides, reefs, and shoals based on hard-won experience. A fully annotated rutter included instructions about how to determine position and plot routes as well as calendars, astronomical and mathematical tables, and calculation instructions, especially regarding the Venetian rule of *marteloio*—literally, hammering, or the racket created by striking a ship's bell to mark the passage of time. It was a method of navigational computation incorporating compass direction, distance, and a trigonometric table, the *toleta de marteloio*. The rule of *marteloio* showed pilots how to plot the zigzagging route between two different navigation courses by means of resolving triangles with basic arithmetic.

Drake in the meantime received information that Diego Garcia de Palacio, a judge of the Supreme Court of Guatemala, was preparing an expedition to the Philippines. He was already building a ship for that purpose. Drake was not about to let him accomplish his mission. He burned the ship, and hanged Garcia de Palacio until he was almost dead. It was Drake's idea of a fine joke—and a dire warning.

He then turned his attention to Colchero, who was considerably older than his colleague. Drake promised to leave him on the first island of the Philippines that he arrived at, but Colchero rather unconvincingly denied he was a pilot. He wished Drake to leave him where they were. Drake explained he wanted only to become familiar with the land. He would ask nothing else of Colchero, who still refused to cooperate. Drake ordered the obstinate pilot to be strung up. Even when hoisted six feet above the deck by a rope around his neck, Colchero refused to volunteer information. With Colchero exhausted and nearly dead, Drake ordered him to be cut down. Despite Colchero's superhuman resistance, Drake succeeded in extracting a description of the northwest coast of America known to the Spaniards, information about typhoons, and other clues concerning the navigation of the Pacific.

Later in March, as the expedition sailed along a tranquil stream toward the coast, "We felt a terrible earthquake, the force whereof was such that our ship and pinnace, riding very near an English mile from the shore, were shaken and did quiver as had been laid on dry land." Earthquakes, generally minor elsewhere in South America, are common in Costa Rica, where Drake was now located. Stretched between tectonic plates on both the Caribbean and Pacific coasts, Costa Rica is among the most earthquake-prone countries in the world. Fletcher's description suggests that they experienced a wild *terremoto*, or violent earthquake, rather than the more common *tremblor*.

The next stopover was the town of Guatalco, population 17. Drake's men streamed onshore as soon as they landed and found "a judge sitting in judgment, being associated with three other officers, upon three Negroes that had conspired in the burning of the town." Drake arrested judges and prisoners alike and brought them on board. Under duress, the "chief judge" wrote to the authorities in town to allow Drake and his men to "fetch water there in safety." And when Drake's men had completed that task, "We ransacked the town; and in one house we found a pot, of the quantity of a bushel, full of reals of plate, which we brought to our ship. And here one Thomas Moon, one of our company, took a Spanish gentleman as he was flying out of the town; and, searching him, he found a chain of gold about him, and other jewels, which he took, and so let him go."

The church custodian, who had served for ten years and knew the contents well, recited a catalog of horrors. The Englishmen shouted "shameless profanations and evil doings" as they stole "two silver chalices, one of them gilt, two pairs of small silver flagons for serving wine and water at mass; one black damask vestment with all that is necessary for saying mass; a similar set of blue damask; another of white damask, also a yellow set; a canopy of crimson satin; a cope of crimson satin, with a border of blue velvet, besides other sacred vestments such as altar-cloths and towels, and surplices for the boys who assisted at mass in said church; and five pairs of altar-cloths, which the Englishmen carried on their shoulders, using them to wipe the perspiration from their faces."

They flung open a box containing unconsecrated wafers "and stamped them underfoot."

They shattered an image of Our Lady, with Our Father and the Holy Ghost, and "hacked and scratched and made holes in it."

They seized a witness to their desecration, and while he was held hostage, they broke into his home, smashed all the religious objects they could find, robbed all the gold and silver they could lay their hands on, and destroyed a writing table.

They were not finished. The boatswain (unnamed but "small, with a scant, fair beard, and his face was pitted with pockmarks") found a crucifix, and wielding it by the feet, struck its head against a table, breaking it into pieces, and declared, "Here it is; here you go!" As the homeowner registered shock, the boatswain said, "You ought indeed to be grieved, for you are not Christians but idolaters."

After sacking homes and desecrating religious objects, Francis Drake decided the time had come to pray. He ordered a table and embroidered cushion placed on the poop (or stern) deck. He then sent for his book of devotion, smacked the table twice with the palm of his hand, whereupon he was joined by nine crew members, each carrying a prayer book. Drake kneeled on the cushion, raised his eyes heavenward, and remained motionless for a quarter of an hour. At last he told the prisoners they could if they wished recite the English psalms with them; otherwise, they were to "keep quiet."

For the next hour he recited the psalms—unintelligible to the prisoners—and then called for four viols to play. He and his men accompanied the instruments, again in English, and the concert ended. There is no evidence that Drake gained a single convert for this trouble, but he stirred up a debate by reading from a rabble-rousing Protestant polemic, John Foxe's *Acts and Monuments*, or, as it was usually known, *The Book of Martyrs*.

Foxe was an Oxford-educated scholar who had mastered Latin, Greek, and Hebrew. In this enormously influential work, he presented accounts of religious martyrs across the ages, with special emphasis on recent English Protestants. Originally published in

Latin, the book later appeared in an English-language version of 1,800 pages. A later edition brought the length to 2,300 pages, more than 3.5 million words. It was considered the most imposing and technically complex work of its day and sold for a mighty sum, ten shillings, a week's salary for many. Despite its popularity, Foxe remained as poor as ever. He was not interested in money, he was a zealous foe of cruelty, especially in the form of religious persecution, and this singular work made him a literary celebrity. Foxe did not pretend to be objective—his bias throughout this encyclopedic work was fiercely anti-Catholic. "Mark the apish pageants of these popelings," he observed in a characteristic aside. The work was lavishly illustrated, and Drake displayed drawings of Protestants martyred in Spain to enlighten his guests in case the meaning of the English-language text eluded them.

When Drake finished he bade a boy to dance the hornpipe for them. This rhythmic sailors' jig, usually performed in hard shoes to mark time, was thought to be salubrious. Drake, along with other English captains, made his sailors dance the hornpipe to maintain their spirits.

"You will be saying now this man is a devil, who robs by day and prays at night in public," Drake declared. "This is what I do, but it is just as when King Philip gives a very large written paper to your Viceroy, Don Martin Enriquez, telling him what he is to do and how he is to govern, so the Queen, my Sovereign Lady, has ordered me to come to these parts. It is thus that I am acting, and if it is wrong it is she who knows best and I am not to be blamed for anything whatsoever."

Revealingly, Drake added, "I am not going to stop until I have collected the two millions that my cousin John Hawkins lost, for certain, at San Juan de Ulúa." Drake was still settling scores. Having

completed his litany of resentments against the Spanish, Drake ordered his captives locked up for the night.

After he had relieved the Spaniards of their gold and silver,
Drake prepared to abandon Nuño da Silva, who quickly drew the
scrutiny of the Mexican Inquisition, an offshoot of the Spanish original, and every bit as relentless and cruel. As in Spain, the Mexican
Inquisition sowed suspicion, fostered cruelty, and taught submission
to Catholic orthodoxy at the point of a sword. Da Silva was convicted
of associating with Francis Drake and "assisting at the Lutheran
prayers and sermons on board the Englishman's ship and of performing heretical acts of reverence and submission, without having
been compelled to do so by force or by fear." (As a Lutheran, Drake
was considered an "arch-heretic.")

Under questioning by representatives of the Mexican Inquisition,
da Silva denied, "even under torture, of having intentionally been
guilty of heresy." But the Inquisitors insisted he had "twice partaken
of Communion according to the English mode of administering it."
In his defense, he claimed he had acted "under compulsion," but the
Inquisitors decided da Silva was not telling the truth. Other prisoners, when examined, had stated that Drake had given them the
option of assisting at the service, or not, as they wished. So it appeared that da Silva could have avoided heresy. Yet it was also true
that Drake had on at least one occasion "willed and straightly commanded" the entire company to receive Communion, on the Sunday
following Doughty's execution.

Found guilty of participating in the Englishmen's heretical ob-
servances, Nuño da Silva was sentenced to perform public penance
and to serve "perpetual exile from the Indies." He was sent to Spain

and languished for several months in Seville, until King Philip summoned the man who had helped the heretic Drake circle the world. Whatever da Silva said to the king—and it was probably hard-won information about the whereabouts, intentions, and modus operandi of El Draque—it was sufficient to win clemency. Philip gave da Silva funds and a commission to convey a "royal dispatch" to Seville. He was back in business as a pilot. Da Silva arrived home safely and rejoined his family.

His story might have ended there, but records suggest that da Silva made his way to England, settled in Plymouth, and employed his piloting skills in the service of clandestine expeditions. To maintain cover, Drake referred to da Silva as "Sylvester," suggesting both a convenient disguise and a special understanding between the pilot and the explorer.

After abandoning da Silva, Drake invited Guatalco's two leading men to share a meal in his cabin, knowing that he was playing a cruel joke on them by stealing personal possessions from them when they were distracted. He later took pity on the townspeople and sent them flour, wine, oil, and sugar, and he released his prisoners. Rather than seeking vengeance or condemning Drake, they commended him to the authorities for his generosity.

Before dawn on April 4, *Golden Hind* captured another Spanish ship, this one from Acapulco, bound for Peru, owned and commanded by Don Francisco de Zárate, a wealthy merchant. Drake immediately established his bona fides by dispatching a boarding party to claim the prize, helped by the fact that all on board were still asleep. The

English pirates roused the drowsy Spanish from slumber, relieved
them of their swords, knives, and other weapons, and locked them
in the hold of their own ship. The pirates singled out Zárate, who
was hauled before Drake aboard *Golden Hind*. El Draque treated his
distinguished hostage with elaborate courtesy, escorted him into the
captain's cabin, relieved him of "certain toys" of his—weapons, most
likely—and interrogated him about his cargo. Drake and his men
treated Zárate with so much formality that they confounded his expectations of how pirates would behave.

After three days, Drake released his Spanish captives, but not
before scattering gold coins among the wide-eyed sailors, who
could scarcely believe their luck, along with a silver chafing dish
and an ornamental curved dagger for Zárate. Two weeks later,
Zárate confided his impressions of the notorious pirate in his
journal. Although the Englishman had bested him, Zárate could
not help but admire his élan. "The English general is the same
who took Nombre de Dios some five years ago," in other words, a
scourge in Spanish eyes. Worse, "He is a cousin of John Hawkins."
Still, Zárate could not contain himself. The man was a genuine
phenomenon.

> He is about thirty-five years old, of small size, with
> a reddish beard, and is one of the greatest sailors
> that exist, both from his skill and from his power
> of commanding. His ship is of near four hundred
> tons; sails well, and has a hundred men, all in the
> prime of life and as well trained for war as if they
> were old soldiers of Italy. Each one is especially
> careful to keep his arms clean. He treats them
> with affection, and they him with respect. He

has with him nine or ten gentlemen, younger
sons of the leading men in England, who form his
council; he calls them together on every occasion
and hears what they have to say, but he is not bound
by their advice, though he may be guided by it.

He has no privacy; these of whom I speak all
dine at his table . . . but who never spoke a word
while I was on board. The service is of silver,
richly gilt, and engraved with his arms; he has
too all possible luxuries, even to perfumes, many
of which, he told me, were given him by the
queen. None of these gentlemen sits down or
puts on his hat in his presence without repeated
permission. He dines and sups to the music of
violins. His ship carries thirty large guns, and a
great quantity of all sorts of ammunition, as well
as artificers who can execute necessary repairs.
He has two draughtsmen who portray the coast in
its own colours, a thing which troubled me much
to see, because everything is put so naturally that
any one following him will have no difficulty.

Zárate was keenly observant (worrying that Drake's detailed
color maps could become a liability), and he was not quite so naive as
he appeared. He had inquired after Drake's standing aboard ship. Did
he have enemies? None, as it turned out, or at least no one willing
to confide in an outsider. And what about the controversial matter of
Doughty's execution? Zárate recalled Drake "speaking much good of
the dead man." Clearly, the English pirate knew how to stay on the
right side of everyone when circumstances demanded.

*E*ven though the Spanish had occasionally frustrated Drake, he had accomplished his primary goals. He had navigated the Strait, and he had seized an immense fortune, which Elizabeth desperately needed to maintain her throne and to keep her kingdom functioning. The next challenge he faced was straightforward: return to Plymouth with his stolen treasure intact.

CHAPTER X

Life Among the Miwok

Drake was far behind schedule. He had originally calculated that the entire circumnavigation would last two years. Almost that amount of time had passed, and he was far from home. If he wanted to keep to his original plan, he would have to make up for lost time. He could attempt to return home through the Strait, but that approach was impractical, reasoned Francis Pretty, "for two special causes; the one, lest the Spaniards should there wait and attend for him in great number and strength, whose hands, he, being left but one ship, could not possibly escape." The other obstacle to his swift return concerned the "dangerous situation of the mouth of the Straits in the South Sea; where continual storms [were] raging and blustering, as he found by experience, besides the shoals and sands upon the coast." For both these reasons, "He thought it not a good course to adventure that way." Winter's return voyage aboard *Elizabeth* demonstrated that sailing east through the Strait was possible, though at that time Drake was not aware of Winter's return. And Drake, unlike Winter, was carrying a fortune in gold and silver. It was best to give the Spanish a wide berth.

Drake decided to follow Magellan's course west to the Moluccas, or Spice Islands, and try his navigational luck from there. But that is not how matters unfolded. He sailed nearly two thousand miles in search of better wind, until June 6, 1579. By that time, he had diverged from Magellan's route, traveling far north of the equator, past the California shoreline, all the way to Oregon Dunes, the longest stretch of coastal sand dunes in North America, indeed, among the longest in the world. Here, in the bleak otherworldly landscape (which later inspired Frank Herbert's popular science fiction novel *Dune*) massive sandbanks extended five hundred feet above sea level. These dunes are unique, formed from sedimentary rock dislodged and transported by water twelve million years ago, shaping and reshaping the coastline until it stabilized about six million years ago. They extend for fifty-six miles. Then as now they were subject to the action of the wind, which generally blows at fourteen miles an hour but sometimes can achieve one hundred miles an hour, and which continually sculpts them into ridges.

*N*ow that Drake had sailed beyond Spanish-controlled waters, he focused on finding a northern ocean route from Europe to the wealth of the Indies: the legendary, long-sought-after Northwest Passage. Today we recognize that no such route exists, but in those days it was an article of faith that a Northwest Passage could be found, much as Magellan took the existence of a strait on faith during his voyage. The English had been actively searching for the shortcut at least since 1497, when John Cabot ventured into the frigid waters of the North Atlantic aboard *Matthew*. Sailing west from Ireland, he expected to reach Asia. Instead, the North American continent intervened. In 1576, just before Drake set out, Martin Frobisher, also backed by Queen Elizabeth, embarked on a quest to find the Northwest Passage. He made three attempts, each one ending in northeastern Canada. Despite his repeated failures, the myth of the passage retained its appeal.

Drake had no more luck than Frobisher in his search for the Northwest Passage. Yet his route was noteworthy and daring. By late June he had traveled nearly five thousand miles north and west, until he reached 42 degrees north latitude.

The weather was clear, the wind plentiful. The only problem was the "extreme and nipping cold." The men complained and feared for their health as they shivered in the "pinching and biting air." It was so frigid that when the sailors tried to adjust the sails, they found "the very ropes of our ship were stiff, and the rain which fell was an unnatural, congealed and frozen substance, so that we seemed to be in the frozen zone." The freezing ropes and tackling grew so rigid that tasks normally requiring three men required six, and even then, "with their best strength and uttermost endeavor" they could barely accomplish the chore.

Everyone despaired except for Drake, who spoke of "God's loving care over his children" and reinforced his message by "cheerful example." He explained they were enduring a "little trouble to obtain the greater glory." In reality, he had just suffered his biggest setback since the execution of Thomas Doughty. He had lost all his ships save *Golden Hind* (and possibly a pinnace) and faced the prospect of perishing at sea with the treasure he had seized. He had hoped to avoid the ordeal of crossing the Pacific by threading his way through the Northwest Passage, but the search had proved futile. Speeches were his last resort to inspire the men to endure their painful circumstances and to seek shelter.

*D*rake approached "that part of America bearing farther out into the west than we before imagined." The nearer he came to shore, the

colder the wind—a miserable, piercing cold. On June 5, the winds
forced *Golden Hind* to "cast anchor in a bad bay," the only refuge
from the "extreme gusts and flaws that beat upon us." When the
winds subsided, the sailors were engulfed by the "most vile, thick
and stinking fogs, against which the sea prevailed nothing" until
more violent gusts blew up and cleared out the miasma.

They were now at 48 degrees north, Fletcher estimated, in the vicinity of the Olympic Peninsula: terra incognita for the English. The
men were "utterly discouraged," but Drake changed his mind once
again and resumed his search for the Northwest Passage. What if
he had come this far only to miss it? Perhaps he needed to sail farther,
and everything would be transformed. But there was no passage, no
escape from their misery, only the huge expanse of the Pacific. "We
had a smooth and calm sea, with ordinary flowing and reflowing,"
The World Encompassed reported, "which could not have been, had
there been a strait, of which we rather infallibly concluded, [and]
then conjectured there was none."

Drake finally recognized that he had been chasing an illusion. He
turned back, hugging the shore, until, at 44 degrees north, he found
a cove where he could safely anchor *Golden Hind*. Even in June, approaching the summer solstice, every hill was blanketed with snow.
Fletcher found the denuded landscape extending to the north and
east dismal to behold: "How unhandsome and deformed appeared
the face of the earth itself shewing trees without leaves, and the
ground without greenness in those months of June and July." Even
the "poor birds and fowl" were trapped in their nests amid the icy
onslaught.

At last they made an agreeable landfall near present-day San
Francisco. "It pleased God to send us into a fair and good bay, with a
good wind to enter the same" where "the people of the country, hav-

ing their houses close by the water's side, showed themselves unto us." These hardy inhabitants were the Coast Miwok, long established in the area. (Other Miwok clusters existed near Mount Diablo and, farther east, in today's Yosemite National Park.) Organized and sophisticated in their fashion, they made a positive first impression on their curious visitors. "Their houses are digged round about with earth," Fletcher wrote, "and have from the uttermost brims of the circle clifts of wood set upon them, joining close together at the top like a spire steeple, which by reason of that closenesse are very warm. Their bed is the ground with rushes strewn on it and lying about the house; they have the fire in the middest." Their appearance was both startling and gratifying. "The men go naked; the women take bulrushes and comb them after the manner of hemp, and thereof make their loose garments, which, being knit about their middles, hang down about their hips, having also about their shoulders a skin of deer, with the hair upon it."

Drake and his crew were only the second European party to set foot in Northern California, preceded by the Spanish explorer Juan Rodríguez Cabrillo years before, in 1542. It was difficult to know who was more amazed by Drake's visit, he and his men or the self-sufficient Coast Miwok, whom they studied with fascination. The Miwok, in turn, seemed to regard their visitors as gods with whom they desired to have peaceful relations.

The English visitors learned that acorns formed the mainstay of the Miwok diet. They were harvested in autumn, dried, and stored in eight-foot-high granaries known as *cha'ka*. Fashioned out of large poles, they resembled large baskets and were lined with pine needles and wormwood, whose pungent odor repelled insects and rodents. The Miwok cracked and shelled the acorns and stuffed the meat in a mortar cup to be pounded with a pestle until it achieved the texture of meal. They poured hot and cold water through the meal to leach out the bitter, inedible tannin. The meal was then sealed in a water-tight container with hot rocks to cook it.

They were endlessly loquacious, these Miwok, never giving their visitors a moment's respite. "One (appointed as their chief speaker) wearied his hearers, and himself too, with a long and tedious oration delivered with strange and violent gestures, his voice being extended to the uttermost strength of nature, and his words falling so thick one in the neck of another, that he could hardly fetch his breath again."

When the Miwok came face-to-face with their visitors, the men placed their bows on the hillside and put their women and children behind, and walked toward Drake as if he were a god. At the same time, "the women used unnatural violence against themselves, cry-ing and shrieking piteously, tearing their flesh with their nails from their cheeks in a monstrous manner, the blood streaming down along their breasts." As if those gestures were not sufficiently alarm-ing, "they would with fury cast themselves upon the ground, never respecting whether it were clean or soft, but dashed themselves in this manner on hard stones, knobby hillocks, stocks of wood, and pricking bushes, or whatever else lay in their way."

The English were both horrified by this behavior and helpless to stop it, or even understand it. "This bloody sacrifice (against our wills) being thus performed, our General, with his company, in the presence of those strangers, fell to prayers; and by signs in lifting up our eyes and hands to heaven, signified unto them that that God whom we did serve, and whom they ought to worship, was above." Drake's men eventually calmed the overwrought Miwok with prayer and psalms and by reading aloud chapters of the Bible, during which the Miwok "sat very attentively: and observing the end at every pause, with one voice still cried, 'Oh, greatly rejoicing in our exercises.' Yea, they took such pleasure in our singing of psalms, that whenever they resorted to us, their first request was commonly this."

This display of piety and self-mutilation presented Drake with a dilemma. These people might deify him one day, but they might destroy him the next.

*W*ord of the visitors bearing gifts and prayers spread, attracting the "king himself, a man of a goodly stature, and comely personage, and with many other tall and warlike men." He wore a crown of feathers and necklaces fashioned of small bones. His followers hailed him with a title that the English took to mean king or leader. A glance at this spectacle was enough to set Drake to dreaming of an empire comprising both English and indigenous peoples, pointedly excluding the Spanish.

The Miwok chattered for half an hour, but their English visitors could not comprehend a word. It emerged that the populace wanted an offering from Drake to give to their king. When the gift had been conveyed, the king himself "marched to us with a princely majesty, the people crying continually after their manner; and as they drew near unto us, so did they strive to behave themselves in their actions with comeliness. In the fore-front was a man of goodly personage, who bare the sceptre or mace before the king; whereupon hanged two crowns, a less and a bigger, with three chains of a marvellous length. After these dignitaries came ten or a dozen people, and eventually the king himself wearing skins. He was followed by the naked common sort of people, every one having his face painted, some with white, some with black, and other colours, and having in their hands one thing or another for a present." It was quite a procession, but there was more.

The ordinary Indians mingled with the English visitors, weeping and tearing "their flesh from their faces with their nails" until copious amounts of blood flowed. The dancing and singing continued as women joined men, bearing bowls filled with drink, "their bodies bruised, their faces torn, their dugs, breasts, and other parts bespotted with blood, trickling down from the wounds, which with their nails they had made before their coming," Fletcher noted. Drake's men frantically encouraged them to look to the sky and pray to God, as they ministered to the Indians' self-inflicted wounds with lotions and ointment.

After they had tired themselves out, the Indians signaled that Drake should sit with them. They wanted the brave adventurer to become their "king and patron" and rule over them. After they surrendered "their right and title in the whole land," Fletcher wrote, they would become his "vassals." To persuade Drake, they resumed singing, a joyful song this time, and reverently placed a crown on his head, "enriched his neck with all their chains, and offering unto him many things, honored him by the name of Hioh." To their way of thinking, "the great and chief god was now become their god, their king and patron, and themselves were become the only happy and blessed people in the world."

Drake thought it best to respect their wishes, partly because he and his men were dependent on them for essentials, and partly because "he knew not what good end God had brought this to pass, or what honor or profit it might bring to our country in time to come." He took the "sceptre, crown, and dignity of the said country into his hand" and spoke of transferring it to Her Majesty Queen Elizabeth. The Indians circulated among the English visitors again, trying to acquaint themselves as individuals this time, "finding such as pleased their fancies," which meant the youngest among them.

The Miwok women circled the young sailors and cabin boys and offered them sacrifices, all the while "crying out with lamentable shrieks and moans, weeping and scratching and tearing their very flesh out of their face with their nails." Making the spectacle even more shocking, elderly Miwok men, "roaring and crying out," joined the women, and despite their age, proved as violent. The sight was deeply disturbing to the English. The more experienced sailors, standing outside the circle, "groaned in spirit to see the power of Satan so far prevail in seducing these so harmless souls." They attempted to display their disapproval, and when that failed to work, they grasped the Indians' hands and violently shoved them upward "to the living God whom they ought to serve," but the Indians broke free of the English and resumed their violent worship.

When the Indians had "a little qualified their madness," they displayed their infirmities to the English—"old aches" and "shrunk sinews," sores and ulcers, and recent wounds—as they were "craving help and cure thereof from us." They had only to blow on or touch the Indians' wounds to cure their suffering and make them whole. Fletcher implied that the Indians' afflictions were no less spiritual than physical. Curing one would ameliorate the other. "We could not but take pity on them," he said, yet they needed to make the Indians understand that Drake and his men "were but men and no gods," and as men, they had no magic, only ordinary means at their disposal such as lotions and plasters. It proved enough for the Miwok.

Once this healing bond had formed, the English sailors found there was no ridding themselves of the Coast Miwok, who spent days on end in the English visitors' shelter, bringing offerings that met with increasing indifference as time passed, "whereupon their zeal abated." Even after the contributions ceased, the Indians persisted in crowding into the English camp, often neglecting to bring food for themselves. Drake, whom they treated as a father figure, provided them with mussels and seals, which only encouraged them to overstay their welcome.

Despite these misunderstandings, Fletcher and his compatriots saw potential in their naive, energetic hosts: "They are a people of a tractable, free, and loving nature, without guile or treachery; their bows and arrows (their only weapons, and almost all their wealth) they use very skillfully, but yet not to do any great harm with them, being by reason of their weakness more fit for children than for men, sending the arrows neither far off nor with any great force."

When Drake and his men had settled in, they traveled inland to inspect the Indians' dwellings. They observed a *hun'ge*, a large round structure that served as the setting for a variety of social gatherings and ceremonial events to mourn the dead or to commemorate significant occasions with dance and music. The Miwok homes varied between eight and fifteen feet in diameter. They were made of cedar poles; a hole at the top let smoke escape. Drake's crew might also have seen a large playing field called a *poscoi a we'a* used for a game similar to soccer, played by both men and women. (In the Miwok version, men could only kick the ball, but women could handle it however they chose.)

Farther inland, Drake's men were agreeably surprised by the change in terrain. The rocky shore gave way to a fertile forest teeming with "very large, fat deer." There were ubiquitous small "conies" with extremely long tails, feet like the paws of a mole, and bags dangling from either side of their little chins, in which they stored meat to ingest themselves or to feed their young. The English considered them a type of rabbit. In fact, they were the rotund California beaver, *Castor canadensis*. The Indians consumed the animal's entire body, and valued their skin highly, "for their king's holiday coat was made of them." Later, their fur would become much sought after for warm, luxurious clothing, and the beaver, once ubiquitous in the Northwest, would be nearly wiped out by the demand.

*I*n all, the land was so fair, the inhabitants so well-disposed and peaceful, that Drake named the country New Albion, using the ancient term for England, partly in recognition of the white cliffs overlooking the sea (the cliffs reminded him of the coast of England), and partly from a growing conviction that the land was free of Spanish taint. "The Spaniards never . . . so much as set a foot in this country," Fletcher noted with satisfaction. They remained "many degrees southward of this place." (The English, of course, had landed here by accident and would have preferred to be navigating the mythical Northwest Passage.)

To commemorate the discovery of "New Albion," Drake set up "a plate of brass, fast nailed to a great and firm post." This was more than a mere marker. It was a "monument" proclaiming "Her Majesty's and successors' right and title to that kingdom." The plate contained the queen's name, the date their ship arrived, and most crucially, "the free giving up of the province and kingdom, both by the king and the people, into Her Majesty's hands." The plate also included "Her Highness's picture and arms," a piece of sixpence affixed to the plate, and under it all, the name of their general, Francis Drake.

"The Spaniards hitherto had never been in this part of the country," Francis Pretty recorded with satisfaction. "Neither did ever discover the land by many degrees to the southwards of this place." England finally had the beginnings of an empire after years of deference to Spain. Drake was still a pirate, but he was becoming much more, a marauder with a mission, a vision. For the sailors who had come so far and risked so much, New Albion served as a charter for the future of their kingdom.

*W*hen it became apparent to the Miwok people that Drake and his company were preparing to leave, Fletcher observed, their "mirth, joy, glad countenance, pleasant speeches, agility of body, familiar rejoicing with one another, and all pleasure whatever flesh and blood might be delighted in" were replaced with "heavy hearts and grieved minds . . . woeful complaints and moans, with bitter tears and wringing of hands, tormenting themselves." The Coast Miwok, as Drake had learned by now, were nothing if not histrionic. The men now considered themselves forlorn "castaways" whom the "gods were about to forsake." But Drake indicated he was resolved to move on. In desperation, the Miwok tried to secure a promise that the English would return. To symbolize this wish, "they stole upon us a sacrifice, and set it on fire 'ere we were aware, burning therein a chain of feathers." Not knowing what else to do, the sailors all fell to their knees and started singing psalms and praying, a gesture that convinced the Indians to suspend their sacrifice, "suffering the fire to go out." Then they imitated their visitors as they "fell a-lifting of their eyes and hands to heaven, as they saw us do." Together, they prayed to their separate gods.

*O*n July 23, *Golden Hind* spread sail, caught a fresh breeze, and glided out of the harbor, ending the five-week idyll in San Francisco Bay. The Miwok, bereft, ran to the hilltops so they could watch the Englishmen in their ship for as long as possible before they disappeared into the haze. (The separation might not have been complete. It appears that Drake took several Miwok with him to present to the queen.)

The following day, *Golden Hind*, with about sixty men, arrived at what is now called the Farallon Islands—the name comes from the

Spanish *farrallón* or "sea cliff"—about thirty miles off the coast of San Francisco. It would be a stretch to call them islands; they are volcanic sea stacks, jagged rock outcroppings surrounded by shoals. At the time Drake visited, even the Indians avoided them, calling them the Islands of the Dead in the belief that only spirits of the departed dwelled there. Juan Rodríguez Cabrillo was said to have skirted these islands in 1542 when he explored the coast of Northern California, but Drake was the first navigator to land there. On arrival, he began provisioning for the voyage ahead with the seals and birds his men found.

The next day they headed west into the never-ending Pacific. Drake still had Pigafetta's crude but relatively accurate account of Magellan's voyage with him, and it warned of the heat, thirst, scurvy, and disorientation they had endured for ninety-eight days before they made their first landfall. Benefiting from Magellan's mistakes, and commanding a superior vessel, Drake covered a similar route in just sixty-eight days, with little recorded harm to his crew.

And so having nothing in our view but air and sea," Fletcher wrote, "we continued our course through the main ocean." Eventually they arrived at an archipelago of 340 small islands known today as Palau, or, in Drake's era, Pelew. They were seemingly in the midst of nowhere, in the vastness of the western Pacific, but these islands, though isolated, were inhabited by settlers who had arrived centuries before from Indonesia or the Philippines.

When Drake's vast ship came into view, a flotilla of canoes set out from Palau, some carrying as many as fifteen men as well as gifts of fish and potatoes and fruit, which would be especially welcome to sailors who had spent weeks at sea. Fletcher noticed their canoes were fashioned from a single tree, "hollowed within with great cunning, being made so smooth, both within and without, that they bore a gloss." They featured a prow and stern curving upward in a high semicircle, and displaying certain white and glistering shells for bravery. He described another feature, "two pieces of timber . . . at the end whereof was fastened crosswise a great cane . . . to keep their canoes from overthrowing"—that is, a pair of pontoons on either side to maintain stability.

Drake's crew was about to make their initial contact in the Pacific.

The very first canoes to arrive beside *Golden Hind* made a show of peaceful trading, "giving us one thing for another very orderly, intending (as we perceived) hereby to work a greater mischief to us: intreating us by signs most earnestly to draw nearer towards the shore, that they might (if possible) make the easier prey both of the ship and us."

The English were determined to avoid this trap. "If they received anything once into their hands, they would neither give recompence nor restitution of it, but thought whatever they could figure to be their own, expecting always with brows of brass to receive more, but would part with nothing."

Drake would not be provoked, especially when his men were outnumbered. "It was far from our General's meaning to requite their malice by like injury," Fletcher explained. "Yet that they might know that he had power to do them harm (if he had listed) he caused a great piece to be shot off, not to hurt them, but to affright them." It worked. "At the noise thereof they every one leaped out of his canoe into the water, and diving under the keel of their boats, stayed them from going any way till our ship was gone a good way from them. Then they all lightly recovered into their canoes, and got them with speed toward the shore." Drake's sense of triumph proved short-lived, for after feigning honesty, "they cunningly fell a-filching of whatever they could." One of the locals got close enough to seize a dagger and knives from the belt of one of the men. When ordered to return them, he brandished the weapons in an effort to get more. The only way the English visitors could rid themselves of this "ungracious company" was to make their attackers "feel some smart"—in other words, sharp pain—"as well as terror" to deter their stealing. This they accomplished with their guns and swords. Then they raised anchor and sailed away, christening their first landfall in the Pacific "The Island of the Thieves."

*I*t took several days for Drake to rid himself of his agile tormentors, but eventually he put them astern. He followed Magellan's course until October 16, when he raised four islands, later known as the Philippines, and by October 21, he dropped anchor at the largest, a dark green bulwark named Mindanao, to take on water, and then hastened away. Drake had no desire to linger in the Philippines because it was here, in the harbor of Mactan Island, where Magellan had been killed, and Drake was always eager to avoid Magellan's missteps, none more than this one.

At the end of the month, they arrived in the Moluccas, the fabled Spice Islands that only a handful of survivors of Magellan's fleet had lived to see:

> *. . . Ternate . . .*
> *. . . Tidore . . .*
> *. . . Makian . . .*
> *. . . Bacan . . .*
> *. . . Jilolo . . .*

In reality, there are more than a thousand islands in this group, which belongs to Indonesia. The sailors beheld a vista unlike anything they had ever seen. The larger islands appeared to float above the surface of the sea, gently climbing to the sky, as if mediating between the temporal and spiritual worlds. These islands were renowned in Europe for a variety of spices, but especially for cloves, the most valuable commodity in the world, itself a form of currency. Drake was far more interested in gold and gems, which he already had stolen in abundance. But now that he was the first English captain to arrive at the Spice Islands, he might as well do business.

Drake arrived in Ternate about November 3, 1579, expecting to negotiate with the sultan for precious cloves, but the little kingdom had turned rigidly isolationist in that era. Drake's men would not be fêted and pampered like their predecessors. Not only that, but *Golden Hind* was already overflowing with treasure taken from *Cacafuego*, leaving little room for spices. Faced with these limitations, Drake chose to negotiate a trade agreement with the local sultans as the best available alternative.

Even that modest goal proved difficult to accomplish. Over time, deadly feuds among the sultans ruling the islands had increased.

*D*rake attempted to overcome resistance with charm and diplomacy, but he had to proceed with extreme caution. Very early one morning, Fletcher recalled, "we came to anchor, and presently our general sent a messenger to the king with a velvet cloak for a present and a token that his coming should be in peace." He wanted to exchange merchandise so that he could be on his way. Through an intermediary, the viceroy of another island, Drake hinted at what an "honour and benefit it might be to him, to be in league and friendship with so noble and famous a prince as we served." Not only that, the Portuguese would consider it a "discouragement" when they learned of the alliance.

Drake's strategy worked. The enemy of his enemy would be his friend. The Sultan of Tidore was so well-disposed to the idea that "before our messenger could come half the way, he had sent the viceroy with divers others of his nobles and councillors to our general with a special message." Drake would have the supplies he needed, and more than that, the Sultan was prepared to give Drake the exclusive right to trade. If that arrangement upset the Portuguese, so much the better. As a sign of good faith, he sent his seal, and he would soon come in person accompanied by other rulers of the island to conduct *Golden Hind* safely into their harbor.

In advance of the ruler of Tidore's appearance, three large canoes bearing the "greatest personages" of his court, all attired in white, approached the *Golden Hind*. Each took his place on a "fine mat" beneath a "frame made of reeds," accompanied by a retinue of "young and comely men," also in white, followed by many others. Soldiers stood guard. When the two sides did meet, "truly it seemed to us very strange and marvellous," Fletcher wrote, "serving at the present not so much to set out his royal and kingly state (which was great) as to do honour to Her Highness to whom we belonged."

A formal procession commenced. "In the forepart of each canoe sat two men, the one holding a tabret," or small drum, "the other a piece of brass, whereon they both at once stroke; and observing a due time and reasonable space between each stroke, by the sound thereof directed the rowers to keep their stroke with their oars." The convoy proceeded "with marvelous swiftness." The English noted that the canoes did not lack for weapons. Each held at least one "small cast piece, of about a yard in length, mounted upon a stock," and every man "except the rowers, had his sword, dagger, and target."

As the canoes approached the *Golden Hind*, one surging after the other, "the men did us a kind of homage with great solemnity, the greatest personages beginning first, with reverend countenance and behaviour, to bow their bodies even to the ground; which done, they put our own messenger aboard us again." With signs, they indicated the course *Golden Hind* should take, and they were prepared to tow the ship. "The king himself was not far behind, but he also with 6 grave and ancient fathers in his canoe approaching, did at once, together with them, yield us a reverend kind of obeisance in far more humble manner then was to be expected." They were able to get their first look at the king: "of a tall stature, very corpulent and well set together, of a very princely and gratious countenance." His counselors dared to speak to him only when they were on their knees, and rose only at the ruler's bidding.

Drake's men fired their weapons to mark the occasion. "Ordnance thundered, which we mixed with great store of small shot, among which sounding our trumpets and other instruments of music, both of still and loud noise."

The ruler of Tidore appeared "so much delighted" by the display that he joined his canoe to the *Golden Hind*, and for the next hour was towed by the larger ship. All the while, "the king being thus in musical paradise, and enjoying that wherewith he was so highly pleased, his brother, named Moro, with no less bravery than any of the rest, accompanied also with a great number of gallant followers, made the like repair, and gave us like respect; and his homage done, he fell astern of us till we came to anchor." With that, the first day of socializing came to a peaceful conclusion.

*T*he Tidorean potentate promised to board *Golden Hind* the following day. Before his arrival, he sent "such victuals as were requisite and necessary for our provision," whereupon "rice in pretty quantity, hens, sugar canes, imperfect and liquid sugar, a fruit which they call Figo" and which Fletcher recognized as plantain, materialized, along with "cocoes, and a kind of meal which they call Sago, made of the tops of certain trees, tasting in the mouth like sour curds, but melts away like sugar." With it, the Tidoreans made a cake that "will keep good at least 10 years."

Despite these elaborate preparations, the sultan did not appear at the appointed time and place, and instead dispatched his brother Moro to invite Drake to go ashore. Moro would remain on board ship "as a pawn for his safe restoring." Drake might have agreed had not the sultan "first broke his word."

Although willing to engage with the locals, he remained extremely cautious. He feared being ambushed or, like Magellan, unexpectedly overwhelmed by the enemy. Without the sultan, Drake took an "utter disliking in the whole company," and a confidential conference with the sultan's brother in the captain's cabin bred "no small suspicion of ill intent" between the parties. Resolved not to go ashore, Drake instead sent a delegation with Moro, bearing a "special message to the king himself."

A thousand Tidoreans surrounding a large structure awaited the tiny English deputation.

*T*he [sultan's] house was in form four square, covered all over with cloth of divers colours," Fletcher recalled. "At the side of this house, next unto the castle, was seated the chaire of state, having directly over and extending very largely every way, a very fair and rich canopy."

While Drake's delegation awaited the ruler, they observed "threescore noble, grave, and ancient personages, all of them reported to be of the king's privy council at the nether end of the house." Outside, four white-haired men, clothed in red, stood guard. At last the sultan arrived, trailing ten "grave senators" arrayed beneath a luxurious-looking canopy embossed with gold. Drake's men, accompanied by Moro, stood to meet the ruler, who responded graciously. He spoke in a "low voice, temperate in speech, of kingly demeanour, and a Moor by nation. His attire was after the fashion of the rest of his country, but far more sumptuous, as his condition and state required: from the waist to the ground was all cloth of gold, and that very rich; his legs bare, but on his feet a pair of shoes, dyed red." His head was "finely wreathed in diverse rings of plated gold, of an inch or an inch and a half in breadth, which made a fair and princely show, somewhat resembling a crown in form. About his neck he had a chain of perfect gold, the links very great and one fold double; on his left hand was a diamond, an emerald, a ruby, and a turquoise, four very fair and perfect jewels; on his right hand, in one ring, a big and perfect turquoise; and in another ring many diamonds of a smaller size."

Decorum prevailed. The sultan took his seat in the chair of state. A page stood at his right, waving a fan "richly embroidered and beset with sapphires, breathing and gathering the air to refresh the king, the place being very hot, both by reason of the sun and the assembly of so great a multitude."

Drake's party concluded that the sultan's abode held little danger. They spied only two cannon, unmounted and unusable, along with other equipment brought there by the Portuguese, who, the English assumed, had been responsible for building the edifice. Fletcher noted with alarm that they were dealing with "Moors," citing their "superstitious observations of new moons, and certain seasons, with a rigid and strict kind of fasting." When the sultan and his retinue came aboard, they "would neither eat nor drink, not so much as a cup of cold water" by day, but at night "would eat three times, and that very largely."

One man, Pausaos, as Fletcher called him, stood apart from this group. He struck the English visitors as a "goodly gentleman, very well accomplished," equipped with an interpreter, and, most surprisingly, "apparelled much after our manner, most neat and courtlike, his carriage the most respective and full of discreet behavior that we have ever seen. He explained that he was in exile from China, having been accused of a capital crime" three years before. He claimed he had heard "strange things" about Drake, and was most curious to know how he had made the journey all the way from England.

Instead of revealing his route, Drake regaled him with stories of England. Pausaos replied that he wanted to see England for himself one day so he could "carry home the description of one of the most ancient, mightiest, and richest kingdoms in the world." Just speaking to Englishmen was enough to make him a "happy man." If only Drake could put in a word for him in China, it "might serve him to recover favour in his country." The man had a talent for flattery, but Drake could not entertain the bizarre request.

*B*y the ninth of November, having gotten what provision the place could afford us, we then set sail," Fletcher wrote, "and considering that our ship for want of trimming was now grown foul, that our cask and vessels for water were much decayed, and that divers other things stood in need of reparation, our next care was, how we might fall with such a place where with safety we might a while stay for the redressing of these inconveniencies." They sailed until November 14, until they reached a small, uninhabited island, where they dropped anchor.

*T*he first thing we did, we pitched our tents and entrenched ourselves as strongly as we could upon the shore, lest at any time perhaps we might have been disturbed by the inhabitants of the greater island which lay not far to the westward of us." They brought their supplies ashore and set up a smith's forge to fashion railing for the ship and repair iron-hooped casks. "We trimmed our ship, and performed our other businesses to our content. The place affording us not only all necessaries (which we had not of our own before) thereunto, but also wonderful refreshing to our wearied bodies, by the comfortable relief and excellent provision that here we found, whereby of sickly, weak, and decayed (as many of us seemed to be before our coming hither), we in short space grew all of us to be strong, lusty, and healthful persons."

Just as remarkable, "among these trees, night by night, did show themselves an infinite swarm of fire-seeming-worms flying in the air, whose bodies (no bigger than an ordinary fly) did make a show, and give such light as if every twig on every tree had been a lighted candle, or as if that place had been the starry sphere." The spectacle ended with "an innumerable multitude of bats," larger than hens, that flew "with marvelous swiftness, but their flight is very short, and when they light, they hang only by the boughs with their backs downwards."

*T*here was more. They were surrounded by the largest crabs on earth. These beasts were the stuff of nightmares, with gleaming blue or black shells, a furry black body, four-foot-long legs, pincers strong enough to snap off a person's finger, a voracious appetite, and a keen sense of smell, especially for blood—human blood. The islanders called them coconut crabs because they were agile enough to scale a coconut tree and strong enough to pierce the coconut's shell and suck out the liquid. They killed small mammals. They attacked unsuspecting birds, dragged them into burrows, and ate them alive. They cannibalized other crabs and even themselves. Closer to our own era, they are suspected of dismembering and devouring the body of Amelia Earhart, the aviatrix, after she crash-landed in the Pacific in 1937.

The giant crabs, despite their horrifying appearance, became an essential source of food for the sailors. A single specimen "was sufficient to satisfy four hungry men at a dinner, being a very good and restorative meat," said Fletcher, who compared its taste and texture to lobster. The resemblance ended there. The giant crabs were "utter strangers to the sea, living always on the land, where they . . . dig great and huge caves under the roots of the most huge and monstrous trees, where they lodge themselves by companies together." Some "did climb up into trees to hide themselves, whither we were enforced to climb after them, if we would have them." He did not exaggerate this peculiar behavior. The giant coconut crab (*Birgus latro*) is the largest land-based arthropod: an invertebrate with an exoskeleton. These creatures weigh nine or ten pounds; they cannot swim, and drown if left in the water for more than an hour. This was the first time Europeans had seen, let alone eaten, giant crabs, although their meat had long been prized by local inhabitants.

Drake's men spent twenty-six days at Crab Island, as they called their refuge, resting and performing repairs on *Golden Hind*. Before departing, they took care to leave behind two or three indigenous women who had served as their consorts. One of them, "the wench Maria," was great with child. It was not clear who was responsible for her condition, but this callous indifference to "Maria" and to the child she would bear was all too common among Drake and other explorers of the era, who viewed the women they encountered as playthings to be used and discarded at will. No one viewed their behavior with remorse, or "Maria's" plight with compassion.

The weather turned nasty. They were forced, Fletcher said, to head south, but "we never had more care to keep ourselves afloat." Conditions left them no choice but to "beat up and down with extraordinary care and circumspection until early January."

They prayed the new year, 1580, would mean "free passage" for *Golden Hind* "when lo, on a sudden, when we least suspected, no show or suspicion of danger appearing to us ... our ship was laid up fast upon a desperate shoal."

They felt a sudden thud followed by a scraping sound, and the ship came to a complete stop. The sails luffed pointlessly. The men strained to look for a landmark but saw none. The ship had become stuck tight on a submerged shoal extending three or even four leagues in every direction: more than ten miles.

CHAPTER XI

Deliverance

*T*here was no chance of escape. "The ghastly appearance of instant death, affording no respite or time of pausing, called upon us to deny ourselves, and to commend ourselves into the merciful hands of our most gratious God." It had been two months since they departed from the Moluccas, and they had little idea of their whereabouts. The sailors prostrated themselves and prayed to God to have mercy on them. "And so preparing as it were our necks into the block, we every minute expected the final stroke to be given unto us."

After they appealed to the Almighty, Drake spoke calmly, "showing us the way thereto by his own example." He explained "first of all the pump being well plied, and the ship freed of water, we found our leaks to be nothing increased, which though it gave us no hope of deliverance, yet it gave us some hope of respite, insomuch as it assured us that the bulk was sound, which truly we acknowledged to be an immediate providence of God alone, insomuch as no strength of wood and iron could have possibly bore so hard and violent a shock as our ship did, dashing herself under full sail against the rocks." Thus, Drake implied, God had not abandoned them, despite the appearance of disaster.

Drake summoned his resolve to reassure the crew. He personally supervised the sounding, and declared that the line was too short to reach the sea floor. A good sign, perhaps, but not for Fletcher. "Our misery seemed to be increased, for whereas at first we could look for nothing but a present end, that expectation was now turned into waiting for a lingering death, of the two the far more fearful to be chosen." Drake, all the while, gave "cheerful speeches and good encouragements unto the rest." Either their ship was stuck fast, and they would remain with her, or they would abandon ship, "to see some other place of stay and refuge, the better of which two choices did carry with it the appearance of worse than 1000 deaths." It was preferable, in Fletcher's estimation, to perish together rather "than with the loss and absence of his friends to live in a strange land: whether a solitary life (the better choice) among wild beasts, as a bird on the mountains without all comfort, or among the barbarous people of the heathen, in intolerable bondage both of body and mind." They had survived crossing the Atlantic, the Strait of Magellan, and thousands of miles of the Pacific, along with mutinies, deadly storms, the Spanish, and giant crabs with pincers capable of snapping off a man's finger, only to come to grief on a wretched sandbar in the unexplored reaches of the ocean.

Fletcher took the measure of their prospects for survival and arrived at a bleak conclusion. "Our boat was by no means able at once to carry above 20 persons with any safety, and we were 58 in all; the nearest land was six leagues from us, and the wind from the shore directly bent against us." Even if they managed to reach the shore, they faced the prospect of being captured by hostile inhabitants, "and though perhaps we might escape the sword, yet would our life have been worse than death, not alone in respect of our woeful captivity and bodily miseries, but most of all in respect of our Christian liberty . . . and continually grieved with the horrible impieties and devilish idolatries of the heathen."

The crew prayed throughout the night, "thereby comforting ourselves, and refreshing our hearts," but daybreak brought no change in their situation. The tide had not lifted the ship free of the sandbar; they were neither sailing nor sinking. They thanked God at least for that much, and "with tears called upon Him to bless our labours." Their entreaties were for nought; they had "nothing to trust but prayers and tears." It seemed to them impossible that any "forecast, counsel, policy, or power of man could effect the delivery of our ship, except the Lord only miraculously should do the same."

To fortify themselves, they celebrated the "sacrament of the body and blood of our Saviour." It was expected this would be their last Communion, and it was laced with dread rather than comfort. (Although Fletcher, Drake, and the crew considered themselves Protestant, their rites were similar to those of Anglo-Catholicism, so they took Communion, went to confession, and followed other rituals of the Catholic Church.)

They attempted one last maneuver. They unloaded the ship "by casting some of her goods into the sea," including their cargo of precious cloves, and when that did not free the ship, they jettisoned sacks of flour, beans, and other provisions, the "very meal for sustenation of our lives." As Francis Pretty recalled, they were so desperate to survive they also unloaded tons of precious cargo. "We lighted our ship upon the rocks of three tons of cloves, eight pieces of ordnance, and certain meal and beans." Still the ship refused to dislodge. Next, weapons were cast into the sea. *Golden Hind* stubbornly clung to the shoal. If by some miracle they survived, they would trust in God to "deliver us out of that most desperate strait wherein we were." They would depend on Him to "fight for us against our enemies" and keep them "safe and free."

Frustrated and exhausted, Fletcher turned on Drake and snarled

that their imminent deaths were divine retribution for his beheading Thomas Doughty in Port Saint Julian.

Doughty! That witch! Infuriated, Drake vowed revenge on
Fletcher for the remark—if they survived this ordeal.

*T*he miracle—everyone called it that—of their deliverance commenced twenty hours after the ship struck the shoal. Wrote Fletcher:
"The place whereon we sat so fast was a firm rock in a cleft, whereof
it was we stuck on the larboard [port] side. At low water there was
not above six foot depth in all on the starboard." At that desperate
moment, the wind "blew somewhat stiff directly against our broad-
side, and so perforce kept the ship upright." Then without warning,
"It pleased God in the beginning of the tide, while the water was yet
almost at lowest, to slack the stiffeness of the wind." Their ship "fell
a-heeling towards the deep water, and by that means freed her keel
and made us glad men."

Drake ordered the crew to set all the sails, and the wind dragged
Golden Hind from the broad shoal into deep water.

The date of their escape from disaster was January 10, 1580.
They would face more hazards in the months ahead—shoals, storms,
and threatening creatures—but "of all the dangers that in our whole
voyage we met with," Fletcher recalled, "this was the greatest." They
were grateful to have overcome it, "but it was not the last."

*W*hen they were all safe, Drake focused his ire on Fletcher. He
ordered his chaplain secured to the forehatch with a padlock, as if he
were a criminal. He summoned all hands as he sat cross-legged on a
sea chest and spoke. "Francis Fletcher, I do here excommunicate thee
out of the church of God and from all benefits and graces thereof,

and I denounce thee to the devil and all his angels." Anyone who approached the chaplain would be hanged. Drake commanded that he wear a band around his arm, removable on pain of death, that declared: *francis fletcher ye falsest knave that liveth.*

Drake made Fletcher wear the band for only a few days. As for being called a "knave," meaning "rascal" or "rogue," there was worse language a sailor could employ. Drake forgave his beleaguered chaplain and allowed him to rejoin the Church of England as arbitrarily as he had excommunicated him. Soon after, Fletcher was again leading the company in prayers, their hour of despair on the reef and the terrible recriminations reduced to a memory that haunted them to the end of their voyage.

A few days later, a rip-roaring "tempest," or monsoon, blew up. They rode out the storm under bare poles, and when the wind weakened, ventured carefully toward another shoal on January 14, where they dropped anchor. After a brief respite, they made their way to a speck of land "and spent a day in watering and wooding." Under sail again, they confronted more foul weather and more shoals. The stress of the storm was unending. There was no time to rest or to eat. Indonesia is comprised of thousands of islands, and the crew passed many of them, hoping to find a safe harbor along the coast of Sulawesi, southeast of Borneo. Even that haven was dangerous for them, for it was the site of a Portuguese base. They decided to stand off but could not sail far enough away to rid themselves of the endless coast of Sulawesi, the eleventh largest island in the world.

On January 20, with the pinnace (including Fletcher) dispatched to reconnoiter, "there arose a most violent, yea, an intolerable flaw and storm out of the southwest against us, making us, on the leeshore among the most dangerous and hidden shoals, to fear extremely not only the loss of our boat and men, whom God should spare, into the hands of the infidels." Again, there seemed no way out, no hope of deliverance, and once again the storm relented, and they reunited with the ship. They moved away from Sulawesi at last, but by January 26, an overpowering wind carried them in a westerly direction "so as we could bear no more sail till the end of that month was full expired."

On February 1, after five days of meandering off course, they spied a "very high land," apparently uninhabited and safe. They would have made for it "to have got some succor, but the weather was so ill we could find no harbor." Wary of sandbars and shoals and other hidden traps, they bore off. On February 3, the sight of another small island tantalized them, but they still could not spread enough sail to reach it. They could only "lie at hull" as another monsoon carried them away, and islands drifted past, recorded in the ship's log, until their arrival.

*O*n February 8, the storm relented enough to allow two canoes to approach, and their genial occupants persuaded Drake and his crew to come with them to their town, called Barativa. Instead of the treacherous inhabitants they had experienced in recent months, the wandering sailors were pleased to find the serene inhabitants endowed with "handsome body and comely stature, of civil demeanour, very just in dealing, and courteous to strangers, of all which we had evident proof, they showing themselves most glad of our coming, and cheerfully ready to relieve our wants with whatsoever their country could afford." They were colorfully attired and adorned, both the men and the women. "The men all go naked save their heads and secret parts, everyone having one thing or other hanging at his ears. Their women are covered from the middle to the foot, wearing upon their naked arms bracelets, and that in no small number, some having nine at least upon each arm, made for the most part of horn or brass, whereof the lightest (by our estimation) would weigh 2 ounces." They were draped in gold, yet seemed not to realize they were wealthy. Their manner was so generous and reassuring that it hardly mattered to Drake's long-suffering crew that they were not Christians.

Displaying newfound horticultural enthusiasm, Fletcher marveled at their cucumbers, lemons, figs, coconuts, nutmeg, ginger, and pepper—all of which the islanders freely donated to the grateful English explorers. "We received of them whatsoever we desired for our need," he said in summary, "so that in all our voyage . . . from our departure out of our own country, hitherto we found not anywhere greater comfort and refreshing than we did at this time in this place."

After three days of this blissful respite from their ordeals at sea, Drake raised anchor. They were due back in Plymouth, and they were weeks, if not months, behind schedule. Day after day they sailed past other verdant islands, each of them mysterious and pregnant with the promise of ease and luxury, never to be sampled. Not until February 18 did *Golden Hind* "cast anchor under a little island" to take on water, only to depart the following day, as the weary sailors watched still more alluring sanctuaries slip past in the mist.

CHAPTER XII

Unbroken Blue Water

In England, Bernardino de Mendoza, the Spanish diplomat and spy, gathered reports of Elizabeth's intense activity against Spain. He revealed that pirates conducted business if not with her approval then at least with her knowledge. And he discussed the furious pace of shipbuilding, ostensibly for commercial purposes, but those same ships, loaded with cannon, could easily have borne down on the Andalusian city of Cádiz in southwestern Spain, with its large and vulnerable harbor.

There was more troubling news. Elizabeth transacted much of her business late at night. In fact, both sovereigns were inclined to insomnia and strange nocturnal behavior. On March 23, 1580, Mendoza wrote, "The Queen receives four or five times a day, and at night, a man who is brought in by secret doors, his face being covered by a taffeta. I have not been able to find out to what country he belongs, nor what he comes about, only that he has been in close conference with Cecil and other Councillors."

The longer Mendoza stayed in London, the more confrontational he became with Elizabeth. He redoubled his appeals to Philip for guidance. But there was none to be had. He was on his own, or nearly so.

*H*aving long passed the point of no return to South America, Drake sailed westward without interruption until March 9, 1580— nearly three weeks of unbroken blue water. Two days later, he arrived at yet another island, where the crew traded with the locals who greeted them. This was not just any island; this was Java, the thirteenth largest island in the world, with Sumatra lying to the northwest and Bali to the southeast.

Java was the setting for tsunamis, volcanoes, and earthquakes, but for the moment, the earth's crust was quiescent. A tropical rain forest covered Java in the west, and dry savanna lay to the east. The island teemed with wildlife. There were Javan rhinos, Javan warty pigs, mouse deer, tigers, elephants, and Javan leopards. Hundreds of species of birds were unique to Java. The exceptional fertility of the soil gave rise to some of the most valuable rice lands in the world and incomparably aromatic coffee. It was an island of hazards and wonders.

Considering this island to be more populated, Drake sent an emissary to present the ruler with linen, wool, and silk, all accepted with thanks. In return, Drake's crew gratefully received rice, coconuts, and hens. Emboldened, he went ashore on March 13 with several of his "gentlemen," to greet the island's ruler, who "joyfully and lovingly" greeted Drake, fed him, and entertained the company. The chief, he learned, governed with the help of lesser rulers, "rajas," who were on good terms with each other, and who sent more food to Drake the following day.

Soon, three rajas came aboard *Golden Hind* to view the ship at close range and inspect the "warlike munition" on display. Thereafter, the rajas visited almost every day, as the Englishmen learned their names: Raja Pataidra, Raja Cabocapalla, Raja Manghango, Raja Boccabarra, and Raja Timbanto, "whom our General always entertained with the best cheer that we could make, and showed them all the commodities of our ship, with our ordnance and other arms and weapons." When Drake performed music for his eminent visitors, "they took exceeding great delight with admiration." Perhaps the captain sang, or played the viola da gamba stored in his cabin. In any case, he was one of the very few explorers who serenaded his hosts. A local ruler, Raja Donan, commanded his own musicians to perform for Drake and his crew. "Though it were of a very strange kind, yet the sound was pleasant and delightful," Fletcher politely commented. More gratifying was the ox conveyed by the raja to his visitors, who reciprocated with "very costly silks, which he held in great esteem."

The crew made the effort, unusual for them, to learn useful words of the "natural language of Java" and to record them in a makeshift phrase book:

Sabuck, silk
Sagu, bread of the country
Larnike, drink
Paree, rice in the husk
Braas, sodden rice
Calapa, coconuts
Cricke, a dagger
Catcha, a looking glass
Arbo, an oar
Vadas, a goat
Cabo, gold
Gardange, a plantain
Hiam, a hen
Seuit, linen cloth
Doduck, blue cloth
Totopps, one of their caps

Quia, black sugar

Tadon, a woman

Bebeck, a duck

All this entertaining and socializing delayed their departure, but the enjoyment they derived helped to justify it. In the end, Fletcher, speaking for the entire crew, lauded the rajas and people alike as "loving, very true, and just-dealing."

As *Golden Hind*, freshly trimmed, cleaned, and shorn of barnacles, prepared to depart, the people of Java presented Drake with hens, goats, coconuts, and plantains. The ship finally set out on March 26, setting a course west by southwest, bound for the rocky headland near the tip of South Africa known as the Cape of Good Hope, a distance of about six thousand miles across the vast expanse of the Indian Ocean, the third largest ocean on the planet. The distances, utter absence of land, and unrestrained storms conjured a sense of loneliness and peril. Their progress felt illusory. At some point, Drake, improvising as he often did, decided not to make for the port of Malacca, where unknown dangers awaited, but instead to head out to sea and ultimately home to England.

The ship sailed on in a void, touching nothing but "air and water" until May 21, when they spied a faint smudge of land in the distance. On June 15, a very fair day, they passed the Cape, which seemed so near that they would have been able "with our pieces to have shot to land." After being suspended for days in the middle of an endless ocean, the proximity to land seemed breathtaking, the stone outcropping unreal.

At the Cape of Good Hope, severe rationing reduced each man's allotment of water and wine. In this rugged landscape, no place appeared safe enough for the crew to risk landing to search for supplies. By now, the shortage of water had become so acute that one man died of thirst. John Drake later recalled, "They were going to take port at the Coast of Guinea but did not do so because they had contrary winds and found no good anchorage. They proceeded directly to Sierra Leone and harbored there for five days, cleaning their vessel and taking in water and wood." They were now about 4,200 miles south of London, on the concluding leg of the journey, and the ordeal of rationing continued. "When they arrived in sight of land at Sierra Leone all the water on board was portioned out and for every three men there was not more than half a pint remaining." If they had been delayed for even two or three days more, they would have died of thirst.

At last, on June 22, they dropped anchor at diamond-rich Sierra Leone, rested, and took on water at last. The days were hot and sticky, the nights not much better. The arrival of the wet monsoon brought blessed relief from dehydration.

*T*wo days later, the restored crew put to sea for the final leg of the voyage. Spanish spies followed their progress. Don Cristóbal de Eraso, the chief of the Spanish Armada, reported on May 14, 1579: "This is an affair of great importance which requires serious consideration. If all three vessels should unite with their artillery and firearms they will constitute a force that could not possibly be vanquished by the ships sent by the Viceroy or those that have left there."

The longer Drake's voyage lasted, the more alarmed Spanish intelligence became; an upstart red-haired infidel pirate had made a mockery of their security. On February 1580, Bernardino de Mendoza, the Spanish emissary to Elizabeth, reported from his post in

London to Philip II that Drake had once again outwitted the Spanish, who had representatives assigned to ports Drake was expected to visit "in order that [the king] may have instant news of his coming." But the local justices in these ports, according to Mendoza, protected Drake rather than arrested him, probably for a price. When the Spanish approached, "they made sure that he got away safely."

Mendoza vowed to speak with Queen Elizabeth about the outrageous situation and to threaten that "if they do not make entire restitution and punish the pirates, your Majesty will issue letters of marque to recover their property, taking possession of English property where they find it." It was a potent threat, he believed, for "this is what they fear most, and the merchants themselves make the greatest outcry over saying that, because two or three of the principal courtiers send ships out to plunder in this way, their property must be thus imperilled and the country ruined. This makes them more anxious to condemn and to give me information."

The information Mendoza received amounted to little more than speculation. "They are apprehensive about Drake's return as the voyage is long and he must be short of ships. They think that if he does not arrive within two months they must give him up as lost." That Drake and his fleet would disappear at sea, as so many other expeditions had, was too much to hope for.

Rather than plan an actual reprisal against Drake, Philip withdrew behind the walls of El Escorial and placed his hopes on a legalistic resolution of the conflict. When he asked Mendoza if Drake had taken out insurance before his voyage, Mendoza patiently explained that in England, "there is a law which was made here to exonerate these pirates, the effect of which is that they have to give sureties before sailing, not to injure anyone excepting those who are the declared enemies of this Crown." However, it was a "dead letter, and when any attempt by a private person made in due form to enforce it, it found impossible to do so." As if explaining to a child, Mendoza reminded the king that "those who sail for the purpose of robbery do not give sureties at all as they are generally under the protection of the principal courtiers, as, for instance, Drake, who was fitted out by Leicester and his friends."

Rumors about Drake's progress bedeviled the Spanish court. Restitution was still out of the question; Drake would never reimburse Spain. The best that Philip could hope for was the opportunity to lodge a protest. Mendoza, more belligerent than his monarch, made a case for invasion—what other way was there to address Spain's grievance?—but Philip shied away from the idea, even as England's imperial ambitions, once negligible, now threatened Spain.

There was still no reliable news of Drake, his men, or his plunder. On June 18, 1580, Mendoza wrote from London, "Very little hopes are now entertained of Drake's return, as he has been so long delayed." By June 30, Drake's adversaries had given him up for lost.

Drake, however, continued to make progress, unseen. He crossed the equator on July 12, the coast of Guinea four days later, and Terceira Island in the Azores on September 11.

*M*endoza finally heard from a courier a few days earlier, on September 5, that Drake "had passed through the Strait of Magellan." That had yet to happen, of course, but the mere thought was alarming. Worse, he "had stolen in the southern sea gold and silver worth 200,000 ducats belonging to his Majesty, and 400,000 the property of merchants." As if to emphasize the calamity, "the adventurers who provided money and ships for the voyage are beside themselves for joy, and I am told that there are some of the councillors amongst them. The people here are talking of nothing else but going out to plunder in a similar way."

Drake's success was Spain's humiliation. He had not simply beaten Spain to distant outposts and trade routes, he had not simply outdone Magellan and the other would-be circumnavigators, he had stolen vast wealth from Spain in a flagrant display of global piracy. The question now was how to bring him to justice.

*D*rake reached home port aboard *Golden Hind* on September 26, 1580, under a full moon. With a sense of relief, excitement, and gratitude, Fletcher wrote of the occasion, "We safely with joyful minds and thankful hearts to God, arrived at Plymouth, the place of our setting forth, after we had spent 2 years, 10 months and some few odd days besides, in seeing the wonders of the Lord in the deep, in discovering so many admirable things, in going through with so many strange adventures, in escaping out of so many dangers and overcoming so many difficulties in this our encompassing of this nether globe, and passing around about the world." He did not exaggerate. It had been an astonishing voyage. They had succeeded where Magellan had failed, survived where he had succumbed to needless bloodshed. They had demonstrated that a circumnavigation was possible, and that England could have a global sea route. Moreover, they had returned with an unimaginable fortune in gold and silver. The fact that it was stolen from their enemy made the haul all the more satisfying to Drake and his highly placed backers. For once, Spain's loss was England's gain.

Drake's young nephew John, writing in the third person, described the anxious moment when the sailors approached home port: "On reaching Plymouth they enquired from fisherman how was the Queen."

This was a matter of critical importance. For almost three years Drake had heard nothing directly from his secret backer. If his voyage was to be considered a success, it was vital that she remain in place. If power had changed hands while he was away, if Elizabeth had been overthrown, or abdicated, or died, he might find himself a Protestant among Catholics, or a loyalist among insurgents, with very uncertain prospects. . . .

But the queen lived.

*D*uring the years of Drake's absence, Elizabeth's life had been in turmoil. She had endured nine months of agony caused by a rotting tooth while physicians in England and Europe hesitated to treat her, fearing for their lives if their efforts failed. Finally, the offending tooth was pulled, and she recovered, although Her Majesty preferred to let her remaining teeth blacken rather than submit herself to the ordeal of extraction again.

The crucial question of marriage and succession loomed. As it became more certain that Elizabeth would not bear a child to inherit the throne, her advisers frantically tried to arrange a match, a notion she strenuously resisted. Her father, of course, had turned marriage into a cause célèbre to remake England's relationship with the Church. His quest for a male heir had provoked violent, grotesque behavior on his part. Elizabeth had come of age in a volatile environment in which a royal marriage often led to instability and bloodshed. She had managed to survive the hazards of matrimony by remaining distant and virginal, at least in her outward behavior. No wonder she announced that marriage "is a thing for which I have never had any inclination." Yet Elizabeth was capable of grasping the other side of an argument. "My subjects, however, press me so that I cannot help myself but must marry or take the other course, which is a very difficult one," by which she meant a life of chastity and the end of the Tudor dynasty. "There is a strong idea in the world that a woman cannot live unless she is married, or at all events that if she refrains from marriage she does so for some bad reason." She allowed that she would have married the Earl of Leicester, but he already had a wife. Even after she died, they still did not wed.

There was another, more fundamental reason why she did not marry: she would instantly become the lesser partner in the union. That was as compelling a reason as any other. Her imperious father, Henry VIII, prophesied that if a lady "shall by chance to rule, she cannot continue long without a husband, which by God's law must then be her governor and head, and so finally direct the realm." With this warning in mind, she avoided addressing the subject. Instead, she sent out artfully mixed messages to get her way, or she took refuge behind obfuscation. Marriage would interfere with her defenses. It was not simply a matter of deferring to her husband. One misstep and she could wind up like her mother, with her exposed neck on a block, a sword poised over it, ready to make her into a victim for all time. With this dire example in mind, she had no choice but to conclude, "I would rather be a beggar and single than a queen and married."

*N*o one believed her. After a long search, the court councillors, who believed they knew what was best for her and for the realm, chose a partner to whom she could feel unquestionably superior. This unfortunate candidate was Francis, Duke of Anjou and Alençon, the youngest son of Henri II and Catherine de Médicis. If his brother, Henry III, did not produce an heir, he would inherit the French throne. Although Catholic, he had made common cause with French Protestants. Elizabeth's secretary of state and chief adviser, Lord Burghley, thought it would be an excellent idea for the House of Valois and the House of Tudor to unite, but in reality, Alençon and Elizabeth made an unlikely couple.

The duke was half the age of the queen—young enough to be her son. And there was his appearance to consider. His spine was somewhat malformed, and severe smallpox scars disfigured his boyish face. Even his mother despised him. "Would to God you had died young," she once wrote to him. On the other hand, popular sentiment in France favored the match, so long as Elizabeth bore a child, but given her age, forty-five, there was no guarantee that she could produce an heir.

Elizabeth's marrying a Catholic might aggravate religious tensions rather than allay them. Negotiations with Alençon stalled. Events moved on, and in July 1579, Elizabeth was nearly assassinated as she traveled on a barge along the Thames. Thomas Appletree, who had fired the shot, was condemned to death by hanging, but as the executioner placed the noose around the condemned man's neck, Elizabeth intervened to spare him.

She also underwent a change of heart regarding the ill-formed yet strangely appealing Alençon. The Spanish diplomat and spy Bernardino de Mendoza conveyed the latest gossip to King Philip. "Since my last I have learnt of some of the presents made by M. d'Alençon," Mendoza related. The frail but determined young duke had gifts for everyone. "He gave the Queen a diamond ring worth, the French say, 10,000 crowns, which he handed to her when he bade her farewell at Cobham. The parting was very tender on both sides, and the Queen presented Alençon with another jewel. He gave Leicester a cord for his cap, consisting of precious stones worth 3,000 crowns," the diplomat-spy reported. "Lady Stafford and other ladies received jewels from the stock brought by Simier, who remains here to continue the negotiations for the marriage and the other French plans, with which object he is winning over the councillors in every possible way."

England was still desperate for wealth, and this decorous bribery partly answered the need. "The Duke of Alençon shall be my husband," Elizabeth publicly declared as she kissed Alençon on the mouth, drew a ring from her hand, and gave it as a pledge. Alençon reciprocated with a ring of his own for her. After that, Elizabeth summoned the ladies and gentlemen in attendance and repeated her declaration. "Alençon and the French are extremely overjoyed at this," Mendoza wrote of the union, which had the potential for realigning nations.

Elizabeth, coming to terms with her advancing age and scarred skin, decided to overlook her suitor's physical shortcomings. Inspired by his hoarse voice, she took to calling him "Frog," and supporters at court inundated her with frog-inspired jewelry. The union of England and France, of Protestant and Catholic, unlikely as it seemed, would soon take place. "I judge that the negotiations for union with the French are proceeding very warmly," Mendoza wrote to King Philip on September 13, 1579. "She kept dwelling upon Alençon's good qualities and praising the Queen mother, whom she formerly abominated, saying how cleverly she had brought France to its present good order. Even if the marriage does not take place, it is probable that a binding union with the French may be effected—all in disservice of your Majesty—from the very evident signs to be seen on all hands." The Spanish nightmare was coming true.

Yet across England voices were raised in protest. In 1579 a young English pamphleteer named John Stubbs expressed his objections in a tract titled *The Discovery of a Gaping Gulf whereunto England is like to be swallowed by another French Marriage*. He stated the obvious: the queen was too old to bear a child, and he went on to say that the marriage would work to the detriment of English customs, morality, and even language by corrupting Protestantism. It would be "an immoral union, an uneven yoking of the clean ox to the unclean ass, a thing forbidden in the law" and destined to humiliate the English public "pressed down with the heavy loins of a worse people and beaten as with scorpions by a more vile nation."

Elizabeth's court prohibited circulation of the offending pamphlet. Stubbs together with his printer and publisher were tried and found guilty of "seditious writing." Elizabeth initially sought the death penalty for all three scoundrels but was persuaded to settle for mutilation. Each man would have his right hand cut off by a cleaver struck with a mallet. Elizabeth pardoned the fortunate printer, but Stubbs and the publisher both underwent the ordeal. On November 3, 1579, Stubbs's right hand was chopped off, but not before he punned, "Pray for me now, for my dismemberment is at hand." After the ordeal, suffering this punishment he removed his hat with his left hand, cried "God Save the Queen," and fainted. He spent the next eighteen months in prison.

*E*lizabeth abandoned the idea of marriage. Alençon was oblivious to a great change in the queen's circumstances and ultimately in England's. She had suddenly lost interest as he stood by, empty-handed. In fact, there was a perfectly good reason she no longer needed to play at romance.

Her ship—*Golden Hind*—had come in. Now she could afford to refuse marriage to the pitiful Alençon and anyone else.

CHAPTER XIII

Return and Reward

*D*rake, for his part, was prepared to deliver a triumphant account of his voyage to his sovereign. There was much to tell and brag about. During his entire circumnavigation with all its natural hazards, not to mention the dangers involved in his pirate raids, he had lost only thirty-seven men, and those who did return were generally in good health. (Magellan, in comparison, lost over two hundred men, nearly his entire crew, and the eighteen survivors of his voyage were gaunt, haggard survivors.) Furthermore, Drake had kept his sturdy flagship, *Golden Hind*, in splendid condition. Her fittings gleamed, and her colorful flags fluttered in the breeze. What could be more pleasing to a queen and a sense of national pride?

More important, Drake's voyage demonstrated a potent idea: England could rule the waves. He had put John Dee's imperialistic theories to the test and found they worked. An empire was there for the taking, and the Spanish were vulnerable, as Drake's raids on their foreign settlements had shown time and again. While the Spanish struggled to overcome habitual indolence and seasickness, Drake had conquered the oceans of the world.

Still, complications abounded. The queen was "in health," he heard aboard ship, "but there was much pestilence in Plymouth." Such infections were unpredictable and deadly. Plague and related contagions were a constant threat. As a result, *Golden Hind* had to delay tying up at home port.

Captain Drake's wife, Mary Newman, arrived in a launch to greet him, accompanied by the mayor, who dispatched a messenger to the queen in London.

There was another anxious interval. Questions abounded. Had Winter, returning first, managed to ruin Drake's reputation? Was Drake, despite all his exploits, in disgrace? If the queen did not acknowledge him, he would have to run the risk of hiding a massive amount of treasure. He drew up alongside tiny St. Nicholas's Island in Plymouth Sound to await word from the queen.

*W*hen it came, the first sign of royal recognition was not at all promising. Drake heard that Her Majesty was embarrassed by his provocations regarding Spain. There was no mention of his three hazardous years at sea, his successful circumnavigation, and the fabulous amount of gold, silver, and gems that he was bringing back to his sovereign, only word that the Spanish ambassador was outraged and seeking compensation for Drake's thievery. The indignant Spanish response was to be expected after all the damage he had done, but the queen's noncommittal attitude was disconcerting. It seemed he had fallen out of favor during his prolonged absence. Perhaps like other explorers he would find himself in disgrace, in prison, or on trial after arriving at home. Perhaps he would have been better off if he had remained among the chattering Miwok, the generous inhabitants of the Moluccas, or the Cimarrons, who looked on him as a leader rather than a liability.

Elizabeth's inexplicable reaction was nothing more than an attempt to mislead the endlessly prying Mendoza and other spies. Soon enough, "The Queen sent him word that he was to go to court and take her some samples of his labours, and that he was to fear nothing. With this he went to court by land, taking certain horses laden with gold or silver. All the rest he left in Plymouth, in custody of one of the principal men there." The town's records, known as the Black Book, after the color of its leather covering, noted that Francis Drake had come home to Plymouth from the "South Sea and Moluccas and was around the world." It noted that he had been away for "two years and three quarters and brought home great store of gold and silver in blocks."

By October 12, the "gold and silver in blocks" that Drake had transported were concealed in a tower near Saltash, guarded around the clock by a detachment of forty men. And what a treasure it was. Drake's ship, *Golden Hind,* returned bearing more of the precious metals than any other vessel during the Age of Discovery. It is difficult to estimate exactly how much, because smugglers set on it the moment she returned. Drake kept an unspecified portion for himself, half belonged to the queen, and the remainder of the treasure was not officially registered. To deflect criticism, Elizabeth declared that Drake was no pirate: he had returned to England empty-handed. No one believed her, least of all the Spanish.

This deception aside, Drake had done little or no actual harm to Spanish subjects. During the entire circumnavigation, he had not killed a single Spaniard, though he had ample opportunity. If he had, those injuries might have aroused more Spanish indignation than his theft, but Drake's humane manner toward his prisoners and victims paid dividends His most notorious act of violence had been toward one of his own, Thomas Doughty, and even that offense was forgotten if not forgiven in the excitement surrounding the value of Drake's haul. Still, one person did remember that infamous act— Doughty's brother John, who had been on the voyage and now lived in Plymouth. He seethed with resentment. Unable to persuade the authorities to try Drake for murder, he complained to everyone, to no avail, calling Drake "the vilest villain, the falsest thief and the crudest murderer that ever was born."

Heedless of this scorn, Drake sailed *Golden Hind* to London in November and unloaded tons of silver for safekeeping at the Tower of London. He conveyed still more booty to an official of the royal treasury; he sent another portion directly to the queen, in residence at Syon House, formerly a luxurious nunnery and now a royal palace on the banks of the Thames. The gifts he bestowed on her personally included a diamond cross and a crown, both fashioned from Peruvian silver and set with emeralds, and he promised more to come.

By now Mendoza had seen through Drake's web of deception and recorded that the red-haired pirate had returned with twenty tons of silver, five boxes of gold in bars a foot and a half long, and countless pearls. The best estimate of the total value of the stolen treasure and spices at that time came to an unheard-of £1,500,000. On October 22, the Queen ordered "our well-beloved Francis Drake" be given another £10,000. His nephew John Drake mentioned that the ship's crew shared £40,000, and the private investors each received double the money they had advanced. News of the payment reached Mendoza and King Philip. If the Englishman had brought nothing of value back to England, as he claimed, why was he being richly rewarded? Why was he always with the queen these days?

*M*endoza and the king were still reluctant to go to war with England even as Mendoza's estimates of Drake's thievery increased. "The plunder is so tremendous," he complained, "and has been seized by the Queen without the intervention of any Minister, Drake having given her £100,000 sterling besides what she has in the Tower, it cannot be believed that she will be contented with arranging with the merchants only, without satisfying your Majesty as well. This is evident, because she thinks, from what I have said, that most of the money belongs to your Majesty's patrimony. My view of the case is strengthened by the fact that, when an English pirate captured an Indian ship with 80,000 crowns in the time of King Edward, they lodged the plunder in the Tower although it was nearly all private property. . . . Restitution was not made until nearly eight years afterwards; and then the restitution was only partial, and was made on the intervention of the Emperor's ambassador here." In other words, the prospects for recovery of the stolen gold looked dim. As a result, "your Majesty's subjects suffer, whereas the English and French go scot free."

Drake, who had set aside plunder beyond Mendoza's reckoning, was not just scot free; he had suddenly become one of the wealthiest men in England. He bought a respectable house in London, in Elbow Lane, so called because it ran west through the City of London and abruptly turned south. He made a habit of appearing at court to visit the queen and bestowing presents, as custom demanded, thus earning more goodwill. At thirty-seven, he appeared destined to play a grand role in English political life. And Elizabeth welcomed him into the fold. In the words of the British naval historian Nicholas A. M. Rodger, she had come to benefit from a situation in which "naval and maritime aggression were becoming identified with a heady combination of patriotism, Protestantism, and private profit." This conviction would motivate Elizabeth and Drake and their successors for centuries to come.

Drake was belatedly recognized as the first English captain to circumnavigate the globe, and the first captain of any nationality to complete a circumnavigation since the arrival of Juan Sebastián Elcano in a battered ship with a skeleton crew in Seville fifty-eight years earlier. The era of Magellan and the Spanish empire was coming to an end; the era of Drake and the British Empire was just beginning.

Queen Elizabeth took extreme measures to conceal word of this geopolitical event. She directed that all accounts of Drake's voyage would belong to the Queen's Secrets of the Realm. Drake, along with the other participants, was sworn to silence on pain of death in order to shield Spain from the specifics of the voyage—the treasure, the navigation route, and Drake's plans.

As expected, Drake gave his queen a jewel to mark the successful circumnavigation. He had found it—more accurately, stolen it—while visiting the Pacific coast of Mexico. It was fit for a queen, fashioned of gold and enamel surrounding a diamond, and it depicted a ship with an ebony hull. The queen in turn honored Drake with a jewel containing her portrait—a lavish gift to confer on a commoner, and one hinting that Drake could expect his status to rise. He is wearing the jewel in a portrait of Drake by Marcus Gheeraerts painted in 1591. The jewel includes an enamel-and-gold case containing a portrait of the queen by Nicholas Hilliard. On the front of the gold case are two cameos in profile, one of an African man superimposed on the profile of a woman who might be Elizabeth. Taken together, the images implied that an alliance between Elizabeth and

Muslims would defeat their mutual enemy, the Spanish, who looked on Drake's success with envy and anxiety. Now the Spanish knew what sort of man they were dealing with in Francis Drake. He was ruthless, violent, and beholden to no one except, perhaps, Queen Elizabeth, the beguiling arch-heretic.

Sic Parvis Magna, "Greatness from Small Beginnings":
Drake depicted with this new heraldry and motto
(National Portrait Gallery, London)

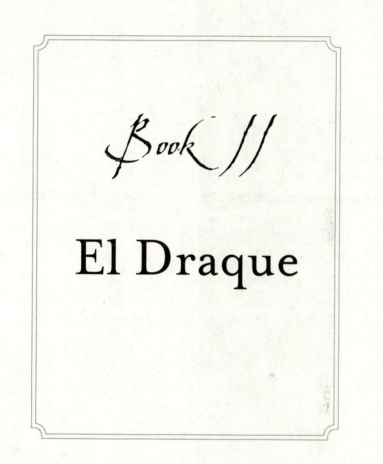

Book II

El Draque

CHAPTER XIV

The Dragon Arrives

Bernardino de Mendoza, the Spanish diplomat turned spy, wrote to King Philip in a state of shock. "I have taken care to announce that Drake's plunder exceeds a million and a half [pounds], and the news has spread all over England, giving rise to much searching of the spirit, as they think that the affair is so enormous that it will lead to a perpetual war between the Queen and your Majesty unless she makes restitution." A million and a half pounds could sustain England for years. Without it, Elizabeth would not have survived much longer. England was perpetually on the brink of being swallowed up by the Spanish. In that event, which seemed all too likely, Spain would annex the island nation, and the Protestant revolution would founder.

Now everything was different, thanks to the gold and silver captured by Drake. Even English government officials were alarmed by the unexpected change in the status quo. "In view also of the greatness of the plunder, the Councilors who are not concerned in the enterprise have become jealous that the others should enjoy the profit and are condemning the matter greatly to the Queen."

The turmoil spilled over into France. "When the Queen saw the French ambassador lately she received him very brusquely, and told him that her ambassador wrote that he saw no means of bringing about a pacification in France, such as he, the French ambassador, had always assured her would take place, which she said she could not help looking upon with suspicion." Mendoza decided he would capitalize on the situation to Spain's advantage. "In order to increase her distrust," he wrote to King Philip, "caused by the rumors that the king of France is arranging with your Majesty, I am treating the French ambassador with more cordiality than usual, inviting him to my house and the like, which arouses great suspicion in the Queen's mind." The shifting alliance threatened to spread to Ireland and Scotland, where Catholics abounded. In the last six weeks alone, "five hundred English gentlemen have been imprisoned here on the charge of being Catholics, there being fears that they might rise in consequence of the news from Ireland."

*D*ays later, on October 30, Mendoza was bursting with developments sure to alarm Spain. "The Queen has ordered Drake to return to Plymouth to bring back the boxes of gold and silver which he had delivered to the Governor of that town. Notwithstanding the declaration, which I mentioned in my last, that Drake had done no damage to your Majesty's subjects, they confess that he has brought twenty English tons of silver, of 2,000 pounds each, and five boxes of gold a foot and a half long, besides a large quantity of pearls, some of great value. According to advices sent from Seville he has even stolen more than this. The Queen has decided that the shareholders in the enterprise shall receive as much again as they invested, and that the rest of the plunder shall be deposited in the Tower of London."

These were crucial findings, and the sheer numbers, though rough calculations at this point, defied credulity. Drake could not have brought back twenty *tons* of silver, could he? He had. All these boxes of gold and silver—*Spanish* gold, and *Spanish* silver—were now in English hands. Even more infuriating, they proved that Elizabeth had been falsely protesting her innocence when she had been in league with Drake all along. Mendoza railed against the pirate, but it was too late.

At the same time, Spain had done little to shore up its defenses against Drake and other pirates. Cannon were installed in Spanish ports to guard against invaders from the sea. They remained unattended and cold. King Philip had dispatched the Spanish explorer Sarmiento de Gamboa in 1579 to track down Drake, but it was too late, the pirate had already escaped into the Pacific, where it was unlikely that anyone could find him. De Gamboa consoled himself by traveling through the entire Strait of Magellan from west to east, a feat to be reckoned with, and returning to Spain. Although Spain tightened its convoy system to protect the ships of the treasure fleet, anything north of Panama remained vulnerable. The western coast of Mexico lacked a single Spanish cannon. Plans for a fort to be constructed at Acapulco to deter pirates and protect Spanish assets were endlessly discussed, but nothing was built. Millions of pesos mined or stolen by Spain were at risk, on which Drake and his successors feasted. Spain had more success defending its interests in the Caribbean, but the Spanish empire had become too big and unwieldy to protect against determined rivals—especially England.

Elizabeth, for her part, intended to keep the wealth Drake had stolen from Spain (and which Spain had stolen from indigenous peoples across the Americas). Restitution was out of the question. The plunder was necessary for the survival of England and, just as important, her throne.

After Drake had landed, Mendoza furiously wrote to the King of Spain on October 16, 1580, "He came hither to see the Queen, and I am assured that he was with her for more than six hours"—*six hours!* "The only members present were Lord Burleigh, [the Earl of] Sussex, the Admiral, James Crofts, the Controller, and Secretary Wilson. They ordered a letter to be written to the effect that all the money was to be registered and handed over to the Queen's possession in the Tower of London."

Mendoza fretted about the possibility that Drake had completed a circumnavigation. "They are very particular not to divulge the route by which Drake returned." He estimated that the English pirate had returned with forty-five crew members, and "the Queen orders that these men are to be taken much care of, and not to be allowed to make themselves ill by eating too much. They are not to disclose the route they took, on pain of death."

Mendoza's summary contained a semblance of the truth, with the notable exception of the assertion that Drake "must have returned by the Strait of Magellan, as he went." In that case, there would have been no circumnavigation, just a round-trip raiding expedition. Mendoza had "sent men to Plymouth to discover the particulars from the men who went on the voyage." Once they did, they would know the truth, which he promised to report faithfully to the king.

Mendoza was still trying to discredit Drake, claiming to the king that El Draque was not the masterly navigator he seemed, even if he had completed a circumnavigation. "Drake asserts that had it not been for two Portuguese pilots, whom he took from one of the ships he plundered and sunk on the coast of Brazil on his way out, he could never have made the voyage. He has given the Queen a diary of everything that happened during the three years he was away, and very long letter about it."

In this terrible state of affairs (from Spain's point of view), "orders should be given that no foreign ship should be spared, in either the Spanish or Portuguese Indies, but that every one should be sent to the bottom, and not soul on board of them allowed to live," wrote Mendoza from London on October 15, 1580. "This will be the only way to prevent the English and French from going to those parts to plunder, for at present there is hardly an Englishman who is not talking of undertaking the voyage, so encouraged are they by Drake's return."

Amid the uproar, Mendoza could not bring himself to admit to his king and perhaps even to himself that Drake had, in fact, completed his circumnavigation.

Drake's confidential meeting with the queen drew attention to his voyage rather than deflecting it. It was a rare adviser who enjoyed such unrestricted access to Elizabeth. The extent of the voyage became an open secret at court, even though the public was still unaware of Drake's accomplishment. The diary of the voyage that Mendoza mentioned—Drake's personal account of the circumnavigation—was irretrievably lost along with whatever secrets and surprises he had confided in its pages. But the treasure remained, along with an immense sense of relief.

Without realizing it, Drake—or rather, the gold, silver, and gems he brought back—had saved Elizabeth from a disastrous marriage, which meant they had saved her throne. If he had returned later, everything might have turned out differently. She might well have married Alençon, who was Catholic, and compromised England's autonomy. King Philip and the pope both would have been delighted. England would have been within their reach. The Protestant rebellion led by Elizabeth would have withered. Instead, Elizabeth kept her throne, and England continued on the course she had set, a course that would ultimately lead to empire. This was Drake's accidental contribution to the idea of Great Britain. He had merely been trying to get rich through piracy, but he could not stop himself from pursuing the glory that came with it. And by doing this in the name of the queen, the effort took on a new dimension, that of preserving queen and country, which, without Drake, might well have disappeared into a Spanish purgatory.

The immediate question was what to do with Drake's spoils. Rumors about its existence were spreading, and there was too much to conceal easily. It could not simply be buried like some pirate's chest in the traditional English fashion. Elizabeth's advisers drafted a letter declaring that "all the money was to be registered and handed over to the Queen's possession in the Tower of London." That appeared to conclude the matter on a defiant note, but Elizabeth, cautious as always, refused to sign the order and urged instead that they disseminate a misleading rumor that "Drake had not brought much money."

Elizabeth moved to safeguard Drake's achievement. She made her inner circle promise to keep her pirate's route secret, in case he had violated international law by sailing through Portuguese waters (he had), or visited lands claimed by the Portuguese (again, he had), or stolen Spanish treasure (he had done that as well).

For now, the queen's bankers were busy counting the fortune she claimed did not exist. The treasure was all the more precious because Elizabethan England, like other European countries, had no paper money or centralized banking system. The Bank of England would not come into existence for another two hundred years. Silver, gold, and gems were what mattered, and English commerce relied heavily on the caprice of the merchants and pirates who supplied them.

By October, an agitated Mendoza wrote to King Philip to discuss Elizabeth's reaction to the controversy over Drake's stolen treasure.

To counteract his credibility, Elizabeth dispatched two Secretaries of
the Council to put him on notice: "They came to tell me that she
had heard that I was talking about Drake's arrival, complaining of
his proceedings and the reception accorded to him here, which I had
no right to do," Mendoza wrote to his king. "She had made careful
inquiry into the details of his voyage and found that he had done no
damage to your Majesty's subjects nor in your dominions. If that
were the case, she would take care that justice was done."

There was more: a scolding from the queen. "She said that I was
not to be annoyed at her not giving me audience, because until she
elucidated the Irish business [concerning a possible insurrection],
she would not receive me as minister from your Majesty but would
perhaps send special envoy of her own." In their combative relationship, a certain redheaded captain proved the most contentious
element of all. "With regard to Drake, I replied that, in consideration of my desire to serve her, felt sorry that she should send me
a message which the many documents and proofs in my possession
contradicted."

To this end, "I showed them some of the evidence I had against
him, consisting of documents sent to me by the consulate of merchants in Seville, particularly one statement of a sum of 385,000
dollars taken from a ship called the Master of St. John, besides the
robberies, insults, and murders that the man Drake had committed
in the same sea, and other places belonging to your Majesty, burning
ships and cutting the rigging and gear of others to prevent pursuit.
These things, I said, I would leave to her judgment, and whether she
ought not to fitly punish them. Your Majesty had great reason to
take offence at them, particularly as the man had stolen a million
and a half of money, which was no small sum."

Mendoza concluded the confrontation on a note of defiance. "I thanked her for the great honour she was willing to extend to me in allowing me, as Don Bernardino, to kiss her hand, and I regretted exceedingly not being able to do so."

King Philip agreed wholeheartedly with his spy's maneuvers. "Proceed with all diligence and promptitude," he ordered on November 14, "in order to recover the booty and punish the corsair," in other words, the pirate Drake. "Do not fail to point out the outrageous nature of the case."

$\mathcal{D}$rake's voyage continued to send ripples of dread through Spain, which in turn threatened England with revenge, as Mendoza explained to King Philip on October 23, 1580: "Leicester sent a secretary of his to say that my talk about Drake's robberies was causing much fear amongst the merchants that your Majesty would declare war, about and this would oblige the Queen to send all her ships to sea and raise troops."

Mendoza's anxiety spiked in November when an informant provided a rough estimate of the amount of wealth Drake had brought back, beginning with weaponry. "He captured . . . about 140 pieces of bronze artillery, some very good and large, and a number of iron pieces as well; some 16,000 or 18,000 ducados' worth of pearls, a little more than 150,000 ducados of gold and silver, and some goods that he took in Santo Domingo. He lost more than 800 men on the voyage."

None of these figures bore much resemblance to reality, nor did his assumption that Drake had failed to return his investors' money. "Not a single real has been given to anyone except the soldiers." Or so Mendoza stated. Without proof, he claimed this shortfall led to rioting, but he truthfully reported that the "rest of the proceeds were placed in the castle," referring to the Tower of London. Mixing

Francis Drake on the eve of the circumnavigation that
would change the course of European history.
INCAMERASTOCK / ALAMY STOCK PHOTO

The symbolic "phoenix" portrait of Elizabeth I, circa 1575, when she was in the middle of her long reign, attributed to Nicholas Hilliard. She considered the phoenix a symbol of virginity and rebirth.
© NATIONAL PORTRAIT GALLERY, LONDON

John Dee, the influential mathematician and magician, appears before the queen and members of her court in this nineteenth-century painting. Dee advanced the idea of a "British Empire."
WELLCOME COLLECTION. ATTRIBUTION 4.0 INTERNATIONAL (CC BY 4.0)

Charred fragment of a letter proposing a circumnavigation,
1577. It was probably written by Sir Francis Walsingham,
Queen Elizabeth's principal secretary and spymaster.

Theodor de Bry, a Flemish-German engraver, produced popular images of the New World, including this impression of Francis Drake and his men surrounded by indigenous people.

A page from Francis Fletcher's journal of Drake's circumnavigation with a drawing and a description of a South American seal glimpsed in 1578.

Dodd delin.

Goldar sculp.

Mr. Doughty beheaded by
order of Sir Francis Drake,
at Port St. Julian, on the Coast
of PATAGONIA.

Published by Alexr. Hogg, No. 16 Paternoster Row, London.

"Mr. Doughty beheaded by order of Sir Francis Drake." The gruesome execution occurred in Patagonia, not far from the spot where Ferdinand Magellan had erected gallows to punish a traitor on his circumnavigation fifty-eight years earlier.

Drake's landing in California depicted in an engraving published in 1590 by Theodor de Bry. At the extreme right, an overwrought indigenous woman tears at her face, as Francis Fletcher described in his journal.

Francis Drake "receiving the homage and regalia of the King of New Albion." The Miwok people of the Northwest wished Drake to become their leader, but he declined. "Albion" is a ceremonial term for England.

Drake's sturdy *Golden Hind* arrives in Ternate, Indonesia, in 1579, near the end of his circumnavigation, as portrayed in this nineteenth-century engraving.
PHOTO © CHRIS HELLIER / BRIDGEMAN IMAGES

Drake appears before the sultan on Ternate in the Moluccas in this illustration by Theodor de Bry. In reality, his reception was cool.
ARTEFACT / ALAMY STOCK PHOTO

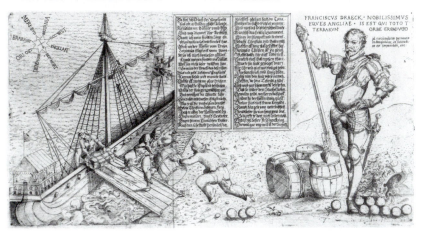

Sailors arduously pack *Golden Hind* with supplies.
PRIVATE COLLECTION / BRIDGEMAN IMAGES

Queen Elizabeth knights Drake on the deck of *Golden Hind*, April 4, 1581. In reality, she arranged for a visiting French ambassador to take over at the last minute to avoid provoking rival Spain. NATIONAL GEOGRAPHIC IMAGE COLLECTION / ALAMY STOCK PHOTO

Buckland Abbey. A former Cistercian monastery constructed in the late thirteenth century, it was seized by Henry VIII and sold to Sir Richard Grenville the Elder, who converted it to a grand residence. Once Drake was knighted, he was able to purchase it, and he lived there with his second wife, Elizabeth Sydenham. Despite his apparent affection for this status symbol, Drake preferred life at sea. BEN BENDER / CC BY-SA 3.0 <HTTPS://CREATIVECOMMONS.ORG/LICENSES/BY-SA/3.0>, VIA WIKIMEDIA COMMONS

Elizabeth Sydenham, Lady Drake, at the time of her marriage to the explorer, in a painting by George Gower, 1585. Drake was by then among the wealthiest people in England. PRIVATE COLLECTION / BRIDGEMAN IMAGES

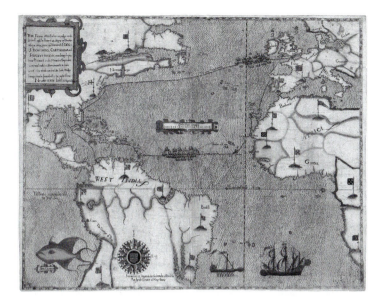

A map of Drake's West Indian voyage, 1585–86. With a fleet
consisting of seven large and twenty-two smaller vessels,
Drake plundered Santiago in the Cape Verde islands,
then crossed the Atlantic to pillage Santo Domingo (now
the capital of the Dominican Republic). The flotilla later
reached the Florida coast, laying waste to St. Augustine,
founded by the Spanish twenty years earlier.

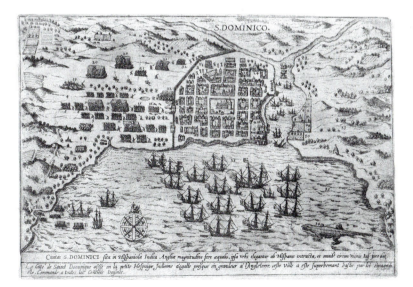

Drake's plan of attack on Santo Domingo.

Philip II (1527–1598), King of Spain, King of Portugal, King of Naples and Sicily, and *jure uxoris* king of England and Ireland. He was also Duke of Milan and lord of the Seventeen Provinces of the Netherlands. Drake was his nemesis.

In April 1587, Sir Francis Drake laid siege to the harbor
of Cádiz for three days, delaying the sailing of the Spanish
Armada by a year. Francisco de Zurbarán's "The Attack on
Cádiz" emphasizes the vast scale of the assault.

Sir Francis Walsingham, secretary of state and spymaster general. He labored long and hard for Queen Elizabeth and died in debt. Portrait by John de Critz.

John Hawkins, Drake's cousin and mentor. He introduced the young Drake to slave trading and later participated in the Battle of the Spanish Armada.

Charles Howard, Second Baron Effingham. He led the English fleet in the Battle of the Spanish Armada. Although he epitomized the desk admiral, he and Drake formed a successful partnership at a time of crisis.

The Spanish Armada menaces England's southern coast, 1588.
HIP / ART RESOURCE, NY

Pedro de Valdes, admiral of *Nuestra Señora del Rosario*,
formally surrenders to Francis Drake aboard HMS
Revenge in the English Channel in August 1588.
THE BOX, PLYMOUTH

The defeat of the Spanish Armada in August 1588 by
Philippe-Jacques de Loutherbourg (1796).

Map of the British Isles showing the circuitous
route taken by the Spanish Armada, 1588.

The "Armada Portrait" of Elizabeth I by George Gower, 1588.
The queen is surrounded by scenes from the Battle of the Spanish
Armada, and her hand rests regally and possessively on the globe.
People familiar with her appearance at the time concluded that
someone younger, perhaps a chambermaid, had posed for it.

AKG-IMAGES

Sir Francis Drake by Marcus Gheeraerts, 1591. Even after all his accomplishments, Drake was still fighting for his place in the official chronicles of the era. Not until 1599 were his achievements made public.

FUNERAL OF SIR FRANCIS DRAKE, 1595.

The funeral of Francis Drake on January 27, 1596. Drake died of dysentery near Portobelo Harbor, Panama. When he realized he was near death, he asked to be dressed in his armor and buried on land. Instead, he was buried at sea in a lead coffin.

spite and hope, he predicted, "Everything has turned out so badly for them that one can guess they will not return to the Indies to sack towns." This guess of Mendoza's was as worthless as his others. In reality, Drake had turned a fantastic profit for his investors, more than 100 percent, more than 1,000 percent, closer to 5,000 percent. All of that in addition to the successful completion of the first English circumnavigation.

Despite its unprecedented success, Drake's expedition remained in danger of being forgotten so long as Elizabeth and her advisers kept it secret. Only a select few were aware of the magnitude of its achievements and its implications for Elizabeth and for England. In the Age of Discovery, many voyages were shipwrecked, sank, wandered off course, and were never heard from again. Drake appeared destined for a similar fate. His principal achievement, from the Crown's point of view, was the treasure he brought back—treasure that no one was to know about. Little was said of the navigational feats he had accomplished, or of his deftness, resourcefulness, and bravado in raiding Spanish ships and towns, facing down storms, and outlasting starvation. His ability to outdo Magellan went unremarked.

Drake, of course, was keenly aware of the importance of his accomplishment. He expected more than a purely material reward in return for all he had risked on behalf of queen and kingdom. He wanted the status that could only come with knighthood: a serious matter in Elizabeth's era. In general, knighthood was conferred on those who glorified the Crown through military service, and Drake certainly thought he qualified for the honor. But matters were more complicated than Drake's wishes.

To confer knighthood on Drake, Elizabeth risked inflaming the

Spanish, whom he had repeatedly and happily humiliated. Fortunately for Drake, she thought of a solution.

On April 4, 1581, almost seven months after his return, she strode onto the deck of the *Golden Hind* at Deptford to join her pirate captain. In his *Environs of London, Being an Historical Tour of the Towns, Villages, and Hamlets within Twelve Miles of that Capital,* Daniel Lysons recorded, "Queen Elizabeth visited Captain Drake's ship, called the *Golden Hind*. Her Majesty dined on board, and after dinner conferred the honour of knighthood on the captain. A prodigious concourse of people assembled on the occasion, and a wooden bridge, on which were a hundred persons, broke down, but no lives were lost."

On the advice of her councilors, the Queen brought along several French commissioners to create the impression that France, with whom England had formed a defensive alliance, lent its wholehearted support to the ceremony. The participants indulged in an opulent banquet while several Miwok warriors apparently imported by Drake from California performed stirring dances for Elizabeth. After the spectacle concluded, Drake described the marvels of the voyage for the queen during a tour of his ship, boasting that King Philip of Spain had demanded his death. In his telling, the circumnavigation was more of a piratical caper designed to embarrass Spain than a great voyage of discovery. When he finished his account, Elizabeth produced her ceremonial sword, waved it about, and playfully said that she would "strike off [Drake's] head."

The moment Elizabeth was supposed to knight Drake did not unfold as recounted in popular legend, with Drake bowing to his queen on the deck of *Golden Hind*. In reality, she handed the ceremonial sword to a French envoy, the Seigneur de Marchaumont, to perform the deed. With this last-minute feint, she still hoped to avoid or at least deflect Spanish fury for elevating Drake to knighthood. And more than that, de Marchaumont was in England to negotiate the marriage between the sovereign and the Duke of Alençon. If not for the vain hope of uniting these two kingdoms, it is unlikely that Marchaumont would have agreed to perform the assignment.

Bloated with feasting, the captain lowered his barrel-chested frame onto the deck in front of the French envoy as Elizabeth looked on, smiling with approval. When the sword, held by de Marchaumont, tapped Drake on both shoulders, Elizabeth's purple-and-gold garter fell down her leg. As she stooped to adjust this intimate accessory, the French envoy begged to "capture" the garment and give it to a French dignitary who would certainly treasure it, but Elizabeth coquettishly explained that she had "nothing else to keep her stocking up." With that, the red-haired pirate became *Sir* Francis Drake.

*O*n April 6, Mendoza reported the entire occasion to Philip in terms calculated to infuriate the king. He told of Drake's attending a "grand banquet" with the queen, "finer than has ever been seen in England since the time of King Henry." There was no question that he enjoyed her special favor. Mendoza continued, "Drake, therefore, has the title of 'Sir' in consideration of the lands he has purchased, and he gave her a large silver coffer, and a frog"—everyone was bestowing images of frogs on the queen at the time to propitiate her courtship with Alençon—"made of diamonds, distributing 1,200 crowns amongst the Queen's officers."

Perhaps this scene, at least as Mendoza recounted it, would motivate Spain to go to war at last. He went so far as to prescribe a military strategy for confronting Elizabeth. If she did not return Drake's plunder, the king should "order the arrest of all English goods." Otherwise, if Elizabeth were allowed to hold it, "she may keep your Majesty at war for two or three years." And in the ensuing peace, he predicted, "all she has done against you will be forgotten." But if she did not have the resources to make war on Spain, "her offenses against you cannot be passed over."

Yet the king avoided the issue; he begged for wheat, not war. "If you can induce the English merchants to send some cargoes thither they shall be welcome and well-treated," he told his ambassador, adding, "do not ask the Queen, but treat only with the merchants." It sounded as though Elizabeth had succeeded in intimidating King Philip, ruler of the most powerful empire in Europe.

Sir Francis Drake appropriated the coat of arms of the early Devon family of Drake of Ash, claiming that he was related to them. In the medieval idiom of "blazoning" heraldry, the arms were described as "Argent, a wyvern"—a two-legged dragon—"Wings displayed and tail nowed," or knotted. (This figure is on page xxii.) The crest was described as "a Dexter arm Proper grasping a battle axe Sable, headed Argent." It was an impressive figure, but some Devonians did not consider the upstart Drake entitled to these armorials. Sir Bernard Drake, who might have been related, was said to have disputed Francis Drake's right to kinship, and when the two confronted one another at court, Sir Bernard "boxed the ear," that is, smacked the arriviste.

At this point, Queen Elizabeth interceded to give Sir Francis a unique coat of arms with a nautical motif: "Sable a fess wavy between two pole-stars argent," referring to the Arctic and Antarctic, along with "a ship on a globe under ruff, held by a cable with a hand out of the clouds." A motto appeared over all: *Sic Parvis Magna*— "Thus great things out of small things come." There was also reference to the "wyvern gules" of Sir Bernard, but it was too late for him to complain.

Although Elizabeth was quick to hail the wealth he brought with him, all of it stolen, Drake's legacy was not immediately apparent. The most ambitious interpretation was that it marked the end of the Spanish empire and the beginning of the British Empire, but it would take years for England to make good on its claim to the high seas.

Soon others were vying to snatch the laurel wreath from Drake's head. Two years after his return, Martín Ignacio de Loyola, a grand-nephew of St. Ignatius Loyola, commenced a circumnavigation going in a westerly direction, completing it in 1584. The following year, he undertook a second circumnavigation, this one in an easterly direction. This globe-trotting priest is considered the most widely traveled person of the century. Then, in 1586, Sir Thomas Cavendish, known as "the Navigator," commenced his circumnavigation, patterned after both Magellan and Drake. He arrived at Plymouth two years later, and soon set off on another circumnavigation, only to die in remote Ascension Island in 1592 at the age of thirty-one. As one attempt to imitate Drake's triumph came to grief, John Dee's vision of a British Empire girdling the globe remained more of an aspiration than a reality.

*D*rake turned his attention to the purchase of a country house that reflected his elevated wealth and status. This was a former monastery, Buckland Abbey, owned by Sir Richard Grenville. It was drafty and gloomy, built to shelter monks in austerity rather than royalty in luxury, but it had an interesting pedigree that might have appealed to its new owner. Established in 1278, it served as a Cistercian abbey (the Cistercians were an offshoot of the Benedictines) until Henry VIII ordered the dissolution of all monasteries, whereupon he sold it to Sir Richard Grenville the Elder, a poet and soldier, who with his son reconfigured the abbey as a residential castle. A grandson, also named Richard Grenville, oversaw the final stages of the conversion in 1576.

The cost of the land, buildings, farm equipment, and other items came to £3,400. The transaction was approved on December 1, and the terms specified that it be purchased by a knight, in this case, Sir Francis Drake. (Mendoza, tracking Drake's every move, conveyed the matter to King Philip to illustrate how high Drake had risen.) The terms of the agreement permitted Drake to hold Buckland Abbey for three years, after which time he could sell it back to Grenville for the amount he had paid for it, but Drake had no intention of surrendering this status symbol. Its most impressive feature was the church, already transformed into a three-story dwelling before Drake moved in. His taking possession of the manor was celebrated with a dinner held by the town of Plymouth at a cost of £10.

In pursuit of enhanced status, Drake commissioned formal portraits. Nicholas Hilliard, who might have been a relative, painted a miniature. Jodocus Hondius also contributed a likeness of Drake. Although it showed only Drake's head and torso at age forty-three, it suggests how dramatically he had aged in the six years since the circumnavigation. He has put on a good deal of weight, and his face shows the effects of age. This is no longer the "robust" Drake, the circumnavigator and pirate, but the well-fed knight and man of property. He had become, in the words of one acquaintance, "more fat than thin." As testimony to his hazardous exploits in distant lands, he bore scars on his right cheek and right leg, but his gait was normal. He had been elected mayor of Plymouth in 1581, but in his official capacity, he was all but invisible. The Black Book, the ledger of public events in Plymouth, scarcely mentioned the famous mayor's deeds. Drake was more interested in real estate. He paid his uncle William Hawkins £1,500 for forty parcels of land, along with other investments. He became one of the major landholders in the area, possessing houses, warehouses, a bakery, two stables, and four gardens.

He had everything a gentleman required except an heir. Drake is not known to have fathered a child, at least not in England. If he did so during his career at sea, no official record survives. Drake's wife, Mary Newman Drake, who had seen him rise from a seaman, slaver, and pirate to a gentleman, died on January 25, 1583, after twelve years of marriage. She was buried at Saint Andrews and noted in the register as "The Lady Marie the wiffe of Sir Frauncis Drake knight." There would be no issue, and no Drake dynasty, despite the impressive trappings.

A favorite son of Plymouth, Sir Francis had few enemies—with the conspicuous exception of John Doughty, the brother of Thomas Doughty, Drake's maritime nemesis. John Doughty was engaged in a long-running, solitary campaign to arrest and try Drake for murder.

At the same time, a Spanish spy, Pedro de Zubiaur, pursued Drake's fortune, only to be jailed. He was working in tandem with an English merchant named Patrick Mason, who possessed documents claiming King Philip promised a reward of seventy thousand ducats in exchange for the head of El Draque. One of these two coconspirators tried to involve John Doughty in their scheme. As a result, he was also confined to prison. Arrested as a spy, Mason was questioned on May 15, 1582, about his knowledge of Spanish plots against the realm in general and Drake in particular.

At first, he denied any involvement. The interrogators were not satisfied, so they questioned Mason again, this time under torture. Now Mason admitted that he had conspired with de Zubiaur. Doughty was confined to Marshalsea prison in late 1583, and there is no report of his ever being released.

For his part, Drake had narrowly escaped the consequences of his treatment of Doughty. Had he not brought back so great a fortune, he might have languished in jail for executing a nobleman, just as John Doughty wished. Samuel Johnson, the critic, biographer, and lexicographer, looking back on the incident from his vantage point in the eighteenth century, remained distrustful of Drake's conduct in the Doughty affair. "How far is it probable . . . that Doughty, who is represented as a man of eminent abilities, should engage in so long and hazardous a voyage other than that of defeating it, is left to the determination of the reader." This remained a minority opinion. Instead, Elizabeth set the tone by looking the other way, and her favorite explorer of the moment got away with murder.

Against this background of intrigue, there was no public celebration of Drake's return, because, as Elizabeth saw things, there was no good reason to provoke King Philip. Instead, Drake's share of the plunder remained under guard in Plymouth. He quietly informed Elizabeth and the other investors of the profit earned by the voyage, now calculated at an astronomical £47 for each £1 invested.

The English public still knew very little of Drake's extraordinary feat of navigation. It would be nine years until a generally available published account appeared, thanks to the persistence of Richard Hakluyt, a young, Oxford-educated historian of Welsh extraction. At the time of the Spanish Armada, Hakluyt, a chaplain assigned to the English embassy in Paris, was busy accompanying Lord Howard's sister during her journey back to England.

In France, he had heard the locals' unflattering comments about England's lack of daring when it came to the exploration of the seas. Hakluyt knew their assumptions were based on ignorance, and he vowed to "stop the mouths of the reproachers" by assembling a massive archive of "the maritime records of our own men, which are hitherto buried in the dust." Hakluyt took it as an article of faith that English navigators and explorers were not the last but first among their European competitors, and he planned to chronicle a century of English maritime achievement in a multivolume work, *The Principal Voyages, Traffics, and Discoveries of the English Nation*, drawing on his extensive personal contacts, and he published the result in 1589.

Hakluyt placed heavy emphasis on English voyages going back to the legendary King Arthur to illustrate that England had always been a seafaring nation, "searching the most opposite corners and quarters of the world." To buttress his case for England's primacy, he omitted essential navigators such as Columbus, Magellan, and Vasco de Gama, all foreigners, and he included secondary figures such as Frobisher and Hawkins and Gilbert, all English.

Hakluyt intended to include Francis Drake in this catalog, or, as he put it, he had "taken more than ordinary pains, meaning to have it inserted in his work, but . . . I have yielded unto those my friends which pressed me in the matter." This artful disclaimer was taken to mean that Drake intended to publish his own account first, and Hakluyt therefore withheld his chapters about Drake's circumnavigation. On closer examination, his language implies that he was pressured to exclude it because the details remained a state secret and publishing them could put national security at risk. As a result, Drake's accomplishment was omitted from the 1589 edition, and his reputation in the world at large languished a while longer. Perhaps Queen Elizabeth censored it to prevent others from stealing information that Drake had risked his life and the Crown's prestige to obtain. Or perhaps the publication of a fuller account would again aggravate King Philip, who would again try to make England pay for this accomplishment in blood. In any case, it would be another ten years until the details of Drake's circumnavigation became public knowledge. Finally, in 1599, Hakluyt published a massive expanded edition, which attracted wide notice, in part because Queen Elizabeth herself was said to have read it.

To set the seal on the accomplishments of Drake and others, Hakluyt included a map by a well-known cartographer, Edward Wright, who had studied with John Dee. Wright's innovative depiction showed the lines of latitude and longitude on a level surface and as such became one of the most celebrated English maps of the sixteenth century. Wright placed England at the center, and the positioning demonstrated that nearly every part of the globe was reachable from England over water. No longer was England seen as an isolated, backward island nation peopled by infidel savages (as some shipwrecked Spanish sailors might have said). Instead, it occupied a crucial position in global affairs. It was a cradle of empire. Wright's map showed how profoundly Drake's voyages had altered the world's perception of England, and England's perception of itself. It bore out John Dee's boast that England was "by reason of situation, most commodious for navigation, to places most famous and rich." The emerging British Empire would be unequaled—even by Spain.

Drake was England's best naval warrior. In light of these superlatives, the question became, what would be his next expedition?

At court, Sir Francis Walsingham, a devout Protestant, secretary to Elizabeth, and spymaster, tried to interest Drake in a plan to launch an English equivalent to Spain's Casa de Contratación to administer distant colonies. Drake would serve as governor and retain 10 percent of the profits: a royal road to riches. It was subject to the shifting strategic goals of Elizabeth, who was reluctant to antagonize Portugal. After all this time, England's navy remained minuscule in comparison to Spain's, and the project lost momentum,

only to be succeeded by an unlikely partnership with Portugal called
First Enterprise, based on Terceira, an island in the Azores. Drake
would command a fleet, Portugal would pay for part of the costs, and
these privileged privateers would prowl the sea. Once again Elizabeth changed her mind, sowing dissension among the would-be pirates and alienating Portugal. A Second Enterprise, backed in part by
Drake, commenced in May 1582, but quickly came to grief.

Matters for Drake grew even more desperate when John Drake,
Francis's young nephew, was captured in Buenos Aires, transported
to Lima, and imprisoned by the unforgiving Inquisition, which continued as virulent as ever. After disavowing Lutheranism, being
forced to wear a yellow sanbenito, and marching in an auto-da-fé,
he was sentenced to spend the rest of his life in Spanish territory.
The forced exile was a humiliating destiny for a close relative of the
despised Lutheran, *El Draque*.

*O*n Christmas Day, 1581, Mendoza wrote an account of Alençon's
taking leave of Elizabeth, and it cast the odd romance in a different
light. "Although she displayed grief publicly at his departure, I understand that in her own chamber she danced for very joy at getting
rid of him." But the potential union was too fraught to be undone at
a stroke, and foul weather delayed his humiliating departure from
England.

Mendoza, closely following events, reported to King Philip that
Alençon felt "hurt that she had been so ready to let him go, knowing
as she must how attached he was to her," but it was obvious to all
that she cared little for him, since she was prepared to dispatch him
"in public disgrace."

On learning of this complaint, Elizabeth launched into a lengthy
self-defense, which Mendoza considered the height of insincerity,

explaining that she was only letting go of Alençon for his own sake, not for hers. In fact, she insincerely claimed to consider his departure "unnecessarily hasty."

The duke replied, "No, no, Madam, you are mine, as I can prove by letters and words you have written to me." Her true feelings for him were "confirmed by the gift of the ring, of which I have sent to the King my brother, my mother, and the Princes of France, all those who were present at our interviews being ready to bear testimony." He hardened his position: "If I cannot get you for my wife by fair means and affection I must do so by force, for I will not leave this country without you."

Elizabeth shot back that she would not be intimidated by his threats. She knew her own mind and what she had written to him better than anyone else, "and as for the ring, it was only a pledge of perpetual friendship and of a conditional contract," contingent on the duke's brother agreeing to it. She was quite certain he never would. In case Alençon's feelings had been clouded by sentiment, this display stopped him in his tracks. Elizabeth might be confused on occasion, or at least act confused, but she could also be dangerous. She backed away from marriage as if it were a noose tightening around her neck. In fact, she claimed to be "entirely free of any matrimonial engagements" and intended to stay that way until she overcame her "natural hatred of marriage"—a remote possibility at best. Having made herself clear, she permitted him to remain in England for a time "as her brother and friend, for mutual companionship, but not as her husband." She sweetened the offer with the promise of funds.

Afterward, William Cecil, Lord Burghley, was assigned to negotiate how much it would take to persuade the unlucky suitor to depart. Still Alençon remained, and according to Elizabeth, he asked her to fund a war in Flanders against Catholics that he claimed he was fighting for her sake. And if she was not interested in that project, she should, at the very least, compensate him for "refusing to marry him." Trying to rid herself of this embarrassing matter, she offered a monthly stipend, and "this has so much brightened him up that you would not know him." But that would not be the end of the affair, at least not in her mind. "As soon as he is across the sea," she said, "I will assure him that my Council will not agree to the arrangement" because "the people will not allow it."

Eavesdropping, Mendoza took her comments to mean that Alençon's true purpose was not to marry the queen, but to extort so much money that England would be weakened. Marriage was merely a means to a darker purpose. Learning about these machinations, Cecil replied that his queen should give the duke only a little money in that case, and the problem resolved itself in spirited laughter among the queen and her advisers, who derided Alençon as "a fine gallant to sell his lady for money." (In Elizabethan usage, a "gallant" suggested a stud.)

After all these negotiations, Alençon still refused to leave. He was pathetic, menacing, and laughable all at once. Elizabeth, her advisers, and the duke continued to bicker over the terms of his departure as 1581 drew to a close. They resorted to persuading him that he should depart before New Year's Day; otherwise, he would have to give the queen expensive presents "according to the custom of the country." The time was drawing nigh. Alençon's ships were readied and brought to the mouth of the Thames to carry him away "almost dead against the wind." It was a cold wind in all senses of the word. Finally, he departed in February 1582. Elizabeth tried to soften the blow by writing a decorous poem expressing her regret concerning the affair:

I grieve and dare not show my discontent;
I love, and yet am forced to seem to hate;
I do, yet dare not say I ever meant;
I seem stark mute, but inwardly do prate.
I am, and not; I freeze and yet am burned,
Since from myself another self I turned.

Alençon returned to the continent and died of malaria two years later. He was twenty-nine years old.

*E*lizabeth, the ultimate survivor, was nearing fifty. Although her motto was *Semper Eadem,* always the same, she was aging rapidly. She would be the last of the line. Paradoxically, the lack of a husband or child gave rise to a cult of virginity. The Virgin Queen had sacrificed personal fulfillment for the sake of England. On a less exalted plane, rumor had it that a deformity prevented her from having sex. The dramatist Ben Jonson, second only to Shakespeare among Elizabethans, whispered that Elizabeth had a "membrane on her which made her incapable of man, though to her delight she tried many"—a morsel of gossip impossible to prove or disprove.

As Elizabeth aged, her striking ashen makeup became heavier than ever to disguise the scars left by smallpox, her natural wrinkles, and her blackened teeth. She stuffed her cheeks with soft fabric to look younger. Thus attired, she presented a simulacrum of herself to her court and her people. White lead and vinegar polished with egg white imparted a ghostly royal sheen to the contours of her face, even as the lead corroded her skin. Her lips were painted a bright vermilion hue containing mercuric sulfide. Mercury is toxic; simply by running her tongue across her lips she was poisoning herself.

Even as her makeup hid her aging, it took a toll on her mind and body. Symptoms of mercury poisoning include muscle weakness; rashes; mood swings; memory loss; impairment of speech, vision, and physical coordination, especially in walking and writing; and numbness or pins and needles in the hands and feet. Elizabeth suffered from all these symptoms at one time or another.

*A*s Drake's great achievement moved inexorably into the past, he was forced to grapple with the vicissitudes of reality. His wife, Mary, had died in 1581 and was buried in Plymouth. The couple had no children, but her nephew Jonas, whose parents were deceased, became Drake's charge. He continued to live at Buckland Abbey after Mary's death during his limited time in England.

By this time, he had become a member of Parliament, although his record lacked much in the way of activity or accomplishment. He filled this position in the same spirit as he did mayor of Plymouth, as a symbol rather than as an attentive legislator. The bills that came before him, mostly on commercial matters, rarely engaged his interest or expertise, with the exception of an odious Bill for the Suppression of Pirates and Piracy, which he could not endorse. He explained his position on the grounds that he considered himself a staunch supporter of the queen. One could never say it enough. Through it all, his claim to fame remained the circumnavigation.

Lost in the excitement over the stolen riches Drake brought back to England was a full appreciation of his extraordinary voyage, the first successful circumnavigation of the globe. No mention was made of those who had died along the way in the service of the Crown, or of their adventures and discoveries. It had been a pirate mission, not a voyage of scientific discovery. Drake was oblivious to the wealth of natural phenomena he had experienced—the tides and storms, the stars and planets in the heavens, the profusion of unfamiliar plant and animal life, the wondrous geological formations, the varied skills and customs of the inhabitants they encountered—except for their immediate strategic value.

Endlessly enterprising at sea, he rarely paused to reflect on all he had seen and done. For a global explorer, the first successful circumnavigator in history, his vision remained surprisingly fixed. He had been abroad for three years, risked his life on dozens of occasions, and seen the world as no other Englishman had seen it, but he remained the same Francis Drake who had left Plymouth in 1577, a combustible blend of faith, greed, restlessness, and fearlessness.

He met with criticism and envy at home. William Cecil, Elizabeth's close confidant, rejected Drake's offer of ten gold bars—an absolute fortune—pilfered from Spain's treasure fleet, loudly declaring that he would not receive stolen goods. Cecil's gesture could only be construed as a slap in Drake's face. And when Drake took to boasting at a dinner party about his daring raids on Spanish treasure ships, the Earl of Sussex, who considered Drake a rude upstart, retorted that it was no great achievement to capture an unarmed vessel. Drake persisted in making his case until the Earl of Arundel called him out as impudent and shameless. Drake *was* a rude upstart compared with the flower of English gentry with which Elizabeth surrounded herself. He was impudent and shameless: but these qualities were what empowered him to become so successful as a pirate. His manner, while not piratical, was coarse by the refined standards of the court, who regarded him as a parvenu. These lesser lights resented his success and sudden wealth. Unlike them, he was not entitled to it.

Coming from the highest echelons of the nobility, these snubs injured Drake's amour propre. He was desperate enough to try to buy his way into their ranks. "Nothing troubled him more," said one observer, "than that some of the principal men at Court rejected the gold which he offered them, as being gotten by piracy." An anonymous offer of fifty thousand ducats was made—by the queen, by Drake himself?—to silence his critics, but it went unclaimed. It was important to condescend to the Devonian. His achievements earned as much resentment as they did praise. He did not know his place, and the queen's favor made him all the more boastful and insufferable.

Elizabeth parried Spanish allegations about Drake. She refused to see Mendoza, even as voices at court urged her to return the stolen treasure to Spain and throw in Drake along with it. That would be a just comeuppance. Ultimately, her stubborn silence and refusal to denounce the ginger-headed Devonian at her side was interpreted as support for him. He was considered her privateer. Mendoza grumbled that "the Queen shows extraordinary favour to Drake" and in public, he was seen speaking with her for long periods of time. He was also seen in her offices and walking with her in the garden, a sure sign of royal favor. To make her intentions clear, she announced her intention of knighting Drake.

Mendoza would not let the matter rest. He wrote to the queen to demand an audience with her. Elizabeth received him, only to spend their time together worrying about Ireland. When Mendoza tried to steer the conversation to his concerns, she "screamed out louder than before at this," Mendoza recalled, "saying that I was to blame for everything that happened, and I smilingly told her that she was speaking as a lady." It mattered little what Mendoza said; he would never be able to manipulate or deceive Elizabeth as he did others in her court, or, for that matter, his own sovereign, King Philip.

*T*he unexpected success of Drake's circumnavigation ignited the idea of the English or, to use John Dee's innovative terminology, *Brit-*

ish Empire. It was to be different from Spain's implacable Catholic monolith. The Spanish empire was rigid and difficult to administrate on a global scale. And it triggered genocides, whether through war or the spread of disease. As a colonial ruler, Spain was known for cruelty and exploitation rather than brilliance or innovation. Christianity was offered, but only as a means of discipline, not as a path to peace or wisdom or salvation. A British Empire could be considered the lesser of two evils, at least from the perspective of indigenous peoples. It would be an open system rather than closed. At times, the English visitors would form partnerships with local people in a primitive form of capitalism rather than indulging in outright confiscation. Its main goals were commercial and strategic rather than military or religious.

By now, England's visionary architect of empire, John Dee, had moved on from real-world concerns to the spirit realm, attempting to commune with angels through an intermediary and wandering across Europe for years on end as his reputation in England deteriorated. Nevertheless, his idea had taken hold and bequeathed Elizabeth a legacy to pursue beyond mere survival. For Drake, a tranquil and prestigious retirement as the squire of Buckland Abbey beckoned, but the interlude would not last. He would eventually resume his career as the queen's pirate. It was the career he knew, and it suited him.

The controversy over Drake's theft of Spanish wealth raged for months. On January 9, 1581, Mendoza again wrote to Philip, this time to register his disapproval that the ministers closest to Queen Elizabeth, including Leicester and Walsingham, were urging her to offer a portion of Drake's loot to "Flemish rebels to maintain war and raise troops in Germany, and also to add with the French Huguenots in their enterprise, by which, they said, her own power and security would be greatly increased and your Majesty involved in a long and costly war maintained with your own money." In reality, England was not prepared to start a series of wars to advance Protestantism on the Continent. The undertaking was entirely too expensive, threatened to turn English Catholics against English Protestants, and set the stage for a civil war.

Rather than going to war, Mendoza told his king, they tried to "tempt me by saying that, if I softened my tone towards Drake's voyage, I might count upon for myself, or for any other person I might appoint, 50,000 crowns profit." He would not agree, of course. "Neither this nor any other offer should cause me to swerve a hair's breadth in my duty to your Majesty." Such a declaration could only sow suspicion that he was considering just the opposite course.

Mendoza continued to obsess about the immense but unacknowledged fortune purloined by Drake. How outrageous "that there will be no proofs against him for the amount he has stolen without registration, which is an enormous sum, as is set forth in the memorials sent to me." Alarmed, or simply straining to get Philip's ear, Mendoza insisted, "Drake is squandering more money than any man in England, and, proportionately, all those who came with him are doing the same."

What about the bejeweled crown that Drake gave to the queen? "She wore it on New Year's Day," Mendoza reminded Philip. "It has in it five emeralds, three of them almost as long as a little finger, whilst the two round ones are valued at 20,000 crowns, coming, as they do, from Peru." He did not need to remind the king that the jewels rightfully belonged to him. "He has also given the Queen a diamond cross as a New Year's gift, as is the custom here, of the value of 5,000 crowns." But not everyone was willing to accept Drake's largesse. Lord Burghley refused 300 crowns, saying Drake had merely stolen it. The Earl of Sussex turned up his nose at 800 crowns offered by Drake for the same reason. But the queen was another matter.

Mendoza groaned as he sketched out the cozy relationship she had fashioned with the red-haired privateer from Devon. "The Queen shows extraordinary favour to Drake and to him when she goes out in public, conversing with him for a long time." There was more. "She has ordered the ship itself to be brought ashore and placed in her arsenal near Greenwich as a curiosity." This was an obvious affront to the Spanish to exhibit the ship that had done so much damage.

This was the world turned upside down, as far as Mendoza was concerned. The pirate Drake would not be jailed, tried, and executed. Instead, he basked in royal favor, and who knew what else, as a reward for his larceny. And all the while Elizabeth, a fluent dissembler, still denied that Drake had returned to England with anything of value after his three-year-long voyage to the ends of the earth.

Mendoza vented his frustration with Elizabeth to the king of Spain on June 24. "It is impossible for me to express to your Majesty the insincerity with which she and her ministers proceed. In addition to repeating to me very opposite of the message she had sent, she contradicts me every moment in my version of negotiations." This was a pretty fair description of Elizabeth's modus operandi not just with diplomats but also with lovers, ministers, and spies. She was at war, she was not at war. She was in love, she was not in love. Everyone was left in doubt as she proceeded through the grand improvisation of her reign.

*I*n mid-January 1581, Mendoza learned that the queen had given ten thousand pounds "of the money lodged in the Tower" to Drake. That was loot Drake had purloined from Spain. Nevertheless, "the signed warrant sent to him states that this is a reward"—a *reward*!— "for the voyage he made." Mendoza suspected the situation was even more sinister than that, and the money was intended to outfit a new expedition devoted to plundering Spain. He learned that the sailors believed that Drake had promised to divide the spoils among them, but, no surprise to Mendoza, "he has not done this, nor has he, indeed, settled accounts with anyone connected with the voyage, but is simply keeping them in hand with sums of money in order that he may get them to return with him on his next voyage."

Already rumors circulated that Drake wanted the queen to back a massive fleet of ten ships bound for the Indies on whatever terms she wished. To Spanish ears, it sounded as though the two of them were conspiring to seize control of the world.

Philip approved of the way his spy handled the queen, Drake, and ministers. He encouraged Mendoza to incite "the public fear that a declaration of war" may result, so "that those who have no share in the plunder may unjustly suffer for those who have." On September 25, 1581, he laid out his evolving strategy to Mendoza: "You did well in pressing Drake's affair as you have done, and it will be advisable to keep alive the alarm of the merchants that reprisals will be used against them unless satisfaction is given. This will cause them to bring influence to bear upon the Queen to restore the booty and moderate her attitude toward me in other things."

In all these matters, Philip misjudged Elizabeth, who was growing more determined all the time. Days later, Mendoza advised that he was not "pressing the matter [of the plunder] furiously" because it might provoke her into a war that Philip did not want. Instead, "I have always kept pegging away at the matter," he advised, "and the sight of so much money in hand incites them to attack your Majesty."

When Mendoza finally obtained his lengthy audience with Elizabeth on October 11, she employed every tactic at her disposal to undercut her adversary. She distracted him with two of her ladies and two of her councilors as she hectored him and warned him not to "try to frighten her." Mendoza smirked as she vented her "fury and perturbation."

Summoning his presence of mind, the ambassador said he would not waste her time making empty threats "as I well knew that monarchs were never afraid of private individuals." He resorted to flattery. "Above all she was a lady," he told her, "and so beautiful that even lions would crouch before her."

It seemed to him that his words worked their charm. "She is so vain and flighty," he later told the king, "that her anger was at once soothed hearing this, and she began to relate how much obliged your Majesty should be to her for having refused to receive the Flemish rebels" who had sought to undermine her. Before taking his leave, he left her with a parting shot: "I told her my firm belief now that if Drake's plunder were not restored your Majesty would order the seizure of all English goods in your dominions to reimburse your subjects for their losses."

Elizabeth was having none of it. Regaining her hauteur, she claimed she had been "first offended and should be the first to receive satisfaction." With that, she took leave of Mendoza "very drily." As she moved out of sight, she sighed, saying, "Would to God that each one had his own and was at peace."

Mendoza recognized that nothing had been settled. Her behavior, he reflected the next day, had been "rude and extravagant." He likened her to "an old rusty weather cock, which long use has worn away, and which will only move at a strong gust of wind, turning back to its old point as soon as the breeze dies away. In like manner I always convince her to be on the side of your Majesty, with truth and reason, but the impression only remains while I am in her presence, after which she veers back again to her old quarter." As Elizabeth vacillated, the affairs of two nations hung in the balance.

To Mendoza's intense frustration, Elizabeth summoned Drake the next day "in a furious hurry," but not, as the ambassador hoped, to make amends for wrongs done to Spain. "They will never restore the plunder," he declared, "unless your Majesty orders the arrest of all English property in your dominions. This, if your Majesty pleases, might be done at once, whilst we see how they proceed on Drake's arrival."

Later that same day he complained to the king to say Leicester and the queen were agitating to have him "expelled" from England. He learned that Leicester had been privy to his negotiations with the queen and had been responsible for keeping her on course when she seemed to vacillate. He would do his utmost to stop her from granting Mendoza any more audiences, "and always introducing me by a back door instead of through the presence chamber." Relations continued to deteriorate. "He is trying every day to get new and greater excuses for my expulsion." He took the extreme measure of arresting one of Mendoza's Catholic servants for baptizing his newborn child according to Catholic rites. By this time, Mendoza was feeling persecuted.

He complained to Philip that Elizabeth, Walsingham, "and their gang are trying to get rid of me, and if necessary, break with your Majesty, which is the real object they have in view every hour of the day, together with the growing distaste with which the Queen looks upon me." If her councilors got their way, he confided, "your Majesty may be forced to resent it, sword in hand." All things considered, "I cannot be of any service to your Majesty here now, with my hands tied and her ears closed against me." For this reason, he urged the king to appoint a successor to Mendoza immediately, "although at first not ostensibly to replace me." This "special envoy" should bring a letter from Philip conferring the power to investigate Drake's various "robberies." In fact, the replacement should bring an entire series of letters authorizing him to investigate on behalf of Spain, wrote an exasperated Mendoza.

Drake was planning elaborate new expeditions, which were certain to damage Spanish interests, the ambassador warned, and England was negotiating with Morocco and Holland to import timber to build more galleys. An expanded English naval presence would present serious obstacles to Spain. That, plus news of reprisals against Catholics across England, alarmed Mendoza. Elizabeth and Leicester were busy "inciting" Protestants "and arousing their hatred of Catholics."

A week later, Cardinal Granvelle, a French minister in the service of Spain, wrote to the king to second Mendoza's sense of alarm surrounding the Protestant insurgency. "It is pitiful to see how the Catholics are suffering, and especially as, the more attempts are made to help them, the harder is their fate." Amid these circumstances, he could only praise Mendoza's efforts. "Don Bernardino is acting exceedingly well in aiding them underhand, in order that they may be the deeper pledged by his solicitude for them."

By late January 1582, the king had become so anxious about Drake's intentions and so dependent on Mendoza's intelligence that he wrote in a state of alarm that a Dutch captain, claiming to have run into Drake near the Isle of Wight, had said that Drake had just sailed from England "with twelve ships, manned with soldiers and colonists, and carrying bricks, lime, and other building materials for forts, bound for the Strait of Magellan. As we have no report of it from you, we cannot believe it, but the doubt causes anxiety." For once, the king need not have worried. At that moment, Drake was thoroughly enmeshed with affairs in England as mayor of Plymouth, member of Parliament, and master of Buckland Abbey. All that Philip could do was to keep Elizabeth aware of his concern.

Mendoza tired of the issue and lost confidence in his ability to put matters right, at least from the Spanish point of view. By March 1, 1582, he was complaining of his own "sluggishness and coldness in the service of God," and he wrote to the king that whoever came next would be "better able to serve your Majesty with greater dexterity and vigilance than I am." He was as confused as anyone concerning Drake's actual whereabouts. The English pirate was at sea, he was headed for Brazil, or for the Moluccas. He was in England. Mendoza hedged his bets by maintaining that Drake was about to set sail. "Drake has not yet left England, but not a day passes that he does not say a thousand shameless things, amongst others that he will give the Queen 80,000 ducats if she will grant him leave to arm ships to meet your Majesty's fleets," he warned Philip, "although of course he has not the slightest idea of doing such a thing." How could Drake have the "impudence" to imagine attacking the "greatest monarch on earth?"

Yet that was exactly what Drake had in mind.

CHAPTER XV

Two Queens, One Throne

At the beginning of 1585, Francis Drake married a wealthy young heiress, Elizabeth Sydenham, the only child of Sir George Sydenham and his wife, also named Elizabeth. Her family dwelled in Somerset, and she was said to be beautiful and intelligent. Drake pledged his estates, including Buckland, for his new wife and their heirs, but he retained the power to dispose of his property as he saw fit.

Now that he was married to his second wife, a tranquil retirement beckoned, but the prospect would not last. "It isn't that life ashore is distasteful to me," he observed, "but life at sea is better." In fact, a life ashore was inimical to his temperament. Drake was not as adept at navigating life on land as he was on the water. On land, he was subject to countless constraints; layers of protocol, etiquette, and decorum interfered with his autonomy. At sea, his authority was unchallenged.

Through it all, Elizabeth remained his champion even as she and her Protestant allies faced trials of their own. Despite her efforts to remain the monarch of Protestants and Catholics alike, she had inherited the Protestant mantle, so she was perceived as Protestant and was vulnerable to attacks from Catholics. Her allies, as proxies for the queen, were also vulnerable to threats, none more so than her closest and most controversial adviser (and presumed lover), Robert Dudley, the 1st Earl of Leicester, who became the target of a vicious screed entitled *Leicester's Commonwealth*. This piece of character assassination was couched as a conversation among a London gentleman, a Catholic lawyer, and a Cambridge graduate who argued that Robert Dudley was a duplicitous Machiavellian out to crown himself king by poisoning all claimants to the throne except for the Earl of Huntingdon, who happened to be his brother-in-law.

With everyone else out of the way, and Huntingdon on the throne, Robert Dudley would overthrow him. Lending this far-fetched scenario credence was Robert Dudley's sinister reputation. He was suspected of murdering his beautiful wife, Amy Robsart, as well as the Earl of Essex, so that Dudley could marry his widow. To add to the case's credibility, the screed reminded readers that his father and grandfather had both been executed as traitors. Embellishing this grim reality, Robert Dudley stood accused of murdering three others: the Cardinal de Châtillon, who had died amid suspicious circumstances in 1571; Sir Nicholas Throckmorton, an English diplomat who had a falling-out with Queen Elizabeth and also died in 1571; and the queen's cousin Margaret Douglas, Countess of Lennox. It was a bloody trail.

Days before her death in 1578, the countess had dined with Robert Dudley, giving rise to rumors that he had arranged for her to be poisoned. It was whispered that his association with Italians, believed to be adept at poisons, gave him the means to advance his evil design.

Then there was the gossip about his numerous affairs. At one time he had hoped to marry Elizabeth, but it was apparent to all that she was opposed to the idea of marriage, which would mean giving up a substantial amount of her hard-won power. In 1578 Robert Dudley secretly wed the queen's cousin, the widowed Countess of Essex, Lettice Knollys, at seven o'clock in the morning. The bride bore a distinct resemblance to Elizabeth, who remained unaware of the marriage for two years, until the Duke of Alençon undertook his ill-fated courtship of the queen. When the truth came out, Elizabeth was stunned and wounded and railed against Robert Dudley. Seven years after the marriage, Elizabeth still shamed him publicly for his transgression. "She doth take every occasion by marriage to withdraw any good from me," he lamented. Eventually, they reconciled, but the queen refused to see Lettice, whom she called a "she-wolf."

King Philip, trapped in his royal echo chamber and increasingly anxious for news, wrote to insist that Mendoza persevere in his reporting on Drake's doings, as well as other English pirates, "as nothing comes from there now except through you." Although it appeared that John Hawkins and Walter Raleigh, who currently enjoyed the queen's favor, might be taking the lead, Philip remained preoccupied with the ginger-haired pirate who preyed on Spain. "Report especially on whether Drake's or any other fleet has sailed, and if so, with what number of ships and men."

By August of 1585, word reached Spain that Drake "was lying at anchor off the Isle of Wight with 24 well-armed ships, although his intentions were not known." Unreliable rumors spread that he awaited instructions from "French Huguenots"—Protestants—and Elizabeth had ordered him not to sail "until further instructions so that the coast might not be bereft of ships."

The ensuing months brought frightening reminders of the vulnerability of the English throne to assassination and subversion. A sequence of events aimed at deposing Elizabeth and putting the Catholic Mary, Queen of Scots, on the throne unfolded during 1583.

It was known as the Throckmorton Plot, after Francis Throckmorton, a cousin of one of Elizabeth's ladies-in-waiting. Throckmorton carried secret and highly incriminating messages between Mendoza and Mary, Queen of Scots. A courier handling the messages tipped off Walsingham, Elizabeth's intransigent secretary of state, and he pounced, arresting Throckmorton in November, and obtaining a list of English Catholic supporters of Mary.

Walsingham discovered that the traitorous Throckmorton had also sent incriminating documents to Mendoza, who, as a diplomat, enjoyed immunity from prosecution. Instead of being arrested, Mendoza was informed that his participation in the Throckmorton Plot had "disturbed the realm of England." By way of reply, he directed English officials to "tell your mistress that Bernardino de Mendoza was born not to disturb kingdoms, but to conquer them."

After this show of defiance, he was expelled from England in January 1584, the last Spanish diplomat of Elizabeth's reign. As for Francis Throckmorton, he was tortured to extract information and executed in July. Mary was placed under strict confinement. No wonder Francis Drake appealed to Elizabeth, besieged as she was on all sides. His loyalty was unquestioned. She needed Drake to defend the realm and to preserve her life, which was very much at stake.

The assassination attempts continued with chilling frequency. In 1586, Walsingham uncovered a complex scheme to assassinate the queen and, once again, replace her with Mary, Queen of Scots. In this case, the head conspirator was Anthony Babington, and documents revealed that Mary of all people lent her support to plans to assassinate Elizabeth and to encourage King Philip of Spain to invade England. How could she? But there was no mistaking her involvement. "Let the great plot commence," she wrote in a letter signed "Mary." With this document she sealed her fate as victim, martyr, and Elizabeth's nemesis.

The conspirators suffered greatly for their transgression. John Ballard, who had advocated a violent Catholic restoration, was executed along with six others on September 20. "You would have killed the queen's majesty," the sheriff declared in public. "You would have sacked London and overthrown the state." Ballard was hanged from a gibbet, cut down, castrated, disemboweled, and quartered. When his head was displayed on a stake to the crowd, they shouted in unison, "God save the queen!" Six additional executions occurred that same day, until the hangman was soaked in blood. More of the same was scheduled for the following day.

To demonstrate mercy, the queen and her council ordered that the condemned should be hanged until dead *before* being quartered. The queen and her council employed these extreme tactics because they believed, with good reason, that her life and the future of Protestant England were in imminent danger. Assassination attempts were frequent, and the newer-model pistols were small enough for a would-be assassin to conceal within a large pocket, making it even easier to carry out an attack.

Yet Elizabeth could not live in seclusion; she understood better than anyone else the importance of showing herself in public, of playing the part of the people's queen. It could be argued that the extreme punishments threatened or carried out on her behalf had the reverse of their intended effect, provoking revolt rather than quelling it. The result was a reign that, for all its brilliance, was beset by mortal threats and constant anxiety.

*T*hrough it all, Elizabeth's Catholic rival for the throne, Mary Stuart, also known as Mary, Queen of Scots, and who was her first cousin once removed, beseeched her for protection. But Elizabeth recognized Mary's plea, in fact, Mary's very existence, for what it was: a mortal threat. There might be two queens, but there was a single throne. In the past, Mary had claimed that she, not Elizabeth, was the legitimate ruler of England, and English Catholics still regarded her as such. And she was backed by Spain.

Working behind the scenes, Elizabeth prodded her agents to confront Mary, who was convicted of treason on October 25, 1586, and sentenced to death. Having come this far, Elizabeth hesitated, as she often did, afraid of the precedent set by regicide. What if Mary's allies sought revenge by killing *her*? What if the execution prompted a Catholic invasion of England, or a Catholic rebellion at home? Elizabeth had faced life-threatening challenges from courtiers, rebellious Irish peasants, and disease. But Mary posed an even greater menace.

Finally, on February 1, 1587, Elizabeth put aside her doubts long enough to sign Mary's death warrant. She felt profound ambivalence: guilt about committing a grievous sin and justification in removing this challenge to her sovereignty.

Mary passed the last hours of her life in prayer. On the morning of February 8, her servants and executioners removed her outer garments, revealing a velvet petticoat in crimson-brown, the color of martyrdom, with a black satin bodice. Mary was blindfolded with a white veil embroidered in gold. She kneeled on a cushion in front of the block, on which she positioned her head, and stretched out her arms, and uttered her last words: "Into thy hands, O Lord, I commend my spirit."

The executioner's first blow struck the back of her skull, and the second cut through her neck. He lifted her severed head to the throng, declaring, "God Save the Queen." At that moment, her chestnut-colored wig separated from her head, revealing short gray hair underneath as it tumbled to the floor. Her terrier remained with her throughout the ordeal, concealed beneath her skirts, covered in her blood, refusing to part with her until he was taken away. Every bloodstained item was consigned to flames.

*E*lizabeth resorted to an array of deceptions to distance herself from Mary's ghastly execution. She protested (too much) that the deed had been carried out against her wishes and without her knowledge. Even if no one believed her denials, she managed to sow some doubt that she was behind a plot to execute Mary. She secluded herself for three weeks in faux mourning; and she wrote a letter of apology to James of Scotland, who calculated that if he went along with her scheme and put aside his Catholicism, he might become heir to the throne of England. Although Elizabeth caused some Catholics in England to soften their stance, Philip saw through her deception and realized the time had come to invade. The project received the grand name of The Enterprise of England.

Even before this, Pope Gregory XIII had been prodding King Philip to invade England. In October 1583, Philip had replied, "This proposal is out of the question." Two years later, he was insisting, "There is little to be said for the English idea." He asked English Catholics "to be patient, for something will be done at some time." This slender hope did not offer much comfort, but by the end of 1585, the discussion in Spain returned to the idea of invading England. The esteemed Marquis of Santa Cruz, undefeated in his fifty-year-long naval career, would lead the Spanish forces. Mere mention of his name, and his flagship, *She-Wolf,* was considered sufficient to strike terror into Spain's enemies. In contrast to England's flimsy naval defenses, the marquis proposed a massive fleet for the invasion: 510 ships and almost ninety-five thousand men. On April 2, 1586, Philip ordered his navy to prepare for the operation.

The cost would be commensurate with this huge fleet, ten million ducats. Simply maintaining the Armada depleted the treasury at the rate of 700,000 ducats per month. (Frugal Elizabeth maintained her threadbare navy at a fraction of that cost.) Philip fretted not about tactics or lives but about the money he was spending on his navy. "Finding money is so important that all of us must concentrate on that and nothing else." To raise the necessary funds, he borrowed unwisely. He sold his deceased wife's jewels, title of nobility, monopolies and trading rights, lordships—a century's worth of royal authority amassed by his predecessors Ferdinand and Isabella.

By June, matters were going awry. Alexander Farnese, Duke of Parma and one of Italy's leading military strategists, proposed a surprise attack on England to be carried out by only thirty thousand troops, without significant naval protection, perhaps just a few flat-bottomed barges. He would first attack Ireland by surprise, distract the diminutive English navy, and proceed to conquer England with the help of an insurrection mounted by English Catholics, liberated at last from their Protestant oppressors.

The Santa Cruz plan had the advantage of brute force; the Parma plan had the advantages of surprise and flexibility. Philip should have chosen one strategy or the other. Instead, he decided to combine the two, even though they were incompatible. The news of Mary's execution arrived in the midst of preparations for this invasion. Philip insisted on continuing, calling his invasion a crusade, but the situation kept changing.

On April 25, 1585, Felice Peretti, a Neapolitan cardinal, was elected Pope Sixtus V, and he brought with him a distinctly anti-Spanish bias. In fact, he went behind the King of Spain's back by contacting Henry III of France to see if he could influence Elizabeth to reconsider her actions and lead her country back to the embrace of the Catholic Church. The initiative failed, infuriating Philip, and

Sixtus V continued to make life difficult for Spain by withholding funds for the impending invasion. Finally, the two Catholic entities came to terms and signed a pact on July 27, 1587, giving Philip a free hand in choosing England's new ruler after the successful Catholic conquest of the island nation.

Through the last part of 1586 and the early part of 1587, arms and matériel accumulated in Lisbon and along Spain's southern coast. Descriptions of this alarming stockpile reached Walsingham, who heard from a Danzig merchant, Hans Frederick, about three hundred "sail of shipping" gathering in "south Spain." And in Lisbon, the authorities were busy confiscating "all the victuals in every ship." Still more alarming, a Portuguese source relayed intelligence concerning four hundred ships and fifty galleys moored in the vicinity of Lisbon as the Portuguese tried to recruit seventy-four thousand soldiers and gather immense quantities of bacon, wine, beef, and cheese to feed the sailors preparing to invade England. At the same time, Philip's supposedly secret plans for conquest were exposed for his adversaries to see. He made matters worse by requiring the College of Cardinals, all seventy of them, to vow that they would carry out the undertakings of Sixtus V in the event of his death. Though sworn to secrecy, the cardinals injudiciously let news of the planned attack slip, and soon it spread around Rome and reached England, where an erroneous rumor of Spanish soldiers coming ashore in Wales unnerved the populace. Reports of sightings of a fleet off the coast of the Isle of Wight and elsewhere circulated.

It was time, in fact it was long overdue, for England to prepare for war. On March 30, 1586, Bernardino de Mendoza, drawing on his sources, provided King Philip with a description of England girding for the conflict: "Four of the Queen's ships fully armed were at the mouth of the Thames. The others were said to be still in course of preparation, but it is asserted that only four of them were seaworthy, all the rest being old and rotten. Some new vessels were therefore being built with all speed at a port at the mouth of the Thames in Kent, at Plymouth, and other places. The Queen has also some armed merchant ships, but with no intention at present of undertaking any particular voyage, they being simply ready awaiting the Queen's orders. Nine thousand mariners also had been notified all over the country to hold themselves in readiness in case of need. Some of the ships are constantly sallying under letters of marque to plunder, as the Queen is quite ready to grant such letters against your Majesty's subjects."

An arms race between Spain and England gathered momentum. Elizabeth, always tightly wound, became even more so. Hearing from a Scottish captain returning from Lisbon that he had seen twenty-seven galleons there, "not ships but floating fortresses," as Mendoza put it, the queen "turned to Secretary Walsingham, who was present, and said a few words to him which the ship master did not understand, after which she threw a slipper at Walsingham and hit him in the face, which is not a very extraordinary thing for her to do, as she is constantly behaving in such a rude manner as this."

As the government tallied the ships available to fight, Elizabeth scrutinized an inventory of two hundred captains fit for service. In the Tower of London, Greenwich, Windsor, and Hampton Court, creaky doors were flung open to retrieve weapons gathering dust in armories. The treasurer of the navy, John Hawkins, declared himself: "In my mind," he wrote to Walsingham on February 1, "our profit and best assurance is to seek our peace by a determined and resolute war." Elizabeth, always reluctant to engage in direct military confrontation and content to parry Spanish aggression with doubletalk, decided she had no choice but to enlist her most daring and successful pirate, Sir Francis Drake, to defend England.

For the previous two years, Drake, rather than remaining in Plymouth with his wealthy second wife, had been roaming the Caribbean in search of loot—Santo Domingo in the Dominican Republic and then south across the Caribbean Sea to Cartagena, on Colombia's northern coast, a distance of about 680 miles. In May 1586 he arrived in St. Augustine, Florida, where he laid waste to a Spanish settlement as the colonizers fled, and in June, he sailed to the failed English community on Roanoke Island, North Carolina, where he rescued survivors and returned with them to England. (This was the first Roanoke Island colony, founded in 1585. Walter Raleigh founded an equally unfortunate "lost" Roanoke a year later.)

By this time, Drake had become expert at transatlantic crossings, and he returned to England on July 26, 1586, just as England's imperial ambitions were giving way to defending the realm against Spanish aggression. Drake was expected to play a major part in the campaign, not as a freelance pirate, but as a captain in the English navy. Could he make the transition from plunder to patriotism? His goal this time was not treasure but securing the English coast against invasion.

On March 15, 1587, Elizabeth signed a commission authorizing Drake to reprimand Spain for colonial ambitions. He was all for urging England to seize the initiative, and on April 2 he wrote to Walsingham to outline his plans. Before long, Leicester, Walsingham, and the Lord High Admiral, Howard of Effingham, aligned with Drake.

Their initial proposal was for Drake to come to the aid of Dom António, a perpetually unsuccessful pretender to the Portuguese throne. As the illegitimate son of Luís, Duke of Beja, the brother of King João III of Portugal, Dom António's claim to power was tenuous. He did serve as the head of the ancient Order of St. John in Portugal and the wealthy priory of Crato. In 1580, António's supporters declared him king, but his title was dismissed by the more powerful Philip II of Spain. Defeated, António fled to Paris. Both France and England attempted to install him as the king of Portugal and in each case met with failure. On this occasion, Elizabeth preferred to set firm limits rather than launch an outright invasion. By deploying El Draque, who had made a career out of humiliating Spain, Elizabeth would send a message that England was prepared to effect regime change in Portugal. After much delay and indecision, Elizabeth agreed to the plan on March 25.

At the same time, King Philip, secluded in the Monasterio de El Escorial, contemplated an even more daring scheme: to kidnap Queen Elizabeth and transfer her to the pope, who would in turn deliver her to the Inquisition. (Philip had apparently forgotten about Sixtus's surprising fondness for the queen.) This striking maneuver would mean the end of the heresy of the Church of England and the return of England to the Catholic fold. He did insist that once they seized Elizabeth, they should treat her with "reverence," another improbable fantasy. An English priest sought to expedite this plan by circulating the papal bull excommunicating her and granting immunity to anyone responsible for murdering her. It was right and fitting to consign heretical sovereigns to death. Elizabeth would face not just life in prison, but execution—after all, she had ordered Mary, Queen of Scots's head to roll.

Philip acted on the confident advice of priests and military advisers, who claimed it would be easy to conquer England, whose military had been declining for years. With an army and navy offering little resistance, and an enthusiastic Catholic population in England rallying to his support, the invasion would be quick and relatively painless, or so it was believed. One battle at sea, another on land, and the damage wrought by Henry VIII and Elizabeth I would be undone. England would be Catholic once again.

Everything was in readiness until it became apparent that England was fully expecting an invasion and prepared to repel it. Spain demanded that Elizabeth stop assisting the Netherlands, which had been an ongoing cause of hers; return the treasure stolen by Drake; and return the abbeys to the Catholic Church.

Instead, she turned to Drake. She would provide four ships—the best in her small fleet: *Elizabeth Bonaventure*, the flagship, a forty-seven-gun galleon; *Lyon*, *Rainbow*, and *Dreadnought*. Nineteen merchants of the city of London would furnish another twenty or twenty-four vessels. They were a motley crew—haberdashers and fishmongers, drapers and grocers—in no way warriors or pirates, but they saw profit in the impending invasion.

Drake agreed with the Merchant Adventurers that "whatsoever commodity in goods, money, treasure, merchandise or other benefit shall happen to be taken by all or any of the aforementioned ships . . . shall be equally proportioned, man for man and ton for ton [and will] be divided at sea . . . as soon as wind and weather will permit." To keep these arrangements secret, southern ports were closed to traffic and officers were informed of preparations on a need-to-know basis.

The ships assembled in Plymouth. Summoning all his eloquence for the great occasion, Drake (or his amanuensis) wrote to Elizabeth's spymaster, Francis Walsingham, to accept the commission:

We all persuade ourselves there was never more likely in any fleet, or a more loving agreement, than we hope the one of the other. I thank God I find no man but as all members

of one body, to stand for our gracious Queen and country
against anti-Christ and his members.

The wind commands me away, our ship is under sail,
God grant we may so live in his fear, as the enemy may
have cause to say that God doth fight for her Majesty as
well abroad as at home, and give her long and happy life,
and ever victory against God's enemies and her Majesty's.

Rumors of the impending conflict reached Spain, inflating the size of the fleet. One report indicated that Drake commanded forty ships, with five thousand men, and this fleet would merge with another of equal size. "We are astonished at the great diligence and secrecy with which this fleet has been equipped," the account concluded, "for up to the moment, not a word of it has reached us here."

Fearful that the queen would change her mind yet again, Drake worked feverishly to ready his merchant fleet. Thomas Fenner, captain of *Dreadnought*, one of Drake's ships, recounted to Walsingham that the admiral "does all he can to hasten the service and sticks at no charge to further the same and lays out a great store of money to soldiers and mariners to stir up their minds." But the sailors deserted in droves, and Drake suspected his rivals at court were luring them away to subvert him. Sir Walter Raleigh, a recent favorite of the capricious queen, had expressed his opposition to the plan. One could never be too careful.

From his new vantage point in Paris, Mendoza filled the king's ear with the latest gossip concerning Spain's chief nemesis.

Still, Mendoza could not say exactly where Drake was, or what he was up to. "It was asserted here as a positive fact that he had returned, and I have delayed sending a report to your Majesty until I could ascertain the truth. Up to the present, however, there is no certain news, except that there has been a strong gale blowing dead against his course."

Drake did strike, but not where Philip or Mendoza expected. At the beginning of 1586, he arrived in Santo Domingo, and departed "on the 22nd of January with all the riches of the island, having also taken five great galleons. He had found great provision of oil, wine, rice, and 350 brass pieces with powder and shot." Drake's latest depredations included two thousand hostages. "He took away with him 1,200 English, French, and Flemish, who were in prison there besides 800 captives of the country." Inspired by Drake, "the rage of the English for plunder is for ever increasing," according to the French ambassador in England, "now that they see your Majesty is not arming."

Weeks later, in March, he took aim at Puerto Rico and Cuba, "as he had done the island of Santo Domingo." Reports from France had reached Mendoza of Drake's ruthlessness. When he arrived, the populace fled to the mountains, "having saved most of the treasure of the country." Drake threatened to torch all their homes unless they agreed to pay him fifty thousand crowns. The fleet remained in the region until May, before moving out, destination unknown.

Drake moved about the Caribbean, bolstering his notoriety. If King Philip would not challenge him, neither would Queen Elizabeth. The situation reminded Mendoza of Drake's offering the queen "to go out and rob your Majesty's fleets," but the current situation was far more volatile. No one knew what to believe. Throughout 1586, Drake was here, there, and nowhere.

Mendoza improvised stories to please and distract Philip. Drake's Caribbean venture had been a humiliating setback for England, Mendoza claimed. El Draque had lost a thousand men. "The best jewel he brings is the cross from the great church of Santo Domingo," and beyond that, he had nothing to show for his time and effort. "The Queen received not a single groat"—a coin of negligible value— "from Drake's voyage, as all the booty was taken by the soldiers in the sacking of the place" Undeterred, the queen ordered cattle to be slaughtered and salted in preparation for another voyage, this time to the Indies, manned by "1,500 shoeless vagabonds."

In Spain, such stories were greeted uncritically. By this time, El Draque with his supernatural powers was liable to appear anywhere, anytime. Or in two places at once. As the legend of this pirate grew, Spain reeled. He was believed to be a sorcerer, and that was why he could overcome Spain. He had sold his soul to the devil. He had the benefit of a familiar. He had a magic mirror on the wall of his cabin, and it showed him the whereabouts of his enemies' ships. He could even peer into it and watch the movements of the men on board and count the crew. Most alarming of all, he could control the winds, summoning a storm or an unexpected calm. In the Spanish imagination, he was all-seeing, all-powerful.

One question remained: Where would he strike next?

CHAPTER XVI

Raid on Cádiz

Mary's death freed Elizabeth to pursue her long-held aspiration to create a Protestant empire. On March 15, 1587, she authorized Drake to attack Spain with a small fleet. It was not to be an all-out war, which England lacked the resources to support, but a gambit intended to put Spain on notice that Elizabeth was prepared to fight. It was war, but, to the queen's way of thinking, a limited skirmish.

Drake departed from Plymouth on April 12, 1587, and proceeded to the nameless body of water now called the English Channel, where he welcomed two ships from Dorset into his fleet of twenty-seven. By April 15, he was within sight of the promontory of Galicia on the coast of Spain, but then disaster struck—five days of storms that scattered the ships and sent one, the pinnace *Martigo*, to the bottom. When the ships reassembled, they met two Dutch vessels, and from their crew, Drake learned that the Spanish were planning to dispatch a massive fleet from Cádiz to Lisbon. The English fleet sailed, hoping to catch the Spanish by surprise.

At about that time, Queen Elizabeth underwent yet another change of heart and sent a swift pinnace to Drake bearing a counter-command. The queen now ordered Drake to restrict his attacks to Spanish ships at sea and prohibited him "to enter forcibly into the King's ports or havens [i.e., Cádiz], or to offer violence to any of his towns or shipping with harbouring, or to do any act of hostility upon land." Instead, he was encouraged to plunder the "shipping of the said king's . . . as shall fall into your hands, to bring them to this realm." That was a level of piracy with which the queen was comfortable and in which Drake had proven himself.

Drake, out of reach, never received this order; headwinds forced the ship carrying the queen's message back into port. Elizabeth probably did not intend to reach Drake; the delay was meant as cover in case he failed in his mission of destruction. In that case, she could protest that Drake had exceeded her carefully calibrated instructions and was acting on his own—and would face the consequences on his own. She needed Drake, who had brought back stolen Spanish wealth; at the same time, she was prepared to sacrifice him to preserve her reign.

An outright invasion of Cádiz was too much for Elizabeth, always seeking to maintain deniability. The last thing she wanted was to upset the balance of fear between England and Spain and to provoke Philip into attacking. With its superior resources, Spain would make short work of England, returning English Catholics to the fold and making as much of an example of Elizabeth as she had made of Mary, Queen of Scots. Spanish forces could overrun her small country in a matter of days. Elizabeth would be seen as a footnote to history, a Protestant aberration, and Philip as a latter-day emperor, ruling the planet in coordination with Rome. She proceeded with caution lest she waken the beast.

ate on the afternoon of April 29, Drake sailed into Cádiz harbor, one of the oldest havens in Western Europe. Over the centuries, Phoenicians, Carthaginians, Muslims, and Romans had swept through the city and port. Julius Caesar once stood there and compared himself to Alexander the Great, humbled that he had accomplished so little in comparison to Alexander. Christopher Columbus had sailed from Cádiz on both his second and fourth voyages. The city had come to represent conquest and Spain's preeminence in the world.

At that moment, tumblers and players in the town square were entertaining passersby, and the surrounding crowds were overindulging in alcohol. Disorder and merriment were everywhere. When Drake's sails appeared, it was at first assumed they belonged to the fleet commanded by Juan Martínez de Recalde, a Spanish naval leader. To preserve the illusion, Drake flew no flags. Two ships under the command of Don Pedro de Acuña, a Spanish military officer known for his bravery in the Battle of Lepanto years before, approached, trying to identify the visitors. When they came within range, Drake opened fire, driving Acuña's ships back. From the quarterdeck of *Elizabeth Bonaventure*, trumpets blared and drums pounded, echoing across the water. The battle was on.

From the shore, the groggy crowd looked on the spectacle with incredulity. After a while, cries of "El Draque!" rang out as women and children hurried to safety in the castle. The rush turned into a panic. The castle's gate slammed shut, and twenty-five women and children were crushed to death before the gatekeeper could act. The townsmen banded together to defend their homes, but they had no weapons or experience to meet this unexpected challenge. Numerous Spanish galleons, packed with men and cannon, made for a reassuring sight, but the ships were large and ungainly and unable to maneuver within the harbor's confines. Each of Drake's ships, smaller and more maneuverable, had more firepower than the entire Spanish naval presence in the harbor.

Though hampered by shallow water, they attempted to repulse Drake's ships. Their cannon took aim at the English invaders and fired, to no avail. No ship was sunk, no English soldier killed. Was Spanish gunpowder too expensive to expend, even in an emergency? Were the Spanish gunners incompetent? Drake had exposed the many deficiencies of the supposedly overwhelming Spanish naval presence, deficiencies with which he had become familiar during his many raids on Spanish-controlled harbors around the world. It was incredible, and irresistible, that a navy of global reach could be so ill-prepared to defend itself.

As Drake's ships entered the harbor, Acuña brought the other Spanish galleys around to fire on the invaders. The English guns with their longer range repelled the Spanish galleys.

Drake next clashed with an armed Genoese merchant ship. He made short work of capturing it, along with a Biscayan galleon. In all, he apprehended five merchant ships bound for the Indies and a galleon owned by the Marquis of Santa Cruz. His men proceeded to plunder these ships, and when they were done, to set them on fire as a warning to those who would challenge him. All in all, it was a very professional demonstration of English piracy.

"We found much shipping," Drake wrote after the incident, "32 ships of exceeding great burthen, laden, and to be laden, with provision and prepared to furnish the King's navy, intended with all speed against England; the which, when we had boarded and furnished our ships with such provision we thought sufficient, we burned."

Within hours of his arrival, Drake had done significant damage to the Spanish, and if he had returned to the open sea at this point, heading for Plymouth, he would have made the point that England was not to be trifled with. But he was just beginning. It was as if a lifetime of resentment against Spain came pouring out, now that he had these ships at his mercy. Whatever the Spanish had done to him and to others he would pay back. The merchant ships riding at anchor in Cádiz harbor were generally without crews or sail. Helpless, they could not move.

For Drake, keen on revenge against the Spanish, they made ideal targets—large, immobile, and well supplied. Drake ordered the pinnaces and other small ships in his fleet to thread their way among these slumbering hulks, board them, and strip them of everything they could carry away. The crew members aboard a few ships stirred and tried to take measures to avoid him, mainly by cutting their cables and drifting toward the inner harbor for safety. Others sought shelter beneath the guns at Puerto Real.

During the night, Acuña's galleys lit up the sky, lobbing cannonballs at Drake's ships. The guns at Puerto Real fired away, to little effect. Spanish galleys did manage to capture an English pinnace and take five sailors hostage: a paltry showing. Drake retained the advantage.

The next day, the Duke of Medina Sidonia arrived with thousands of reinforcements, artillery, infantry, and cavalry. Drake appeared overwhelmed by the enemy's sheer numbers, but their proximity placed the Spanish forces at risk. Medina Sidonia's best option, in fact his only option, was to thwart Drake's troops from going ashore and looting unsuspecting towns.

Fearless, Drake shifted his fleet to the inner harbor, looking for the vessels that had escaped the night before. This part of the bay was shallow, and *Elizabeth Bonaventure* ran aground. Drake transferred his troops to smaller boats and pinnaces and sacrificed the larger ships. Meanwhile, other ships joined the fray, as shouting and the concussive roar of cannon reverberated across the harbor, and ominous smoke drifted across the sky.

For the next two days, wrote Drake, "we were still endangered both with thundering shot from the town and assaulted with the roaring cannon of 12 galleys, we yet sunk 2 of them and one great argosy, and still avoided them with very small hurt; so that our departure we brought away 4 ships of provision, to the great terror of our enemies and honor to ourselves, as it might appear by a most courteous letter, written and sent to me with a flag of truce by D Pedro, general of the galleys."

*M*edina Sidonia busied himself fortifying the bridge across the Rio Sancti Petri to secure an entrance by land to Cádiz. With Drake's fleet within range, Medina Sidonia prepared two bronze guns dragged to the promontories to fire on the invaders. Now that Spanish troops commanded all the forts and the approaches to Cádiz, it was no longer feasible to land any soldiers to sack the city, as it seemed Drake might have done when his ships first appeared.

As was his habit, Drake had left for the inner bay without informing his second-in-command, William Burroughs. Oblivious, he entered the harbor, looking for Drake, only to hear that he had returned to the flagship. While Burroughs was gone, Medina Sidonia's heavy guns on the promontory bombarded Burroughs's ship, *Golden Lion*. One ball pierced the hull and landed on the gun deck, where it shattered the leg of the master gunner.

Secure on his own flagship, Drake busied himself giving instructions to the fleet. The plunder would be divided among the ships. Some captured vessels were fitted for the sea. The others were burned. Though Drake was unperturbed, the master of *Golden Lion* was thoroughly frightened. With his ship becalmed, he put men into boats and ordered them to drag the stricken vessel to the entrance of the harbor. There Burroughs rejoined his ship as Acuña harassed him until other English ships arrived on the scene and repelled him. Drake would never have allowed himself to be put in such a vulnerable position.

Drake had a busy morning of it, and by noon he had pillaged more than twenty ships. Assembling his fleet at the mouth of the bay, Drake attempted to sail out, but the wind had died. At the sight of English ships drifting helplessly, the Spanish floated small boats filled with barrels of burning pitch in the direction of the fleet, but scant damage was done to Drake's ships.

Finally, about midnight, the wind came up and they sailed out of the bay. Right behind them came Acuña and the Spanish galleys. Just beyond the bay, the fleet lost wind and became ensnared in a brief battle. Again, the galleys proved they could not measure up to the heavily armed, highly maneuverable English fighting ships.

About noon the galleys lay within sight of the English fleet. Drake sent a messenger to see whether the Spanish ships had the five English prisoners aboard. The answer came back that they did not have the prisoners at that moment, but if Drake waited for another day, perhaps an exchange could be arranged. Suspecting a trick, Drake decided against the offer.

In the raid on Cádiz, Drake had resupplied his fleet, loading the ships with wine, oil, biscuits, and dried fruits. Four Spanish ships, laden with provisions, were added to his fleet, as dozens more left behind at Cádiz were burned to the waterline. The Spanish estimated their loss at 172,000 ducats. In addition to the ships, the payloads

amounted to a huge loss. A Biscayan ship of seven hundred tons was
filled with iron. A Portuguese ship carried almost five thousand tons
of wheat. Not all of these payloads were intended for the Armada;
some were bound for Brazil or Italy. In all, ten thousand tons of
Spanish shipping had been destroyed. El Draque had struck again,
having accomplished an act of consummate piracy that exposed him
to a minimum of danger and a maximum of profit.

Perhaps by coincidence, Spain's top naval officer, the Marquis of
Santa Cruz commenced a steep decline and died several months later.
With him went Spain's best hope for defending itself against Drake.

*W*e were encountered with a violent storm, during the space
of five days, by which means our fleet was put asunder and a great
leak sprang upon the *Dreadnought*," Drake wrote. When they recovered from this mishap, Drake boasted that they "sank a Biscayne
of 1200 tonnes, burnt a ship of the Marquis of Santa Cruse of 1500
tonnes and 31 ships more, of 1000, 800, 600, 400, to 200 tonnes the
piece, and carried away four with us laden with provision, and departed thence at our pleasure with as much honor as we could wish,
notwithstanding that during the time of our abode there we were
both oftentimes fought withall by 12 of the King's galleys (of which
we sank two)." Fortunately, they "always repulsed them and were
(without ceasing) vehemently shot at from the shore, but to our little hurt, God be thanked."

Drake wrote to the queen herself the next day, summarizing reports he had heard about the rich prizes to be taken at Cádiz. If he
did not act, he warned, Spain would deploy them against England.
"These great preparations of the Spaniard may be speedily prevented," he advised the queen, "by sending your forces to encounter
them somewhat far off, and more near their own coasts, which will

be better cheap"—that is, strategic—"for your Majesty and the people, and much the dearer for the enemy."

He cautioned her not to be distracted by Spanish deception: "The
promise of peace from the Prince of Parma and these mighty preparations in Spain agree not well together."

*E*ager to put the troops crowded aboard his ships to work, Drake
summoned his captains to announce a plan to land at Sagres, to the
south. But his second-in-command, William Burroughs, captain of
Golden Lion, objected in writing that Drake's proposal was terribly
ill-conceived. Moreover, he considered Drake's manner of command
insulting to experienced captains, which was another way of saying
that Burroughs resented Drake's success, sudden wealth, knighthood, and access to the queen.

In a spiteful mood, he took up his pen to savage Drake's strategy
and seamanship. "In all this voyage since our coming . . . I could
never perceive any matter of counsel or advice touching the action
& service for her Majesty, with the fleet now under your charge, to
be effectually propounded, & debated," he began, and launched into
a detailed complaint. "You have used us well by entertaining us with
your good cheer, & so most times after our stay with you most part
of the day, we have departed as wise as we came, without any consultation or counsel held. This manor of assemblies (albeit it may please
you to term them either counsels or courts) are far from the purpose
& not such as by any reason they ought to be. You also neglected
giving instructions to the Fleet in time and sort as they ought to
have had and as yet ought to be,—for which I have been sorry."

Worse, according to Burroughs, "I have found you always so
wedded to your own opinion & will, that you rather disliked and
showed as that it were offensive unto you that any should give

you advice in anything (at least I speak it for myself) for which case I have refrained often to speak that which otherwise I would." It seemed to Burroughs that Drake treated him with inexplicable disdain: "Nay, you deal not so with me as you do to others." He merely asked of Drake "to be well used by you, in respect of, and according to, my place." It was a show of false modesty, but affecting nonetheless.

Burroughs had more to get off his chest. It was bad enough that Drake played favorites, but he overlooked their central objective: to frustrate the Armada, "to seek, by all the best means you can, to impeach their purpose, and stop their meeting at Lisbon." If Drake troubled to review what was said, "I think the words will not bear you out."

Did Drake forget that "to land men, requireth a land wind, or calm weather & smooth water, that the ships may be brought at anchor near the shore"? What if "the wind should chop off into the sea upon the sudden, what then, do you think it meet that the ships should remain at anchor, & put all in hazard to be lost and cast away?" Burroughs urged Drake to "consider effectually of these points, for I have done so, and thereupon am resolved in opinion that it is not meet nor convenient that you attempt to land hereabout: which I thought good to advertise rather by writing which you may keep to yourself."

Drake had been conducting daring raids for two decades and did not take kindly to this extended reprimand. His plan to sail to the volcanic Isle of Terceira in the Azores drove Burroughs to disobey Drake's orders, prompting Drake to relieve him of command and place him under arrest. On May 21, he wrote that Burroughs "had not carried himself in this action so well as I wish he had done for his own sake, and . . . hath committed a double offense not only against me, but it toucheth further." As a result, "I dismissed him."

Burroughs's challenge to Drake's authority was pointless. Drake was recognized as the most capable captain in the English navy, with a series of accomplishments stretching back more than twenty years, not the least of which was his successful circumnavigation of the globe. Burroughs, in contrast, was known for sending a procession of men to be hanged, ten in all. Yet he now sought to condemn Drake's matchless record.

Drake was furious with Burroughs but resisted the urge to reply in kind. He conferred with his captain, Thomas Fenner, and his chaplain, Philip Nichols, to compile a list of charges against the offender. Then he summoned Burroughs to the flagship, where, in the presence of Fenner and Nichols, he charged him with insubordination and formally removed him from command.

Stunned, Burroughs belatedly realized he had gone too far and penned a letter of apology, but it did not sway Drake. The former captain suddenly found himself a passenger on his own ship. Soon Burroughs was leading a mutiny, although he later claimed to be unaware of it. Ultimately, the troublemaker was sent back to England, leaving Drake with a freer hand but with only nine ships.

*D*rake looked forward to a battle that would dwarf the one he had just survived. He evoked the "great forces we hear the King of Spain has out in the Straits. Prepare in England strongly," he urged, "and mostly by sea."

He concluded: "Stop him now, and stop him ever."

*O*n May 14, Drake and his fleet arrived at the harbor at Lagos, a small port on the extreme southern coast of Portugal where steep cliffs loomed above shimmering cobalt and emerald water. Lagos was known for its flourishing slave trade. Drake put a thousand soldiers ashore, who made for the nearest stronghold. The fort offered no resistance, and Drake captured it. A mile away, on the cape, the castle of Sagres proved to be a more stubborn objective. The garrison there held a hundred well-armed soldiers, defending a site and protecting their families, huddled inside. Drake set fire to the castle gate and besieged the fort for two hours, until the commander surrendered.

The next day, Drake marched his men to a nearby monastery from which the monks had already fled for their lives. According to a possibly biased Spanish report, Drake's men vandalized the monastery, destroyed religious images, and set fire to the structure: "They committed their usual feasts and drunkenness, their diabolical rampages and obscenities. They stole everything they found and then set the place on fire, having first committed a thousand excesses and diabolical desecrations on the images of the saints, like wicked heretics."

Drake did not participate in the free-for-all. He and the other gentlemen in the company returned to the ships and permitted the sailors to do their worst. The raid ended with the desecration of a Catholic church. Nothing could have made Drake and his men more despised in Spain. Oblivious to such concerns, Drake, in his own mind, was still bent on gaining a measure of revenge for the brutality that he and his late cousin Robert Barret had suffered years before at the hands of the Spanish.

*D*rake proceeded toward Sagres, on the southern tip of Portugal, traditionally considered the seat of Prince Henry's school of navigators, established in 1418. As if in defiance of that ancient mariner,

Drake positioned himself offshore and captured almost a hundred Lusitanian ships and caravels, relieving them of their supplies of hoops and oars and pipe staves: wood strips used to make the sides of barrels. He sent an inventory of his haul to Walsingham—"I assure your honour that the hoops and pipe staves were above 16 or 17 hundred ton in weight." He commanded that all of it "be consumed into smoke and ashes by fire, which will be unto the King no small waste of his provisions, besides the want of his barques." Without these humble items, crews could not function, and Spain could not prevail.

With the concern for sparing human life that occasionally marked his raids throughout the world, Drake released the Portuguese sailors. "The Portuguese I have always commanded to be used well and sent them ashore without the wanting of any of their apparel." He explained that he did not want to hurt them, "but I found them employed for Spanish services which we hold to be our mortal enemies." After dispensing with the Portuguese, Drake burned the items he had captured, along with small boats and fishing nets, ruining the tuna-fishing season. ("The nets we have consumed," Drake observed, "will cause the people to curse their governors to their face.")

Emboldened, Drake headed for Lisbon, which was now in a state of alarm concerning the destruction he had brought about, and dropped anchor near Cascais, a onetime royal refuge. Natural splendor abounded. Crisp, scented breezes wafted over glistening hills. The Marquis of Santa Cruz appeared, but perhaps intimidated by Drake's ferocity, the admiral stood by, doing nothing. Drake sent the Spanish leader a message that he was prepared to engage in combat, but the marquis feebly replied that he had not been authorized by the king to respond.

Another version of their interaction held that Drake merely inquired if the admiral was prepared to negotiate for the return of prisoners, but "the Marquis sent me word that as he was a gentleman he had none and that I should assure myself that if he had had any he would surely have sent them to me, which I knew was not so." In fact, English and Portuguese spies had informed Drake that the marquis held "divers Englishmen both in his galleys and prisons," but required authorization from both the king and the clergy to release them.

Drake anticipated still more maneuvers to humiliate the Spanish monarchy. "As long as it shall please God to give us provisions to eat and drink, and that our skies and wind and weather will permit us, you shall surely hear of us near this Cape of St. Vincent," he wrote of the windswept point at the extreme southwest of Portugal.

Drake was never more powerful in his career than he was at this moment. He felt he was shaping the political destiny of Spain, or, to be more precise, undoing it by attacking its most vulnerable component: Portugal.

$\mathcal{D}$rake's two-week-long rampage in Cádiz had done more damage than anyone had foreseen. The queen expected a quick skirmish, nothing more, to put the Spanish on notice, not a sustained campaign of terror. Even Drake was surprised by the outcome and mystified as before by the Spanish passivity in the face of his attack. There were other lessons to be learned from this unexpected piece of good fortune. Most important, Portuguese carracks, in addition to being richly laden, proved easy to seize. If anything, it was even easier to steal from the Portuguese than from the Spanish. Then there was the wealth of the East Indies to consider. It would profit England to exploit this previously unfamiliar source of abundance. An empire in the east was there for the taking.

*D*rake shaped his course for the Azores, a spectacular archipelago situated a thousand miles to the west. Steep cliffs ascended from ultramarine waters, and lush vegetation flourished on ancient volcanic outcroppings. Yet all was not well in paradise. He reported to Walsingham that his men were falling ill and supplies growing short. Although disease had spread to all his ships, and Drake's men were reluctant to extend the voyage and risk their lives, he insisted on proceeding.

Less than a day into the voyage, a storm struck, which the merchant ships took as an excuse to seek safety. When the storm abated on May 22, *Golden Lion*, formerly commanded by Burroughs, was heading north with forty-six sick men aboard. They had given the captain a written demand to return home. Offering no resistance, Captain John Marchant, who had replaced Burroughs, simply abandoned ship.

By June 5, *Golden Lion* had arrived in Dover with Burroughs still aboard. Seeking to avoid prosecution, Burroughs immediately set about writing his own account of events to the Lord High Admiral:

> Objection: Sir Francis Drake allegeth against me,
> William Burroughs that I am in fault and guilty for
> the *Golden Lion*'s coming away from him at the sea,
> without his consent; which fault he, his associates,
> and followers, think worthy to be punished by
> death, which they urge and prosecute as they may.
>
> Answer. My answer is: That I am not guilty any
> manner of way; for procuring the coming away of
> that ship in such sort, but the ground and cause
> thereof was the company of the ship, which did

mutiny against the Captain and Master, whereof I
had no knowledge or suspicion. . . . I spoke unto the
company, and told them that they had entered into
a matter that might hazard their lives, and therefore
wished them to be better advised, and prayed them to
stay till they had spoken with the Admiral, and made
him acquainted with their wants and griefs. They
answered they would not stay to speak with him, for
they had had many fair promises, but found nothing
performed; and if they should go back unto him
he would shift them out of that ship, and use them
with tyranny, and therefore they would go home and
rather stand to the Queen's mercy for their lives,
or be hanged at home, amongst their friends.

Drake, intensely annoyed by this challenge to his command, convened a court that hastily found Burroughs guilty of desertion and pronounced the sentence: death.

Rallying his remaining men once again, Drake reminded his crew they were looking for a rich prize: "I assure your honour our sickness is very much, both of our soldiers and mariners. . . . But if God will bless us with some little comfortable dew from heaven, some crowns or some reasonable boo[ty] for our soldiers and mariners, all will take good heart again, although they were half dead." The best medicine was gold and silver.

He approached the Isle of St. Michael (São Miguel), where he encountered a Portuguese carrack called *Saint Philip*. He made short work of capturing it and sending its crew home bit by bit in merchant vessels. Of greater importance, the plunder was sufficient to assure all of Drake's men a very substantial reward for their effort.

Emboldened, Drake ordered his squadron to sail home to Plymouth, where he boosted his reputation by bringing another infusion of wealth to his sovereign. The English decided that it was easy enough to plunder such carracks, and, in the process, they gained a better appreciation of the riches of the East Indies that they carried, and that realization in turn added further impetus for England to develop its own global empire. If the Portuguese navy could do it, why not England?

The Portuguese navy was said to be the oldest in the world, and Drake retained a mariner's respect for the accomplishments of Portuguese seafaring. The Portuguese explorer Vasco da Gama's epic voyages to India, from 1497 to 1499, again in 1502 to 1503, and finally in 1524, pioneered an ocean route from Western Europe to the East by way of the Cape of Good Hope. Da Gama made sure that history would remember his first voyage by depositing *padrões*, or stone pillars, along his route. He erected one on an island near Mossel Bay, South Africa; two in Mozambique; and another in Calicut, India, to demonstrate that his fleet had visited there. And Ferdinand Magellan, of course, was Portuguese, even though he sailed under the auspices of Spain.

When it came to Spain, however, Drake's grudging respect turned to contempt, and even to hatred. He had seen and suffered the excesses and brutality of the Spanish empire and the monstrous indignity of the Inquisition. Laying waste to a Spanish vessel was for him as natural as breathing. They were clumsy, slow, top-heavy, and poorly commanded. Nor was Drake alone in his opinion. Even the Duke of Parma, regarded as Spain's best admiral, had scant confidence in the prowess of the Spanish navy. And now, thanks to Drake, the English navy, despite its improvised nature, was poised to replace Spain as the dominant seafaring force.

*A*s England gained confidence, Spain faltered. Philip suffered excruciating episodes of gout and was often confined to bed. Occasionally he hobbled through his sweet-smelling garden or sat at his desk, arranging pieces of paper representing aspects of his empire's destiny. As always, he believed God would guide Spain to achieve victory. (Meanwhile, Elizabeth was constantly on the move. She rode horseback and hunted and worried over the wisdom of her decisions and the future of her country.)

A prisoner of his geopolitical preconceptions, Philip assumed that English Catholics would rise up spontaneously to join the invading Spanish troops in their campaign against Elizabeth. But there was no sign of that response. He assumed that Spain had the capability of invading England by sea. Again, a miscalculation, as was his expectation that the Duke of Parma would stake his reputation on the outcome. Nevertheless, Philip wrote to the Marquis of Santa Cruz and the Duke of Parma to describe every detail of the planned invasion as if they were maneuvering toy ships on a tabletop rather than actual vessels on a treacherous sea.

Throughout Spain, anti-English feeling ran high. Priests and writers joined politicians to proclaim Spain's impending victory over the English. A scrap of anti-English doggerel fanned Spanish hopes of enslaving the English:

My brother Don John
To England is gone,
To kill the Drake
And the Queen to take,
And the heretics all to destroy:
And he will give me

When he comes back
A Lutheran boy
With a chain round his neck;
And our lady grandmamma shall have,
To wait upon her, a Lutheran slave.

Heedless of such threats, Drake continued to infuriate Spain. Before he left the Azores, on the night of June 8, his lookout discerned the sails of a large ship in the lee of the Azores Isle of St. Michael. In the morning, Drake, benefiting from a breeze coming from astern, approached the ship. On closer inspection, he made out her flag as it was being raised. It contained a red cross; it was Spanish. Those aboard the enemy ship wanted Drake, hiding in anonymity, to show his colors immediately, but he waited, and waited, until he came within cannon range.

All at once Drake ran up the flag of England along with battle streamers and pennants flapping smartly in the breeze. Drake opened fire, and the ship tried to return it, but with little conviction. Drake's cannonballs killed several crewmen, injured several others, and tore through the hull. Two small vessels in Drake's fleet sidled up to the hawseholes—openings cut through the bows of a ship on each side of the stem, through which the cables passed—and prepared to board.

As usual, the Spanish put up little resistance, as if the loss of one ship out of their enormous fleet hardly mattered. The captain surrendered without a fuss. Drake boarded her to see what sort of trophy he had bagged. It turned out to be the king's ship *San Felipe* from the East Indies with a cargo of china, velvet, silk, gold and jewels, and slaves—all fit for a king, in this case the King of Spain.

*D*rake commandeered *San Felipe* and led her, along with the rest of the fleet, to Plymouth, where they arrived on June 26. This should have been a signal event, to arrive in England with the King of Spain's ship, but there were complications. Burroughs, preceding Drake, had asserted that crew members aboard Drake's ships had been stricken with the plague. It seems he was exaggerating, because Drake was able to return to Plymouth, where his new wife, Elizabeth, joined him aboard ship. But fear of the plague remained.

Much of Drake's fleet had already returned home, and they awaited their share of his plunder. *San Felipe*'s cargo was valued at £114,000, of which £40,000 went to the queen. Drake had done it again; he had brought home a fortune in stolen Spanish goods for his sovereign. An inventory listed £40,000 of pepper "of which much is decayed"; 115 packs of calico, at fifty to the pack, worth £5,750; 400 fardels of cinnamon, worth £8,000; cloves worth £1,600; ebony worth £1,000; and an astounding 110 chests containing "divers other kinds of merchandise" such as saltpeter, silk, and wax; and of course the ship itself, valued at £2,000.

The remaining inventory consisted of trinkets in caskets: six gold forks, a dozen golden hafts for knives, six gold chains, as well as rings, beads, and bracelets, a flask of musk, pomanders, crosses, and ambergris, most of them made from or decorated with gold. The grand total came to £108,049. (And there might have been even more. Mendoza claimed that an additional 300,000 ducats had been removed from *San Felipe* but had not been accounted for. Drake was a prime suspect for this pilfering, at least in Mendoza's imagination.)

Drake presented all of these precious items to the queen, but if he expected a reprise of the honors that she had conferred on him after his circumnavigation, he was mistaken. Instead, she let it be known that she was highly displeased with his violating Spanish territory. Burghley went so far as to inform Flanders, their ally, "those actions were committed by Sir Francis Drake, for the which Her Majesty is as yet greatly offended at him." This was on July 18, 1587. Burghley's unconvincing letter gave every evidence of an after-the-fact attempt to obscure the embarrassing reality of Drake's actions. In fact, by October, Burghley was deliberating how to persuade Drake to "yield up his account for this last voyage."

As before, Drake's bravado and plunder covered a multitude of his sins. All of a sudden, the English could boast that Drake had "singed the King of Spain's beard" during the raid. In time, the "singeing of the King's beard" came to signify the entire Cádiz operation, suggesting that Drake had taught the implacable Catholic monarch, and by extension his empire, a thing or two. With such captains in the service of the queen, England could be a deadly foe.

Just when it appeared that Drake had made the case that war between England and Spain was imminent, Elizabeth in her inscrutable fashion decided the time had come to withdraw, to the point of expressing regret about sending troops to the Netherlands, where she had expended £60,000 more on troops than planned. She remained conflicted concerning Drake's uproarious adventure in Cádiz harbor. Yes, it had put Spain on notice that England was not to be trifled with, but it had also shattered the appearance of neutrality and a peaceful if uneasy coexistence with Spain. When Leicester reminded her of Drake's prowess in battle, she shot back, "I do not see that he has done much damage to the enemy, except to scandalize him at considerable loss to me."

With that, she initiated peace talks with Spain. Her closest adviser, Leicester, realized that Elizabeth was mistaken if she thought that Spain would come around to her point of view. Drake, under no illusions, tried to impress the urgency of the situation on Walsingham. This was not the time to discuss peace; England should prepare for war. "I assure Your Honor, the like preparation was never heard of, nor known, as the King of Spain hath and daily maketh to invade England."

Drake's report was correct. Although slow to prepare, Spain had every intention of attacking England. Philip was pleased that Spain's strategy of appearing to be receptive to England's peaceful overtures was working, but he reminded his military chief, Parma, that the goal was distraction, not a treaty. "All this is done," he wrote of the English, "to deceive and cool them in their preparations for defence, by inducing them to believe that such preparations will be unnecessary." In the meantime, he advised Parma to apply "the greatest diligence in our efforts for the invasion of England."

At the same time, Drake pursued the highly unpleasant matter of Burroughs. A court was convened, and on July 25 at Theobalds, Lord Burghley's house north of London, Drake read from his diary the charges and the evidence against Burroughs. In addition to insubordination, Burroughs was now charged with cowardice and desertion. The accusations were based on Drake's interpretation of Burroughs's actions at Cádiz. In this version of events, Burroughs had come aboard his ship "in trembling sort" on the morning after they entered Cádiz and urged Drake to move out of the harbor. Burroughs's *Golden Lion* had not fought the Spanish galleys, Drake said, she had deserted.

When his turn arrived, Burroughs played his strongest card and reminded the court of Drake's execution of Thomas Doughty. In his defense, Burroughs feared that "the Admiral would have executed upon me his bloodthirsty desire as he did upon Doughty." And he went on to describe his heroic efforts at Cádiz, battling the Spanish galleys while the other ships plundered.

Burroughs's testimony amounted to a fairly convincing reply to the charges leveled against him with one exception: the charge of inciting mutiny. There was every indication that he had played an important role in the uprising. On that basis, his fate might be the same as Doughty's, but Burroughs was in luck. At that moment, Elizabeth sought to appease the King of Spain and to present a serene facade to the world. There would be no execution of Burroughs.

The matter did not end there. It emerged that two of Drake's captains had visited the imprisoned sailors from the *Golden Lion*, who were in the Marshalsea prison, to induce them to give false testimony. As a result, the case that Drake had been building against Burroughs fell apart.

The entire convoluted proceeding forcefully reminded Drake just how capricious Elizabeth could be, and how precarious his position, no matter how much gold and silver he had brought back to England. That was all in the past. At the moment, Burroughs was free, and Drake labored under a cloud of suspicion.

CHAPTER XVII

Signs and Portents

In the early months of 1588, the English populace dwelled on predictions of events "afflicting mankind with woeful destiny." The credulous saw signs and portents everywhere. Regiomontanus (Johannes Müller von Königsberg), an influential fifteenth-century German mathematician and astrologer, had predicted that 1588 could witness "the final dissolution of the world." Such pronouncements placed everyone on edge.

Gossip dwelled on matters such as the number of fleas gathered on the window of the "Queen's Presence Chamber at Court," as well as "thirty great fish" swimming up the Thames. The latter curiosity attracted the attention of King Philip himself. Mendoza noted with satisfaction that a cannon exploded aboard one of Drake's ships on April 5, killing thirty-five men and wounding seven more. The English regarded the accident as "an evil omen." Mendoza naturally thought otherwise.

To calm the populace, the Privy Council commissioned an expert named Dr. John Harve to write a book to put cosmic matters in perspective. There would be one solar and two lunar eclipses in 1588, he conceded, but he was not worried in the slightest, and those who thought that the planet Mars was stirring up trouble were misinformed. As he saw things, Mars was "greatly unlike to infect, terrify or astonish the world."

Heedless of this foreboding, Elizabeth pursued the illusion of a peaceful understanding with Spain, despite the many voices at court counseling otherwise. Greatly alarmed, Howard, Elizabeth's recently appointed Lord High Admiral, wrote to warn Walsingham of a trap. "Sir, there was never, since England was England, such a stratagem and mask made to deceive England withal as this is of the treaty of peace."

Elizabeth preferred to take encouragement from the elderly and befuddled Sir James Croft, who was secretly in the pay of Spain. Doing as told, he assured the queen that Spain was only interested in peace. Realizing that he and the queen were working at cross-purposes, Howard feared that he was becoming "a jest to many, and they have reason." Despite his doubts, Elizabeth kept trying to negotiate a peace settlement, or maintain the appearance that she was, until the Armada set sail.

The English public was exposed to a completely different message by William Allen, one of the leaders of the "Spanish Party" among the Roman Catholics in England and in Ireland. King Philip recommended that Allen be made a cardinal in 1587, and he subsequently warned in a book that should Spain invade England, the populace would do well to enlist in Philip's army and drive out the queen, who was, the cardinal wrote, "an infamous, deprived, accused, excommunicate heretic; the very shame of her sex and princely name; the chief spectacle of sin and abomination." With Leicester, she had conspired in an "unspeakable and incredible variety of lust" that had turned her court into a moral cesspool. Even when these accusations reached Elizabeth's ears, she continued to negotiate with Spain, although with less conviction.

To complicate matters, the Spanish admiral Santa Cruz, with

whom Philip had been planning the invasion, suddenly died on February 9, 1588, at the age of sixty-one. He had been the most capable and trusted naval officer in Spain, and his demise could not have come at a worse moment. Ever since Drake had carried out his successful terror attack in Cádiz harbor, Santa Cruz had lost the goodwill and confidence of Philip, who held him responsible for the delays in readying the Armada. Afterward, it was said that Philip's scorn had contributed to Santa Cruz's death.

Santa Cruz's replacement was Alonso Pérez de Guzmán, Seventh Duke of Medina Sidonia. He enjoyed a favorable reputation and had helped to assemble the Armada. He was not at all happy with the promotion. By his own description, he had "neither aptitude, ability, health nor fortune" to meet the challenge, "for I know by the small experience that I have had afloat that I soon become sea-sick." Beyond that, he was deeply in debt: "My family owes 900,000 ducats, and I am therefore quite unable to accept the command. I have not a single real to spend in the King's service." Nor was he the right person for the assignment, claiming he had no experience of seafaring. No matter, he met Philip's criteria for a leader. He came from the highest echelons of the nobility, was unquestionably loyal to the crown, and, most important, was a man of unswerving Christian faith. If Medina Sidonia hoped to escape the assignment by pleading lack of naval qualifications and material resources, he soon learned that this gambit failed to convince the powers that be. In reality, he was well versed in navigational theory, and he was generally capable, except that he did suffer from seasickness. More important, his misgivings had a basis in reality. In his professional judgment, the Armada was doomed to failure. He wrote to Philip that only a miracle could save the fleet and Spain from disaster.

The king's advisers dreaded showing the warning to the king. "Do not depress us with fears for the fate of the Armada because in such a cause, God will make sure it succeeds," they advised the new admiral. They flattered him—"Nobody knows more about naval affairs than you"—and they threatened him—"Remember that the reputation and esteem you currently enjoy for courage and wisdom would entirely be forfeited if what you wrote to us became generally known (although we shall keep it secret)."

*E*lizabeth dodged the issue of an all-out naval battle even as she took steps to strengthen the English navy. She now had at her disposal twenty-five warships, plus many others available for charter. John Hawkins, Drake's former mentor, having won her confidence, served as treasurer for the navy. He updated the fleet by replacing ships that rode high in the water, or sported obsolete towering castles, with lower, sleeker, faster vessels.

The Lord High Admiral, Charles, Lord Howard of Effingham, took it upon himself to inspect the fleet and was heartened by what he saw. "I have been aboard every ship that goeth out with me, and in every place where any may creep, and I do thank God that they be in the estate they be in; and there is never a one of them that knows what a leak means," he told Walsingham, and "there is none that goeth out now but I durst go to the Rio de la Plata in her," and a good thing that was, because by this time Walsingham considered war with Spain inevitable. Other insiders, including the queen's newest favorite, Walter Raleigh, identified locations where Spanish forces were likely to land, and these were strengthened against the growing likelihood of invasion. Preparations became still more serious in April 1588, when the call went out to thirty-seven seaside towns to ready private ships as the first line of defense against a Spanish attack.

By then, Francis Drake urged a more active strategy, leading his fleet to the coast of Spain to destroy the enemy before it could inflict any damage. He explained his thinking to Elizabeth: "The advantage of time and place in all martial actions is half a victory," and he argued to the council that "fifty sail" could do more damage off the coast of Spain than many times that number closer to England.

Elizabeth fretted that the Spanish Armada might evade her ships and invade defenseless England. Her Lord High Admiral agreed. Drake initially took issue with Howard, the embodiment of a desk admiral, with little experience at sea, let alone in combat, but then something surprising occurred. The admiral recognized expertise when he saw it, and he allowed himself to be convinced. A grateful Drake repaid Howard for coming around to his point of view by determining to behave "lovingly and kindly" toward the admiral at all times. Whether expedient or sincere, it was a wise decision. Drake secured his connection with Howard by attending church with him on Whit Sunday (the seventh Sunday after Easter) and receiving the sacrament with him. Drake's attentiveness bore fruit when Howard made sure to tell Walsingham "how lovingly and kindly Sir Francis Drake bearest himself, and also how dutifully to her Majesty's service and unto me. I pray that he may receive thanks." And Drake returned the compliment by letting Burghley know that he found Howard "so well affected for all honorable services in this action as it doth assure all his followers of good success and hope of victory." The alliance between Howard and Drake would prove lasting and crucial to the smooth functioning of the overmatched English navy.

For all Drake's experience and daring, Spain retained the advantage at sea. Elizabeth and her ministers had failed to protect the kingdom from invasion for the simple reason that England, nearly insolvent, could not afford to take precautions. There were no ramparts, no standing army, and only a few isolated garrisons—often as not deserted—near Dover Castle on the channel. A 1588 survey listed only a hundred experienced soldiers, most of them too old to fight. Elizabeth and her ministers estimated that half of the English populace was Catholic and feared they would side with the Spanish invaders, whom they would consider their deliverers, and help them rid England of Protestants.

Robert Dudley, the queen's intimate, warned against "rebels and traitors and other offenders and their adherents attempting anything against us, our crown, and dignity," and vowed to "slay or kill and put to death by all ways and means" insurgents who dared resist. Catholic recusants—those who refused to attend Anglican services—were disarmed and imprisoned without trial. The sense of urgency could not have been greater.

If Spain's Armada landed as expected at Margate, on the southeast coast, the marauders would arrive in London within days, make straight for the queen, and execute her after a brief trial. The Spanish flag would fly over British soil, and Philip II, the king of Spain and Portugal, would return England to his Catholic realm.

As protection against this dire outcome, Elizabeth relied on her ships, which she called her kingdom's "walls," and again Drake was responsible for maintaining their integrity. Whenever she needed someone to achieve a brilliant victory, she called on Francis Drake. She had called on him to confront the Spanish in the New World and to claim territory for her, and so he did. Now she urgently needed him to defend the realm against the Spanish: the greatest challenge of all.

It was time for England to go to war.

*T*he stakes could not have been higher for England or Drake. This contemplated attack was not some consequence-free pirate mission on a distant shore. In those operations, as long as he came away with life and limb, he would fight another day. Now, against Spain, he had to find a way to trounce the Spanish, as unlikely as it seemed. And if he went down in defeat, Protestant England might perish along with him. Elizabeth had escaped death time and again since she was a child, but Spain's cruelly methodical approach to conquest held special peril for her. If Catholic Spain prevailed, they would come for her, the Protestant queen who had condemned a Catholic queen to death, and she would find herself subjected to the same torture that her countrymen had inflicted on Catholics. This was not just war, this was a holy war.

In the meantime, Howard swelled with pride at the sight of the English fleet ready to do battle with Spain. From Plymouth he wrote to Burghley, "My good Lord, there is here the gallantest company of captains, soldiers, and mariners that I think ever was seen in England."

Drake wrote to the Lords of the Council from Plymouth on March 30, 1588, carefully preparing them for the inevitable: a war with Spain intended to protect England from all-out invasion. He stressed the advantages possessed by King Philip and his partner in conquest, the Duke of Parma:

> *If her Majesty and your Lordships think that the King of Spain meaneth any invasion in England, then doubtless his force is and will be great in Spain, and thereon he will make his groundwork, or foundation, whereby the Prince of Parma may have the better entrance, which in mine own judgment is most to be feared. . . .*
>
> *To prevent this I think it good that these forces here should be made as strong as to your Honors' wisdoms shall be thought convenient, and that for two special causes: first, for that they are like to strike the first blow, and secondly,*

it will put great and good hearts into her Majesty's loving
subjects both abroad and at home, for that they will be per-
suaded in conscience that the Lord of all strengths will put
into her Majesty and her people courage & boldness not to
fear any invasion in her own country, but to seek God's en-
emies and her Majesty's where they may be found, for the
Lord is on our side, whereby we may assure ourselves our
numbers are greater than theirs.

Drake ended on a note of caution. He needed firepower as soon as possible. He had already sent for weapons and was awaiting delivery. And he would soon need more, for he had requested only a third of the total number of armaments that he expected to use. Above all, it must come quickly, "for if we should want it when we shall have most need thereof, it will be too late to send to the Tower for it."

*F*our weeks later, on April 28, Drake, perturbed and frustrated in Plymouth that he was not being listened to, alerted the queen to his urgent concerns. He hammered away at the argument that Spain would negotiate a peaceful settlement with England. That was a trap. His instincts told him that Philip was preparing for war and hoping to lure England into a false sense of security.

Although Drake embellished his correspondence with declarations of loyalty, his message was unsentimental: do not be fooled by the Spanish. As such it was likely to appeal to Elizabeth, who habitually peered below the glossy surface of affairs for darker impulses. And she grasped the reason why English ships should go out to meet Spain, rather than the other way around. The farther these potential invaders were kept from vulnerable English shores, the better.

*S*oon after Drake wrote these words of warning, the Armada was under sail. There had already been numerous delays. Every day they waited gave England the opportunity to arm, protect the queen, and seize the initiative. Not until May 19 did the "most fortunate Armada," as the fleet was called, finally depart for England.

The Armada was among the largest fleets ever assembled, a testament to Spain's wealth and pride. It was divided into ten squadrons, the largest of which belonged to Portugal, consisting of fourteen ships, including *São Martinho*, the flagship of the seasick commander in chief, Medina Sidonia. Another squadron, Viscaya, was comprised of fourteen ships; eleven from Castile; fourteen from Guipúzcoa; ten Levantine ships from Sicily and Lisbon, plus many others. Philip, always pious, assigned religious watchwords to the ships to identify themselves during their crusade. Sunday: Jesus. Monday: Holy Ghost. Tuesday: Most Holy Trinity. Wednesday: Santiago. Thursday: The Angels. Friday: All Saints. Saturday: Our Lady. In all, 132 ships made up the great Spanish Armada, manned by 8,766 sailors, 21,556 soldiers, and 2,088 convict rowers.

The Armada was made up for festivities rather than for combat. Flags and pennants snapped gaily in the wind. The warships displayed decorative freeboard; gilt flashed everywhere. Ornamented shields protected the cannon, and the sails carried the billowing sword, the symbol of Spanish might. The officers and men dressed in a dazzling variety of attire. Nobles wore jewel-encrusted armor; gentlemen wore silk and velvet. Crimson, purple, royal blue, and violet were the predominant colors of their capes, clothes, and flags, all of it highlighted with gold thread: flamboyant costumes better suited for the stage than for battle at sea. Even the lower ranks of soldiers wore finery. One sergeant, later captured, went into combat wearing stylish blue velvet hose accented with gold and silver lace and a jerkin of finely worked velvet, cushioned with taffeta. Musketeers displayed a red ribbon around one arm and wore hats with expansive brims bearing plumes. Finery for all to see, right down to the slaves toiling in bright red jackets to accent the waterborne pageant. Yet the regalia gave the Spanish no military advantage.

Under sail, the ships of the Armada ranged across seven miles of open water, a fearsome sight to behold as they crested the whitecaps. "You could hardly see the sea," said a bystander, Juan Bentivollo. "The Spanish fleet was stretched out in the form of a half moon with an immense distance between its extremities. The masts and rigging, the towering sterns and prows which in height and number were so great that they dominated the whole naval concourse, caused horror mixed with wonder. . . . It came on with a steady and deliberate movement, yet when it drew near in full sail it seemed almost that the waves groaned under its weight and the winds were made to obey it."

The triumph of Spain, with its superior fleet and resources, seemed inevitable, but those in the know realized that English ships, though smaller and fewer in number, were faster and more agile, their cannon more maneuverable and muskets more potent—all that, plus the combination of daring and surprise contributed by Francis Drake.

The English navy, comprised mainly of merchant ships hastily converted for battle, was far more informal than Spain's vast Armada. The appearance of the English ships and soldiers could be summed up in a few words: dull, drab, and functional—with the important exception of the Cross of St. George emblazoned on the sails. Lord Charles Howard Effingham led a fleet consisting of *Ark Royal* (the flagship), *Elizabeth Bonaventure, Rainbow, Golden Lion, White Bear, Vanguard, Revenge* (Francis Drake's ship), *Victory* (John Hawkins'), and dozens of others: a navy of more than a hundred ships seemingly summoned out of thin air. Said a Spanish naval officer, "Unless God helps us by a miracle, the English, who have much faster and handier ships than ours, and more long-range guns, and who know their advantage just as well as we do, will never close with us at all, but stand aloof and knock us to pieces with their culverins [small cannon], without our being able to do them any serious hurt. So we are sailing against England in the confident hope of a miracle."

The journey from Lisbon cruelly exposed the unwieldy nature of the Armada's ships. The larger galleons, designed for boarding enemy ships and hand-to-hand combat, proved slow and unweatherly. Many of the merchant vessels in the Armada were designed for the calmer conditions found in the expanses of the Mediterranean Sea, their crews accustomed to sailing before the wind. In adverse conditions, they would anchor and wait for the wind to shift. Some ships carried large oars suitable for the Mediterranean, but such equipment was useless in the heavy Atlantic seas.

Burdened by these limitations, the Armada took three weeks to sail three hundred miles from Lisbon to Cape Finisterre. Already the crew suffered from disease and hunger, and the battle had not begun. When they did arrive, Medina Sidonia expected to replenish his supplies, but at that moment a violent storm struck, scattering many ships toward the Isles of Scilly, more than four hundred miles to the north, and smashing others on the coast of France. Weather wreaked more havoc than the enemy. When the storm relented, the remnants of the Armada limped into La Coruña in northwest Spain, where the battered ships loaded supplies, and pinnaces went in search of vessels scattered across the Bay of Biscay, the large gulf between the western coast of France and the northern coast of Spain.

Medina Sidonia's worst fear for the Armada had come to pass. "I am bound to confess that I see very few, or hardly any of those in the Armada with any knowledge or ability to perform the duties entrusted to them," he wrote to the king. "Your majesty may believe me when I assure you that we are very weak. Do not be deceived by anyone who may wish to persuade you otherwise." To be absolutely clear, he asked, "How do you think we can attack so great a country as England with such a force as ours is now?" Instead, he recommended that Spain agree to "some honorable terms with the enemy" while the damaged ships of the Armada underwent repairs in La Coruña.

Unnerved by the reversal of fortune, Philip spent all "day and night in prayer, although suffering from the gout in his hand." Even worse, Alexander Farnese, Duke of Parma, who commanded the invasion army, warned that the flat river barges intended to convey Spanish troops to England were in peril. "If we came across any armed English or [Dutch] rebel ships they could destroy us with the greatest ease," he wrote, and in the margin, he noted, "God grant that no embarrassment may come from this." No matter what hazards his men faced, Philip remained steadfast. He instructed Medina Sidonia: "I have dedicated this enterprise to God. Pull yourself together then and do your part!"

*B*y that time, the English navy had taken control. Elizabeth had previously ordered Howard's ships to "ply up and down" the waters near home, an empty exercise but a necessary one. As it happened, Philip had ordered his fleet to sail all the way to England, even if English sails appeared off the coast of Spain. The queen had guessed correctly. English ships carried only half the ammunition that the Spanish ships did, twenty-five rounds to fifty. If they met in the English Channel, Elizabeth's navy could easily restock and reload, but if they clashed a thousand miles away, off the coast of Spain, they would not be able to avail themselves of this strategy.

Howard replied to the queen with irritation, declaring that he was "glad" that others far away were better able to judge the situation than he. His acid words had their intended effect, and Elizabeth once again reversed herself, but by the time Howard set out, the wind had become southerly, and he was concerned that it would carry Spanish ships all the way to England before he could reach Spain. In June, he wrote to Walsingham in alarm: "And if her Majesty do think that she is able to detract time with the King of Spain, she is greatly deceived; which may breed her great peril."

Howard was still was not getting through. In desperation, he warned Elizabeth: "For the love of Jesus Christ, Madam, awake thoroughly, and see the villainous treasons round about you, against your Majesty and your realm, and draw your forces round about you, like a mighty prince, to defend you."

Fortunately for England, storms repeatedly forced the Spanish ships to turn around and head back to Spain, but by the afternoon of July 19 the full strength of the Armada, a seven-mile line of ships, appeared out of the mist near Lizard Point in Cornwall. (The name derives from the Cornish word *lezou*, meaning "headland.") At that moment, both Howard and Drake were supervising repairs to their ships. According to legend, Drake was engaged in playing a game of lawn bowls, a cross between billiards and curling, and when he heard about the sighting of Spanish sails, he quipped, "There is plenty of time to win the game and thrash the Spaniards too."

The English lit fire beacons along the shore from Devon to the Scottish border to warn the populace. They discharged heavy-duty cannon, trying to pick off Spanish vessels emerging from the gloom. It was a terrifying sight. There was no mistaking that the massive fleet was bent on conquest. And this time, luck was with the Spanish, because the ships would be close enough to grapple with the English, who would be unable to maneuver while confined in the harbor. In fact, both the wind and the tide ran contrary to England's advantage.

Maneuvering the English ships into position against the Spanish Armada proved arduous and painstaking. In the face of oncoming wind, a small craft would sail out, position a sea anchor, and then the ship would be dragged forward against the wind to a new, more secure position. Fifty-four English ships were dragged, or warped, out of the harbor by this method. Though awkward and time-consuming, warping moved the ships from their vulnerable location inside Plymouth harbor, where the Armada could have ensnared them, to the relative safety of the open sea. Just as important, it gave the English ships the all-important benefit of the weather gage, that is, the direction of the wind, which now favored them at Spain's expense.

At about the same time, Lord Howard, urged on by Drake, led his ships into the Bay of Biscay, where they planned to attack Spanish ships in La Coruña harbor. But the wind prevented Howard's fleet from sailing south. Howard returned to Plymouth, where he anticipated the arrival of Spanish ships in the Channel.

Philip instructed Medina Sidonia to sail along the Channel, clinging to the English shore until he reached Margate, where he was to rendezvous with ships from Dunkirk carrying Parma's army. Then Medina Sidonia would ensure that Parma landed in England. Parma understood Philip's orders to require the Armada to eliminate the English and Dutch fleets from the Channel and then escort his transports from Dunkirk to England. But Parma had no intention of leaving Dunkirk without the protection of the Armada.

On the night of July 20, Howard's and Drake's ships arrived at the Eddystone, a heavily eroded rock formation in the English Channel off Plymouth. Although it was dark, the two fleets caught sight of each other. That night Howard's vessels worked their way to the west, gaining a strategic advantage over the Spanish. With its greater maneuverability, the English navy provoked Spanish fire while keeping safely out of range. The English then approached, firing broadsides into the hulls of the enemy ships, damaging them below the waterline. The ships were so close that men exchanged fire from opposing decks. Drake's ship sustained heavier damage than the others, "pierced with shot above forty times" according to Hakluyt, "and his very cabin was twice shot through." All of this maneuvering happened as if in slow motion as the ships approached one another and bore off with stately precision. After eight hours of fighting, the English ships exhausted their supply of ammunition, and about four in the afternoon, the English fired off their final shots and pulled back.

The Armada might have succeeded despite all these obstacles had not King Philip overlooked the critical question of where his two commanders, Medina Sidonia and Parma, would merge their fleets.

Parma's resources were fully deployed in the Netherlands, yet Philip expected him to land in England, conquer the country, and seize Elizabeth. Parma knew an attempted invasion of England would end in disaster for Spain, yet he could not disobey Philip (Parma's mother was the king's half sister), so he offered token assistance. If any single event determined the outcome of the battle of the Spanish Armada, it was Parma's decision to withhold support at this decisive point. Without a rendezvous of the two fleets and a subsequent landing of soldiers in England, Spain could not prevail. Despite their superior size, the forces of King Philip had been lured into a perilous situation.

The ungainly Spanish ships, arrayed in a crescent extending seven miles, lumbered under full sail. The following day, Howard, the Lord High Admiral, sent a pinnace, *Disdain*, toward the fleet, blasting away at the Spanish. That was merely a distraction. At the same time England's preeminent naval warriors broke into squadrons—Drake, captain of *Revenge*; Hawkins, captain of *Victory*; and Frobisher, captain of *Triumph*. They approached the Spanish ships commanded by Admiral Juan Martínez de Recalde, who, suffering embarrassing losses, tried to pull out of range of English gunfire to no avail. His ship was disabled, her rigging in tatters, and shot wedged in her foremast.

The Duke of Medina Sidonia attempted to gather his fleet, but they were still at a disadvantage, as the wind favored the English. The rivals skirmished for two hours. Although the English kept forty ships in reserve, Howard decided to halt hostilities for the moment.

Drake sent a bulletin to Lord Henry Seymour to describe the peril facing the English at that moment. "The army of Spain arrived upon our coast. We had them in chase and so coming up unto them there hath passed some common shot between some of our fleet and some of theirs and as far as we perceive they are determined to sell their lives with blows."

He added as an afterthought, "This letter, my honorable good Lord, is sent in haste; the fleet of Spaniards is somewhat about a hundred sails; many great ships, but truly I think not half of them men of war."

Even as Drake was dictating, the battle continued. A Spanish ship caught fire, set, or so the English believed, by a rogue Dutch gunner. The fire spread quickly, and flames consumed two decks plus the roof, or poop, deck. The galleon commanded by Don Pedro de Valdez accidently collided with another Spanish ship, dislodging her foremast. The afflicted ship floated helplessly along the high seas at night, with no prospect of rescue. The Armada, rather than break its progress, sailed on, abandoning the galleon: another rich prize that fell into the hands of Drake thanks to Spanish indifference.

Drake took it upon himself to loot the abandoned Spanish ships. He captured badly needed gunpowder and, for good measure, gold. But then things went awry. He had been guiding the English fleet with a lantern, which he extinguished as he slipped away from the Spanish ships. The English ships following him became disoriented, and by dawn they had dispersed. As the scattered ships began reassembling, the Armada recovered.

The English fleet, meanwhile, had sailed past the Armada at night, undetected, and by the morning of July 22, they were west of the Spanish, with the weather gage still conferring a tactical advantage. Their determined adversary responded by ordering its warships to run interference for their slower, less agile supply ships, with galleons arrayed on either side of the formation. The English fired on the forward galleons for hours, to no avail.

The English ships attacked with renewed fury, sending the most "terrible value of great shot" hurtling toward the Armada, but they might as well have been firing at sea monsters, for they failed to take out even one Spanish vessel. The next day, the English came as close as they dared to their adversary, trading volleys off the coast, about 150 miles west of Plymouth. So it went for the next several days. The Armada proceeded along the English Channel, firing now and then, mostly for effect. To do real damage, they needed to get closer to the English ships, close enough to grapple and overwhelm those on board, but the maneuverable English vessels stayed out of range. Those lofty, ornate Spanish ships looked intimidating beside the low-slung English craft, but the armaments and other supplies they carried weighed them down. Occasionally a Spanish ship would attempt to draw up even with an English vessel, but at just the right moment, the queen's sleek craft would veer off, out of harm's way.

The English fleet and the Spanish Armada engaged once more off Portland, a land-tied island in the English Channel. During their maneuvering, the wind shifted, giving Spain the all-important weather gage, but as they prepared to attack, the English ships' superior maneuverability conferred a vital advantage. Howard ordered his ships to form a line of battle. Arrayed thus, they could fire their cannon without fear of hitting other English ships.

Howard decided not to press the attack despite having the advantage and withdrew. The ships of the Armada sought a sheltered area to await the promised arrival of Parma's army, but the army never came. Medina Sidonia, leading the Spanish ships, became desperate for sanctuary before the English attacked again. He was forced to order his ships to head northeast, all the way to the coast of France and Calais. And still Parma failed to appear.

To add to the general confusion, the ships of both countries displayed sails with a red cross on a white background. For the ships of the Armada, the red cross symbolized a crusade to depose a heretic queen. For the English, the red cross signified St. George, their patron saint.

By the end of July, the battered Spanish Armada was sailing off the coast of Calais en route to Dunkirk, where Parma's forces were waiting.

The Spanish fleet remained in a tightly knit group to reduce the danger of being picked off by Howard's ships. All were aware that this tactic rendered the Armada particularly vulnerable to attack by fireships, and that was exactly the strategy deployed against them.

At midnight on July 28, eight vessels filled with combustible material and manned by skeleton crews, or no crews at all, sailed toward the Armada. As they approached the anchored fleet, the eight ships erupted into flames. Medina Sidonia described the scene of horror that unfolded. "The alarm was raised. Men began to think they were terror-ships." The Duke, hasty and inexperienced, dashed out to the open sea to fight his adversary. Alert to the danger of such an attack, the Spanish had posted vessels that attempted to tow the fireships into shallow water where they could be beached until they burned out, but the plan failed. Explosions hurled debris into the sky, where it drifted on the wind and descended onto Spanish ships. The Spanish panicked under the assault, cut anchor, and fled through the darkness to the open sea.

*T*he next day, Drake vanished. He was supposed to lead his fleet; instead, he turned pirate and plundered his newest victim, *Nuestra Señora del Rosario*, a year-old warship carrying 50,000 gold ducats intended to pay the Spanish. The night before, the unlucky ship had collided with another Spanish vessel, *San Salvador*. The resulting horrific explosion killed two hundred of *San Salvador*'s crew members, cracked her bowsprit (the spar extending from the ship's prow), and brought down her sails and rigging. Ever the opportunist, Drake claimed the disabled ship as his personal prize the following morning. He would not rely on others—not even the queen—to reward his efforts. As before, he would do it himself.

Drake later provided 23,300 ducats, presumably taken from *Nuestra Señora del Rosario*, to Howard, but questions arose about the missing portion of the treasure. Suspicions about who might have stolen it fell on Spanish sailors, on English sailors, and on Drake, who was rumored to have kept 15,000 ducats, or gold coins. A *Revenge* crew member said that Drake had paid £2,000 to two officers. Another crew member claimed that Drake had been authorized by the queen to give some of the booty to various "gentlemen" on the voyage. Howard preferred to look the other way, but Martin Frobisher, the captain of *Triumph*, condemned Drake as a "cowardly knave or a traitor"—he could not decide which. As a result of this diversion, Drake's role in the defeat of the Armada was diminished as rival captains, notably Hawkins and Frobisher, rushed to take credit for the victory.

Spain, in contrast, still considered Drake its chief adversary.

*B*y the end of July, the Armada had anchored off Calais. Medina Sidonia sent further urgent messages to Parma in an attempt to discover his intentions and for the first time received a reply; Parma was not yet ready. The loss of the main anchors in this way was to have devastating consequences when ships later attempted to anchor off the coasts of Scotland and Ireland in fierce storms but were driven onto the shore.

*T*he small coastal town of Gravelines sits on the promontory of France, just south of Belgium between Dover and Calais. The name derives from the Dutch *Gravenenga*, meaning "Count's Canal." Charles V, Emperor of the Holy Roman Empire, and Elizabeth's father, Henry VIII, once met here, in 1520. And in 1558, thirty years earlier, it was the scene of a battle between Spain and France—and Spain won.

It was now August 1588, and once again Spain threatened. English ships streamed from every port to join meet the challenge. By this time, they held a numerical advantage, with 140 craft at the ready, along with their superior firepower.

English artillery was more advanced than that of the enemy. Spanish cannon were heavy, hard to move, and they were so difficult to load, prime, and shoot that it took everything the crews had just to fire a ball once or twice during a battle, whereas the English stored their ordnance on wheeled carts that moved rapidly across the decks, making it possible to fire much more frequently, which was precisely what they did off Gravelines. And all the while, they kept enough distance from the Spanish ships to avoid being grappled, which would have left them at the mercy of the larger Spanish ships. Even so, the two fleets came so close to each other that the English could hear the Spanish shouting "Lutheran chickens! Cowards!"

When the smoke dispersed, it became apparent that the English ships had crushed their Spanish counterparts. Medina Sidonia's flagship nearly sank and had to be saved by frantically plugging divers leaks. Two other disabled Spanish ships ran aground, and another sank with all hands—275 souls—frantically clutching the rigging as the water swirled and claimed their lives.

The Armada had no choice but to return home. In despair, Medina Sidonia admitted, "The enemy pursue us night and day, but will not grapple. There is no remedy for they are swift, and we are slow."

The Armada under Medina Sidonia lacked pilots familiar with the Netherlands coast and could not safely approach any harbors, which were situated along treacherous sandbanks.

Unable to retrace his route, Medina Sidonia was forced to order his Armada to sail for home around the tip of Scotland and along the west coast of Ireland. This was an unnerving prospect for a fleet short of food and water, with many of the ships already damaged in battle. The Spanish, who never expected to find themselves in this predicament, lacked charts to guide them on their perilous way. Their finery was of no help. The best Medina Sidonia could do was to give his captains abbreviated directions. Beset by violent squalls, with ships taking on water and sail ripped to shreds, the Armada scattered in the heavy seas.

*T*here was worse in store for the Spaniards. The next day, the floating castles of the Armada nearly ran aground. A strong northwest wind pushed the ships toward the coast of Zeeland, north of Germany, in Denmark. This was a circumstance the Spanish Armada had never anticipated. The Spanish ships were badly deteriorated, some of them held together with cables. They were running out of victuals and water. They might have considered sailing off the west coast of Scotland and Ireland, before heading to the open sea. By now Howard's ships had stopped menacing them.

But the Armada's pilots, unable to measure longitude to confirm their position, did not realize that the Gulf Stream bore them toward the north and east even as they tried to sail west. They had no maps of the region, and their pilots were unfamiliar with it. If only they had managed to lure the English ships closer to Spain, they would have been able to disable them, but here, on this remote coast, they were simply trying to stay afloat. To make matters still worse, the last years of the sixteenth century in general and especially the year 1588 saw a series of powerful North Atlantic storms in a climatic anomaly known as the Little Ice Age, a period of cooling that lasted until the end of the nineteenth century. The arrival of the Little Ice Age meant that the greatest adversary Spain faced was heavy weather. Frigid temperatures and storms claimed more lives than combat with England. In this phase of the battle of the Spanish Armada alone, five thousand men drowned, many of them in sight of land but unable to reach it before succumbing, or were killed by local inhabitants on the shores of Scotland and Ireland.

Drake wrote to Walsingham to convey the exhilarating sight of the once great Spanish Armada fleeing English ships: "We have the army of Spain before us, and mind with the Grace of God to wrestle pull with him. There was never anything pleased me better than the seeing the enemy flying with a southerly wind to the northwards."

Even the unflappable Howard was elated by the prospect of success. He had written to Walsingham: "God knoweth whether they go either to Norway or into Denmark or to the Isles of Orkney to refresh themselves, and so to return; for I think they dare not return with this dishonour and shame to their King, and overthrow their Pope's credit." Now that was something to contemplate. "A kingdom is a great wager," Howard ventured. "Some made little account of the Spanish force by sea; but I do warrant you, all the world never saw such a force as theirs was; and some Spaniards that we have taken, that were in the fight at Lepanto, do say that the worst of our fights that we have had with them did exceed far the fight they had there." Lepanto was the scene of the victory that served as Prince Philip's claim to fame, until the English thoroughly undid it. Howard guessed the Armada would return no more because "they dare not go back with this dishonour and shame; for we have marvellously plucked them."

The defeat of the Spanish Armada marked a new phase in naval tactics. Smaller and more maneuverable, the English ships were better able to manage the weather. They could fire from windward, directly at the enemy's hull and rudder. English cannon made it possible to mutilate the enemy's vessels without putting men at risk by boarding. In addition, Spain's unwieldy tactics depended on coordinating the invasion fleet with Spanish soldiers on land. Bringing all these elements into alignment slowed the Spanish response and gave the advantage to English ships and cannon, despite England's smaller fleets. Of necessity, the English had transformed the technology and tactics of naval warfare.

Throughout the extended battle, the English, helped greatly by the favorable wind, seized and held the advantage. At the same time, their cannon alone sank a fifth of the Spanish ships. Four thousand Spanish sailors died, and another four thousand were wounded. Many ships that had survived the mêlée barely stayed afloat, and now the wind carried them, helpless, into the North Sea, where squalls tore their sails to shreds. They took on water, and without anchors, made their hazardous way around Scotland and Ireland.

Violent storms destroyed many Spanish ships. Twenty-six came to grief off the coast of Ireland. Six thousand sailors drowned, and a thousand more were killed on land by the Irish. One of the beleaguered captains described the terrible scene as his ship came to grief on the rocks near Sligo, on the northwest coast of Ireland. "Many were drowning," he recollected. "Others, casting themselves into the water, sank to the bottom without returning to surface; others, on rafts, and barrels, and gentlemen on pieces of timber; others cried out aloud inside the ships, calling upon God; captains threw away their chains and crown and pieces into the sea, the waves swept others away, washing them out of their ships."

The captain was helpless, paralyzed with fear, "as I did not know how to swim, and the waves and storm were very great on the other hand and the shore full of savages, who went about jumping and dancing with delight at our misfortunes, and when anyone of our people reached the beach, 200 savages and other enemies fell upon him and stripped him of what he had on him until he was left in his naked skin."

On September 10, 1588, *San Estéban* and another Spanish ship ran aground off County Clare, Ireland. The sheriff, Boetius Clancy, executed all the survivors. (Since that time, a service has been held at a church in Spain every seven years to curse the name of Boetius Clancy.) On September 15, several Spanish ships came to grief along the Sligo coast. A thousand bodies were said to have washed up along the beach.

The storms continued until September 24, ending with a violent tempest that terrified everyone who experienced it. Another twenty-one ships sank on this leg of the journey home. Of the original Armada and its 132 ships and thirty thousand men, only 67 ships and ten thousand men survived, and many of those survivors perished as they tried to return to Spain.

Sailors who washed up in Scotland were often treated with a measure of compassion and eventually repatriated. In his compendium, Hakluyt wrote that four hundred Spanish soldiers "after their shipwreck were brought into Edinburgh in Scotland, and being miserably needy and naked, were there clothed at the liberality of the King and the merchants, and afterward were secretly shipped to Spain." Local authorities, "in regard of their manifold miseries, though they were enemies, winked at their passage." A few Spanish sailors settled in the Orkney Islands, an archipelago extending north of Scotland, where their descendants are known as the "Dons." Chickens that survived the wrecks created a special strain of fowl called "Armada chickens."

In contrast, those unfortunate Spanish sailors who washed up on Irish shores fell prey to looters. These were not ordinary opportunists. To the Spanish, they appeared as primitive savages who feared foreigners speaking in a strange tongue, and who wanted only to destroy the intruders. One Irishman, Melaghin McCabb, claimed he slaughtered eighty Spaniards with his axe.

The tally of wrecked ships of the "invincible" Spanish Armada, as the English mockingly called it, reached overwhelming proportions. *San Marcos* was wrecked on the Irish coast. *San Felipe* and *San Mateo* were grounded in the Netherlands and captured by the Dutch. *Florencia* was scrapped after her return to Spain. *La Maria Juan* sank during the Battle of Gravelines. *San Juan* was wrecked off the coast of Ireland. *La Trinidad* sank somewhere in the Atlantic. *San Juan Bautista* was scuttled by Admiral Recalde. *Urca Duquesa*

Santa Ana was wrecked off the coast of Ireland. *Santa Ana* exploded on arrival at the north coast of Spain. *Santa Maria de la Rosa* foundered off the southwest coast of Ireland. Only one member of the crew survived, a sixteen-year-old Italian named Giovanni, who was questioned by English officials and then hanged. *San Estéban* foundered off the coast of Ireland. The surviving crew members were hanged. *La Lavia* foundered off the Irish coast. *La Rata Encoronada* ran aground and was burned in Blacksod Bay, County Mayo. *San Juan de Sicilia* blew up in Tobermory Bay in Scotland. *La Trinidad Valencera* sank in Kinnagoe Bay, Donegal. *La Anunciada* was abandoned in the Shannon estuary. *Juliana* sank off Donegal. *Falcon Blanco Mayor*, a Hamburg ship requisitioned by the Spanish, was seized by Drake in the Channel. *Castillo Negro* sank off the coast of Ireland, as did *Barca de Amburg*, whose crew sought refuge on other ships, all of which sank. *San Pedro Mayor* smashed up on the Devon coast. *Santiago* foundered off Ireland. *San Lorenzo* came to grief off Calais. *Patrona* reached Le Havre in a state of disintegration. *Princesa*, off Bayonne, yielded to the mayhem, as did *Diana*. *Girona* was wrecked off Antrim, splitting into two over a deadly reef, hurling men and matériel into the seawater. Some men tried swimming to safety. Hundreds more were trapped inside, assaulted by gear and spars turned into deadly missiles, weighed down with their water-soaked clothing forcing them to the bottom.

As part of its invasion force, the Armada carried many horses and mules. It was determined there was not enough water on board for the animals to survive the journey back to Spain. Sailors forced the animals over the sides of their ships into the North Sea. Later, an English ship caught sight of the abandoned beasts swimming in the dark green sea on a journey to oblivion.

The remaining ships of the Armada, less than half of the original fleet that had sailed in June, reached La Coruña on the extreme northern coast of Spain. Most of the crew had subsisted on starvation rations and had already run out of water. Several more ships were scuttled, and the remnants of the once proud Armada straggled back through October 1588. The losses were appalling. Starvation and disease claimed the largest number of Spanish lives, and soldiers continued to die even after they reached Spanish ports. "To conclude," said Hakluyt, "there was no famous nor worthy family in all Spain which in this expedition lost not a son, a brother, or a kinsman."

*E*nglish casualties in battle were relatively light. Perhaps a hundred sailors lost their lives. Notably, not a single English ship was lost—other than the eight sacrificial fireships.

In despair, Philip II said, "I sent the Armada against men, not God's winds and waves." The gale of which he spoke became known as the Protestant Wind, favorable to England, and shattering to Spain. The heavens had undergone a mysterious realignment, as if Earth's magnetic sphere had reversed itself, and as a result now favored England over the Spanish Empire.

*W*hen news of the defeat of the Armada arrived in Paris, one man in particular denied the reality of the conflict; he was Bernardino de Mendoza, who had taken refuge there after being expelled from England. While in Paris, he printed a false account of a *Spanish* victory, despite all the evidence to the contrary. Even his friends were appalled by this dishonorable performance. "I marvel, good Sir," said one, "to see a man of so noble a lineage, and no less imbued with gifts of nature than others, should have your ears so opened to hear the rumours and lies which the scoffing and gibing flatterers do write you; and I wonder not so much in that you credit them, as at the speed wherewith your honour doth write them."

He did not fool many. When he mounted his mule and ventured beyond the ambassadorial residence, children jeered at him and mocked him with cries of "Victory!" And when word reached Mendoza that Philip himself was displeased, the veteran diplomat realized he had no choice but to retire, citing his worsening eyesight.

*A*lways aware of appearances, Elizabeth sat for a portrait designed to capture the grandeur of the occasion. In the painting, her right hand gently, even protectively, rests on a globe to symbolize her newly acquired power in world affairs. The Spanish Armada occasionally regained the upper hand in subsequent engagements but had ceased to dominate global politics and trade. In her mind, Drake's victory heralded the dawn of British mastery of the high seas and, beyond that, a new world order.

Nevertheless, the Armada's defeat met with doubts and criticism at home. The "famous victory" would live on in memory, but it soon became apparent that it had come at great cost.

CHAPTER XVIII

Disdain, Revenge, Victory

The English forces faced new challenges from Spain. Although badly battered, the remnants of the Armada had veered northward, toward the English ships, who chased the invaders toward the Firth of Forth, a Scottish estuary running into the North Sea, until they lacked the resources to continue. The English had expended their ammunition and exhausted their supplies of food, not to mention the strength of their sailors. If they had been able to pursue the Spanish fleet, they could have annihilated the enemy, or so they believed. Instead, they consoled themselves with the thought that the Armada might not be able to survive the journey home to Spain.

That judgment proved correct. Storms would do what the English could not: punish the fleeing Spanish ships. The English took this situation as God's judgment on the Armada. Said one righteous English sailor, "Many of them will never see Spain again, which is only the work of God, to chastise their malicious practices, and to make them know that neither the strength of men, nor their idolatrous Gods, can prevail when the mighty God of Israel stretcheth out but his finger against them."

Howard, aboard *Ark*, reported to Walsingham that the formerly "invincible" Armada was finally disintegrating. "We sank three of their ships, and made some to go near the shore, so leak, as they were not able to live at sea. After that fight, notwithstanding that our powder and shot was well near all spent, we set on a brag"— that is, bold—"countenance and gave them chase, as though we had wanted nothing, until we had cleared our own coast and some part of Scotland of them; and then, as well to refresh our ships with vict- uals whereof most stood in wonderful need, as also in respecte of our want of powder and shot, we made for the Firth, and sent cer- tain pinnaces to dog the fleet until they shold be past the Isles of Scotland." Now Howard was confident that the Spanish "either are past about Ireland, and so do what they can to recover their own coast, unless that they are gone for some part of Denmark." In other words, the wind had carried them much farther north than intended, and they were in danger of perishing.

Some ships were missing, others presumed destroyed. "We left a pinnace of her Majesty's, the *Advise*," wrote Drake to the queen, "and a fine caravel of my own to attend the fleet of Spain when we left them, but what has become of them, that great storm, or whether they maybe stayed in any other country, I know not." He recom- mended sending a "good ship, and some fine barque, with some very sufficient persons to deal effectively from her Majesty with the King of Denmark, as he shall find the cause to require; and to send the true report back with all speed possible that they may be the better prevented: for no doubt, but that which they are able to do they will presently put it in execution [before] the winter will overtake them else in those parts. If they stay in the sound this winter, I hope many of the Spaniards will seek Spain by land."

*D*rake in contrast went about his business with such élan that even the Spanish regarded him favorably. Pedro de Valdes, admiral of

the *Nuestra Señora del Rosario,* captured by Drake, compared El Draque favorably to Juan Martínez de Recalde, the second-in-command
of the Armada. While attempting to contact Recalde, Valdes had become entangled in a collision with another boat "lying so in the way
as I could neither pass by nor bear room," as he wrote to King Philip.
His own vessel was disabled, unable to steer, and before he could clear
the first obstacle, "another ship fell foul with her likewise in the self-
same manner, and brake her bowsprit, halyards, and forecourse."

As he appealed to Recalde for assistance, rough seas continued
to assault the ship, and it became "impossible to repair that hurt but
in some good space of time." He complained to the king that he repeatedly tried to send word to Recalde, to the point of firing his guns
several times so that "all the fleet might know what distress I was
in," and here was the disheartening part: although Recalde was close
enough to Valdes "and saw what case I was, and might easily have
relieved me, yet he would not do it."

Instead, he fired his own gun to summon his fleet, "leaving me
comfortless in the sight of the whole fleet, the enemy being but a
quarter league from me," and closing fast. Abandoned, Valdes "resisted them and defended myself all that night till the next day,
hoping still that the Duke [Recalde] would send me some relief and
not use so great inhumity and unthankfulness towards me," but in
the end, Valdes found himself alone and "beset with enemies," and
worse, "Sir Francis Drake, admiral of the enemy's fleet, bearing towards me with his ship."

Drake sent word that if Valdes surrendered, he would be treated
well. To his surprise and gratification, Drake "gave us his hand and
word of a gentleman and promised he would use us better than any
others." Valdes took a moment to think it over, deciding "this was our
last and best remedy," and so "I thought it good to accept his offer."

*O*n August 10, Drake tore himself away from the conflict to declare his latest "poor"—that is, humble—"opinion" of events to Francis Walsingham. It was late, Drake was tired, he was under siege, and he wrote as quickly as he could, reliving the traumatic events:

"The army of Spain I think certainly to be put either into Norway or Denmark; there are divers causes which moveth me so to think. The first we understood by divers prisoners which we have taken, that generally through all their whole fleet there was not one ship free of sick people. Secondly, their ships, masts, sails, and ropes were very much decayed and spoiled by our great shot. Thirdly, at Calais . . . we forced them to cut many of their cables, whereby they lost many of their anchors, which of necessity they must seek to supply. Further, if they had had none of these former great causes of distress, yet the winds and storm with the wind westerly as it was hath forced them thither." Even if they traveled as far as Scotland, Drake surmised, they would not find the supplies and especially the water they so desperately needed. "Norway, or the outer isles of Scotland, can relieve them but with water and a few cows, or bad beef, and some small quantity of goats and hens, which is to them as nothing; and yet these bad reliefs are to be had but in few places, and their roads [are] dangerous." In these desperate circumstances, "the only thing which is to be looked for is, that if they should go to the King of Denmark, and there have his friendship and help for all their reliefs," including "great anchors, cables, masts, ropes, and victuals, and what the King of Spain's whole crown will do, in cold countries, for mariners and men, I leave to your good Lordship, which can best judge thereof."

Concerning the Duke of Parma, "I take him to be as a bear robbed of her whelps; and, no doubt, but being so great a soldier as he is, that he will presently, if he may, undertake some great matter, for his rest will stand now thereupon."

Despite this threat, Drake glimpsed deliverance. "If we may recover near Dunkirk this night or tomorrow morning, so as their power may see us returned from the chase." In that case, anything was possible, and the Spanish might even mutiny against the Duke of Parma. It was only a hope, but hope was all England had at the moment.

The same day, August 10, Lord Howard, in Margate, wrote to Burghley to warn about the rapidly deteriorating health of the fighting men who had risked their lives to save England from the Spanish, a crisis to which Drake had alluded only in passing. The brave crew of *Elizabeth Jonas*, for instance, suffered an outbreak of infection from the start of the campaign. More than two hundred of her roster of five hundred were already dead, and the number was growing by the hour.

Alarmed, Howard ordered the ship to land, with all her crew going ashore and her ballast removed, so that she could be cleansed of her "infection" with three or four days of fire treatments. He replaced the crew with "new men, very tall and able as I ever saw." Yet the infection returned "in greater extremity than ever it did before, and the men sicken and die faster than they ever did." He erroneously conjectured that the source of the infection was the "pitch" used to waterproof the planks. The problem was not confined to one ship; it was fleetwide, he warned. The ships had been at sea for months on end, and "have so little in the way of clothing, nor any money to buy it" that he "would think it a marvellous good way that there were a thousand pounds worth or two thousand marks worth of hose, doublets, shorts, shoes and such like sent down" and soon. If not, Lord Howard would "look to see most [of] the mariners go naked."

*H*oward's heart-rending appeal had no effect on Burghley. He refused to squander money to rescue the vulnerable sailors, even though they had imperiled their lives to protect their country. Cruel financial logic dictated Burghley's decision to let the infected men die in place, whether it was at Margate or aboard the ships in which they had served. He estimated the forces defending England at twelve thousand men, which came to £16,800 "in wages and victuals." The Crown could simply not afford to let them all live.

On August 26, John Hawkins wrote to Burghley to correct this reasoning. "Your Lordship may think that by death, by discharging of sick men, and such like, that there may be spared something in the general pay." If so, he was mistaken. "First, those that die, their friends, require their pay. In place of those which are discharged sick and insufficient, which are indeed many, there are fresh men taken, which breedeth a far greater charge, by means of their conduct in discharge, which exceedeth the wages of these which were lastly taken in, and more lost by that than saved." And he reminded Burghley, "If anything be spared, it is to Her Majesty's benefit only," in case Burghley implied that Hawkins or anyone else happened to be lining their pockets in the transaction. "The ships I have paid, of those which were under Sir Francis Drake's charge, I find full furnished with men, and many above their numbers."

*W*hen Howard returned to Dover on August 21, he summoned Drake, Hawkins, and the other commanders to assess the "state of the fleet." Despite victory, theirs was a tale of woe "which with sorrow and grief I must deliver unto your Lordships."

To begin, "the most part of the fleet is grievously infected, and men die daily." The ships themselves were considered so badly diseased that plague was suspected. Simply replacing the fallen mariners did not alleviate the problem: "We find that the fresh men that we draw into our ships are infected one day and die the next, so as many of the ships have hardly men enough to weight their anchors." Howard recommended to the council that the fleet be divided into two parts to receive fresh food and minimize illness. In the most solemn terms, he warned, "We do not see, amongst us all, by what other means to continue this service, for the lost of mariners will be so great neither realm shall be able to help it."

The fast-spreading infection, for which there was no remedy, did far more damage than the enemy, and he implored the council to explain the urgent situation to the queen. And there was another matter, perhaps more mundane, but of equal importance to the men. They harbored "great discontentment" that their pay, which they had expected to receive in full, arrived "scantly unto them; it breeds a marvellous alteration amongst them." Some had not been paid at all. It was imperative for the Crown to pay them by August 25, or else England would not have a navy when it was most needed.

Drake, still aboard *Revenge*, unburdened himself once more to Walsingham on August 23, assessing both England's and Spain's prospects in battle with notable objectivity. No one had a keener eye for such a survey: "The uncertainty of the reports which daily come unto us out of Calais, Dunkirk, Ostend, Flushing, and from my Lord of Huningsom, Scotland, and such ships and pinnaces which have been sent out for discovery by my Lord Admiral, make me rather to rest upon mine own conjecture than upon any of them, they disagreeing so much as they do; the one, affirming that the Duke of Medina Sidonia, which his fleet, is coming back again, that the Duke of Parma is marching presently to embark to be conducted by him, the other affirming that it is for certain that the fleet of Spain is past without Scotland for their way homewards. Which reports are quite contrary."

Drake had his own thoughts about navigating to Spain. "If their fleet chance to return, it is altogether for that the wind will not permit them good passage to go about the other way at this time of the year, because it is now must subject to westerly winds. This wind that now bloweth, if it be not more easterly there than it is here, could hardly permit such a fleet . . . to pass on the back side of Scotland and Ireland." Both the Duke of Medina Sidonia and the Duke of Parma needed "fair weather" to effect a rendezvous, and if the wind failed to cooperate, "they shall never perform as much as they have promised to the King, their master." The Duke of Parma required a moderate breeze because his ships were small. And the Duke of Medina also depended on it because there was no safe harbor within reach.

So much for Spanish hopes. In Drake's opinion, "the Duke of Parma should be vigilantly looked upon for these 20 days, although the army of Spain return not this way," because they remained a threat to England. And that brought Drake around to the painful subject of weakness in Her Majesty's army. Reluctant to disparage the queen and her ministers, he proposed in vague terms that the powers that be "should animate us forward."

Even as Drake proposed these measures, the scope of battle moved beyond his comprehension.

*I*n case the Armada tried to seek shelter along the Scottish coast, Elizabeth had induced James VI of Scotland to promise that he would assist England in repelling her enemies. James's allegiance to Elizabeth was all the more remarkable because his mother was Mary,

Queen of Scots. Despite his traumatic history, James VI had switched his loyalty from Catholicism to Protestantism, guided, perhaps, by the hope that this childless queen would ultimately name him as her heir. With such a prize at stake, religious scruples could be set aside.

Elizabeth did not take James's newfound commitment at face value. He had made a number of anti-English speeches and publicly allied himself with Spanish interests. Elizabeth had reason to believe he might be posturing. Philip, for his part, always believed that James would refuse to help Elizabeth because of the harrowing history involving Mary, Queen of Scots. "The blood of his murdered mother is not yet congealed," Philip insisted, yet James had other ideas. To encourage James to remain loyal to her, Elizabeth had dispatched an envoy to Scotland just before the beleaguered Armada arrived to promise him a dukedom and £5,000 a year—two generous offers that he hastened to accept, and which Elizabeth later withdrew when the crisis passed. She was, after all, trying to save her life, her kingdom, and some money—all at the same time.

*I*n place of funds, which were in short supply, Elizabeth relied on her royal authority and abundant charisma. This boost in morale was needed because the battle of the Spanish Armada, begun on the sea, threatened to move onto land. Rallying to his sovereign's support, the Earl of Leicester, holding a new title, "Lieutenant and Captain General of the Queen's armies and companies," assembled a division of soldiers at Tilbury in Essex, about twenty miles from the mouth of the Thames River. Even Leicester believed that in a land conflict between England and Spain, Spain would emerge as the victor. The troops commanded by Parma, for instance, had the reputation for being "the best soldiers at this day in Christendom," while English soldiers were said to be more interested in "fashion" than "discipline."

On the other side of the divide, Parma was beset by his own set of worries. He wanted at least thirty thousand troops in England but had only eighteen thousand at his command, and their numbers were being rapidly decimated by disease. England mustered twenty-six thousand soldiers, but after only a week, supplies ran short, and some of them drifted home before they started to fight. Privately, Philip did not hold out much hope for victory over the Protestant infidels. He gave the Duke of Medina Sidonia sealed instructions authorizing him to negotiate with England "if (God forbid) the result be not so prosperous that our arms shall not be to settle matters." In that regrettable case, he was authorized to offer "limited concessions" to England, and if he failed to obtain those, Philip would settle for Elizabeth's agreeing to allow Catholics in England to worship freely—which in theory they already could. Suddenly the most powerful monarch in Europe did not seem so invincible. He looked more like a ruler who had overstepped his bounds and wanted to save face. In the end, Philip was reduced to saying that he hoped God would not let him fail.

At this critical moment, Elizabeth interjected herself into the fray, accepting an invitation from Leicester to inspect the troops fighting in her name and to impress the force of her personality on them. She might be a woman, but she was also a warrior.

On August 9, Elizabeth had arrived in the village of Tilbury, overlooking the River Thames at a point where the waterway narrows to about seven hundred feet. The queen was on horseback, dressed in armor, apparently prepared to fight to the death with her soldiers if necessary. She appeared before them, resplendent in white, stiffened by a snug silver breastplate, astride a gray gelding, flanked by the

Earl of Leicester and the Earl of Essex. She appealed to the tribal instincts of her soldiers by giving her most memorable address.

"My loving people, we have been persuaded by some that
are careful of our safety, to take heed how we commit our
selves to armed multitudes, for fear of treachery; but I assure
you I do not desire to live to distrust my faithful and loving
people. Let tyrants fear. I have always so behaved myself,
that under God, I have placed my chiefest strength and safeguard in the loyal hearts and goodwill of all my subjects, and
therefore I am come amongst you, as you see, at this time,
not for my recreation and disport, but being resolved in the
midst and heat of battle, to live and die amongst you all, to
lay down for my God, and for my kingdom, and for my people, my honour, and my blood, even in the dust."

And more memorable words tumbled out.

"I know I have the body but of a weak and feeble woman;
but I have the heart and stomach of a king, and of a King of
England too, and think foul scorn that Parma or Spain or any
prince of Europe, should dare to invade the borders of my
realm, in which, rather than any dishonour shall grow by
me, I myself will take up arms, I myself will be your general,
judge and rewarder of everyone of your virtues in the field.
I know already for your forwardness, you deserved rewards
and crowns, and we do assure you, in the world of a Prince,
they shall be duly paid you . . .
    "We shall shortly have a famous victory over these ene-
mies of my God, of my kingdom, and of my people."

That was the magic word: *shortly*. The time had come. Her words had worked their charm.

It was said the troops "gave a mighty shout or cry." Leicester, for his part, believed the queen had "so inflamed the hearts of her good subjects, as I think the weakest among them is able to match the proudest Spaniard that dares land in England." From the day of her coronation she behaved according to the belief that her authority derived in large part from the English people, to whom she was responsible, according to the dictates of God. Now, at Tilbury, she demonstrated this pact; in her woman's voice she declared that she had the heart and stomach of a king, and these blunt images conveyed exactly what her presence meant for England. For years, England had labored under an inferiority complex, unspoken but nonetheless potent, concerning the seemingly invincible Spanish empire. Even Drake's victories against the Spanish had been mostly vandalism, or, as Drake memorably phrased it in connection with his raid on Cádiz, singeing the king's beard. Now, at last, England could claim victory.

*I*n the coming weeks, silver coins were struck to commemorate England's glorious victory over Spain. They showed the English fireships—a fine symbol—driving off the Spanish. Some carried the Latin motto *Venit, vidit, fugit* ("It came, it saw, it fled") to drive home the humiliation of the Spanish. Drake and other courtiers commissioned the renowned Armada portrait of Elizabeth in which her hand rests regally on a globe. Floating around her head are scenes of battle, those fireships again, and the wreck of the Armada on a rocky coastline. It was now her world. Those who studied the portrait realized that Elizabeth, getting on in years, had probably not posed for it; rather, a younger chambermaid had been substituted.

Elizabeth understood that image was all, and it would not do to look gaunt and aged in a portrait, especially at a time of triumph.

The battle of the Spanish Armada had come to an end, or so it seemed, with Elizabeth's speech. The Armada's death ships did not return. No Spaniards overran what Shakespeare would a few years later describe as: "This royal throne of kings, this sceptered isle, This earth of majesty, this seat of Mars, This other Eden, demi-paradise, This fortress built by Nature for herself Against infection and the hand of war. . . . This blessed plot, this earth, this realm, this England."

Yet the English began to second-guess their historic victory. Why had they run out of ammunition at the critical time? They could have sunk so many more Spanish ships if only they had had an adequate supply. Why had they neglected to capture Spanish ships? The council assailed Howard for failing to grapple and board the enemy's vessels.

England's war fever cooled quickly. The day after Elizabeth gave her stirring address, apparently a call to arms, she reversed herself and ordered the soldiers assembled at Tilbury to break camp. The Crown could not afford to keep them on duty. As for the navy, which had served as England's walls, as she put it, almost everyone would be discharged, and most ships promptly decommissioned. At the beginning of August, Elizabeth commanded 197 ships. At the beginning of September, just 34. Francis Drake complained that the drastic reductions could jeopardize England's security, to no avail. The Lord Treasurer was relieved, and that mattered more.

The war, though short-lived, had proved ruinously expensive, just as Burghley had feared. Elizabeth had raised money from the wealthy but at a high rate of interest—10 percent. She borrowed additional funds from the City of London. She tapped into the country's financial reserves for an extraordinary £100,000. She had contributed some of her personal fortune to the effort. Now England teetered on the brink of a financial emergency as Burghley ran about trying to obtain additional loans. Before August was over, he confided to Walsingham: "I see a general murmur of people, and malcontented people will increase it to the comfort of the enemy."

Even the sailors who had risked their lives to defend their country were not paid. The Crown spent a paltry £180 on "rewards to the injured." Many of these injured were soon to die. Ultimately, starvation and sickness claimed the lives of half the survivors, with worse to follow.

*E*lizabeth felt one death especially keenly, although it was not directly connected to the conflict. As England celebrated the miraculous victory over Spain, Elizabeth's most trusted minister and possible lover, Robert Dudley, Earl of Leicester, decided to visit a spa at Buxton in the rolling hills of Derbyshire. He had been in failing health, and he traveled at a moderate pace. He lodged at Cornbury, in Oxfordshire, where, according to one account, he "supped heavily" and "forced himself to vomit" during the night.

He had come down with what Shakespeare called "the ague"— malaria. It was one of the most serious and widespread diseases of the era, borne by mosquitoes breeding in swampy areas along the Thames. Malaria caused fever, chills, vomiting, seizure, coma, and ultimately death. It was a major factor in London's mortality rate. The average lifespan was only thirty-five years; Leicester was now fifty-five. With his wife, Lettice, in attendance, Robert Dudley, the 1st Earl of Leicester, died on September 4, 1588, leaving debts of more than £20,000.

Upon learning of Leicester's passing, Elizabeth gave herself over to mourning in her private chambers "until the treasurer and other councillors had the doors broken open and entered to see her." She was nothing if not histrionic, and she had occasionally treated him as cavalierly and as cruelly as she treated others, but at the same time, she was deeply devoted to Leicester, who, in a world of traitors and assassins and incompetents, had stood with her and supported her and her reign ever since he had appeared at court as a young man. For the rest of her life, she kept in a safety box beside her bed an emotional, slightly maudlin letter he had written to her just before he died.

I most humbly beseech your Majesty to pardon your poor old servant to be thus bold in sending to know how my gracious lady doth, and what ease of her late pains she finds, being the chiefest thing in this world I do pray for, for her to have good health and long life. For my own poor case, I continue still your medicine and find that [it] amends much better than with any other thing that hath been given me. Thus hoping to find perfect cure at the bath, with the continuance of my wonted prayer for your Majesty's most happy preservation, I humbly kiss your foot.

From your old lodging at Rycote, this Thursday morning, ready to take on my Journey, by your Majesty's most faithful and obedient servant,

R. Leicester

On it, she had written "His last letter."

His funeral cortege proceeded from Kenilworth to Warwick, with two absentees: his wife, Lettice, who sent in her place a letter calling Leicester "the best and dearest of husbands." Elizabeth, by custom, stayed away from the funeral. Worse, she refused to forgive the huge debt that Leicester had accumulated in a lifetime of service to the queen. Lettice would have to pay, a task made much more difficult by Elizabeth's confiscating his lands, Leicester House overlooking the River Thames, and the art within. Burdened with £50,000 of debt, thanks to Elizabeth's vindictiveness, Lettice became entangled in years of legal fighting. In desperation, she married a commoner to avoid being sued for debt.

Elizabeth would have to carry on alone, without the benefit of Dudley's advice, one more intimate whom she would never glimpse again in this life. The loss took its toll on her. She locked herself within her bedchamber, refusing to come out. Two months later, in November 1588, Elizabeth appeared "much aged and spent, and very melancholy."

She made an effort to put the death of Leicester behind her by celebrating England's victory over the Armada. That month, attired in white and silver, a monarch for the ages, she stepped out of her bedchamber and into a chariot drawn by a pair of white horses, preceded by royal trumpeters, and trailed by her gentlemen and footmen.

Amid the privileged group was the vain, ambitious, and hot-headed Robert Devereux, 2nd Earl of Essex, nearing his twenty-fourth birthday, who had become the new favorite of the queen, who, incidentally, was more than thirty years his senior. It was said the earl aspired to take Leicester's place, and at that moment, his prospects looked excellent. The queen had already conferred Leicester's title, Master of the Horse, on the young man, and now he was seen with her constantly. They often played cards at night, and rumor had it that he did not return to his own lodgings "till the birds sing in the morning." Elizabeth encouraged him to move into Leicester's apartment at St. James, where he would be at her beck and call.

Yet troubling signs emerged. The earl violated protocol by daring to complain about Elizabeth for siding with Walter Raleigh, a commoner, in a dispute, and turned his back on the queen before striding out of the room in a huff. One did not turn one's back on the queen. She launched into a memorable tirade against him. Even so, the young earl continued to revel in his status. He engaged Nicholas Hilliard to portray him as *The Young Man among the Roses*, legs crossed, leaning insouciantly against a tree festooned with white roses. Ten years hence, his arrogance would be his undoing.

*O*nly one hundred men had been lost in battle, but now disease ravaged the crew—typhus, food poisoning, and scurvy. As his men died from these conditions, Howard could only look on with a sense of fatalism. "It is a thing that ever followeth such great services," he lamented.

Spanish sailors, farther from home and more vulnerable, faced more devastating losses. Since many of their ships had fled north of Scotland, they headed west before entering the Atlantic and shaping a course for Spain. They accomplished the crossing on short rations, their wretchedness increased by the humiliation of losing to England. Howard's Spanish counterpart, Medina Sidonia, told King Philip, "The troubles and miseries we have suffered cannot be described to your Majesty. They have been greater than have been seen in any voyage before."

Loyalists dared not pass on this disastrous news, so the initial reports of the great battle that reached Philip's ears sounded a triumphant note. Spain was victorious, they declared, and El Draque had been captured. When the true dimensions of the drubbing that Spain had received became apparent, Philip remained infuriatingly stoic: "In the actions of the Lord, there is no loss or gain of reputation; one should simply not talk about it." In private, however, he confessed that he soon would wish he had never been born, so terrible would be the retribution for the loss, unless a miracle delivered him. No miracle was forthcoming, and as time went on, Philip developed an irrational but characteristic response: he redoubled his efforts to conquer England. War, he believed, had "become all the more necessary because of what happened."

*I*n the midst of this unlikely victory, the English treasury wrestled with financial disputes. Hawkins and Burghley persisted in sniping at one another, and neither would back down. Hawkins adopted an injured tone for his reply to the skinflint Burghley. "I am sorry I do live so long to receive so sharp a letter from your Lordship, considering how carefully I take care to do all for the best," he complained. "I had but one day to travail in, and then I discharged many after the rate that I thought my money would reach; but after that day, I could hardly row from ship to ship, the weather hath been continually so frightful." In his efforts to distribute pay "in the best order" possible, "some are discharged with fair words; some are so miserable and needy that they are holpen with tickets to the victuallers for some victual to help them home; and some with a portion of money, such as my Lord Admiral will appoint, to relieve their sick men and to relieve some of the needy sort." Taking care of them "required 19,000 pound," Hawkins reminded Burghley. "I will go with this as far as I can, and never demand more till extremity compel me."

Howard added his voice to the urgent appeal for funds. English casualties had been light, it was true, but the members of the council should not be deceived. Starvation and illness were doing more damage than the Spanish had to English mariners. "It were too pitiful to have men starve after such a service. I know her Majesty would not, for any good. Therefore I had rather open the Queen's Majesty's purse something to relieve them, than they should be in that extremity; for we are to look to have more of these services; and if men should not be cared for better than to let them starve and die miserably, we should very hardly get man to serve. . . . Before God, I had rather have never penny in the world than they should lack."

Oblivious to the suffering and sacrifices of their mariners, the English commemorated their miraculous delivery. Victory medals were struck. One memento depicted a family of four praying, above the motto, in Latin: "Man proposes, God disposes." The obverse shows a sailing vessel breaking apart, and the motto: "The Spaniards are put to flight and perish with no man in pursuit." Another showed England's principal Catholic enemies blindfolded and menaced and tortured; the reverse side depicted a ship from the Armada coming to grief on the rocks, as sailors plummeted into the waves. Prayers were written and read aloud. Bells rang, and guns were discharged on November 19 to celebrate the victory.

An elaborate play, *The Three Lords and Three Ladies of London*, composed by a certain "R. W.," was published. It described how pugnacious English schoolchildren defeated Spanish personifications of pride and shame and other vices. Pamphlets about the Armada flooded London, and one in particular discussed whether it was safe to eat fish that had fed on Spanish sailors and caught their venereal diseases, only to declare later that it was safe for the English to continue their usual diet. Ballads and poems celebrating the defeat of the Armada appeared everywhere, most of them dwelling on the cruelty of the Spanish: "They made such whips, wherewith no man would seem to strike a dog. . . . That they would force at every lash, the blood abroad to spin."

Adding his voice to the clamor, Burghley sent an essay to Bernardino de Mendoza to explain that English Catholics disapproved of Spain's attempt to return England to Catholicism by force. Was it possible that this "Reformation . . . is not allowable in the sight of

God?" At least one Spanish prisoner in London, remarking on the overwhelming English victory, declared, "In all these fights, Christ showed himself a Lutheran." Several "Armada Portraits" of Elizabeth appeared, depicting the defeat of England's enemies and her global influence. For once, it seemed God was on their side.

*T*he English triumph over the Spanish Armada was so convincing that Spain reluctantly conceded that Providence favored the Protestant cause. On August 20, 1588, a service was held at St. Paul's Cathedral in London to thank God for the miraculous English victory over the Spanish Armada. At noon, the royal chariot appeared at the Great West Door of the cathedral, where members of the clergy, attired in their silver cloaks, awaited Elizabeth. They proceeded to hold a service of thanksgiving for England's victory. When the queen was seated, she could see the Armada's captured standards suspended aloft, stirring in the breeze.

Spanish fatalism set in with a vengeance. Philip admitted that the defeat "lost us the respect and good reputation that we used to have among warlike people." Spanish religious authorities were unable to explain why God had allowed the Armada to fail. Eventually a reason was found: the Spanish had taken too long to drive the Moors from Granada. Yet the defeat had resulted not from the machinations of Providence or from individual heroism. Rather, it had resulted from mundane factors: the weather, first and foremost, and also the hoops and staves that Drake had destroyed during his raid on Cádiz months before.

Without casks, the Armada quickly depleted essentials such as water, wine, salt meat, salt fish, and biscuits. Replacement barrels hastily fashioned from unseasoned wood did not serve nearly as well, and so the mighty Spanish Armada was effectively disabled.

*D*rake too saw the hand of Providence in the outcome. This victory over the Spanish Armada solidified Elizabeth's claim to empire. The memory of the campaign helped to sustain England during the Napoleonic Wars at the dawn of the nineteenth century and again during World War II. Winston Churchill, in a speech celebrating an English victory over the Germans, echoed Elizabeth's zeal for battle at Tilbury: "Now this is not the end. It is not even the beginning of the end. But it is, perhaps, the end of the beginning."

Beginning or end, Elizabeth could not say. She boarded her barge and made for London, where she lay low at St. James's Palace until the beginning of October. By then, still more Spanish vessels had come to grief off the north coast of Ireland, and she felt safe enough to return to her capacious residences at Whitehall and Greenwich.

*I*f the Battle of the Spanish Armada had ended then and there, it would have remained fixed for all time as an unalloyed victory for England and Drake. But over the next few years, the balance of power and influence between victor and vanquished shifted back and forth. After the battle ended, illness and starvation claimed the lives of half of those men who fought for England, so it took months to reckon the true cost of victory, and if those throngs celebrating the victory in November along with the queen had known this, they might have muted their celebration, or paused to recognize the lives lost, the suffering, and the economic peril.

The wisdom of Philip's stoic reaction, which seemed at odds with the reality of the Spanish defeat, would slowly become more apparent. Spain, too, suffered from self-inflicted wounds. Spanish soldiers died cruel deaths on distant shores, savaged by opponents they never intended to confront in Ireland and elsewhere, and

Spanish soldiers starved to death in far greater numbers than their enemy did.

Of greater importance, the late summer battle of the Spanish Armada did not end the conflict, as seemed likely at the time; it marked the beginning of more violent clashes that would take an enormous toll on both countries. Over time it became apparent that the Spanish empire had reached its apogee and was beginning a long, slow decline, as England, although suffering its own internal conflicts between Catholic and Protestant, Irish and Scottish, presented a united front to its geopolitical rivals.

It was a measure of England's new commitment to the cause of empire that Drake, despite his singular accomplishment as the first and only circumnavigator and his less respectable but critical contribution to the English treasury as a pirate, was now seen as something he was not—a military leader—and he was valued for his contribution to the cause of England's defense more than anything else.

Drake had always been a maverick throughout his career at sea, attacking whenever, wherever, and whomever he pleased, and despite his loyalty to the queen, keeping for himself whatever he wanted. Drake's apparent dereliction of duty was not as serious as it seemed, even though his peers expressed disapproval. Drake had always been the initiator, a rogue pirate, and so he remained. More important, the geopolitical movement that started with his circumnavigation had become a cause célèbre for England, an introduction to an empire to rival and ultimately overtake Spain's. Drake's contribution to the cause of a British Empire came together as a happy accident. His circumnavigation was simply the raid to end all raids on the Spanish rather than a grand geopolitical statement, although it came to seem that way in retrospect. Given Drake's devil-may-care temperament, it was as much a product of cheekiness as calculation. Spain, with all its resources, proved unable to manage its empire; how would diminutive England manage the task? The cause had grown far beyond Drake himself. It encompassed all of England, and as time passed, he increasingly became a bystander in this new world he had helped to open. It would be left to others—Elizabeth, Raleigh, and subsequent waves of colonizers—to follow up. In time Great Britain gained its empire as Spain gradually ceded its global influence to the upstart.

Drake's piracy was both his inspiration and his limitation. Once he had circumnavigated the globe, there were no new worlds for him to conquer, only ships to plunder. It was time for Drake to move on, but he had nowhere to go. Buckland Abbey might have been a showplace for the ages, but the scant amount of time he spent there suggests he had no more interest in it than he did in serving as a member of Parliament, or as a husband to his second wife. The defeat of the Spanish Armada was a great victory for England, but the beginning of the end for Drake.

*P*hilip remained outwardly calm in the face of defeat, except when it came to his chosen leader, Medina Sidonia, whose military failure had infuriated the king. He ordered the duke never to show his face in court again. (Later, the duchess persuaded the king to soften his stance.) Diego de Valdez was sent to prison for eighteen months. A Neapolitan who sent guns and powder to England was caught and sentenced to be drawn and quartered not by horses, but by galleys dragging his limbs in opposite directions. And passing through Valladolid to reach his home, Medina Sidonia was jeered with calls of "Drake! Drake!" and earned the humiliating sobriquet "*El duque de gallina*"—the Chicken Duke.

The pope, for his part, was also furious about the outcome of the Armada. He was supposed to be infallible, but England had made a mockery of him.

*M*endoza, the former Spanish ambassador to London, had completed the transition from semireliable spy to unreliable propagandist, manufacturing lies about the queen, Howard, and especially Drake, claiming that El Draque had been taken prisoner.

Usually indifferent to Spanish propaganda, Drake took the unusual step of answering Mendoza's insults. "They were not ashamed to publish in sundry languages in print, great victories in words, which they pretended to have obtained against this realm, and spread the same in a most false sort over all parts of France, Italy, and elsewhere; when, shortly after, it was happily manifested in very deed to all nations, how their navy, which they termed invincible, consisting of one hundred and forty sail of ships, not only of their own kingdom, but strengthened with the greatest Argosies, Portuguese carracks, Florentines, and large hulks of other countries, were, by thirty of Her Majesty's own ships of war, and a few of our merchants, by the wise, valiant, and advantageous conduct of the Lord Charles Howard, High Admiral of England, beaten and shuffled together even from the Lizard in Cornwall, first to Portland, where they shamefully left Don Pedro de Valdez, with his mighty ship; from Portland to Calais, where they lost Hugh de Moncado, with the galleys of which he was captain; and from Calais, driven with squibs from their anchors, were chased out of the sight of England round about Scotland and Ireland," Drake roared. These wretches were "hoping to find succour and assistance" from other Catholics in those regions. Instead, "a great part of them were crushed against the rocks, and those other that landed, being very many in number, were, notwithstanding, broken, slain, and taken; and so sent from village to village, coupled in halters to be shipped into England, where Her Majesty, of her princely and invincible disposition disdaining to put them to death, and scorning either to retain, or entertain them, they were all sent back again to their countries to witness and recount the worthy achievement of their invincible and dreadful navy." To Drake, their suffering and humiliation seemed fitting.

Beyond that, the enemy's performance had been utterly incompetent, as Drake reminded his readers. "They did not, in all their sailing round about England, so much as sink or take one ship, bark, pinnace, or cockboat of ours, or even burn so much as one sheepcote [sheep's pen] on this land." Parma, for his part, did not remain idle. He called upon a cardinal in Rome (who happened to be his uncle) for help, and he conveyed his version of events in detail to Philip, who said nothing publicly against Parma but held him responsible for the outcome nonetheless. Amid this climate of resentment, Parma announced the official end to the Enterprise of England, at least for the time being.

After a prolonged wait, Elizabeth's government finally released funds. The wounded sailors received a total of £80, and the hundred seamen who heroically manned the fireships near Calais received £5. These amounts were not per sailor, they were to be shared among them. Not knowing what else to do, Howard authorized licenses permitting wounded sailors to beg for their daily bread. One such certificate gave William Browne, a gunner who had been "shot through his body and grievously wounded in sundry places and . . . maimed forever," permission to panhandle in churches for just one year.

Such were the meager rewards for soldiers and sailors of England's great naval victory.

*S*pain, despite having lost the battle, took much better care of its soldiers. When Philip heard that some had been released without full pay, he wrote a blistering letter warning that such behavior was "contrary to Christian charity and also very much alien to my will." Therefore, "Those who have served, and are serving me, should not only be paid what they are owed, but rewarded as far as our resources permit." He assigned a scrupulously honest representative to supervise payment of benefits for the survivors, as well as widows and orphans of those who had perished in battle. He even dispatched two boats filled with emergency reserves intended for Spanish ships still lost at sea. Although the imminent arrival of still more booty from the New World helped to defray the cost of the Armada, Spain sank further into debt, and Philip was forced to declare bankruptcy.

CHAPTER XIX

A "Top-Earning Pirate"

The triumphant mood in London proved short-lived. Elizabeth and her advisers remained vigilant about Spain. Despite the great victory they had won, Drake's men were starving aboard ship, and he was perplexed—outraged, in fact. To make matters worse, a contrary wind prevented his leaving Plymouth.

By April 1589, plainly exasperated, he unburdened himself to the Lord High Treasurer. "I did never write to your Lordship with so discontented a mind as I do now. The cause is (as it may please your Lordship) in that it pleaseth God to stay our forces in harbor by contrary winds; whereby our victuals have been and do daily consume without doing any service," he protested. "We have used our best means as longe as we could to uphold the service, as far as our own abilities, and the credit of our friends could any way be stretched to serve our turns, but for that the numbers of our men are so many, and our daily charge so great by reason of our stay, we are no further able to continue the same as we have done."

His men recovered their health in time, and Drake, having pried at least some wages from the queen's grip, put to sea. A month later, on May 8, 1589, he wrote to Lord Burghley about the latest English success off the coast of Galicia, in northwestern Spain, due south of

London: "The 23rd of the last month we fell with Ortingall in Galicia, the wind blowing very much easterly. And the day following we landed at the Groyne [La Coruña, Spain] 7000 of our men, where we had attempted the taking of the Base Town the same night, if extreme rain and very foul weather had not [prevented] us. The 25th we assaulted the Base Town both by sea and land and took it with the only loss of 20 of our men, and 500 of the enemy. The winds have been always contrary since our coming here, blowing very much with a great sea and continual showers of rain."

Despite these obstacles, he achieved some notable successes. "We found at our coming thither four great ships, making ready with all expedition for a fresh Armada against England. Amongst which there was the Gallion St. John, the Vice Admiral of the King's last fleet, which is burnt, and the other three taken. We have taken of the enemies in this place, out of the ships, and town, very near 150 pieces of ordnance; and have made spoil of many great provisions in readiness for this new army. To defer the time, being stayed in by contrary winds, we laid battery to the higher town, finding it to be strongly defended, by reason of divers companies of old soldiers which were remaining there ready to go forth in this army." They numbered fifteen thousand in all, and Drake was extremely concerned about being overwhelmed. "Being shortly advertised that they had entrenched themselves within 5 miles of us, we thought it meet, upon consultation had the next morning, to sally forth with 7000 of our men, who understanding our forces to come nigh unto them resolved to fight, where it pleaseth God to allot us the victory, which is no little quailing to the enemy."

He boasted of the importance of his victory to Elizabeth and her ministers. "My opinion is that great happiness is fallen to our Queen and country by our coming hither, where we stay until God send us a fair wind."

*N*ot everyone hailed the Armada's defeat with the same fervor. Sir Walter Raleigh dared to blame Elizabeth for failing to crush the Spanish for good: "Her Majesty did all by halves, and by petty invasions taught the Spaniard how to defend himself." Perhaps he was correct. It was a matter of speculation. On an even more serious note, typhus decimated the ranks of English sailors. Drake was among the handful of survivors.

*T*his was not the final conflict between Spain and England; the Spanish Armada would occasionally regain the upper hand but no longer dominated global politics and trade. Drake's victory proclaimed British mastery of the high seas and, beyond that, the arrival of a new world order.

On April 4, 1589, Drake and Sir John Norreys—a friend to the queen—joined forces to lead another attack against Spain. Norreys was a controversial figure, having massacred two hundred Scots at Rathlin Island on July 26, 1575. In a separate campaign, Norreys led English volunteers against the Spanish in support of Dutch Protestant rebels. He was later knighted by Leicester, known to confer knighthood left and right, unlike Elizabeth, who was sparing about conferring honors.

Theirs was an ambitious plan, designed to capitalize on the recent English victory. They would set fire to the Spanish fleet, sail to Lisbon, and inspire a popular uprising against the king. The English fleet would then establish a base in the Portuguese outpost of the Azores and capture the Spanish treasure fleet en route to Cádiz. With these maneuvers, Elizabeth rather unrealistically hoped to force an alliance with Portugal, even though Philip's sovereignty was already accepted there. England's insurgent candidate was the luckless António, Prior of Crato, who had tried to establish a government in exile in the Azores until more qualified Portuguese noblemen beat him to it.

*E*lizabeth and Drake were soon disabused of the notion that they could repeat the success of Drake's lightning raid on Cádiz two years earlier. In the original attack, Drake had enjoyed the element of surprise; Spain was unprepared to contend with his audacious raid. Also, the "Protestant wind" had favored his cause by driving Spanish ships on the rocks. Now, as the much-delayed English fleet advertised itself and its purpose, the element of surprise had vanished. And the weather failed to cooperate with English intentions. There was no more Protestant wind favoring the maneuvers of the English ships. Drake's fleet on this occasion consisted of six galleons, sixty armed merchantmen, twenty pinnaces, with about 5,500 men. (Other accounts offered different numbers.) Drake divided the fleet into five. He was captain of the flagship, *Revenge*, Norreys in *Nonpareil*, Norreys's brother Edward in *Foresight*, Thomas Fenner in *Dreadnought*, and Roger Williams in *Swiftsure*. Brave names and bold ships, but this time, Spain was ready for them, having repaired and refitted its own fleet.

To complicate matters, Elizabeth's headstrong intimate, the Earl of Essex, chose this moment to flout her wishes, jump on his mount, and bolt from London to Plymouth, where he stowed away aboard *Swiftsure*, intending to make himself into a naval hero. By the time Elizabeth learned of this development, *Swiftsure* had sailed, and the impetuous young earl was out of reach. Elizabeth dictated a scathing missive to be delivered to him: "Your sudden and undutiful departure from our presence and your place of attendance, you may easily conceive how offensive it is, and ought to be, unto us. Our great favours bestowed on you without deserts have drawn you thus to neglect and forget your duty, for other constructions we cannot make of your strange actions." She ordered him to return immediately. "See you fail not," the queen warned, "as you will be loath to incur indignation and will answer for the contrary at your utmost peril."

As if that threat was not sufficient, she wrote to Drake and Norreys that the captain of *Swiftsure* would be hanged from a yardarm for participating in this conspiracy against her. If Drake and Norreys, who briefly fell under suspicion, did not comply with her demand, "you shall look to answer for the same." She cautioned, "These be no childish actions," and warned them not to respond with cunning, or evasions, or "anything associated with lawyers." When they doubted her seriousness, she declared, "We look to be obeyed. . . . Otherwise we will think you unworthy of the authority ye have." There was no mistaking the threat she conveyed.

Reviewing the text, Walsingham commented that the fierce letter "is in as mild terms as may be, considering how Her Majesty standeth affected."

*T*his was a novel situation for Drake. He had been a pirate, and he had been the queen's favorite. Now he was serving the queen, and praising or protecting him, she threatened him. (She was, after all, her father's daughter, and threats were part of her strategic arsenal.) Drake and his partner Norreys assessed the situation. For one thing, they were far from home, and for another, Elizabeth's words did not carry the same weight as a man's, no matter how severe her tone. Drake figured he was irreplaceable. Instead of obeying her wishes—which she often contradicted—they did exactly what they wanted.

Drake and Norreys headed south toward La Coruña. They had been led to believe that two hundred Spanish supply ships rode at anchor, as rich a target as could be imagined, but when they arrived, they were disappointed to see just five. At that point, Drake and Norreys should have headed north to Plymouth. Instead, they gradually became ensnared in one of the worst disasters in English naval history, all the more shocking for its coming on the heels of the victory over the Spanish Armada less than a year before.

The fleet headed for Lisbon, hoping to set fire to Portuguese and Spanish ships, plunder them, and, if possible, install the hapless Dom António on the Portuguese throne, contrary to Elizabeth's wishes. To add to the fleet's rogue nature, they met up with Essex, who led the attack on the fortress of Peniche, miles from Lisbon but considered a safe destination.

The fleet took control of the edifice in the name of Dom António, an impressive but pointless feat. Drake and Norreys now went their separate ways, Norreys leading his foot soldiers along the coast to Lisbon, and Drake leading his fleet to rendezvous there. Norreys's men had a wretched time in the heat, as his soldiers sickened and lost heart as they confronted Lisbon's formidable defenses, with Dom António dispensing useless advice as they went. With the English forces depleted, Norreys warned Dom António that if the pretender to the throne failed to rally the troops and obtain desperately needed provisions, Norreys would lead his men back to England. Drake, in the meantime, tried to navigate the tortuous curves of the Tagus estuary, which would take his ships to Lisbon. His plans frustrated, he resorted to pillaging ships as he came across them, including sixty German vessels bearing wheat, copper, masts, and wax—not a bad haul, but not what he had come for.

At this point, Essex repelled an attack. According to a contemporaneous account, he approached the city walls and "ran his spear and broke it against the gates of that city: demanding aloud, if any Spaniard mewed therein, durst adventure forth in favour of his mistress to break a staff with him. But those gallants thought it safer to court their ladies with amorous discourses, than to have their loves written on their breasts with the point of his English spear." Essex heard laughter coming from within the walls. He made a show of clearing his possessions from his carriage to make room for wounded English soldiers: a noble gesture of defeat.

On June 8, Drake and Norreys held a council of war to discuss with their captains the options available to them, none of them good. In the original defeat of the Spanish Armada, fortune had favored the English at every turn—the weather, the tides, and Philip's indecisiveness—but on this occasion no divine intervention came to their aid. Their primary goals now involved saving lives and saving face. On the return journey, eager to salvage the expedition, Drake broke ranks and made for the Azores, again, beyond Elizabeth's limited orders, but his flagship was badly in need of repair, and he was forced to return to Plymouth with his tail between his legs, arriving in late June 1589.

The defeat of the Spanish Armada in 1588 had been England's greatest naval victory. The defeat of the English Armada less than a year later amounted to a severe setback. Drake still had a name and reputation to reckon with, but now he seemed not just fallible but also corrupt. Elizabeth implied that he had abandoned the mission and reverted to self-dealing, in other words, to mere piracy. He had almost nothing to share with the Crown on this occasion—neither gold nor pearls nor glory, only defeat.

By this late date in his career as a pirate, Drake had become a victim of his own success. After the raid on Cádiz and the unprecedented victory over the Spanish Armada, the expectations for Drake's plunder and piracy exceeded his ability to meet them. Elizabeth did not bother to conceal her disappointment. She accused him of theft and dereliction of duty. Drake could not fail to have been humiliated, especially because other adventurers such as Walter Raleigh were rising in her esteem.

In decline, Drake stubbornly persisted in raiding Spanish ships long after he had made his fortune. He could have spent his last years languishing at Buckland Abbey in the company of his wealthy, wellborn second wife. Instead, he took command of a ship north of Venezuela, fighting the Spanish as always, hunting for their gold and gems, professing loyalty to the queen even as he quietly set aside plunder for himself.

On August 28, 1595, he joined forces once again with his cousin John Hawkins to look for treasure in the West Indies. It was to be the final expedition for both of these legendary pirates and former slavers. In the course of their campaign, they attacked San Juan in Puerto Rico, not once but twice, without managing to overcome its fortifications. They attacked San Juan in Puerto Rico only to go down in defeat when Spanish gunners fired a cannonball right through the cabin of Drake's flagship. During this voyage both men suffered from dysentery, a painful and generally lethal infection of the intestines brought on by ingesting contaminated food or water. Hawkins succumbed on November 12, 1595, and was buried at sea off Puerto Rico.

Drake fought on a while longer, although he lost more skirmishes than he won. Panama. Curaçao. Riohacha. Nombre de Dios. Being in the thick of things mattered more to him than the outcome. If he gave any thought to his wife, Elizabeth Sydenham, or his home, Buckland Abbey, while he was in the heat of battle, there is no record if it. He was absorbed in life aboard ship, more at home marauding than attending civic meetings in Plymouth or intriguing at Elizabeth's court.

In the midst of his struggles, dysentery, agonizing and bloody, overwhelmed him. Preparing for the end, he asked to be dressed in his armor.

Francis Drake died in Portobelo Harbor, on the northern coast of Panama, on January 27, 1596. Sheathed in his armor, he was buried in a lead-lined coffin between the wrecks of two ships, *Elizabeth* and *Delight*.

*T*hose who knew Drake praised him as the great sailor-explorer of his day. A mariner called "R.M." compared him favorably to his nearest rival, John Hawkins—"They were both of many virtues"— but found Drake by far the more impressive navigator and character. "John Hawkins had in him mercy and aptness to forgive, and true of word; Sir Francis [was] hard in reconciliation and constancy in friendship; he was withal severe and courteous, magnanimous, and liberal." Both were ambitious, but Drake burned with an "insatiable desire of honour, indeed beyond reason. He was infinite in promises, and more temperate in adversity than in better fortune." He could be too quick to anger, too bitter in condemning others, and "too much pleased with open flattery," but he had none of Hawkins's malice and tight-fistedness. Both were "great commanders," R.M. acknowledged, "but there was no comparison to be made between their well-deserving and good parts, for therein Sir Francis Drake did far exceed."

*D*rake always emphasized the value of the treasure he had stolen over the far-flung lands he had explored. A recent survey in *Forbes*, the business magazine, awarded him second place on its list of the "top-earning pirates" in history. His wealth, estimated at $115 million, nearly equaled the $120 million acquired by Samuel "Black Sam" Bellamy, who terrorized the coast of New England in the eighteenth century.

Drake's plunder, much of it taken from Spanish ships and settlements, dramatically affected England and the world. The economist John Maynard Keynes, writing in 1930, expressed the conviction that Drake's lust for gold and silver heralded the birth of the British Empire and the modern British economy. "I trace the beginnings of British foreign investment to the treasure which Drake stole from Spain in 1580. In that year he returned to England bringing with him the prodigious spoils of the *Golden Hind*. Queen Elizabeth was a considerable shareholder in the syndicate which had financed the expedition." Keynes enumerated the benefits Drake's treasure purchased. "Out of her share she paid off the whole of England's foreign debt, balanced her Budget, and found herself with about £40,000 in hand. This she invested in the Levant Company—which prospered. Out of the profits of the Levant Company, the East India Company was founded; and the profits of this great enterprise were the foundation of England's subsequent foreign investment. Now it happens that £40,000 accumulating at 3 per cent compound interest approximately corresponds to the actual volume of England's foreign investments at various dates, and would actually amount to-day to the total of £4,000,000,000 which I have already quoted as being what our foreign investments now are. Thus, every £1 which Drake brought home in 1580 has now become £100,000. Such is the power of compound interest!"

Just as remarkable as Drake's winnings was the transformation in his attitude toward the people he encountered around the world. He had started his career as a slaver, but he came to despise slavery and those who profited from it, especially Spain. He had lived among the Cimarrons in Panama and almost became their leader. In North America, he contemplated a similar offer from the Miwok, who wept when his ships left. He had a measure of sympathy for nearly everyone, even his avowed enemies. Among the grim adventurers of the era, his robust and generous nature set him apart. He was at home in the world in a way that Columbus, who encouraged slavery, and Magellan, who set himself in opposition to everyone, were not.

His rough gallantry won him recognition even in Spain, where the historian Francisco Caro de Torres, another contemporary of Drake, assessed him this way: "In his profession as a seaman he was one of the most outstanding mariners the world has ever seen: in sailing around it only Magellan preceded him." Drake, never known to be modest, would have gone de Torres one better. In his own mind, he was "such a good sailor, so learned, that . . . there was no one in the world who understood better the art of sailing."

Drake's ability to navigate the seas was just the start. In an improvised partnership with Elizabeth, he came to represent the idea of English daring and heroism in the minds not only of his countrymen, but also across Spain and western Europe. He set in motion the idea of the British Empire, partly to challenge Catholic countries and partly to promote a particularly English sense of camaraderie, of a new blend of freedom and loyalty. Philip II lived on to 1598, ruling Spain with inflexible authority as always, and on his death, he was succeeded by his twenty-year-old son, Philip III. Together, they represented the old order and the burden of the past, while Elizabeth and her successors looked forward to an expanding universe, summarized by Shakespeare in *The Tempest* as a "brave new world / That has such people in't." Drake set out in search of gold and gems, but his quest expanded to include countless raids, a circumnavigation, and an attack on the

Armada that rearranged the geopolitical balance. He remade the map of empire, for better and for worse, securing a leading role for England. And he did so with a sense of humor. Quick to anger, he never stayed angry for long, and he found the internal resources to treat his most despised enemy with humor, courtesy, and gallantry—a mode of behavior that demonstrated his victory over them. He was both celebrating his accomplishment and mocking his adversaries: the essence of Drake at sea. Some of the people he encountered in his travels—in Central America, along the California coast, and on the island of Java—recognized his charisma and leadership abilities, and even offered him, the outsider from a distant, unknown land, speaking a strange tongue, a chance to rule over them: an extraordinary testament to the sense of vigorous protectiveness that he emanated. In each case, Drake considered and refused. He would not be confined.

In fact, he could scarcely stay put in his sprawling manor in Devon with his wealthy second wife. He was more at home on the water, where boundaries did not apply, and where wind and waves ruled over men and their ships. He was always morally dubious to a greater or lesser extent, evolving from slaver—a task he came to detest—to royally sanctioned pirate—a role he relished. Yet he was not malicious, at least according to the standards of his time, nor was he especially cruel, even though meting out punishment was part of a captain's job description. Insouciant, superstitious, and unswervingly loyal to his queen (except when concealing his plunder), he fashioned a standard of action readymade to transmute into history and eventually folklore.

*E*lizabeth died eight years after Drake, on March 24, 1603, at Richmond Palace. She was buried in Westminster Abbey beside her half sister, Mary I, who had tried to undo the Protestant Revolution.

Situated thus, the two could vie for eternity. Elizabeth had survived against long odds. She was celebrated, childless, and destined to give her name to an era.

A year later, her chosen successor, James I, the son of Mary, Queen of Scots, ascended to the throne. He became the king of England, Ireland, and Scotland, and thus the first monarch of Great Britain.

Acknowledgments

$\mathscr{F}$rancis Drake played many parts in his flamboyant career: pirate, explorer, naval hero, and, less admirably, slaver and thief. He both craved and avoided honor and status, and he was more at home at sea pursuing a ship laden with gold and silver than he was at court jockeying for recognition dispensed by his queen, who often withheld it on a whim. Drake seemed to be master of his fate, yet his daring circumnavigation, outdoing even that of Ferdinand Magellan, and his prominent role in the Battle of the Spanish Armada were both undertaken at Elizabeth's request. He learned to become an instrument of her will in order to survive and thrive.

I had wanted to write about this ebullient explorer since completing my narrative of Magellan's circumnavigation, *Over the Edge of the World,* and I am grateful to HarperCollins/Custom House for making that possible. Peter Hubbard, vice president and executive editor, offered the ideal combination of support and goal setting. His skillful assistant, Molly Gendell, patiently brought out the best in the story. At HarperCollins, I am also grateful to the publisher, Liate Stehlik; the associate publisher, Ben Steinberg; the marketing director, Kayleigh George; the production editor, Stephanie Vallejo; the designer, Nancy Singer; the diligent copyeditor, Shelly Perron; Nick Amphlett; the publicist, Christina Joell; and to Richard Aquan, who brought welcome flair to the cover. I had the good fortune to persuade Jeff Ward to draw the maps of Drake's circumnavigation and the Battle of Cádiz.

In my years of research on Drake I have benefitted from the expertise and interest of many libraries and archives. I am particularly indebted to Widener Library at Harvard University, where the now former director, Sarah K. Thomas, facilitated my research. My only regret is that I did not encounter Sarah twenty years ago. At John Carter Brown Library at Brown University, Director Neil Safier provided access to crucial documents of the Age of Exploration. My search for materials relating to John Dee led me to the New York Society Library, where I am a trustee, with its collection of rare Dee materials, including books from his library containing his extensive marginal notes. My thanks to the head librarian, Carolyn Waters, for her seemingly omniscient knowledge of the library. I also conducted research at Butler Library at Columbia University and at NYU's Bobst Library. I was fortunate to profit from the enthusiastic legwork performed by my longtime research assistant, Anna Basoli. My former editor, the talented Henry Ferris, kindly offered me his literary expertise. I am indebted to my old comrade Dan Dolgin for his wise counsel and simply for being Dan Dolgin. Also in New York, my tireless friend Susan Shapiro proved to be a capable sounding board.

In Washington, DC, and in Lisbon, Portugal, Dr. James Garvin, chief scientist of the NASA Goddard Space Flight Center in Greenbelt, Maryland, was as inspirational and perceptive as always when it came to placing Drake in the context of exploration and discovery.

At William Morris Endeavor, I wish to thank my longtime agent, Suzanne Gluck, as well as her capable assistants and colleagues Andrea Blatt and Eve Attermann for their help in making this book a reality.

In London, I consulted the British Library's John Dee collection, including its assortment of Dee's polished, black "spirit mirrors." I was not sure such devices existed until I laid eyes on one displayed there. I am indebted to my London-based researcher, Christina Bucher, and to my good friend and fellow naval chronicler, George Ermakoff, who joined the hunt for Drake. I must also acknowledge the generous help of Michael Turner, the author of *In the Wake of Sir Francis Drake*, a voluminous compendium of original Drake research. "When I have been to Cape Horn, I shall have seen all Drake's world." Also, in London, I spent hours of vicarious exploration aboard the replica of *Golden Hind* tied up at St. Mary Overie Dock. Sturdy and compact, this ship could be considered analogous to the Mercury space capsule in which John Glenn orbited the globe in 1962, bringing the world into the Space Age in the way Drake once brought the world into the Age of Exploration.

Far from London, I washed up on the same inviting Brazilian shores as Drake and retraced his route through the Strait of Magellan aboard M/V *Terra Australis*.

In Brazil, New York, and elsewhere, my wife, Jacqueline Philomeno, offered unfailing inspiration, support, and encouragement throughout the time I worked on this book, and for all that, plus more, I will always be thankful.

Notes on Sources

*B*ooks and articles about Francis Drake are varied and numerous, and even more so concerning Elizabeth I. Most are straightforward accounts. Few, if any, make a concerted effort to demonstrate how their accidental relationship led to the British Empire, and the extent to which Elizabeth relied on Drake to expand England's presence at sea, which I have endeavored to do in this book. The most detailed modern biography is Harry Kelsey's 1998 work, *Sir Francis Drake*, a thorough if dry compendium of Drake particulars. Still, anyone who writes about Drake will eventually find themselves in debt to Kelsey's labors. I should also mention Michael Turner's *In Drake's Wake*, which is both a website and a privately published record of his exhaustive Drake research. Turner has retraced many of Drake's landfalls, and the heavily illustrated website in particular is worth consulting.

Primary sources about Drake abound, and the most important are listed in the Bibliography. He has often been a controversial figure (except in folklore, where he assumes the stature of a heroic legend). Although the eyewitnesses often have their own issues with Drake, their accounts take the reader on board his ships as the circumnavigation unfolds and thus have a compelling immediacy.

Sources

CHAPTER I: THE ISLAND AND THE EMPIRE

Drake's intentions concerning the circumnavigation are discussed by Kelsey, Sir Francis Drake: The Queen's Pirate, pp. 207ff. And for his preparations, see ibid, pp. 82ff.

For more on Plymouth, see R. N. Worth, *History of Plymouth*, W. Brendan, 1890, and Sugden, *Sir Francis Drake*, 5–9, which also provides details of Drake's youth, and Kelsey, pp. 3ff. See also Crispin Gill's *Drake and Plymouth*.

The term "pirate" was relatively new, dating to 1387, according to the *Oxford English Dictionary*. Later, Shakespeare evokes a "notable pyrate" in *Twelfth Night*, a term that may have derived from the Greek *peiratēs*, or bandit.

Accounts of Hawkins's life and career are numerous and varied. For more, see Barrow, *Sir Francis Drake*; Davis, *Proof of Eminence*; Hazlewood, *The Queen's Slave Trader*; Kelsey, *Sir John Hawkins*; and Unwin, *The Defeat of John Hawkins*.

It has been estimated that eleven million slaves were transported across the Atlantic between the fifteenth century and the nineteenth.

Ronald's *The Pirate Queen*, pp. 61ff, describes the rough and undisciplined English navy as Drake first encountered it, as well as its profitability, 73. It was also an efficient organization. Hawkins needed only 170 sailors to manage the entire enterprise. The cruel treatment accorded the slaves he transported and sold to Spaniards in the New World is described in the same work, 93. No matter, he became a "national hero" in Ronald's words, 95 and 102, and helped to give the slave trade semi-official status in England. Drake, as Hawkins's "cousin," is mentioned in Ronald, 105.

For more on Hawkins's to-the-manor-born lifestyle, see Bicheno, *Elizabeth's Sea Dogs*, pp. 72ff.

Barrow's *Sir Francis Drake* gives a complete account of Hawkins's and Drake's early careers in piracy, pp. 101ff.

Ronald describes King Philip's style of rule in *The Pirate Queen*, 76–86.

Accounts of the hydra-headed Spanish Inquisition, including graphic descriptions of the auto-da-fé, are drawn from Thomas McCrie's *History of the Progress and Suppression of the Reformation in Spain in the Sixteenth Century*, 1829. See also Lea, *A History of the Inquisition of Spain*, Vol. VIII, 1–233; Liss, *Isabel the Queen*, 311–27.

See also Liebman, *The Jews in New Spain*, 89–111; Margolis and Marx, *A History of the Jewish People*, 470–76; and Roth, *Conversos*, 253–55. Painful detail concerning devices and procedures of the Inquisition can be found in William Andrews, *Bygone Punishments*; Baker, *The History of the Inquisition*, 195–201; and Marchant, *A Review of the Bloody Tribunal*, 342–63. In addition, see *The Inquisition*, 1931, 138–48 and *The Inquisition: A Bilingual Guide*, 1985.

The cruel fate of Drake's cousin Robert Barret at the hands of the Inquisition is recounted in Fuller-Eliott-Drake, *The Family and Heirs of Sir Francis Drake*, 25.

Drake's date of birth is variously given as 1540 or 1541. See Corbett, *Drake and the Tudor Navy*, appendix A.

Barrow's *Sir Francis Drake* supplies details about Drake's modest origins and youth, pp. 62ff.

For more on the traumatic events of San Juan de Ulúa, see Bicheno, *Elizabeth's Sea Dogs*, pp. 90ff.

Elizabeth's youth: See Aikin, *Memoirs of the Court of Elizabeth*, 19–21; Lipscomb, "Did Thomas Seymour Sexually Abuse the Teenage Princess Elizabeth?"; Ronald, *The Pirate Queen*, pp. 3ff; Starkey, *Elizabeth: Apprenticeship*; Stevenson, *Naval History of Queen Elizabeth*, vol. 1, pp. 407ff; Strong, *Coronation*, pp. 222ff and Rowse, *The England of Elizabeth* and "The Coronation of Queen Elizabeth."

For poverty in England, see Mapp, *Three Golden Ages*, 134–35, and Williamson, *The Age of Drake*, 10.

CHAPTER II: THE MONARCH AND THE MYSTIC

An enigmatic, mystical character, John Dee is one of the most important figures of the era, part brilliant mathematician and part sorcerer. For more on Dee, see Bicheno, *Elizabeth's Sea Dogs*, 111–31; Kenneth Andrews, *Trade, Plunder, and Settlement*, 35; Ronald, *The Pirate Queen*, 20, 182–83, 200–1, and appendix I.

I examined the John Dee collection at the British Library, London, where I viewed several of his books and possessions: https://www.bl.uk /collection-items/john-dees-spirit-mirror.

Closer to home, I examined John Dee's annotated books adorned with his extensive marginalia in the Winthrop Collection at the New York Society Library, where I serve as a trustee.

Elizabeth's excommunication is described in Ronald, *The Pirate Queen*, 146–47.

The secrets of Queen Elizabeth's Privy Chamber and Bedchamber are exposed in Anna Whitelock's *The Queen's Bed*, 18–31.

CHAPTER III: "CONTRARY WINDS AND FOUL WEATHER"

See Corbett, *Drake and the Tudor Navy*, 95, for a detailed description of a caravel.

The most comprehensive account of Drake's circumnavigation belongs to Henry R. Wagner's *Sir Francis Drake's Voyage around the World*, 1926, an extended labor of love written by a California-based businessman and Drake aficionado. Williamson's *The Age of Drake* places the explorer in the larger landscape of the Age of Discovery.

The first published account of Drake's circumnavigation did not appear for nine years, when it was finally included in the 1589 edition of Richard Hakluyt's landmark *Voyages.* Until then, its existence was known mostly among insiders at court. It is assumed that Drake agitated for its publication to secure his place in English naval history. Rivals were making claims almost from the moment he returned from the circumnavigation.

For other contemporaneous accounts, see Zelia Nuttall's *New Light on Drake,* 18–56, 236–37, and pp. 328ff. This is an idiosyncratic but useful collection of accounts, especially that of the pilot Nuño da Silva, pp. 242ff. The best-known early account is *The World Encompassed by Sir Francis Drake . . . Carefully Collected out of the Notes of Master Francis Fletcher,* 1628.

For a useful summary of Drake's circumnavigation, see Morison, *The Southern Voyages,* 637–87. For Magellan's circumnavigation, see ibid, 380–99. If Morison's frame of reference occasionally seems to belong to a bygone era, his nautical data remain reliable.

Two other important naval histories, Julian Corbett's *Drake and the Tudor Navy,* first published in 1889, and his *Sir Francis Drake,* from 1890, are rather dry and less informative but useful accounts of the circumnavigation.

John Winter's account, rescued from obscurity by E. G. R. Taylor, was published in *Mariner's Mirror,* 16 (April 1930), in an article titled "More Light on Drake," 134–51.

Peter Carder's account of his wandering can be found in *Purchas his pilgrimage; or, Relations of the World and the Religions observed in all ages and places.* London, 1626.

CHAPTER IV: TRAITOR

Drake's adventures with the Cimarrons are recounted in Roche's *The Golden Hind.* See also Kenneth Andrews, *Drake's Voyages,* pp. 37ff.

CHAPTER V: GOLDEN HIND

For more on the St. Bartholomew's Day Massacre of August 24, 1572, see Holt, *The French Wars of Religion,* 79–80, and Knecht, *The French Religious Wars,* 51–52.

Roche's *The Golden Hind* presents a detailed "biography" of the ship.

There are two replicas in England, one in Brixham, Devon, and the other at the St. Mary Overie Dock in London.

For Drake's servant Diego, see Miranda Kaufmann, www.history .com/news/the-untold-story-of-how-an-escaped-slave-helped-sir-francis-drake-circumnavigate-the-globe, August 31, 2018, and *Black Tudors*, 2018, by the same author.

For Nuño da Silva's account, see his sworn deposition in Nuttall's *New Light on Drake*, 303.

CHAPTER VI: "THE MOST MAD SEAS"

For more on Montaigne and cannibals, see his outstanding discussion of the subject in *The Essays of Michel de Montaigne*, 1946. Montaigne, despite his reasoning and eloquence, changed few minds regarding the relative merits of the indigenous peoples of the New World.

Details of Drake's postcircumnavigation activities and knighthood are drawn in part from Corbett, *Drake and the Tudor Navy*, pp. 311ff.

CHAPTER VII: "CRUEL COURTESY"

For more on young John Drake, see Fuller-Eliott-Drake, *The Family and Heirs of Francis Drake*, appendix I.

CHAPTER VIII: TREASURE FLEET

Las Casas's account, unmatched for clarity and outrage, showed how cruelly the Spanish treated the people they encountered in the New World and exposed the veneer of religiosity as a cover for exploitation and avarice. Although his treatise had little immediate impact, it became part of the permanent historical record of the era.

CHAPTER IX: *CACAFUEGO*

For more detail about Drake's adventures off the coast of Chile, see Kelsey, pp. 137ff.

For the capture of this ship, see the account by Pedro Sarmiento de Gamboa in Nuttall, *New Light on Drake*, 56–88. See also Roche, *The Golden Hind*, pp. 111ff.

For more on John Foxe, see Mozley, *John Foxe and His Book*.

Chapter X: Life Among the Miwok

For the giant crabs Drake's men encountered, see Shea, "Colossal Crabs."

The appalling treatment of "Maria" is recounted in Kelsey, 201. And the following pages discuss Drake's stay in Ternate and on Java. Here some of the men took advantage of the readily available women only to contract "the French pox," apparently syphilis.

Chapter XI: Deliverance

See Drake, *The World Encompassed*, published in 1854, for the best record of this part of the journey.

Chapter XII: Unbroken Blue Water

Details of the tortured courtship of Francis Duke of Anjou and Alençon and Elizabeth can be found in Anna Whitelock's *The Queen's Bed*, 180–89.

For Mendoza's account, see *Calendar of Letters and State Papers Relating to English Affairs: Preserved Principally in the Archives of Simancas, Elizabeth, 1558– ,* pp. 226ff.

For Drake's return to England, see Nuttall, *New Light on Drake*, 54, and especially Barrow, *Sir Francis Drake*, pp. 161ff.

For more on Spanish attempts to achieve restitution of Drake's booty, see *Calendar of Letters and State Papers*, Vol. 3, *Elizabeth, 1580–1586,* pp. 55ff.

Chapter XIII: Return and Reward

Drake's return to Plymouth is described by Kelsey, pp. 210ff. For more on Drake's wealth, see Kelsey, pp. 216ff.

Hilliard portrait is described in Kelsey, p. 225.

Mendoza's shocked reaction to Drake's return can be found in *Calendar of Letters and State Papers*, Vol. 2, *Elizabeth, 1568–1579,* pp. 59ff.

Drake's newfound wealth and status in England after the circumnavigation can be found in Kelsey, pp. 216ff. House on Elbow Lane, ibid.

Elizabeth's "natural hatred" of marriage can be found in the *Calendar of Letters and State Papers: Preserved Principally in the Archives of Simancas: Elizabeth, 1558– ,* 343.

The Black Book, or official annals of Plymouth, is mentioned by Kelsey, 228.

For more on the varied aftermath of Drake's circumnavigation, see also Ronald, *The Pirate Queen,* pp. 240ff.

CHAPTER XIV: THE DRAGON ARRIVES

Drake's six-hour audience with Queen Elizabeth is described in Kelsey, p. 211ff, and in Corbett, *Drake and the Tudor Navy,* 311. There is also a tantalizing reference to a diary of his on p. 214, but this document has apparently been lost.

The details of Drake's taking possession of Buckland Abbey and its long history are related by Kelsey, pp. 219ff.

Drake described as "more fat than thin" comes from Kelsey, 227.

For more on de Zubiaur, see Kelsey, pp. 232ff.

For more on Walsingham, see Budiansky, *Her Majesty's Spymaster,* for a thorough review of this remarkable figure's career. The hurled slipper incident is recorded in the *Calendar of Letters and State Papers,* Vol. 3, p. 573.

Drake's surprising reticence and passivity as a member of Parliament are noted by Kelsey, 236–37.

For Elizabeth's attempting to silence Mendoza, see *Calendar of Letters and State Papers,* Vol. 3, *Elizabeth, 1580–1586,* pp. 61ff. These heated letters penned by Mendoza, the King of Spain, and others reek of paranoia and insecurity regarding Drake's giant haul and Elizabeth's skillful concealment of the treasure. They realize she is outflanking them but are powerless to stop her.

For more on Drake's start-and-stop activities after the circumnavigation and before the Battle of Cádiz, see Ronald, *The Pirate Queen,* pp. 256ff, and Bicheno, *Elizabeth's Sea Dogs,* pp. 155ff.

Drake's receiving a coat of arms and the surrounding controversy is given a thorough airing in Kelsey, pp. 222ff.

John Doughty's long-running enmity regarding Drake is described by Kelsey, pp. 231ff. See also Corbett, *Drake and the Tudor Navy,* pp. 226ff. Doughty's boast about having been intimate with Drake's wife is reported by Kelsey, who wrote the entry on Drake in the *Oxford*

Dictionary of National Biography. See also Sugden, *Sir Francis Drake,* and Cummins, *Francis Drake.*

For Elizabeth's resolve to knight Drake, see *Drake and the Tudor Navy,* 315. My account is also drawn from Weir, *The Life of Elizabeth I,* 336–37.

For Drake's appearance in Hakluyt's work, see Kelsey, pp. 367ff.

CHAPTER XV: TWO QUEENS, ONE THRONE

For the complete text of Leicester's Commonwealth and related documents, see Peck, *Leicester's Commonwealth.*

Singh's enlightening *The Code Book* discusses Walsingham as spymaster and "Elizabeth's most ruthless minister," pp. 39ff.

CHAPTER XVI: RAID ON CÁDIZ

See Aikin's *Memoirs of the Court of Queen Elizabeth,* pp. 367ff, for the growing enmity between Spain and England.

Barrow's *The Life, Voyages, and Exploits of Admiral Sir Francis Drake,* pp. 213ff, provides a meticulous account of the Battle of the Spanish Armada, as well as letters among the principals.

Kelsey, usually an admirer of Drake, questions his judgment and motives in the raid on Cádiz, pp. 281ff.

CHAPTER XVII: SIGNS AND PORTENTS

My narrative of the Battle of the Spanish Armada is told largely from Drake's point of view. For a comprehensive overview of the conflict, see Winston Graham's *The Spanish Armadas;* Neil Hanson's *The Confident Hope of a Miracle;* Robert Hutchinson's *The Spanish Armada;* Garrett Mattingly's *The Armada,* 1959; and Whiting's *The Enterprise of England: The Spanish Armada.* Kelsey covers much of the same ground, 306–39.

For a poignant account of the Armada's tragic misadventures in Ireland, see Fallon's *The Armada in Ireland,* 97 and passim. And for a personal version of the search for the wreckage of the Armada, see Sténuit's detailed *Treasures of the Armada.*

For background of Hakluyt, whose compilation of accounts of English voyages subtly shaped naval history, see Herman, *To Rule the Waves*, 132–33.

Chapter XVIII: Disdain, Revenge, Victory

For more on Drake and the Spanish Armada, see *State Papers Relating to the Defeat of the Spanish Armada*, Vol. 2. And for the heartbreaking account of illness spreading among the sailors, see pp. 96ff.

Chapter XIX: A "Top-Earning Pirate"

Matt Woolsey summarizes the rewards of piracy in "Top-Earning Pirates," *Forbes*, September 19, 2008.

Bibliography

ARCHIVES CONSULTED

LONDON
British Library
British Museum
Tower of London
Public Record Office
Golden Hind: St. Mary Overie Dock on Cathedral Street, in Bankside,
    Southwark, London

UNITED STATES
Bobst Library, New York University
Butler Library, Columbia University, New York
John Carter Brown Library, Providence, RI
New York Society Library (John Dee Collection)
Widener Library and Archives, Harvard University, Cambridge, MA

SPAIN
Archivo General de Indias, Seville
Archivo General de Simancas

PRIMARY SOURCES

State Papers Relating to the Defeat of the Spanish Armada, ed., John Knox
    Laughton, Vol. 2. London: Navy Records Society, 1894.

Calendar of Letters and State Papers Relating to English Affairs: Preserved Principally in the Spanish Archives of Simancas. Vol. 2, *Elizabeth, 1568–1579,* ed. Martin A. S. Hume. London: Eyre & Spottiswoode, 1894.

———. Vol. 3, *Elizabeth, 1580–1586,* ed. Martin A. S. Hume. London: Eyre & Spottiswoode, 1896.

Calendar of State Papers Relating to English Affairs in the Archives of Venice. Vol. 7, *1558–1580,* eds. Rawdon Brown and G. Cavendish Bentinck. London: Her Majesty's Stationery Office, 1890.

Calendar of State Papers Relating to English Affairs in the Archives of the Vatican. Vol. 1, *July–December 1568*, January–July 1569, ed. W. H. Bliss. London: His Majesty's Stationery Office, 1916.

Collection of State Papers Relating to Affairs in the Reign of Queen Elizabeth from the Year 1571 to 1596. London: William Bowyer, 1759.

ARTICLES AND JOURNALS

Andrews, Kenneth R. "Aims of Drake's Expedition of 1577–1580." *American Historical Review* 73 (1967–1968): 724–41.

———. "Beyond the Equinoctial: England and South America in the Sixteenth Century." *Journal of Imperial and Commonwealth History* 10 (1981): 4–24.

———. "Caribbean Rivalry and the Anglo-Spanish Peace of 1604." *History* 59 (1974): 1–17.

———. "Elizabethan Privateering." In *Privateering and Colonisation in the Reign of Elizabeth I.* Raleigh in Exeter 1985, ed. Joyce Youings (Exeter, UK, 1985): 1–20.

———. "English Voyages to the Caribbean 1596–1604: An Annotated List." *William and Mary Quarterly* series 3, 31 (1974): 243–54.

———. "Sir Robert Cecil and Mediterranean Plunder." *English Historical Review* 87 (1972): 513–32.

Bayne, C. G. "The Coronation of Queen Elizabeth." *The English Historical Review* 22, no. 88 (October 1907): 650–73.

Drake, Francisco, and G. Jenner. "A Spanish Account of Drake's Voyages." *English Historical Review* 16, no. 61 (Jan. 1901): 46–66.

Fessenden, Marissa. "A Painting of John Dee, Astrologer to Queen Elizabeth I, Contains a Hidden Ring of Skulls." Smithsonian.com. January 15, 2016.

Gentle, Peter. "Dr. John Dee—the Original 007." www.woe.edu.pl /content/dr-john-dee-original-007.

Heizer, Robert F. "Francis Drake and the California Indians, 1579." Project Gutenberg Online Catalog, 2011.

Lipscomb, Suzannah. "Did Thomas Seymour Sexually Abuse the Teenage Princess Elizabeth?" *HistoryExtra* (BBC), July 10, 2018.

Loomie, Albert J. "Religion and Elizabethan Commerce with Spain." *The Catholic Historical Review* 50, no. 1 (April 1964).

Mello, Amilcar D'Avila de. "Peter Carder's Strange Adventures Revealed." *Mariner's Mirror* 91, no. 4 (August 2007).

Pollard, A. F. "The Coronation of Queen Elizabeth." *The English Historical Review* 25, no. 97 (January 1910): 125–26.

Rodríguez-Salgado, M. J., ed., and Simon Adams, tr. "The Count of Feria's Dispatch to Philip II of 14 November 1558." Camden Miscellany, 18, series 4, vol. 29. London: Royal Historical Society, 1984.

Rowse, A. L. "The Coronation of Queen Elizabeth." *History Today* 3, no. 5 (May 1953).

Shea, Rachel Hartigan. "Colossal Crabs May Hold Clue to Amelia Earhart Fate." *National Geographic*, August 20, 2019.

Taylor, E. G. R. "More Light on Drake," *Mariner's Mirror*, 16 (April 1930), 134–51.

Von Bülov, Gottfried. "Journey through England and Scotland Made by Lupold von Wedel in the Years 1584 and 1585." *Transactions of the Royal Historical Society*, new series, 9 (1895): 223–70.

Wigington, Patti. "Biography of John Dee: Alchemist, Occultist, and Advisor to a Queen." ThoughtCo. January 26, 2018.

Wilson, H. A. "The Coronation of Queen Elizabeth." *The English Historical Review* 23, no. 89 (January).

Woolsey, Matt. "Top-Earning Pirates," *Forbes*, September 19, 2008.

BOOKS

Aikin, Lucy. *Memoirs of the Court of Elizabeth, Queen of England.* New York: G. P. Putnam & Sons, 1870.

Aker, Raymond, and Edward Von der Porten. *Discovering Francis Drake's California Harbor*. Drake Navigators Guild, 2000.

Andrews, Kenneth R. *Trade, Plunder, and Settlement: Maritime Enterprise and the Genesis of the British Empire, 1480–1630*. New York: Cambridge University Press, 1984.

———. *The Spanish Caribbean: Trade and Plunder, 1530–1630*. New Haven: Yale University Press, 1978.

———. *Drake's Voyages: A Reassessment of Their Place in Elizabethan Maritime Expansion*. London: Weidenfeld & Nicolson,1967.

———. *Elizabethan Privateering: English Privateering During the Spanish War, 1585–1603*. Cambridge: Cambridge University Press, 1964.

Andrews, William. *Bygone Punishments*. London: W. Andrews, 1899.

Archer, Elisabeth, et al. *The Progresses, Pageants, and Entertainments of Queen Elizabeth I*. Oxford: Oxford University Press, 2007.

Baker, J. *The History of the Inquisition*. Westminster, UK: O. Payne, 1736.

Barrow, John. *The Life, Voyages, and Exploits of Sir Francis Drake*. London: J. Murray, 1844.

Bawlf, Samuel R. *The Secret Voyage of Sir Francis Drake, 1577–1580*. New York: Walker, 2003.

Bergreen, Laurence. *Columbus: The Four Voyages*. New York: Viking, 2011.

———. *Over the Edge of the World: Magellan's Terrifying Circumnavigation of the Globe*. New York: William Morrow, 2003.

Bicheno, Hugh. *Elizabeth's Sea Dogs: How the English Became the Scourge of the Seas*. London: Conway, 2012.

Birch, Thomas. *Memoirs of the Reign of Queen Elizabeth from the Year 1581 until Her Death*. 2 vols. London: A. Millar in the Strand, 1754.

Black, J. B. *The Reign of Queen Elizabeth I*. Oxford: Clarendon Press, 1959.

Boorstin, Daniel J. *The Discoverers*. New York: Random House, 1983.

Bourne, Edward Gaylord. *Spain in America: 1450–1580*. New York: Harper & Brothers, 1904.

Braudel, Fernand. *The Mediterranean and the Mediterranean World in the Age of Philip II*. 2 vols. New York: Harper & Row, 1972–73.

Brimacombe, Peter. *All the Queen's Men: The World of Elizabeth I*. New York: St. Martin's Press, 2000.

Budiansky, Stephen. *Her Majesty's Spymaster: Elizabeth I, Sir Francis Walsingham, and the Birth of Modern Espionage.* New York: Viking, 2005.

Campbell, John. *The Spanish Empire in America.* London: M. Cooper, 1747.

Caro de Torres, Francisco. *Relación de los Servicios de Don Alonso de Sotomayor*, vol. 5. Santiago: Imprenta del Ferrocarril, 1864.

Clule, N. H. *John Dee's Natural Philosophy: Between Science and Religion.* New York: Routledge, 1988.

Cooper, J. P. D. *The Queen's Agent: Sir Francis Walsingham and the Rise of Espionage in Elizabethan England.* New York: Pegasus Books, 2013.

Coote, Stephen. *Drake: The Life and Legend of an Elizabethan Hero.* New York: Palgrave, 2005.

Corbett, Julian Stafford. *Drake and the Tudor Navy.* Aldershot, Hants, England: Temple Smith: Brookfield, VT: Gower, 1988.

———. *Sir Francis Drake.* London: Macmillan and Co., 1902.

Cordingly, David. *Under the Black Flag: The Romance and the Reality of Life among the Pirates.* New York: Random House, 1995.

Corn, Charles. *The Scents of Eden: A Narrative of the Spice Trade.* New York: Kodansha International, 1998.

Crane, Nicholas. *Mercator: The Man Who Mapped the Planet.* London: Weidenfeld & Nicolson, 2002.

Crow, John A. *Spain: The Root and the Flower.* New York: Harper & Row, 1975.

Cummins, John. *Francis Drake: The Life of a Hero.* London: Weidenfeld & Nicolson, 1995.

D'Avenant, Sir William. *The History of Sir Francis Drake.* London: Henry Herringman, 1659.

Deacon, R. *John Dee: Scientist, Geographer, Astrologer and Secret Agent to Elizabeth I.* Letchworth, Hertfordshire: Frederick Muller, 1968.

Dee, John. *General and Rare Memorials Pertayning to the Perfect Arte of Navigation.* London: Iohn Daye, Anno 1577.

Doran, Susan. *Elizabeth I and Her Circle.* New York: Oxford University Press, 2015.

Drake Manuscript in the Pierpont Morgan Library, The. London: André Deutsch, 1996.

Drake, Sir Francis. *The World Encompassed.* London: Hakluyt Society, 1854.

——. *The World Encompassed by Sir Francis Drake, being his next voyage to that of Nombre de Dios formerly imprinted; Carefully collected out of the notes of Master Francis Fletcher.* London: Nicholas Bourne, 1628.

Davis, Bertram H. *A Proof of Eminence: the Life of Sir John Hawkins.* Bloomington, IN: Indiana University Press, 1973.

Ellis, Sir Henry. *Original Letters. Report of the sig. Re Giovanni Michele on His Return to England, 1557.* London: Harding & Lepard, 1827.

Fallon, Niall. *The Armada in Ireland.* London: Stanford Maritime, 1978.

Felch, Susan, and Donald Stump, eds. *Elizabeth I and Her Age.* New York: W. W. Norton & Co., 2009.

French, Peter. *John Dee: The World of an Elizabethan Magus.* New York: Routledge, 2002.

Fuller-Eliott-Drake, Elizabeth Douglas, Lady. *The Family and Heirs of Sir Francis Drake.* England: Smith, Elder, 1911.

Gill, Crispin. "Drake and Plymouth." *Sir Francis Drake and the Famous Voyage, 1577–1580: Essays Commemorating the Quadricentennial of Drake's Circumnavigation of the Earth.* Berkeley: University of California Press,1984.

Graham, Winston. *The Spanish Armadas.* Garden City, NY: Doubleday, 1972.

Green, Toby. *Inquisition: The Reign of Fear.* New York: St. Martin's Press, 2007.

Guy, John. *Elizabeth: The Forgotten Years.* New York: Viking, 2016.

——. *Tudor England.* Oxford: Oxford University Press, 1988.

Hakluyt, Richard. *The Principal Navigation, Voyages, Traffiques and Discoveries of the English Nation.* London: G. Bishop, R. Newberie, and R. Barker, 1599–1600.

——. *Voyages and Discoveries.* New York: Penguin Books, 1972.

Halliwell, James Orchard. *Private Diary of Dr. John Dee and the Catalogue of His Library of Manuscripts.* Camden Society, Old Series, 19. Cambridge, UK, 2011.

Hampden, John. *Francis Drake, Privateer.* University: University of Alabama Press, 1972.

Hanson, Neil. *The Confident Hope of a Miracle: The True History of the Spanish Armada.* New York: Knopf, 2005.

Haring, Clarence Henry. *The Spanish Empire in America*. New York: Harcourt Brace & World, 1973.

Harrison, G. B., ed. *The Letters of Queen Elizabeth I*. Westport, CT: Greenwood Press Publishers, 1981.

Hazlewood, Nick. *The Queen's Slave Trader: John Hawkyns, Elizabeth I, and the Trafficking in Human Souls*. New York: William Morrow, 2004.

Held, Robert and Marcello Bertoni. *The Inquisition: a bilingual guide to the exhibition of torture instruments from the Middle Ages to the industrial era*. Florence: Qua D'Arno, 1985.

Herman, Arthur. *To Rule the Waves: How the British Navy Shaped the Modern World*. New York: HarperCollins, 2004.

Hibbert, Christopher. *The Virgin Queen: Elizabeth I, Genius of the Golden Age*. Reading, MA: Addison-Wesley, 1991.

Holt, Mack P. *The French Wars of Religion 1562–1626*. Cambridge: Cambridge University Press, 2005.

Hort, Gertrude M. *Dr. John Dee, Elizabethan Mystic and Astrologer*. London: William Rider & Son, Ltd., 1922.

Hume, Martin Andrew Sharp. *Philip II of Spain*. London: Macmillan, 1899.

Hutchinson, Robert. *The Spanish Armada*. London: Weidenfeld & Nicolson, 2013.

Johnson, Paul. *Elizabeth I: A Biography*. New York: Holt, Rinehart and Winston, 1974.

Johnson, Samuel. *The Life of Mr. Richard Savage, Son of the Earl Rivers. The Third Edition. To which are added, the Lives of Sir Francis Drake, and Admiral Blake*. London: F. Newbery, 1777.

Kamen, Henry. *Philip of Spain*. New Haven: Yale University Press, 1999.

Kaufmann, Miranda. *Black Tudors: The Untold Story*. London: Oneworld Publications, 2018.

Kelsey, Harry. *The First Circumnavigators: Unsung Heroes of the Age of Discovery*. New Haven: Yale University Press, 2016.

———. *Sir Francis Drake: The Queen's Pirate*. New Haven: Yale University Press, 1998.

———. *Sir John Hawkins: Queen Elizabeth's Slave Trader*. New Haven: Yale University Press, 2003.

Kinney, Arthur F. *Elizabethan Backgrounds: Historical Documents of the Age of Elizabeth I*. Hamden, CT: Archon Books, 1975.

Knecht, Robert J. *The French Religious Wars: 1562–1598*. Oxford: Osprey, 2002.

Kraus, H. P. *Sir Francis Drake: A Pictorial Biography*. Amsterdam: N. Israel, 1970.

Las Casas, Bartolomé de. *A Short Account of the Destruction of the Indies*, tr. Nigel Griffin. New York, Penguin Books, 1994.

Lea, Henry Charles. *A History of the Inquisition of Spain*. Vol. 3. New York: AMS Press, 1988.

——. *A History of the Inquisition of Spain*. Vol. 8. New York: AMS Press, 1988.

Leng, Robert. *The True Description of the Last Voiage of that Worthy Captayne, Sir Frauncis Drake, Knight*. Camden Miscellany, Fifth Series. London: The Camden Society, 1964.

Leonardo de Argensola, Bartolomé. *Conquista de las islas Malucas al rey Felipe Tercero nuestro señor*. Zaragoza: Imprenta del Hospicio Provincial, 1891.

Léry, Jean de. *History of a Voyage to the Land of Brazil*. Berkeley: University of California Press, 1990.

Liebman, Seymour B. *The Jews in New Spain: Faith, Flame, and Inquisition*. Coral Gables, FL: University of Miami Press, 1970.

Limborch, Philippus van. *The History of the Inquisition*. Translated by Samuel Chandler. London: J. Gray, 1731.

Liss, Peggy K. *Isabel the Queen: Life and Times*. Philadelphia: University of Pennsylvania Press, 2004.

Mapp, Alf J., Jr. *Three Golden Ages*. Lanham, MD: Madison Books, 1998.

Marchant, John, et al. *A Review of the Bloody Tribunal; Or the Horrid Cruelties of the Inquisition*. Perth: G. Johnston, 1770.

Markham, Clements, tr. *Early Spanish Voyages to the Strait of Magellan*. London: Hakluyt Society, 1911.

——. tr. *The Letters of Amerigo Vespucci*. London: Hakluyt Society, 1894.

Martin, Colin, and Geoffrey Parker. *The Spanish Armada*, rev. ed. Manchester, UK: Manchester University Press, 1999.

Martyn, Trea. *Queen Elizabeth in the Garden: A Story of Love, Rivalry, and Spectacular Gardens.* Katonah, NY: BlueBridge, 2012.

Mason, A. E. W. *The Life of Francis Drake.* Garden City, NY: Doubleday, Doran, 1942.

Mattingly, Garrett. *The Armada.* Boston: Houghton Mifflin, 1959.

McCrie, Thomas. *History of the Progress and Suppression of the Reformation in Spain in the Sixteenth Century.* Edinburgh: W. Blackwood, 1829.

Merriman, Roger Bigelow. *The Rise of the Spanish Empire in the Old World and the New.* New York: Macmillan, 1925.

Montaigne, Michel de. *The Essays of Michel de Montaigne,* tr. George B. Ives; with an introduction by André Gide. New York: Heritage Press, 1946.

Morison, Samuel Eliot. *The European Discovery of America: The Northern Voyages.* New York: Oxford University Press, 1971.

——. *The European Discovery of America: The Southern Voyages.* New York: Oxford University Press, 1973.

Mozley, James Frederic. *John Foxe and His Book.* London: Society for Promoting Christian Knowledge, 1940.

Nichols, Philip. *Sir Francis Drake revived: calling upon this dull or effeminate age, to follow his noble steps for gold & silver. Set forth by Sr. Francis Drake Baronet (his nephew) now living.* London: Printed by E. for Nicholas Bourne, 1626.

Norton, Elizabeth. *The Temptation of Elizabeth Tudor: Elizabeth I, Thomas Seymour, and the Making of a Virgin Queen.* New York: Pegasus Books, 2016.

Nuttall, Zelia. *New Light on Drake.* London: Hakluyt Society, 1914.

Parker, Geoffrey. *Imprudent King: A New Life of Philip II.* New Haven: Yale University Press, 2014.

Parry, J. H. *The Age of Reconnaissance.* Berkeley: University of California Press, 1963.

——. *The Discovery of South America.* New York: Taplinger, 1979.

——. *The Discovery of the Sea.* Berkeley: University of California Press, 1981.

——. *The European Reconnaissance: Selected Documents.* New York: Walker, 1968.

———. *The Spanish Seaborne Empire*. New York: Knopf, 1970.

Peck, D. C., ed. *Leicester's Commonwealth: The Copy of a Letter Written by a Master of Art of Cambridge* (1584). Athens, OH: Ohio University Press, 2006.

Picard, Liza. *Elizabeth's London: Everyday Life in Elizabethan London*. New York: St. Martin's Griffin, 2003.

Quinn, David B. *Sir Francis Drake as Seen by His Contemporaries*. Providence, RI: John Carter Brown Library, 1996.

Roche, T. W. E. *The Golden Hind*. New York: Praeger, 1973.

Rodger, N. A. M. *The Safeguard of the Sea: A Naval History of Britain 660–1649*. New York: W. W. Norton, 1998.

Ronald, Susan. *The Pirate Queen*. New York: HarperCollins, 2007.

Roth, Norman. *Conversos, Inquisition, and the Expulsion of the Jews from Spain*. Madison: University of Wisconsin Press, 1995.

Rousmaniere, John. *The Annapolis Book of Seamanship*. New York: Simon & Schuster, 1989.

Rowse, A. L. *The England of Elizabeth: The Structure of Society*. New York: Collier Books, 1950.

Rule, William H., Rev. *The Brand of Dominic, or, Inquisition*. London: John Mason, 1852.

Sáiz Cidoncha, Carlos. *Historia de la piratería en América española*. Madrid: Editorial San Martín, 1985.

Savile, Henry. *A Libell of Spanish Lies*. London: John Windet, 1596.

Sherman, William H. *John Dee: The Politics of Reading and Writing in the English Renaissance*. Amherst: University of Massachusetts Press, 1995.

Singh, Simon. *The Code Book: The Evolution of Secrecy from Mary Queen of Scots to Quantum Cryptography*. New York: Doubleday, 1999.

Somerset, Anne. *Elizabeth I*. New York: Knopf, 1991.

Starkey, David. *Elizabeth: Apprenticeship*. London: Chatto & Windus, 2000.

Sténuit, Robert. *Treasures of the Armada*, tr. Francine Barker. New York: E. P. Dutton, 1973.

Story Donno, Elizabeth, ed. *An Elizabethan in 1582: The Diary of Richard Madox*. London: Hakluyt Society, 1976.

Stow, John. *The Annales, or General Chronicle of England*. London: T. Adams, 1615.

Strong, Roy. *Coronation: A History of Kingship and the British Monarchy*. London: HarperCollins, 2005.

Sugden, John. *Sir Francis Drake*. New York: Henry Holt, 1990.

Thomson, George Malcolm. *Sir Francis Drake*. New York: William Morrow, 1972.

Turner, Michael. *In Drake's Wake*. Burnham-on-Sea, Somerset, UK: 2016.

Unwin, Rayner. *The Defeat of John Hawkins: A Biography of His Third Slaving Voyage*. London: Allen & Unwin, 1960.

Verrill, A. Hyatt. *The Inquisition*. New York: D. Appleton & Co, 1931.

Wagner, Henry R. *Sir Francis Drake's Voyage around the World*. Glendale, CA: Arthur H. Clark, 1926.

Weir, Alison. *The Life of Elizabeth I*. New York: Ballantine Books, 1999.

Whitelock, Anna. *The Queen's Bed: An Intimate History of Elizabeth's Court*. New York: Sarah Crichton Books, Farrar, Straus and Giroux, 2014. [In the UK, *Elizabeth's Bedfellows: An Intimate History of the Queen's Court*. London: Bloomsbury, 2013.]

Whiting, J. R. S. *The Enterprise of England: The Spanish Armada*. Gloucester, UK; Wolfboro, NH: Sutton, 1988.

Williamson, James Alexander. *The Age of Drake*. London: A. and C. Black, 1946.

Woolley, Benjamin. *The Queen's Conjuror: The Life and Magic of Dr. Dee*. New York: Henry Holt, 2001.

Wright, I. A., ed. and tr. *Documents Concerning English Voyages to the Spanish Main 1569–1580*. London: Hakluyt Society, 1932.

Index